OTHER BOOKS BY WILLIAM SAFIRE

LANGUAGE

Watching My Language
In Love with Norma Loquendi
Quoth the Maven
Coming to Terms
Fumblerules
Language Maven Strikes Again
You Could Look It Up
Take My Word for It
I Stand Corrected
What's the Good Word?
On Language
Safire's New Political Dictionary

POLITICS

The First Dissident
Safire's Washington
Before the Fall
Plunging into Politics
The Relations Explosion

FICTION

Sleeper Spy
Freedom
Full Disclosure

ANTHOLOGIES

Lend Me Your Ears: Great Speeches in History

(WITH LEONARD SAFIR)

Good Advice on Writing
Leadership
Words of Wisdom
Good Advice

SPREAD THE WORD

Spread the Word

William Safire

Illustrations by Terry Allen

TIMES BOOKS
RANDOM HOUSE

Published in the United States by Times Books, a division of Random House, Inc., New York, and simultaneously in Canada by Random House of Canada Limited, Toronto.

Grateful acknowledgment is made to *The New York Times* for permission to reprint 165 "On Language" columns by William Safire from January 3, 1993, through December 2, 1994.

Library of Congress Cataloging-in-Publication Data
Safire, William
Spread the word / by William Safire.
p. cm.
A collection of the author's weekly columns "On Language" from the New York Times Magazine.
Includes index.
ISBN 0-8129-3253-6
1. English language—Usage. 2. English language—Style.
I. New York Times Magazine. II. Title.
PE 1421.S2335 1999
428—dc21 99-13812

Random House website address: www.atrandom.com

*Printed in the United States of America on acid-free paper**

2 4 6 8 9 7 5 3

FIRST EDITION

* *Acid-free* is a slogan, not a description; "this book is printed on alkaline paper," he said acidly. —WS

Spread the Word

William Safire

Illustrations by Terry Allen

TIMES BOOKS
RANDOM HOUSE

Published in the United States by Times Books, a division of Random House, Inc., New York, and simultaneously in Canada by Random House of Canada Limited, Toronto.

TIMES BOOKS and colophon are registered trademarks of Random House, Inc.

Grateful acknowledgment is made to *The New York Times* for permission to reprint 165 "On Language" columns by William Safire from January 3, 1993, through December 2, 1994.

Library of Congress Cataloging-in-Publication Data
Safire, William
Spread the word / by William Safire.
p. cm.
A collection of the author's weekly columns "On Language" from the New York Times Magazine.
Includes index.
ISBN 0-8129-3253-6
1. English language—Usage. 2. English language—Style.
I. New York Times Magazine. II. Title.
PE 1421.S2335 1999
428—dc21 99-13812

Random House website address: www.atrandom.com

*Printed in the United States of America on acid-free paper**

2 4 6 8 9 7 5 3

FIRST EDITION

* *Acid-free* is a slogan, not a description; "this book is printed on alkaline paper," he said acidly. —WS

for Coral Samuel

The limits of my language mean the limits of my world.

—Ludwig Wittgenstein

INTRODUCTION

"The two were not only made for each other," wrote *The Washington Times* about star-crossed lovers, "they deserve one another."

The editorialist, grappling with the rules of correctness, was undoubtedly torn. Question: When writing about a relationship between two people, is it proper to use *each other* or *one another*? The writer refused to choose and the editorial went both ways.

At *The New York Times,* we have firm guidance to keep us from such pushmipullyu style. Our style manual, now embedded in software so that century-old judgments can be amended in a flash, is sternly prescriptive: "*each other, one another:* two persons look at *each other;* more than two look at *one another.*"

It's a comfort to have a rule. That's our style. If you write for *The New York Times* (or the A.P., or *The Wall Street Journal,* whose stylebooks present a united front and follow one another on this), that's the way it is, like it or lump it. If I were to write, "Two stylebooks disagree with *one another,*" an alert copy editor would demand I change it to: "two . . . *each other.*" Sometimes a kindly copy editor will call to say, "Are you deliberately trying to slip this egregious error into the paper, thereby generating mail from infuriated grammarians and giving you a subject for your language column?" (I don't do that, as a rule.)

What if I were to respond to the corrector-in-chief at my newspaper: Samuel "Dictionary" Johnson once wrote about "six ministers who meet weekly at *each other's* houses," breaking the rule. And Bishop Lowth, the nineteenth century's high priest of usage, instructed that "two negatives in English destroy *one another,*" breaking the rule the other way. In 1926, Fowler—St. Henry himself—wrote that "the differentiation is neither of present utility nor based on historical usage," and in his recent revision of Fowler, Bob Burchfield declares that the belief of the rulemakers is "untenable," citing recent breakings by classy writers like Anita Brookner and Nadine Gordimer. E. Ward Gilman, editor of Merriam-Webster's indispensable *Dictionary of English Usage,* often unfairly dissed by me as "Dr. Roundheels," assembles these authorities and concludes about each rule:

"There is no sin in its violation," adding from his loosey-goosey perch, "It is, however, easy and painless to observe if you so wish."

I so wish. If I did not, and instead chose to break the stylebook rule, a great contretemps would take place. Citations all over the floor. (No sentence fragments!—Ed.) In the end (at the denouement of the contretemps but never *at the end of the day*), a Sanhedrin of copy editors might permit my dissenting usage, but only if accompanied by an explanation of my departure from the Stylebook Team, including their punchy rebuttal and my stinging surrebuttal. (Sometimes they let me win; that's why *Times* style is now to spell Rumania *Romania.*)

In the same way, the three newspaper stylebooks stand foursquare for the *between/among* rule. The A.P. cites "the maxim that *between* introduces two items and *among* more than two. . . ." Thus, it's "between you and me" and "among the three of us." But here comes Old Roundheels again (Mr. Gilman is honorably retired but comes out swinging at my request) trotting out a parade of authorities who disagree, and denouncing as a waste "the enormous amount of ink spilled in the explication of the subtleties of *between* and *among.*" And no doubt he has common usage on his side.

But not good usage. (You really ought to do something about those sentence fragments—Ed.) What's wrong with an obeisance to sharp edges in a world of fuzz? If we adopt as a rule the practice of using *each other* and *between* to two, and rigorously apply *one another* and *among* to three or more, our world of words is a little more tightly organized. We're operating comfortably within agreed guidelines. We have a Style.

A style is a set of conventions, not a fundament of grammar fixed in our brains like subject-verb agreement. A stylistic rule is not a law. No cellblock in Reading Gaol is reserved for those condemned of using *between the three* (and indeed a medal is pinned on writers careful to use *between* when expressing a relationship of several items considered a pair at a time).

But when you play by the rules of grammar—that is, when you agree to adopt a style that befits a certain level and tone of discourse—and then stick to the rules you've learned, you get a subtle intellectual kick that the anything-goes crowd never experiences. And when you break any rule for effect, as when you use sentence fragments now and then for emphasis, or begin a sentence with *and* to foster an illusion of spontaneity or afterthought, you are like an actor playing a drunk and performing an exquisite stumble.

The respecter of the rules of an adopted style becomes a member of a club so determinedly inclusive as to be truly snooty. You're in, and nobody can cancel your membership as long as you consult the rulebook. The secret handshake and the code ring are yours. With these symbols come the sense of belonging, of serene security, of smug noninferiority that suffuses all those who clothe themselves voluntarily in the golden chains of good usage. (I learned psychology from the *Story of O.*)

If you take language as a metaphor for life, your respect for the gently arbitrary rules of style signifies your willingness to respect the rules of civility in the way you behave. Breaking a rule of style or even of civility gains force and meaning only when you know what code you are violating and why.

Imagine, two centuries ago, the copy editor for the Committee on Style of the Constitutional Convention coming up to Thomas Jefferson and pointing to the last line of his proposed Unanimous Declaration of the Thirteen United States of America: ". . . we mutually pledge to each other our lives, our fortunes and our sacred honor." "Not only is *mutually* redundant, Tom, but you're referring to more than two people, so it should be *one another.*"

And Jefferson would reply, "We're the Committee on Style, right? Leave it the way it is."

SPREAD THE WORD

Advert

Let me advert here to the phrasing of an apology to reporters made by George Stephanopoulos, the White House communications chief. Bill Clinton claimed never to have been asked about normalization of relations with Saddam Hussein; when this was shown to be wrong, the press aide said his boss "*inadvertently* forgot that he had been asked that specific question."

Vertere, in Latin, is "turn"; *ad* is "to"; to *advert* is "to turn attention to," as every advertiser knows. The adjective *inadvertent* originally meant "heedless, inattentive"; the predominant sense now is "unintentional."

The adverb *inadvertently* thus covers a mistake with innocence: It was caused by lack of attention, rather than malice. But while you can *inadvertently injure,* or *inadvertently stumble,* you cannot *inadvertently forget.* That is either redundant or recalls the existence of the opposite—of intentionally forgetting—which politicians have been known to do.

Ah, Ur

Ur recently surfaced in the pages of *The New York Times Magazine* in Ron Rosenbaum's piece about the spy Kim Philby: "after Philby has been exposed as a long-term Soviet mole, indeed the *ur*-mole, the legendary Third Man, the most devastatingly effective known double agent in history."

Got a call from Richard Helms, the legendary Director of Central Intelligence in the 60's, the *ur*-secret-keeper, the most devastatingly effective American spy master, a man on whose watch not a single mole—or, as he calls it, "penetration agent"—infiltrated the C.I.A.

"What's an *ur*?" this longtime Lexicographic Irregular wanted to know. Fearful that we might be overheard, I said I'd get back to him.

Couple of weeks later, a clipping appeared in my Farragut Square dead drop, a mode of secure communication I use instead of E-mail. Helms again: "I'm not trying to worry the *ur* thing, but here it is again in your own magazine."

The article by Michael Kelly referred to "the signal event in the development of Clinton's character—the *ur*-compromise from which all later compromises would flow."

The pattern of usage calls for immediate research; it cannot wait for the appointment of a presidential commission to shake up the agency or the magazine.

Ur is an ancient Sumerian city on the Euphrates in what was then Mesopotamia and is now Iraq; the Sumerians, in the fourth millennium B.C., developed the cuneiform system of writing, which may have preceded Egyptian hieroglyphics. This information about the origin of language has nothing to do with the prefix *ur-* but is what intelligence agencies call noise.

The prefix that has so entranced *Times* writers comes from the Old High German and means "original, primitive, prototypical." In German, *Ursprache* means "primitive language." In English, it has been in use only for a century: Joseph Jacobs wrote in 1889 about William Caxton's translation of *Aesop's Fables,* in favor of "any light he can throw on the *Ur*-origin of the Fables."

The term most often appears in literary discussions of the *ur-Hamlet,* the undiscovered text of Shakespeare's earliest version of that play (from whose bourn no deconstructor returns). The poet W. H. Auden wrote in 1947, "For Long-Ago has been Ever-After since *Ur*-Papa gave the Primal Yawn that expressed all things."

It's pronounced "oor," as in "tour," and not "err." Sometimes it is capitalized, but that conflicts with the name of the Sumerian city, so drop the capital. The prefix *ur-* is shorter, and certainly trendier, than "prototypical," but it is not the word to use if you're striving for aboriginality.

Alpha Male

"O.J. was so graceful, so ingratiating," Robert Lipsyte wrote in *The New York Times,* "that it was easy to forget how he got there, a ghetto gang leader, a high school, junior college, major college *Alpha male* who had learned to knock down anything in his way."

Gary Muldoon writes from Rochester: "*Alpha?* The reference is unclear to me. First thought—fraternity—nah. In *Brave New World,* there are different strata of people, with the Alphas on top—could be."

Nah. The fairly frequent phrase *Alpha male*—135 uses in Nexis, 134 in Dialog—though not in dictionaries yet, nor even in *The Barnhart New-Words Concordance,* is from ethology.

No, not *ethnology,* the branch of anthropology that compares cultures; *ethol-*

ogy, the study of animal behavior. In two words, an *Alpha male* is "top dog"; to ethologists, it is "the dog at the top of a troop's dominance hierarchy."

"An *Alpha male,*" says Dr. Katherine Houpt, director of the Animal Behavior Clinic at Cornell University, a high human among ethologists, "is the top rank in the hierarchy. From *Alpha* as the first letter in the Greek alphabet, this term is usually used of the top male in wolf packs, the one that gets to breed and to aggress and has first access to scarce resources like food and the best place to sleep."

Alpha male is the second contribution of ethology to pop psychology and politics. The first was *pecking order,* a discovery of the Norwegian zoologist Thorleif Schjelderup-Ebbe, who called it *hackordning,* "peck order." In the social order of chickens, the one at the top is the hen that pecks but is never pecked in return; the novelist Aldous Huxley picked this up in his *Point Counter Point,* and it was adopted in political analysis in 1954 by the Alsop brothers.

I was the owner, though not the master, of a wonderful Bernese mountain dog named James who was an *Alpha male.* Had he been a chicken, he would have been at the head of the pecking order, but he was no chicken. The trainer said James had "great character," which meant he resented being told what to do. We finally taught him to sit. How does an *Alpha male* respond to the "sit" command? He waits for you to say it the third time, then sits in the most begrudging way, but to show he's not being submissive, barks, as if to say, "I'm sitting only because I feel like it."

Aphetic Verbal Doppelgänger

David Brinkley welcomed Vice President Al Gore on his Sunday morning ABC program with a cordial "Thank you for coming." Mr. Gore—as so many guests now do—answered with the aphetic "thank you," with a slight emphasis on the *you.*

"*You're welcome* used to be the standard response to *thank you,*" writes Daniel Kocan of Orlando, Florida. "Now *thank you* is the stock response to *thank you.* Since when, and why? Can you explain this recent doppelgänger phenomenon?"

First to *doppelgänger:* This is from the German for "the ghostly double of a living person," and is an apt description of the returned *thank you.* Next to the *aphetic,* or shortening of words or phrases by the elimination of the unstressed word or syllable: The *I* is lost in *I thank you.*

Now to the rampant Alphonse-Gastonism on the airwaves. ("After you"; "No, after *you.*") Richard Weiner, author of *Webster's New World Dictionary of Media and Communications,* thinks it is a subtle form of one-upmanship, or at least the aversion of one-downmanship. "Say that Dan Rather and Connie Chung are on the air, and Dan says, 'Thank you.' If Connie replies, 'You're welcome,' then Dan may appear to have the advantage. A returned 'thank you' equates their positions."

We have here what psycholinguists call *focal stress.* The primary emphasis in a spoken sentence often affects its interpretation, as in "What do you THINK?" vs. "What do YOU think?" In the current abandonment of welcome, the riposte "Thank YOU" means "Thank you for having me," or less suggestively, "Thank you for inviting me"; in unspoken words, it says, "I can match you thank for thank" in the gratitude contest.

With assertive humility, the new counterappreciation avoids the appearance of acknowledging a favor that the responder may have done for the thanker. Listen for it; the aphetic verbal doppelgänger has all but abolished what used to be the polite response.

Henry Kissinger never used to have that problem. I recall a woman rushing up to him when he was Secretary of State to gush, "Thank you, thank you, Dr. Kissinger, for saving Western civilization from nuclear catastrophe!" His reply was more honest than modest: "You're welcome."

Doppelgänger? Not at all—as should be apparent from the change in stress: "Thank you" followed by "Thank YOU." Nor is it Alfonse vs. Gaston. What would you make of a French exchange in which "Merci mille fois" *is answered by* "C'est moi"*? This is very current in France. The* "C'est moi" *is short for* "C'est moi qui vous remercie" *(which also is heard very often). It is only a gracious acknowledgment of* mutual *indebtedness, and a whole lot shorter and sweeter than "I am the one who should be thanking* you*."*

Carolyn Silver
Charlottesville, Virginia

In the mid-1960s when I lived in the U.K. as an American graduate student, I was startled to discover that "you're welcome" was not in their speech. For me, this was quite an ear-opener because, in most other respects, the average Englishman in the 1960s was more courteous in language and actions than the average American.

I soon realized that while there was no standard reply to thanks in the U.K., I would sometimes get a spoken "thank you." More often, one simply received a nod, a smile or just a grunt "ta" in return. In England, "you're welcome" was simply understood in ordinary conversation.

James N. Rudolph
New York, New York

With respect to the new thank-you response, it might be that Chinese is the real culprit! In Mandarin Chinese, "thank you" is xiè-xiè *(approximately). As for "you're welcome," two responses are probably predominant:* bú-xiè, *literally "no thanks (necessary)" or "don't mention it," and* bú-kè-qi, *literally "not guest (visitor, customer) atmosphere," that is, "not the atmosphere of a guest (visitor, customer)." In the former, there is the negation of "thanks," and in the latter, there is the appreciative equality of positions without the assertiveness.*

Go figure (aphetic for "go figure it out"?).

David Bernklau
Brooklyn, New York

Dear Bill:

Very likely the first instance of the practice occurred in The Play's the Thing *by Molnar, which was produced in New York in the mid-1930s. In it, the middle-aged playwright-hero has a servant named Dvornitchek who does a great deal for his master, including serving an elaborate supper. As each bit of service is completed, the valet and butler says, "Thank you" in the traditional manner. To which his master says: "No, no, no, Dvornitchek, thank* you.*"*

This little scene repeats a dozen times during the play, and it induced a wave of imitation, at least among us young students and theatergoers. But we outgrew the habit as it got silly, and I am sure it is a precedent, but not the origin of the bright new custom you record.

Jacques [Barzun]
New York, New York

Babes Up in Arms

Words, like spies, can be taken prisoner, turned and used against the enemy.

Consider *babe,* not in the sense of "infant," but in its slang meaning cited in *Dialect Notes* in 1915 of "pretty girl," as in "She's some *babe.*"

Despite its use as the name of Paul Bunyan's blue ox, and as the nickname of home-run king George Herman Ruth and the best-dressed Mrs. William S. Paley, the slang noun *babe* was most often a word for *bimbo, skirt, doll, dame, broad, chick* and other derogations, sometimes admiring, more often patronizing.

In the late 1960's, that began to change. Sonny and Cher's theme song, "I Got You, Babe," used the word in an affectionate, unisex manner; applied by women to men in the 70's, it was synonymous with *dude;* in the 90's, feminists made their move.

" 'Culture Babes' Fill Goddess Rolodex" is a recent headline in *The New York Observer* over an article by Peter Stevenson about Naomi Wolf, a feminist writer who sends letters to friends with the salutation "Dear Babes" and the sign-off "Yours in babehood." Ms Wolf espouses "power feminism" in her book *Fire with Fire,* and her network of media friends is called "Culture Babes."

What cooks with the babes? I turned to the lexicographic babe, Anne Soukhanov: "This is an example of a feminine-gender in-group's private language in action," she responded. "A word used *about* women is now being used *by* women *to* other women, about themselves, in a specific, new way."

She has heard women greet one another with "Hi, babe—you look fabulous!" In this use, "*babe* denotes affection and intimacy between women as friends or relatives. It is synonymous with *hon, dear, sweetie, sweets* and *darling,* and is of virtually the same register as the famous Kennedy 'Hi, kid!' directed to special friends."

But when a man says, "Get a load of that *babe* at the bar," he uses the word in the same derogatory sense as *dame, wench* and *fox.*

"*Babe* lives a double linguistic life," Ms Soukhanov observes. "It's alive and well with Major Sexual Attitude in the parlance of males; at the same time it is used in the in-parlance of women, now taking on Major Feminosexual Attitude in Ms Wolf's salons. Let's hope that the twain never meets; imagine the results if a man approached a group of Culture Babes enjoying smokes by the window of a New York bar, and said: 'Hi, *babe.* Buy you a drink?' "

I would take exception to Ms. Soukhanov's view where, with reference to the Major Sexual Attitude and the Major Feminosexual Attitude, she says, "Let's hope the twain never meets." On the contrary, let's hope they does *meet!*

Göran Kjellmer
English Department
University of Göteborg
Göteborg, Sweden

I was somewhat disturbed by your assuming that a man's admiring statement, "Get a load of that babe *at the bar," is derogatory. In my book that statement may have been rude, but its complimentary intent is just the opposite of your meaning. Only a* femifascist *or PC dweeb would take such a tribute and turn it into a pejorative phrase. So the real question is what's gotten over you? Your normal critical senses seem to elude you when writing on issues touching on feminism. As the* Times *resident language maven you also seem to have become their chief* spokeswimp. *Get a grip on yourself, man! Let's get back to that old eagle-eyed, razor-tongued, wickedly skillful wordsmith we all remember so well.*

Stephen Somerstein
Mountain View, California

Batch File: Aim at Foot, Fire!

I.B.M. has had a difficult time lately, and I hate to pile on, but Jacques Barzun has just sent me its annual report. It suggests why the company may have had dark days the following year.

The report writer wanted to say that I.B.M. was making better products, which would allow it to compete successfully. But after the thought went into the word process, the headline in the report proudly read: "Competing With Better Products."

As Professor Barzun notes, "The text does not say whose products are better than I.B.M.'s, very likely because that is not what the man who wrote the head thought he was saying."

Betwixt *Among* and *Between*

Charlotte Thorp of Brooklyn was struck by the subtitle of Lester Thurow's recent book, *Head to Head: The Coming Economic Battle Among Japan, Europe and America.*

"I was taught, as a child," she writes, "that *between* was for two things, *among* for three or more." True, that's what most people are taught. Even copy editors are taught that: *The Associated Press Stylebook and Libel Manual* repeats the maxim that "*between* introduces two items and *among* introduces more than two." That stylebook directs that *between* also be used when expressing the relationships of three or more items considered one pair at a time, as in "negotiations between the network and the Clinton, Bush and Perot committees."

But Ms Thorp, a native speaker, feels uncomfortable about that subtitle, *The Coming Economic Battle Among Japan, Europe and America.* She writes: "The editors goofed, no? It should be '*Between* Japan, Europe and America.' " To her ear, it's a battle between, not among, the three powers, no matter what she had been taught as a child. Her ear (her innate feel for the language) is fighting her eye (her instruction from teachers and stylebooks). This conflict leads to cognitive dissonance, despair and her plea to the language maven for an all-day succor.

To all those caught in Charlotte's web, this advice: Consider the possibility that your ear may be right and the "rule" not a real rule. *The New York Times* stylebook buttresses her concern by going further than its A.P. counterpart: "*Between* is correct in reference to more than two when the items are related [both] severally and individually." *The Times*'s example is "The talks between the three powers ended in agreement to divide the responsibility among them."

Where did the "rule" begin? Who laid this guilt on Ms Thorp? "*Between* is properly used of two," Samuel Johnson wrote in his dictionary of 1755, "and *among* of more." He saw *tween* as meaning "twain, two," and therefore decided that it would be "proper" to limit the division to two. He did notice, however, that not everybody was as fastidious as him (or, as he would say, as *he*): "But perhaps," he added, "this accuracy is not always preserved."

Noah Webster considered himself an observer more than a prescriber, and in 1828—reporting what he was seeing and hearing—took sharp issue with Johnson: "We observe that *between* is not restricted to *two*." Sir James A. H. Murray, editor of the early volumes of the *Oxford English Dictionary,* published in 1888, took a long look at usage both before and after his fellow lexicographers Johnson and Webster, and found, "In all senses *between* has been, from its earliest appearance, extended to more than two." He concluded that *between* "is still the only word available to express the relation of a thing to many surrounding things severally and individually, *among* expressing a relation to them collectively and vaguely." Henry W. Fowler, the great twentieth-century usagist, labeled the Johnson distinction a "superstition" and warned that it "dies hard."

Here we have a rule that doesn't really rule; it hangs on with no real authority but is useful enough in most cases to satisfy a general craving for direction. It is a correctionmonger's delight: "Whatsamatter, don't you know the difference between *between* and *among,* or among *between, among* and *amidst*?" People like Charlotte Thorp and other sisters of Norma Loquendi tolerate the derision of the correctionmongers but mutter to themselves and their local language columnist that something does not sound quite right.

Let's not knock moorings. Certain rules of grammar are immutable: Subject-verb agreement is one, and any variation from that is dialect. Certain distinctions are clarifying and should be preserved: *Inference* is *taken,* while *implication* is *given.* But beware of the shibboleth masquerading as a rule.

I usually use *between* when separating two, and *among* when discussing more than two, because I want to, not because I have to. However, I would feel more comfortable with "the battle *between* Japan, Europe and America" because it is a battle between Japan and Europe, between Europe and America, and between Japan and America. (Maybe there is another possibility, but I am a language maven, not a mathematician.) Another reason for choosing *between* is that a battle is not necessarily a melee; if discussing a battle among Japanese, Europeans and Americans, I use *among* because there are more than a half-billion people involved in that free-for-all.

Never use *among* when dealing with only two because (among you and me) it sounds funny. What kind of reasoned analysis is "it sounds funny"? It's as good as Dr. Johnson's blithe assumption of propriety, but don't whisper that—or the permissibility of following *between* with more than two—to linguistic amateurs who presume to be grim guardians of good grammar. Keep it between you, me and the lamppost.

The "between-among" discussion brings this question to my mind: Shouldn't Professor Thurow's book have been more properly titled Head to Head: The Coming Economic Battle*s* Between Japan, Europe and America*? For unless there is a two-against-one gang-up, aren't we witnessing three battles? (As a former teacher of mathematics, I like to deal with the higher numbers, as you can see.)*

Julian B. Grafa
La Jolla, California

You identify the coming fights in Lester Thurow's prediction as happening between Japan and Europe, Japan and America, Europe and Japan, Europe and America, America and Japan, America and Europe. Therefore what we have is a war among Japan, Europe and America, a war involving Japan, Europe and America, with battles involving all three facing varying opponents. Singular war. Plural battles within that war. Therefore if Thurow's subtitle is to be corrected, it should be changed to plural: "The Coming Economic Battles Among Japan, Europe and America." I would prefer "The Coming Economic War Involving Japan, Europe and America."

Fifty years ago I had a discussion with my mother, a kindergarten teacher. She noted that Southerners called the Civil War "The War Between the States." She wanted it changed to "Among the States." I said we couldn't make such a change, because if we used "among" in that context we would be implying that Alabama would be fighting New York and Georgia, that Mississippi would be fighting Alabama and Massachusetts, that all states involved would be fighting each of the other states at one time or another. What the Southern folks meant when they called it "The War Between the States" was that it was a war between two groups of states, two different federations of states. But as a catchy title that's too awkward, so it was okay to chop it down to "The War Between the States," with the "between" underlining the fact it was two sides involved and with the implied "groups of" preserving accuracy.

Much the same reasoning applies to Thurow's subtitle. In his case, however, it's turned on its head—he did *want to imply that all participants were at one time or another fighting each other. Hence "battles among" instead of "battle among." The better, cop-out version would be "battle involving" or "war involving" and get rid of "among" entirely.*

Richard Patrick Wilson
Mobile, Alabama

The Bloopie Awards I

Every year Madison Avenue thrills to the much-deserved recognition given the most egregious examples of confused copywriting. Here come the Bloopie Awards, or as they are known in the advertising community, the *covetedbloopies.*

To the New York Palace, one of The Leading Hotels of the World (a phrase with a copyright—be careful, hoteliers, if you call your fleabag one of the leading hotels of the world), a free gift Bloopie for this ringing claim: "$20 more includes Continental Breakfast for two or free parking." As Elizabeth Horgan of Carmel, Indiana, who sponsors this entry, writes, "There may be no such thing as a free lunch, but not until now did I find out that there is no such thing as free parking; it costs $20."

To Target Stores, which zapped Wal-Mart with "This Never Would Have Happened If Sam Walton Was Alive," goes a Bloopie not for what Wal-Mart claimed—mere "grossly unfair and exploitative" advertising—but for fumbling the subjunctive in a statement contrary to fact. Mr. Walton is not alive; therefore, the line should have read, ". . . if Sam Walton *were* alive." Later, Target hit the bull's-eye again with "We want . . . the consumer to win. Just like Sam Walton did."

Language slobs since the perpetration of "Winston Tastes Good Like a Cigarette Should" have been pushing *like* as a synonym for *as,* reflecting dialectical use. It's rampant: Arneson automatic pool cleaner boasts that it will "clean your pool like no other pool cleaner can!" But this bit of dialect still belongs in fiction or in quotations, and we are right to resist the sloppiness in print. Just as Sam Walton did.

A dry-to-the-point-of-flaky Bloopie goes to Chanel, whose Day Lift Refining Complex (a small jar of moisturizer, not a huge oil refinery operating on a single shift) is recognized for a lack of parallel structure in "recognized by leading dermatologists as highly effective in improving skin's texture, smoothness and counteracting the appearance of photoaging." My nose wrinkles at that unsupported "smoothness"; either two parallel gerunds should be used, "*improving* the skin's texture and smoothness, and *counteracting* the appearance of photoaging," or—if this is the meaning—"*improving* the skin's texture, *promoting* smoothness and *counteracting* the appearance of photoaging." (And if your photos are aging, I suggest you put them in an album with those cellophane envelopes.)

In a dry heat for the Parallel Structure Bloopie is the actor and director Kenneth Branagh's highly acclaimed (is anything ever moderately acclaimed?) film *Much Ado About Nothing.* Across the top of the movie's full-page ad are these five words, separated by marks that look like plus signs: "Romance + Mischief + Seduction + Revenge + Remarkable." That's four nouns and an adjective; the line is out of joint. (O cursed spite, that ever I was born to set it right!) Right author, wrong play; try again. (Speak low if you speak grammar.)

"You Can't 'Clean' Germs, You Have to Kill Them," says Lysol's Direct, which may be designed to clean and presumably kill multi-purposes. (Do I have that right? The product is called a "multi-purpose cleaner.") This is the Comma Splice Bloopie for 1993, misusing a comma to jam together two sentences. To end a thought, the proper punctuation is a period or a semicolon; then you have to begin the next thought, which in this case is the need to kill the germs. You Can't 'Fiddle Around' with Headline Copy. You Have to Get It Right.

"Here's the details," errs Marine Midland Bank in direct-mail advertising for its Marinextra account. For this year's prime example of subject-verb disagreement, here are my Bloopie. Runner-up is the Ford Motor Company, with its "we encourage everyone, in every area of the company, to share their ideas." Recall that one, fellas; I know you want to avoid the sexist *his,* but *their* doesn't go with *everyone;* try "all our employees" instead.

For the fuzziest line of the year, wind up your Rolex: "It makes her very good at guiding high-strung half-ton animals over the formidable series of obstacles on the Grand Prix show-jumping circuit, and why she's won virtually all of the major championships both here and abroad." A key verb must be missing before the "why she's won."

Challenging Rolex by misplacing a modifier is Paladion wristwatches, offering "watches for men and women reminiscent of the Italian Renaissance." What is it that reminds us of the Renaissance, the watches or the men and women? Better to write about "men's and women's watches reminiscent of the Italian Renaissance." (This entry has been helpful to those like me who need practice in spelling *Renaissance.*)

And speaking of spelling, here is one Bloopie on a label from Dr. Scholl's Soft Corn Cushions: "Eases painful shoe pressure and fiction." My favorite former publisher comments, "Apparently, if you wish to improve your writing, you should wear Dr. Scholl's Soft Corn Cushions." But that's just a typo; the real misspelling Bloopie goes to Land's End, whose catalogue copy reads: "So he bought six of our shirts, put them through the ringer for three years and here are the results."

A *ringer* is a look-alike; a *wringer* is a mechanical device, popular in the days before electric dryers, through which you rolled a wet shirt to squeeze out the water. A "dead ringer" is the spit 'n' image, while a "dead wringer" is a defunct attachment to your antique wash pail.

The punctuation Bloopie goes to Hofstra University, which boasts "a 1.3 million volume library, larger than 95 percent of the nations's universities." Neither for the singular nor for the plural possessive will "nations's" do, according to all stylebooks, including the *Times*'s. Also, hyphens would help in "a 1.3-million-volume library," which is "larger than *those of* 95 percent. . . ." Hofstra, with one of the nation's larger libraries, might leave space on a shelf for *Fowler's Modern English Usage,* which Robert Burchfield is bringing up to date for publication.

Finally, in a supplement to a recent issue of *Columbia Journalism Review,* the Times Mirror Center for the People and the Press offers a self-assessment that mistakenly construes *media* as singular. Examples: "the media was 'fair and objective' " and "the media to lower its profile." Unless you believe that the media is a monolith, treat these diverse publications and broadcasters as plural—in these cases, using *were* and *their.* I stumble over this myself on occasion, receiving a small bloopie from the Gotcha! Gang every time; maybe the temptation to lump the media together strikes us because the older term, *press,* is singular. Mnemonic: In everything we do, including awarding the not-so-coveted Bloopies, the press is fair; the media are not.

A copyright *protects "original works of authorship" from being copied, distributed, displayed or performed without the author's permission. A* trademark, *on the other hand, protects "any word, term, name, symbol or device" from uses that are likely to cause confusion, mistake or deception "as to the origin, sponsorship, or approval" of goods or services.*

Copyright protection extends to creative expression such as may be incorporated in your columns, in novels, musical compositions and performances, works of visual art, computer software, multimedia works, and even architectural works. It does not, however, extend to names (e.g., The New York Times*) or brief advertising slogans (e.g., "Things go better with Coke"). Both names and such slogans (which are usually called "taglines") are protectible under trademark principles. Thus, the statement in your May 31 column that the phrase "The Leading Hotels of the World" is "a phrase with a copyright" sounded unlikely to this intellectual-property lawyer.*

A quick perusal of on-line data bases revealed no registered copyright for the phrase "The Leading Hotels of the World." There are, however, four trademark *registrations for "The Leading Hotels of the World." Three registrations (one for the words alone, one for the words in stylized letters and one for the words together with a design) are for hotel reservation services; the fourth registration is for "bath soap, perfumery . . ." and other items presumably likely to be found in bathrooms of those hotels in which rooms are reserved through such services.*

Priscilla A. Walter
Chicago, Illinois

What does one call a blooper on *a blooper.*

Yes, I am one of the thousands who noticed that you "corrected" the title of the company, "Lands' End." Yes, it is "Lands' End," not "Land's End" as you wrote in your recent blooper article.

Vincent O'Keeffe
Akron, Michigan

You referred to "The Leading Hotels of the World" as "a phrase with a copyright." What you meant was a registered trademark. One cannot claim a copyright in a phrase, slogan, or trade name.

Robert C. Cumbow
Seattle, Washington

Master—

As regards "sexist his,*" currently "his or her." Couldn't we agree on "their" as good enough usage? People in my work, men people that is, live in dread of the TV interview in which you leave out "her." Marine Midland has not paid me to send in this suggestion. But they (?) are a Buffalo bank now owned in Hong Kong and you never know.*

Daniel P. Moynihan
Senator, New York
United States Senate
Washington, D.C.

The Bloopie Awards II

For those of you unable to get a seat in the white-tie audience at this year's televised Bloopie Awards ceremony, here are this year's winners. Missing is the tension felt by the advertising copywriters nominated by their peers for grammatical gaffes, as well as the acceptance speeches blaming sponsors who demand language that dumbs down to the lowest denominated consumer.

The yawning lion bloopie to Dreyfus Asset Allocation Fund, for the headline "Some Don't Know How to Choose Between Stocks, Bonds and Money Markets. We Do." Sell short on *between* when that preposition, from the same root as *twain* meaning "two," precedes more than two items. Go long on *among* for three or more, especially when your motto is "Survival of the smartest."

The Bloopie Awards Committee of the Lexicographic Irregulars is not hung up on the rule to use *between* only for two when it conflicts with Norma Loquendi's rule "When *among* sounds funny, stick with *between.*" Goldman Sachs, in wishing *The Economist* magazine a happy 150th birthday, chose to use "Between the fire, the wheel and *The Economist,* mankind will continue to evolve." The new age investment bank was undoubtedly influenced by the idiom *between you, me and the lamppost,* and cannot be given a bloopie for its usage, but it's crowding the border.

The could-care-less, we-meant-the-opposite semi-bloopie to the Lands' End clothing advertisement for its "But we keep tinkering with it—to see if we can't improve it somehow." The meaning is "to see if we *can* improve it," not the opposite, but here, too, an idiom takes over. A loosey-goosey usagist of my acquaintance, chastising my occasional prescriptivism, sent me this note: "See if you can't do better than 'I could care less.' " The meanings of both are reversed; you can read that line as "See if you can do better than 'I couldn't care less.' " Don't fight quirks in the language; idioms is idioms.

Which brings us to agreement bloopies. The Honda Motor Company offers, "One day your child turns 16 and you let them borrow the keys to the wagon." One child is not *them.* The copywriter might argue that he—or she, as the sex may be—felt that *them* would be better than *him* or *her,* either of which imputes a sexist preference to the ultrasensitive. How about "One day your children turn 16 and you let them . . ."? No good, unless they're twins or better. Solution: Recast the sentence a little. "One day your child turns 16 and wants to borrow the keys to the wagon." There's always a way out.

Another agreement bloopie was proposed for the Ford Motor Company, for "In each of us, there's a dreamer and a realist. But now they can share a ride." This proposal argued that *they* reinforced the plurality of *a dreamer and a realist,* disallowing a contraction of *there is.* It was defeated because the correction, "there *are* a dreamer and a realist," while grammatically in agreement, sounds funny. Norma strikes again. Otto Jespersen, the great grammarian, explained the disagreement as an attraction between *is* and the first part of the compound subject, in this case the singular *dreamer.* (Jespersen's example, from Shakespeare's comedy *As You Like It,* is "There comes an old man and his three sons.") Way out: "In each of us, we can find a dreamer and a realist. But now they can share a ride."

The misplaced-indicative bloopie goes to Eddie Bauer, purveyor of deeply striped shirts made in Singapore, for "If life was full of Saturdays. . . ." Unfortunately, six-sevenths of life is not Saturdays, making Bauer's dream a condition contrary to fact and requiring the subjunctive "If life *were.* . . ."

Can you *voice* an *audible*? Sprint advertises its voice-activated Foncard (with a macron over the *o,* to help us pronounce it "oh," instead of spelling it "Fonecard") by telling customers to dial "just by voicing an audible when they are on the line. And that means ten less numbers to remember." You can *voice* an opinion, and a football quarterback can call an *audible,* but this combination stretches the verb form of *voice* too far, even for a Fon company; worse, it means ten *fewer* numbers to remember. For the diet-conscious, Sprint's new TV ad makes the ominous offer to take "50 percent off the person you call most."

The dramatically misplaced modifier bloopie goes to Estée Lauder for "New Advanced Suncare protects you against the sun's most damaging rays without harsh chemical sunscreens." Are the rays without the sunscreens? No; the modifying phrase belongs next to the product it modifies: "New Advanced Suncare, without harsh chemical sunscreens, protects you. . . ."

This year's capitalization bloopie goes to I Can't Believe It's Yogurt! for urging us to "Try a lowfat Fruit Parfait featuring our Nonfat frozen yogurt." This sort of crazed capitalization can be found in the Declaration of Independence, which begins, "When in the Course of human Events, it becomes necessary for one People to dissolve the Political Bands. . . ." In the past two centuries, the trend has been to decapitalize. Even if the incredulous company has a trademark on fruit parfait, it has no reason to capitalize *Nonfat* and lowercase *lowfat.* (I Can't Believe They Did That!)

The bloopie for most pernicious pronoun goes to Barneys New York, which listed under "Some of Our Favorite Things" this salute to a supposedly well-brought-up child answering the telephone: "Kids who say 'Whom may I say is calling?' " Send that pretentious little pedant back to calling all boys to Seventh Avenue and Seventeenth Street; after placing the needed commas after the first "say" and around "may I say," the copywriter should quote Fauntleroy as using *who,* not *whom,* because when *may I say* is dropped out, the question is *"who is calling?"*—not *"whom is calling?"*

The last envelope, please. The spelling bloopie to *The New York Times Magazine,* in an ad for an advertising supplement from the same issue as last year's Bloopie Awards, for suggesting advertisers "snuggle into something warm and envelope yourself in the pages of 'Fabulous Furs.' " That was faux spelling; *envelop* is the verb, *envelope* the noun.

Dear Bill:

You begin your awards for misbehavior by citing for obloquy a mutual fund which, in my opinion, showed excellent judgment in writing: "Choose Between *Stocks, Bonds, and Money Markets." You want them to say* among, *which to my mind would suggest choosing among all the stocks, bonds, and markets, whereas the intended meaning is choosing between pairs in sequence: A & B, and B & C.*

If you turn to Follett, you will find an eloquent article against rigidly applying the rule of between = *only two. You would be the first to admit that the etymological* twain *should not petrify usage. One might as well say that* either or *ought never to be followed by a second* or.

Jacques [Barzun]
New York, New York

You did no service to the language by resurrecting the old superstition that between *is used for two,* among *for three or more. Fowler put it to rest long ago but it is apparently persistent enough for you to restore it to some credit. When it's not the* number *of parties but their relations that you want to stress,* among *doesn't do the job because all it means is "in the middle of," just like* amid. *There can be excellent relations* between *the U.S. and a hundred other countries, but Iran is not* among *them.*

Albert L. Reiner
Greenbrae, California

As to your citing the Declaration of Independence for "crazed capitalization," did you note that your quote capitalizes only the nouns, as the Germans do? Couldn't the close relationship between the two languages have made this still "correct" in the eighteenth century?

Hope Hale Davis
Cambridge, Massachusetts

It's not just pretentious little pedants who say whom *when they mean* who. *Here are some citations from* The Times *(the offenders shall be nameless): "Mr. Guzmán, whom officials said was being held in Lima," "subordinates whom he felt spoke too freely to the press," "a Russian native . . . whom even his prosecutors concede is an indefatigable businessman."*

*Louis Jay Herman**
New York, New York

I believe the expression is "between you and me and the lamppost," which is grammatically correct. In use there would probably be a tiny pause or change in inflection, not worth a punctuation mark, after the "me."

John Granbery
Salisbury, Connecticut

*Louis Jay Herman, my most frequently quoted correspondent, died on May 13, 1996.

The Bloopie Awards III

Time once again for the coveted Bloopie Awards, recognition of Madison Avenue solecisms that sends thrills of *Schadenfreude* through the ranks of advertising copywriters.

Because the top of this column gets the lowest rating (the audience increases as we approach Prime Space), we begin with the least important award, "For the most egregious abuse of the comma." Push the envelope, please:

We have a five-way tie, or quintuple dead heat, as racing fans say. CBS erred in a spot for the mini-series *Scarlett.* (That's the sequel to *Gone With the Wind,* but CBS says Ted Turner's outfit, which owns that film, won't let CBS use the title in its ads; this column, however, is keenly aware of its First Amendment rights.) The network printed on screen: "Frankly my dear, I don't give a damn" as a voice-over intoned, "It was the most controversial statement of its time."

Let us set aside the affected pronunciation of *controversial* as "con-tro-VER-see-ul"—the preferred form is "contro-VERSH-ul"—and zero in on the statement that first used the word *damn* in movies. The Hays Office would never have permitted it, Will Hays once told me, had not Clark Gable, playing Rhett Butler, de-emphasized the profanity, delivering the line as "don't GIVE a damn."

The CBS line has no comma after the sentence adverb *frankly,* although the *Gone With the Wind* screenplay has it with the comma, and an exclamation mark to boot: "Frankly, my dear, I don't give a damn!" (In Margaret Mitchell's novel, she never used the *frankly:* "He drew a short breath and said lightly but softly: 'My dear, I don't give a damn.' ") In direct address, the name or its substitute (as in *my dear* or *my fine feathered friend*) must be set off by commas.

The comma is also needed in Sherlock Holmes's famous line "Elementary, my dear Watson." Holmes, however, never spoke that line, at least not in Arthur Conan Doyle's stories. (Basil Rathbone did use the phrase when he played Sherlock Holmes in movies.) With the comma for direct address, the familiar saying would also answer the question "What school did you go to, darling?" Without that comma, dear reader, the copywriter has made a mistake.

As has Toyota in this line: "To us, a successful business shouldn't just try to make a profit, it should try to make a difference as well." That's a comma splice: two complete sentences incorrectly joined by a comma. Toyota could have used a semicolon after "profit," or put a period after that word and started a new sentence, or added a conjunction: "profit, but it should try. . . ."

Catching Toyota on the test-track turn is Mercedes-Benz, with its "Technologically speaking it had no rivals. . . . Even standing still the S 320 easily leaves other cars behind." Both *Technologically speaking* and *Even standing still* are used as introductory participial phrases that cry out for punctuation to separate them from their sentences' main thoughts. Also, nothing in the first sentence has to do with speaking, and the result is a dangling modifier; it should read

"Technologically, it had no rivals," or "Technologically speaking, we are sure it had no rivals" (though Toyota can rival it on comma splicing any day).

Not to be outdone by foreign rivals, the Ford Citibank credit card, in conjunction with Hertz and Texaco, offers an ungrammatical rebate: "To apply see your Ford or Lincoln-Mercury dealer." An introductory infinitive phrase, like *To apply* or *To run up a whopping bill,* calls for a comma to separate it from the main clause, especially when misreading is possible. The comma should be left out only if the infinitive phrase is the subject of the main clause, as in "To apply is to get rejected."

Fifth entry is "The Coca-Cola Company in collaboration with Franklin Heirloom Dolls, authorizes their first-ever heirloom collector doll." The comma after "Dolls" requires a balancing comma after "Company"; you could get away with no commas at all, but if you're going to start down the comma road in this instance, you need both.

In the non-comma bloopie group, the winner is Attends, the incontinence product: "Attends' patented Perma-Dry fibers pull in wetness faster than other leading retail brands to help protect you." This is a misplaced modifier; for clarity, it should read, "To help protect you, Attends'. . . ." Also, I'd put another *s* after that apostrophe, though some authorities disagree; the possessive should sound like "Attends-ziz."

In the field of word choice, an ad writer for the realty division of *The New York Times Magazine* wins the coveted bloopie: "Whether it's a city tower . . . manor house . . . or seaside cove, it's here for you to dream on. And one day (soon, perhaps) to act on." The writer was reaching for a parallelism—*dream on* and *act on*—but *dream on* is a different idiom, something you tell a copywriter when he tells you he thinks he will one day be a poet. We *dream about* and *dream of;* nobody ever dreamed on Jeanie with the light brown hair.

And now—in Prime Space, with readers breathless with suspense—we come to the Most Horrendous Solecism of 1994, submitted by Thomas Luskin of Bayside, Queens. By virtue of the prestige of the sponsors, it is the Super Bloopie.

It goes to eighty-seven Nobel laureates—in chemistry, economics, literature, medicine, physics and peace—who signed an ad titled "A Call to Reason" in support of measures to control population growth.

"The survival of mankind, and of the earth which sustains all of us, are in serious jeopardy," it begins, and is proudly signed by wreathed worthies from Christian Anfinsen to Geoffrey Wilkinson. Linus Pauling signed it, too, though he is dead.

Let us not nitpick about *mankind,* a word embracing male and female that is being replaced by *humankind.* And there are those who will let the Nobel laureates get away with the *which* when *that* is better to introduce a dependent clause not set off by commas. No; the inescapable root problem here is subject-verb disagreement.

The simple subject is *survival.* That takes the singular verb *is.* Everything between the word *survival* and the verb *is* falls in the domain of prepositional phrases, not part of the subject of the sentence. Only if the subject had been repeated—"The survival of mankind and the survival of the earth"—could you correctly use the plural *are.*

The Nobel laureates, or their petition copywriter, would do well to study the similarly constructed statement posted at the entrance to Busch Gardens amusement park in Virginia: CLOTHING WITH SUGGESTIVE OR EXPLICIT LANGUAGE OR INSULTING STATEMENTS IS NOT ALLOWED. Although *explicit* is a foolish euphemism for "obscene," the sentence's simple subject—*clothing*—leaps over the intervening phrases to agree with the singular verb *is.* You can learn plenty at amusement parks.

One thing about the language dodge: A cat can look at a king.

We enjoyed your column on the Bloopie Awards. In fact, we relished it to such an extent that we forwarded it to our local Chamber of Commerce—presided over, we believe, at this period by none other than that inconclusive character—Sammy Colon.

Ellie and George Shearing
New York, New York

A Bridge Too Far

Connie Chung, following weeks of interviews about her elevation to co-anchor with Dan Rather on *The CBS Evening News,* gave her reaction to the ordeal to *USA Today:* "I'm *fartumelt! Fartootst! Farmisht!*"

For those without a copy of Leo Rosten's* *Joys of Yiddish* at hand, here is the synonymy:

Fartumelt (rooted in the German *tummein,* "to rush about") means "bewildered."

Fartootst (from the German *verdutzt,* "confused") means "mixed up."

Farmisht (from the German *vermisch,* "mingled") is the strongest of the three, meaning "all balled up, totally confused."

The alliteration, not to mention the perfectly calibrated increase in emphasis on confusion demonstrated by the choice of the three synonyms, suggests that Ms Chung has a fine command of Yiddishisms.

She did not add *farblondjet* (from the Slavic "to roam"), which means "wan-

*Leo Rosten, a great source about the Yiddish language, died in 1997 at the age of eighty-eight.

dering about with no idea where you are," presumably because that word is frequently used by worried ABC executives to describe CBS News.

Concerning Connie Chung's knowledge of Yiddish: After noting that the three Yiddish past participles she used, all beginning with the prefix far, *originally came from German verbs beginning with* ver, *you bring up a similar Yiddish word,* farblondjet. *Fine, but how did you ever reach the far-out conclusion that* farblondjet *comes "from the Slavic 'to roam' "? What's wrong with the German* verblendet *(akin to English* blinded*), which surely could well mean "wandering about with no idea where you are"?*

Mary Lou Pacepa
Arlington, Virginia

A Bridge Too Fur

"The aim of NATO's future expansion," the Clinton Administration's National Security Council staff writes in its strategy statement, "will not be to draw a new line in Europe further east, but to expand stability, democracy," etc.

Quoting this line in a recent polemic, I put a [*sic*]—the Latin word for "so, thus" to mean "error in the original"—after *further.* That's because the word for distance is *farther,* and the word for degree or expressing a sense of "beyond" is *further.* Furthermore (only say "farthermore" in the Situation Room), you can use *further* to mean either degree or metaphoric distance, but you should use *farther* only for physical distance.

But a language maven has to be careful with his bracketed thuses because he cannot then let anything go by. A colleague circled "will not be to draw a new line" and swung the *not* behind the *be* to read "will be not to draw a new line . . . but to expand." The Nitpickers' League has a new member.

Bungee Jumping

"One scene from the last Judson Welliver Society meeting stayed with me," writes Mary Kate Cary, recollecting the assemblage of former White House speechwriters, of which she is one. When that ghostly gathering learned that President Clinton had reviewed a speech on the prompter for the first time only minutes before airtime, she notes, Anthony Snow, with whom she served on the Bush staff, exclaimed, "That's bungee jumping!"

As the group chuckled, Arthur Schlesinger Jr.—a Kennedy adviser and writer, and the coiner of such phrases as "the Imperial Presidency," "the vital center" and "permanent government"—turned to Tony Dolan, the author of Ronald Reagan's "evil empire" phrase, to ask, "What's bungee jumping?"

"Tony explained something about people tying a rope around themselves and jumping off a cliff," Ms Cary recalls. "Schlesinger peered through his glasses at Tony for a time, and made a 'harrumph' noise."

The sound, I think, was not a disapproving *harrumph;* it was more of a *hmpf* of wonderment from a lover of vivid metaphors.

A few days later, the phrase was back in the news. Dick Thornburgh, the former Attorney General who spent a year decompressing as United Nations Under Secretary for Administration and Management, issued a farewell report that described the financing of peacekeeping operations as "much like a financial *'bungee jump,'* often undertaken in blind faith that timely appropriations will be forthcoming." A *New York Times* editorial on this subject was titled "Bungee Jumping at the U.N.," which the International *Herald Tribune* improved with "Enough Bungee Jumping."

Bungee, which is sometimes spelled *bungie,* is defined in the *Oxford English Dictionary* supplement as British slang for "india rubber." A 1934 citation says, "The piece of india-rubber for erasing purposes was referred to as 'india-bungie' or 'bungie.' "

However, Punch Coomaraswamy, a former Singapore Ambassador to the United States, who grew up in a Malaysian rubber-growing area, challenged this assumption and sent me an entry from *Hobson-Jobson,* a glossary of colloquial Anglo-Indian words that defined *bangy,* rooted in the Sanskrit *vihangama,* as "a shoulder-yoke for carrying loads, the yoke or bangy resting on the shoulder, while the load is apportioned at either end in two equal weights, and generally hung by cords."

Other Lexicographic Irregulars have noted the word used for elastic ties for parachutes—"we always snapped those *bungies* to make sure they still had their elasticity"—and in a 1946 book, Theodore H. White described a model airplane driven by a propeller worked by a rubber band as "her wretched *bungee* airplane."

Whatever the correct etymology, the ideas of elasticity and load-bearing cords are present. We are now ready for a bungee jump.

You are hoisted high aloft by a crane or attain some altitude in your hot-air balloon. Attached to your ankle is a *bungee cord,* a thick elastic that is also tied to your jumping-off point. You then leap, screaming, into the blue; well before you hit the ground, the elastic cord begins restraining your fall, until you are bouncing up and down. After a while, you are just hanging there, gently bobbing, and your friend at the jumping-off point hauls you back in.

"Modern bungee jumping," *The New York Times* reported in 1991, "using the wrist-thick bundles of rubber strands wrapped in woven nylon, was born on April Fool's Day, 1979, when members of the Oxford Dangerous Sports Club attached bungee cords to themselves and dived from the 245-foot Clifton Bridge in Bristol, England." At the time, the *Sunday Telegraph* quoted one member as saying, "Quite pleasurable, really."

Its current political and financial meaning, Professor Schlesinger: Any unnecessarily risky undertaking, especially a stunt that gives the participant a feeling of living dangerously and onlookers a thrill of trepidation.

Dear Bill:

You're right! It was a hmpf *of wonderment, not a* harrumph *of dis*approval. *And now at last I know about bungee jumping.*

Arthur [Schlesinger Jr.]
New York, New York

Centered on Focused

"By sticking fast to a *focused,* no-nonsense strategy," *Fortune* writes about Laurence A. Tisch, the chairman of CBS, "Tisch, 70, has triumphantly built CBS back to the No. 1–rated television network."

In an *Arkansas Times* article about the apparent suicide of the deputy White House counsel, John Brummett quoted a stunned former employer as saying of Vincent Foster, "He was the most *focused* person I ever knew, with the possible exception of his friend Hillary."

In current use, *focused* is one of the two vogue words for "purposeful, dedicated, resolute," replacing the last generation's vogue word, *committed.* The other word for those with their eye fixed determinedly on the ball is *centered.*

Self-centered was and is pejorative. "The wretch, concentered all in self" was denounced in *The Lay of the Last Minstrel* by Sir Walter Scott in 1805. But Quakers had long spoken of "peace at the center," describing one at peace with oneself; the past participle *centered* began a century ago with the simple sense of "being on center," which led to a sense of "emotionally stable and secure" in twentieth-century psychology.

Fred Mish of Merriam-Webster comments: "I don't think *centered* and *focused* are synonyms. *Focused* means something more like 'intent,' 'concentrated,' and it seems more often to refer to a temporary condition than to a continuing state of mind and soul, as *centered* does." For an early citation, he offers William Faulkner's 1957 description of a character involved in "all sorts of things that would have made a weaker or a less *centered* man blench and falter, but not him."

With this purposeful sense, *centered* was right in the middle of the psychobabble that featured ways to *get in touch with your feelings,* and saw the explosion of the verb *relate to.*

In this argot, *space* shook off its *spaced-out* connotation and became a desired *place:* You needed space, said those who were "into distancing," to explore your own needs or luxuriate in your delicious uniqueness. *Dynamic* changed from a hard-charging adjective (campily reappearing in Batman's "dynamic duo") to become a noun of interaction, playing emotions off against one another to avoid *closure,* the dread end of the affair. *Interface* has been a verb at the heart of this post-space age, denoting the point of interaction among systems, groups and—best of all—*processes.* During this period, even peace became a process.

In this psycholingo, metaphor is strangely absent; the vocabulary is bloodless, and such phrases as *at the heart of* in the previous sentence were eschewed. Anne Soukhanov, who brought the third edition of the *American Heritage Dictionary* to fruition, has a theory about that: "Psychobabble avoids the metaphors and sense extensions rooted in biology, because biological changes inevitably involve decay and death. Instead, psychobabble chooses words from the physical sciences: *centered, focused, dynamic, space.* By extension, these words depersonalize, creating vague abstractions from things once concrete. They redefine people in terms of mass, energy and process—the physical sciences, not the flesh and blood, growth and death of biology."

This department is open to emendation or refutation from those who embrace the physics-based vocabulary (or who boast the facile facility of facilitators), but this notion of the linguistic influence of the physical sciences offers food for thought: *center* and *focus* come from mathematics and optics. The *center* is rooted in the spike on a pair of compasses; "an early meaning of *focus,*" Ms Soukhanov points out, "was the 'burning point' of a lens. Moreover, in Latin *focus* originally meant a hearth or fireplace, the focal point of a home. And if highly *focused* and *centered* individuals inexplicably *stress out,* can *burnout* be far behind?"

Metaphors follow cultural trends. A University of Maryland physics professor, Robert L. Park, threw a large thought into an Op-Ed piece in *The New York Times:* "Society will change even more rapidly as we leave the century of physics and enter the century of biology." O.K., everybody—off center, out of focus. We'll soon let life, death and growth interface with our space.

I am surprised at you. Surely you cannot agree one iota with Professor Park's assertion that we are leaving the century of physics and entering the century of biology. The simple truth is that biology's current hot topic, genetic engineering, is made possible by quantum mechanics (through the interpretation of X-ray diffraction data as well as an understanding of molecular binding). Other modern offshoots of physics include: microchips, new drugs, cloning, and lasers used for fiber optic communication, compact disks, and microsurgery. In fact, all of what we really know about chemistry is based on physics. Things that go bump at the atomic and molecular level do not follow the rules (of classical science), which is why physics' own spin doctors (who declared that a particle must turn around twice to get back where it started) resemble political spin doctors.

President Clinton is obviously aware of all this and that is why he has promised to "focus like a laser" *on the economy. I am sure no one wants to get in his way. No doubt you will remember from Bronx Science that* laser *is an acronym for "light amplification by stimulated emission of radiation," a feat made possible by—you guessed it—quantum mechanics. Even former President Bush chose his metaphors from physics, when he expressed concern with (his) position and momentum, which he referred to simply as the "Big mo." What Bush never learned from quantum mechanics, though, is that you cannot look at something without changing it. I believe that the late Senator E. Dirksen also equated physics with politics when he said, "When I get the heat, I see the light."*

In this time of uncertainty, what better source of metaphor than physics, which holds uncertainty as a central principle. Einstein, who, ironically, introduced the notion of probability into atomic theory, could not bring himself to accept the uncertainty principle, hence his famous statement, "God does not play dice."

You say, "We'll soon let life, death and growth interface with our space." Not a chance. At least not with my cyberspace.

Michael S. Spataro
Brooklyn, New York

Chat Me Up

The columnist Richard Cohen, writing about that unabashed advocate of traditional virtues William Bennett, noted, "Few members of what the Brits call the *chattering class* hail from conservative Christian backgrounds."

Evidently a need exists for a phrase that columnists, pundits, commentators and other harangutangs can use to flagellate themselves and one another. *Punditocracy,* a 1988 coinage of Eric Alterman, and *mediacracy,* blending *media bureaucracy* with *mediocrity,* are too intellectual. *Talking heads* is limited to television and lacks zing. Besides, with the rise of the radio talk shows (*chat shows* in England) as well as the televised food-for-thought fights, commentary today has become more oral than written; to characterize the participants in this panelization of opinion-mongering, Americans have seized on this Britishism, which has become the most important contribution of the mother country to the lingo we call Murkin since *not to worry* and *spot on.*

Its first appearance over here: "Political commentators and supposed insiders," Joseph Lelyveld, a reporter with an uncertain future at *The New York Times,* wrote from Blackpool, England, in 1986, "—sometimes referred to in Britain as 'the chattering classes.' " Recently, Susan Estrich, who managed Michael Dukakis's campaign, wrote in *USA Today* that the press has been savage in its criticism of President Clinton: "The turn against him by the *chattering classes* has been much documented."

The columnist Charles Krauthammer noted that, a decade ago, the notion that Ronald Reagan had his finger on the button "was enough to send the *chattering classes* into a nuclear frenzy." North Korea, he added, may be developing a bomb: "Yet this time the *chattering classes* appear rather calm about the danger." In the *San Francisco Chronicle,* Jerry Carroll used the phrase to derogate liberals in recounting the backlash against high taxation: "Keep this thumbnail history in mind next time you hear the *chattering classes* bash Proposition 13."

Meanwhile, it flourishes in the British press: "There's a tendency among the *chattering classes,*" writes the cultural critic Will Self in *The Guardian,* "—another of our great coinages—to trash our own before anyone else can." And an *Evening Standard* sportswriter provided a subdivision when blasting opponents of pay-TV soccer as "the Syncopated Hand-wringers and Whingers (the bleating faction of the *chattering classes*)."

From these usages, we can determine that *classes* has triumphed over *class,* and the disparaging thrust of the phrase is directed by the chic populist set against liberals, intellectuals and others of that ilk who do go on. It is defined in *Bloomsbury Neologisms* as "the opinionated, usually liberal, usually metropolitan middle classes; the main chatterers are employed by the media. . . . The implication, much derided by the usually right-wing enterprise culture, [is] that . . . they talk a good deal, but create very little."

Who coined the much-needed phrase, on the analogy of *working classes*? In a November 25, 1989, piece in *The Guardian,* Alan Watkins of *The Observer,* the undisputed popularizer, attributed coinage to a journalist, Frank Johnson, in a conversation in the late 70's or early 80's, when the two lived in neighboring apartments. After noting this burst of honesty by the popularizer, the 1991 *Oxford Dictionary of New Words* defined the phrase he made famous as "educated members of the middle and upper classes who read the 'quality' newspapers, hold freely expressed liberal political opinions and see themselves as highly articulate and socially aware."

(How did I dig up the origin? The time-saving *Barnhart New-Words Concordance* lists all the new terms cited in the ten main reference works on neologisms. That directed my chief research aide, Jeffrey McQuain, to the *Oxford Dictionary of New Words,* as well as to *Bloomsbury Neologisms,* which I did not have, but David K. Barnhart, the concordance editor, faxed us the entry from his copy. Next time I'm in Foyles on Charing Cross Road, I'll pick one up. We all help one another in this dodge.)

The early English *chatter,* like *twitter* and *jabber,* came from imitating the rapid sounds of birds. "Human 'chattering' was originally transferred from the chattering of birds," the *Oxford English Dictionary* reports, but nowadays the figurative use of "chattering" for magpies is thought to come from the noise of humans.

How does *chattering* differ from *nattering*? While barnstorming with Spiro Agnew in 1970, I churned out the *nattering nabobs of negativism* to alliteratively eviscerate the pack of professional pessimists, in an updating of Adlai Stevenson's *prophets of gloom and doom.* Stewart Alsop, a longtime student of British English and the best political columnist ever, was on the campaign plane and argued that *nattering* meant only "chattering," with no connotation of complaint. (Yeah, but I needed a word beginning with *n.*) I held that "natter, natter" was the dialect equivalent of "bitch, bitch," and that the echoic or onomatopoeic verb "to natter" conveyed a message of nagging criticism. The sainted Stew later accepted that grudgingly when shown a 1943 book of service slang defining the verb as "to chide or chatter in an irritatingly aimless fashion."

Since then, however, I have come up with the clincher: In his 1829 *Glossary of North Country Words,* John T. Brockett defined *natter* as "to scold, to speak in a querulous or peevish manner." And the novelist George Eliot, in her 1859 *Adam Bede,* wrote of a character "whose motherly feeling now got the better of her 'nattering' habit."

Both *chattering classes* and *nattering nabobs of negativism* are attacks on critics, usually *eggheads* (another derogation of intellectuals, coined by Carl Sandburg in 1918 and popularized, coincidentally, by Stew and Joe Alsop's brother John). The phrase *politically correct* is another current attack on liberals, especially those in the academy. Where is the counterbalancing attack on the populists? Over a generation ago, liberals could deride their opponents as *little old ladies in tennis shoes* or *rednecks,* and long before that, the Swiftian *yahoos* and the turtle-based *mossbacks.* Of late, however, leftists have neglected the art of vituperation. The phrase for the anti-intellectual intellectual has yet to be coined.

The reason I clipped the fast-rising Mr. Cohen's column, however, was to question his use of "hail from . . . backgrounds." Ever since 1841, *hail from* has been limited to specific places. One hails from Brooklyn, as Mr. Cohen does, not from a background or culture or other abstraction. I point this out to show the difference between *chattering* (what he does) and *nattering* (what I do).

Clinton Defender

"What you call subject-verb disagreement is frequent and justified when it serves the subtle purpose of suggesting the unity of two ideas," writes Jacques Barzun, a member of "On Language" 's Board of Octogenarian Mentors (Olbom), objecting to my nitpicking of William Jefferson Clinton's inaugural address. "Your very example of *toil and sweat sends us* is such a nuance, for obviously the sweat is one with the toil. A plural verb would imply two separate causes propelling *us.* In the second example, *will and conscience,* your objection is sound, because you are able to show that the phrase refers to two distinct situations.

"In the *each in our own way* you are entirely right," Professor Barzun continues, setting me up for the kill, "but might have pointed out that when *each* precedes the verb, the plural follows; *each* is not always singular. Hence the tendency to slip into error. But when you reprove *each other* as wrong for *one another,* you go against usage and logic both. 'Each the other' surely will take in a crowd in pairs as quickly as 'one another.' See Fowler (*Modern English Usage*)."

I don't see Fowler much these days. But surely the man in the house of intellect cannot object to my purist criticism of President Clinton's use of *raised* when the proper verb is *reared*?

"I agree that *raised* for *reared* lacks elegance. But it is perfectly clear and no blunder. Indeed, there are contexts in which *raised* is called for: 'Born on a rundown farm and raised on pork and beans and hard work.' *Reared* would be silly here, wouldn't it?

"Finally," writes Olbom's Barzun, in a Parthian (not a parting) shot, "in disallowing *nor* after a negative, you are only expressing a modern preference. In the 19th century, the opposite was generally preferred. G. B. Shaw almost invariably used *nor* where we use *or.* Swift had done the same, and there you have the two greatest masters of plain English."

Ordinarily I would raise an eyebrow at the placement of *only* in "are only expressing," but I think it's a trap.

Don't let that rascal Barzun snow you regarding the use of or *and* nor. *Of course you are "only expressing a modern preference" when you disallow* nor *after a negative. However, that preference is so well established today that Shaw's and Swift's usage is completely beside the point. Let Barzun try* nor *after a negative in a few simple sentences, and he will see how absurdly it strikes the modern ear: "I don't like this nor that." "I haven't seen John nor Mary." "I didn't eat nor drink."*

Louis Jay Herman
New York, New York

Compellence or *Compellance*?

"The case for 'Compellance' " was the headline over a particularly insightful essay in *The New York Times* last month, calling on President Clinton to bomb the Serbians in Bosnia into a cease-fire. "Needed also is strategic coercion," wrote the columnist: "*compellance* is the word now being heard in the Pentagon. It means the use of air power to persuade by punishment. *Compellance* is not obliteration. . . . Rather, its sudden infliction of national pain . . . is intended to encourage negotiation by leveling more than playing fields."

I spelled it wrong, twice in the copy and once in the headline. A Pentagonian sent me a speech by Les Aspin, then a mere Representative and later Secretary of Defense, on September 21, 1992: "The debate . . . will hinge on two questions—one, something called escalation and, two, something called *compellence.*" After defining *escalation,* which we all know and I can spell, Congressman Aspin dealt with the new word: "*Compellence* is the use of military force against an adversary to influence his behavior elsewhere. The issue of compellence is at the heart of the argument made by the limited objectives camp."

Where did he get the word? In came this missive from a Princeton professor, Avinash Dixit: "This is a rare instance where the person who coined the word gave an explanation for his choice." He attached a page from the 1966 book *Arms and Influence,* by Thomas C. Schelling.

"There is, then, a difference between *deterrence* and what we might, for want of a better word, call *compellence,*" Mr. Schelling wrote. Searching for a relationship similar to *statics* and *dynamics,* Schelling synonymized: "*Coercion* covers the meaning but unfortunately includes 'deterrent' as well as 'compellent' intentions. *Intimidation* is insufficiently focused on the particular behavior desired. *Compulsion* is all right but its adjective is 'compulsive,' and that has come to carry quite a different meaning. *Compellence* is the best I can do."

He did well, making a noun out of an adjective used first by Elizabeth Barrett Browning in 1847 with the spelling *compellant.* Professor Dixit notes: "Schelling spells his neologism *compellence.* Is there any reason to prefer *compellance*?"

In an attempt to brazen it out, I tried Fred Mish, editor in chief of Merriam-Webster, whose avidly awaited *Tenth Collegiate Dictionary* recently hit the bookstores. He's cool: "The ending with *-e-* is the more etymological choice, but as one of the very few users of the word, you could plausibly argue that you're entitled to make your own choice and etymology be hanged."

But not with "Ipse" Dixit on my case. *Compellence* it is.

Dear Bill:

I beg your pardon, but compulsive *is not the regular adjective for "compulsion"; it is* compulsory. *The* -ive *form was created by psychoanalysts to describe the behavior of neurotics who can't keep themselves from doing what they know is foolish or harmful.*

As for the hideous compellance, *what is the need for it? I can detect no difference in meaning from* coercion. *It's only a euphemism of the kind people are so fond of nowadays, forgetting that they soon wear out their cloakiness and stand out as naughty words like those they replaced.*

What is worse, this kind of pointless neologism breeds imitations. We'll soon have impellance, propellance, *and* repellance, *just as we got* basal *and* supplemental *doubling* basic *and* supplementary.

Jacques [Barzun]
New York, New York

Dear Bill:

In the column on compellence/compellance *(if I may second-guess Fred Mish), he said that* compellence *would be "the more etymological choice" because it is closer to the Latin source:* compellere, *as also such other forbidding words as* deterrere/obstruere, *whence* deterrent/obstruent. *On the other hand, there are the* -ant *words as Latin* resistare, *to resist,* repugnare, *to oppose, whence* resistance/repugnance. *So we are still using Latin to tell us how to spell English—if we accept this. On the other hand, the* -ant *spelling comes more naturally to the English speller, since* -a- *comes closer than* -e- *to the central or "neutral" vowel with which we say it. So, despite the Latin source,* -ance *is gaining ground over* -ence. *It is unrealistic to expect people who know no Latin to consult it before spelling English, or (unless they are utterly at home in Latin) to think in Latin when spelling English. The alternative would be to know each English word as an individual case, which is what winners of spelling bees end up doing. Dictionaries, being normally conservative, will choose for the Latin form, or list it first. But if the non-Latin form seems more natural, it will gradually come in and dictionaries will have to list it. Of course, these days, the hand that rocks the computer cradle will be the hand that rules the world, and it may become* compellant.

Fred [Frederic G. Cassidy]
Chief Editor
Dictionary of American Regional English
Madison, Wisconsin

I always knew that the English language would need Latin's future passive paraphrastic, e.g., Cato's delenda est Carthago. *Les Aspin's use of* compellence *suggests that the time has come for* compellenda est Serbia.

Alice Coyle Lunn
Olmstead Falls, Ohio

Not Easy Being

In the same column misspelling *compellence* (ten uses and they have to put it in the next unabridged, and that makes ten, counting Mrs. Browning's adjectival pioneering), I predicted that the next Chairman of the Joint Chiefs of Staff will be "wearing a uniform not of Army khaki but of Air Force blue."

Ran into the present Chairman, who offered this correction: "The color of the U.S. Army uniform is *green*." General Colin Powell was wearing his civvies at the time and couldn't prove his point, so I called the Pentagon the next day.

Forget *khaki,* which we wore forty years ago and became so unchic that it was picked up in this generation by Ralph Lauren. Forget *olive drab,* too. Corrected prediction: The next Chairman of the Joint Chiefs will not be wearing *green.*

The Core Corps

"On those things that are at the core of our contract," said incipient Speaker Newt Gingrich, "on those things that are at the core of our philosophy . . . there will be no compromise."

Core is in. To get right to the heart of the matter, as we used to say, such terms as *center, hub, nucleus, crux* and even *quintessence* have been rendered hopelessly old-fashioned.

Those who remember *core* mainly for "rotten to the core" had better get down to the kernel of the nut: The vogue word's power is shown by its use not merely as a noun but also as a modifier.

Newtonians speak of *core beliefs;* virtuous William Bennett holds forth on *core values;* liberal alliterators worry about *core concerns* in the *core city* (*inner* is out). Thus has *core* established itself as the year's hottest attributive noun, ousting yesteryear's *executive* summary and *killer* whale.

Bryce Harlow, the speechwriter and adviser to Presidents, liked to express the center's center as "peeling the onion down to where the tears are." Shakespeare's Hamlet swore that if he could find a man that is not passion's slave, "I will wear him in my heart's *core,*" immediately defining that for slow audiences as "in my heart of heart." Shakespeare used the singular *heart of heart* correctly. By 1806, Wordsworth was pushing the plural, which is now the familiar form: "Yet in my *heart of hearts* I feel your might."

When did we start using *core* as a modifier? In the nineteenth century, *core bar* and *core box* were used in metal-casting. In 1926, a guide to Stone Age implements in the British Museum observed "the change from a *core*-industry to a flake-industry." (Flake-industries today range from head shops to political commentary.)

To get to the nub, I turned to the *Barnhart Dictionary of Etymology.* The noun is suggested there to be derived from the French *coeur,* literally "heart," from the Latin *cor* for the same word, which does not lead to a *coronary* (from the Latin *corona,* "crown"). The etymologists report that the first use of *core* to mean "the part of a nuclear reactor containing fissionable material" was recorded in 1949, and note that the verb form—"to take out the core of fruit"—dates to the mid-fifteenth century.

But this excellent reference work about linguistic roots has no coverage of the attributive noun that today's deep thinkers have taken to their innermost lexicon. For that, you have to go to the cover of the dictionary, which advertises itself as covering "the *core* vocabulary of Standard English."

Cut Them Some Slack

"Americans of my generation," Bill Clinton told U.C.L.A. students, "have been bombarded by images on television shows, and even one book, about the so-called 'Generation X' filled with cynics and slackers. Well, what I have seen today is not a generation of slackers, but a generation of seekers."

The Clinton use of the word *slacker* calls to mind the reaction of Franklin D. Roosevelt when Republicans complained of continuing depression: "There is an old and somewhat lugubrious adage that says, 'Never speak of rope in the house of a man who has been hanged.' In the same way, if I were a Republican leader speaking to a mixed audience, the last word in the whole dictionary that I think I would use is that word 'depression.' "

The last word we might expect from Mr. Clinton, frequently accused of using deception in avoiding the draft during the Vietnam War, is *slacker.* Perhaps he took a current sense from the title of Richard Linklater's 1991 film, *Slacker,* celebrating the lazy life of Texas drifters and castoffs in their twenties who are now more frequently called *Generation X'ers* than *twenty-somethings.* (That term is derived from the title of the TV series *Thirtysomething.* Curiously, the longer *-something* has replaced the suffix *-ish.*) And perhaps a young speechwriter wanted to contrast those *slackers* with *seekers,* presumably from "seekers of truth," as in Jeremiah's efforts to "find a man . . . that seeketh the truth."

The noun *slacker*—from the adjective *slack,* meaning "loose"—first appeared in 1898 to refer to "one who avoids work or physical exercise; a shirker." During World War I, it was a derogation of anyone avoiding military service, including conscientious objectors. In World War II, it was used interchangeably with *draft dodger.*

Since the late 1960's, it has regained its original, general meaning as a second sense, which may be what Bill Clinton had in mind. The harsh edge of the word may have been softened by the influence of *cut him some slack,* derived from loosening a taut rope in sailing, its meaning extended to "ease up on him; allow room for maneuver."

Slacks are also casual trousers, not part of a suit; in the 90's, *slacking* now denotes the wearing of loose jeans: "The hip-hopsters' trademark blue jeans five sizes too big (a.k.a. *slackin'*)," wrote the magazine *Essence,* "created such a noise that clothing giants like Levi Strauss & Company began manufacturing oversize jeans to quench demand." (Take it from me: Baggy or "relaxed fit" jeans have long been the favorite of sixty-somethings.)

And what of *Generation X,* that nonslacker but often happily slacking cohort of seekers referred to by the President? "The Myth of Generation X" was the cover line of a recent *Newsweek,* with the subtitle "Seven Great Lies About 20-Somethings." These myths include "They're *slackers* . . . whiners . . . white . . . psychically damaged children of divorce . . . [devotees of the suicide] Kurt Cobain . . . [and they'll] buy anything." Seventh "myth" is that Generation X exists at all; the writer held that many in the cohort thought that their stereotyped X-hood was a plot by the previous generation—the middle-aged baby boomers—to put them down.

Although the coinage is usually attributed to the title of a 1991 novel by Douglas Coupland, the philologists John and Adele Algeo note in the Fall 1994 issue of *American Speech* magazine that it was also the title of a 1964 book by Charles Hamblett and Jane Deverson about the "alienated" generation of that time.

Everybody wants to be part of a generation; it's an exclusive cultural club. According to Ernest Hemingway, Gertude Stein found a there there in France with *the lost generation* after World War I; Winston Churchill, in 1930, called it "a generation shorn by the war." Jack Kerouac is credited with coining *the Beat Generation.* John F. Kennedy, in his inaugural, said, "The torch has been passed to a new generation of Americans." And we have recently seen the series finale of *Star Trek: The Next Generation.*

Generation comes from the Latin *genus,* "birth, kind," also generating *general* and *generous.* Grammarians clasp the related *genitive* to their bosoms, a case showing possession. We all have that yearning to belong.

You wonder if Gertrude Stein (with the help of Ernest Hemingway) coined the phrase "lost generation." According to the well-written biography Gertrude and Alice *by Diana Souhami, the phrase definitely did originate with Monsieur Pernollet, a hotelier in Belley, France. On page 168 of the text, Ms. Souhami explains that Monsieur Pernollet believed "that men became civilised between the ages of eighteen and twenty-six. Those who fought in the First World War were de-*

nied the opportunity and so were a lost generation." Gertrude Stein liked the phrase, repeated it to Hemingway, and the rest is history.

Roberta Dawson Chabalko
Wilmington, Delaware

Cyberlingo

Sir Winston Churchill is turning over in his grave.

Peering into the mists of the future, the keepers of all the books and papers of the past and present at the Library of Congress came up with a dreary name for its plans to reproduce a core of its holdings as on-line digital bits: the National Information Infrastructure.

When Sir Winston in 1950 heard an opposition politician use *infrastructure,* the lover of forthright English prose rose in the House of Commons to heap ridicule on the uppity member: "It may well be that these words 'infra' and 'supra' have been introduced into our current political parlance by the band of intellectual highbrows who are naturally anxious to impress British labor with the fact that they learned Latin at Winchester."

Vampire-like, *infrastructure* has returned in the dead of night to suck the blood out of the colorful language of the information age. A *Washington Post* editorialist had a livelier idea, infradigging up the scene of the linguistic crime as "The 'Cyberbrary' of Congress."

Let's interface it: *cyber-* is the hot combining form of our time. If you don't have *cyberphobia,* you are a *cyberphiliac.*

When a Los Angeles think tank started the experimental Democracy Network to let politicians interact on line, the move was headlined as "Campaigning in *Cyberspace*"; that word was coined by William Gibson in *Neuromancer,* his 1984 sci-fi novel. Bill Howard, executive editor of *PC Magazine,* modems me that "originally *cyberspace* was the future network created when people melded their brains with computers. It then came to mean the romanticized non-place where hackers met to carry on electronic conversations. *Cyberspace* in the past year or two has come to be more broadly equated with the Internet (a.k.a. the information highway, infobahn, autostrada, etc.)." Gibson's novel was the forerunner of what has come to be called *cyberpunk* fiction; John Markoff of *The New York Times* was co-author of a book about computerdom titled *Cyberpunk.*

In what it hailed as "the first interactive election event of its kind," *U.S. News & World Report* labeled its election night on-line forum a *cybercast.* The Popcorn Channel, a service for moviecomers (as contrasted with *moviegoers*), took an ad in *Variety* to denounce pretentious interactivists as *cybercrats.* Sean Piccoli wrote in *The Washington Times* that "battlefield valor belongs not to the brawny soldier but to the astrophysics major who invented smart bombs," somebody who's called a *cyberwonk.*

Newsweek, which calls its page covering the virtual virtues "Cyberscope" (on the analogy of its "Periscope" page), informs us that "steamy computer bulletin-board exchanges" form what is called *cybersex.* Naturally, the climax induced by computer-transmitted stimuli is a *cybergasm,* as safe as sex gets.

A New York advertising agency, Biederman, Kelly & Shaffer, issued a glossary of "the new *cyberlingo*" titled *"Cybertalk";* its definition of *cyber-,* the combining form, is "just a slang hand-me-down from *Cybernetics.*"

Which brings us to Norbert Wiener, the early automation genius, who settled on *kybernan,* the Greek word for "to steer," hence "govern," and declared in 1948: "We have decided to call the entire field of control and communication theory, whether in the machine or in the animal, by the name *Cybernetics.*" (That's how to coin a word authoritatively. Wiener was apparently unaware of the 1834 use of *cybernétique* by the French physicist A. M. Ampère to mean "the art of governing.")

"There is no doubt that *cyber-* is now a combining form," says the lexicographer Cynthia Barnhart, "though it seems to have slipped by dictionary makers." A pub in London where you can get a vodka is named after the frozen wastes of *Cyberia.*

Defuse Those Participles

When a former naval person chose to credit the news media, and especially me, with his withdrawal from the public arena, I discovered what it was like to be staked out, besieged and otherwise intruded upon by the pushy, pesky Nosy Parkers of the press.

How to put them off? What message could I leave on my answering machine that would make my privacy impenetrable and yet not offend my hard-working colleagues?

The solution: "Sorry I can't take your call, or be on your show or whatever, because I have a language-column deadline on the subject of fused participles."

Fused participles stopped 'em all cold. Every interviewer, booker and volunteer confessor accepted that as irrefutable evidence that I could not be disturbed and must not be faulted for going into deep isolation. Participle fusion, much like thermonuclear fusion, is a subject too widely dreaded to be approached lightly.

One reporter from Australian (or was it Austrian?) radio responded with exquisite wit: "Tell Safire I can understand him ducking." In that sentence, *him ducking* is what the usagist H. W. Fowler named a "fused participle" and what others call a "false participle."

Grammar-destroying participle fusion takes place when a noun or pronoun is not made possessive before a gerund. When you treat a gerund as if it were a participle, argued Fowler, the author of *Modern English Usage,* you defy grammatical analysis and make a mess of the language.

As an activity, *ducking* is a gerund (from the Latin *gerere,* "to carry out"), which is a noun formed from a verb. Another example: In "Withdrawing can be newsworthy," the subject, *withdrawing,* is a noun formed from the verb *to withdraw.* Now you want to know what a *participle* is: It's often an adjective that grows out of a verb, like a *ducking* columnist.

Here comes the part that traps the unwary. In these examples, you will note that the same word—*ducking,* coming from the informal verb "to duck"—can be used as a noun-like gerund ("can understand *ducking*") and also take the form of an adjective-like participle ("a *ducking* columnist"). Just because the word is the same, that doesn't mean its function is the same. *Ducking* the gerund acts like a noun, while *ducking* the participle acts like an adjective. When you mix them up, you confuse everybody.

Thus, the correct message would be "I can understand *his* ducking." The ironic Aussie (that's to cover *Australian* and *Austrian*) broadcaster, whose number I inadvertently wiped from my voice mail so I am answering in this column, knew that *him ducking* failed to put the possessive pronoun before the gerund *ducking* and incorrectly turns it into a participle. Other examples abound:

On the TV show *Roseanne,* daughter Becky says about sexism, "It's a matter of women being exploited by men for centuries." No, it's not "a matter of women"; it's "a matter of women's being exploited."

The pseudonymous Walter Scott writes in *Parade* of "the cliché about love being blind," which should be "love's being blind."

Writing about *Jurassic Park* in *Variety,* Don Groves noted, "Nobody foresaw the dinosaur movie ringing up monster receipts overseas." But it was the foreign business, not the movie, that was not foreseen; that should have been "the dinosaur movie's ringing up."

In a piece about Dan Quayle in *TV Guide,* Harry Stein wrote about a "report on comics having a field day." The report was not on "comics"; it was on "comics' having a field day," with the apostrophe placed after the plural *comics* to have it take possession of the gerund *having.*

On this subject, even Homer nods to the point of falling off his chair. I recently wrote in a polemic about "New York liberals . . . who did not appreciate the President lecturing them about how their anti-incumbent votes were motivated by racism." V. F. Oathout of Vero Beach, Florida, wrote: "The pot is calling the kettle black! The gerund takes the possessive case." It was not the President that the liberals did not appreciate; it was *his* lecturing them, and the possessive form should have been "the President's lecturing them." As Thomas Volet of New Canaan, Connecticut, noted, "There are those who question your (please note the possessive) lecturing, as well as the President's."

Waxing philosophical about this, Fowler wrote: "It is perhaps beyond hope for a generation that regards *upon you giving* as normal English to recover its hold upon the truth that grammar matters. Yet every just man who will abstain from the fused participle . . . retards the progress of corruption."

The reader is entitled to know that the great Danish grammarian Otto Jespersen thought this was all a lot of hooey. He issued a tract arguing that what Fowler considered gerund-abuse was a useful means "to provide the English language with a means of subordinating ideas which is often convenient and supple where clauses would be unidiomatic or negligible." Fowler snapped back with "I confess to attaching more importance to my instinctive repugnance for *without you being* than to Professor Jespersen's demonstration that it has been said by more respectable authors than I had supposed."

When the giants of linguistics clash, who decides what is correct? We turn to our inner ear. In written prose at least, Fowler's sense of order makes sense, and sharpens our writing; however, Fowler's hooting at those who fuse their participles in speech would be out of place, because the tongue can be more loosey-goosey. Jespersen would not be so strict about using the possessive before the gerunds *writing* and *hooting.* (Note me ducking, as Jespersen would permit, or my ducking, as Fowler would say.)

Illustrating the point that you can't always tell a participle from a gerund without a scorecard are the two phrases swimming man *and* swimming pool. *In* swimming man, swimming *is a participle; the man swims. In* swimming pool, *on the other hand,* swimming *is a gerund, i.e., a noun used adjectivally to modify another noun. The pool doesn't swim; it is used for swimming.*

Louis Jay Herman
New York, New York

The English language seems to create much confusion among its speakers. I attribute this to the near total loss of inflexion and the consequent fusion of forms. Thus in taking your example, "Note me ducking the issue," ducking is not a gerund, but a gerundive which agrees with me *and has sufficient verbal strength to take a second object. The gerundive is an adjective derived from the verb (once theoretically fully inflected), while the gerund is a noun which perhaps found its origin as a neuter of the gerundive. Its most primitive sense seems to be to impart a quality. One may speculate further that both derive as participles from a long lost qualitative aspect of the verb. When you say, "Note me ducking," you are calling attention to yourself. When you say, "Note my ducking," meaning, "Note the ducking of me," you are calling attention to the act of ducking.*

*Now let me note that in Latin the gerund and gerundive are clearly defined by their inflexion. Thus we have a way of living (*modus vivendi*) or a way of doing* *things (*modus operandi*), but the gerundive of the former is* vivendus, -a, -um, *so neatly inflected for agreement that we have no difficulty deciding whether it is nominal or adjectival in nature. Jespersen is correct in saying that it overcomes the need for a cumbersome subordinate clause such as, "Note me who ducks," and indeed both Latin and Greek ducked subordinate clauses in a similar manner. So you can enjoy your fish living in its bowl and rest easy. It would be silly logically to enjoy the fish's living as opposed to the fish.*

Lawrence Feinberg
Brooklyn, New York

You wrote, "Just because the word is the same, that doesn't mean its function is the same." We could not find any grammatical problems with this sentence, but we felt that it should be seriously revised. Using "just because" as your line of reasoning is poor at best; I remember saying "just because" in elementary school when I couldn't think of a good reason to back my argument. The second half of the sentence is even worse. You state, "that doesn't mean its function," which, to be generous, is poorly worded. A possible revision of the sentence might be, "Even if the word is the same, its function can be different." I think you should consider including a revised version of this sentence in one of your future articles with an apology.

Graham Stone
Haddonfield, New Jersey

Diddle-Daddle

Limited air strikes around Sarajevo and other besieged cities in Bosnia, opined Representative Lee Hamilton of Indiana, "would mark an end to the endless *diddle-daddle.*"

This is not a new formulation combining *fiddle-faddle* and *diddly squat.* On the contrary, the *Dictionary of American Regional English* traces *diddle-daddle,* a third-order reduplication, to an 1899 citation: "You go diddle-daddling about all day and do nothing."

Diddle as a verb has been in use since the early seventeenth century meaning "to walk unsteadily." Other senses include "to copulate, to engage in amorous genital play," as well as the similar-sounding "to dawdle."

Diddly squat, used with great force by Justice Thurgood Marshall at the time of his retirement, means "very little" or "hardly anything worth noticing." Its origin is in baby talk, in the mid-twentieth century: "It is euphemistically but correctly defined," Fred Cassidy of *DARE* reports, "as 'the product of a child who squats to do his duty.' "

Though *diddly squat* should be used sparingly in light of its origin, and *to diddle* used cautiously because of its sexual undertone, *diddle-daddle* is acceptable in any dithering situation.

Dog's Breakfast

Grown dogs don't eat breakfast. Oh, I give my Bernese Mountain dogs, James and Heidi, a hard cookie apiece to shut up their racket in the morning, but they know that one session a day wolfing down their kibble is their lot, which is called their "meal."

That is why I wondered at this figure of speech in a report by Michael Wines in *The New York Times* during last fall's campaign: "Aides repackaged a *dog's breakfast* of White House trade and fiscal policies into an 'agenda for American renewal.' "

"How did a repast not usually associated with our canine companions," asked

Thomas Zekov of New York, "come to represent a repackaging of old ideas into a new program?" Added Mary Lou O'Brien of Brooklyn: "A *dog's breakfast*? I love it. Where does it come from?"

Since it came from Mike Wines down the hall, I asked him for an explanatory memo. He wrote: "A *dog's breakfast* is any kind of smorgasbord prepared, in haste or at random, from life's castoffs. In this case, it was the chicken bones and half-eaten pizzas of policies that the Administration had proposed earlier and Congress had rejected. . . . Cat people wouldn't understand, but anyone who has ever walked a dog down an alley would."

A Scottish terrier would say the phrase has a long pedigree. The slang lexicographer Eric Partridge cited Glasgow circa 1934 as its place and time of origin, though he noted that Australians also used the phrase with the same meaning as "confusion, mess, turmoil." (After a *three-dog night,* one so cold it required three dogs to keep you warm, a *dog's breakfast* could be quite a mess.)

About the same time, a *dog's dinner* appeared with a quite different sense. "Why have you got those roses in your hair?" asked a character in *Touch Wood,* a 1934 novel by C. L. Anthony. "You look like the *dog's dinner.*" This expression was defined by the *Oxford English Dictionary* supplement as "dressed or arranged in an ostentatiously smart or flashy manner," probably derived from the 1871 usage "to *put on the dog.*"

The early 30's, a time for many canine coinages, also saw the expression *dog's bait* appear in the Ozarks, with a meaning of "too much to eat," as in "Enough's enough, but too much is a *dawg's bait.*"

While we're going to the dogs, here's a query from Alan Geller of Elmwood Park, New Jersey, who attached an article in *The New York Times* by John Darnton, writing from Sinj, Croatia: "Another town official . . . brought out a *dog-eared* diary."

Many a dog's ears do not stand up straight, but lap over. (Heidi, when especially alert to the prospect of leftovers from what she must call a master's breakfast, seems to perk up her ears, but they still lap over; German shepherds' ears are different.) The two words were first used together as a verb in the mid-seventeenth century in a book of essays by Francis Osborne: "To ruffle, dogs-ear, and contaminate by base Language and spurious censures the choicest leaves."

When you turn down the corner of a page in a book, you *dog's-ear* it. "Lady Slattern Lounger," wrote Richard Brinsley Sheridan in his play *The Rivals* in 1775, ". . . had so soiled and dogs'-eared it, it wa'n't fit for a Christian to read." Thus, a book that has had many pages turned down is *dog's-eared,* or as it is more frequently written, *dog-eared.*

We have strayed. What alternatives are there to a *dog's breakfast* for the writer who wants to describe a mixed bag?

Farrago is a favorite of mine, a 1632 noun rooted in the Latin for "mixed fodder." *Mishmash* also does the hodgepodgian trick: It's a reduplication of the German *mischen,* "to mix," which some say was introduced into English via Yiddish (while others hold it was a reduplication of the English *mash,* but if that's true, how come it's pronounced mish-mosh?). The aforementioned *hodgepodge,* also known as *hotchpotch,* comes from the French *hocher,* "to shake," and *pot* (similar to *olio,* from the Spanish *olla podrida,* "rotten pot"). Another term formed of rhyming syllables is *ragbag,* while another French-based word for "jumble, tangle, muddle" is *gallimaufry,* "hash."

Taken together, this synonymy amounts to a *dog's breakfast.*

Growing up in England in the 40's, the expression "done up like a dog's dinner" was applied to any woman who wore an excessive amount of make-up. The apparent reference is to the biblical Queen Jezebel who (II Kings 9:30–37) "painted her eyes, arranged her hair" and was subsequently thrown to her death through a window and her body eaten by dogs!

George W. Sleigh
Livingston, New Jersey

Don't Worry, Be Peppy

Lloyd Cutler, the seventy-six-year-old Washington legal establishmentarian, was asked by a reporter if he would consider staying on as President Clinton's White House counsel beyond the short period that had been announced. Mr. Cutler replied that he limited his planned stay "in part because I'm married fairly recently to a very young and peppy wife and I want to spend some more time with her."

Peppy is a swell word. Like *swell,* it is Old Slang, part of the razzmatazz language used by Generation Z (the incipient geezer set), which can still recall the lyrics of Ira Gershwin and Cole Porter. I can remember my mother telling me how to do well on television in the early 50's: "Be *peppy*!"

Mr. Cutler's wife of four years was assumed by some Generation X members of the press corps to be their age. Not so; Mrs. Cutler is the artist Polly Kraft, widow of the columnist Joseph Kraft, and sister of Kay Evans, wife of the columnist Rowland Evans. Her age is her own business, but she is in my cohort and I am no spring chicken, to use another example of Old Slang.

But *peppy* Polly is. (In a generation, she will be said to be *sprightly,* and as a nonagenarian, *spry*.)

Pep is a shortening of *pepper,* which took place about the time, 1912, that *gin up* was spawned from *ginger.* Advertising copywriters used it before that industry found its home on Madison Avenue: "This newest Overland Four," went a Canadian car ad in 1916, "has more power, *pep,* punch and speed." Sports

coaches were said to be giving lethargic athletes *pep talks.* A breakfast cereal named Pep did well before flaking out.

The adjective *peppy* appeared at the close of World War I, according to *Merriam-Webster's Tenth Collegiate,* and was used by Sinclair Lewis in *Babbitt,* his best-selling 1922 novel: "Wouldn't it be a good idea if I could go off to China or some *peppy* place?" (That locution may have been repeated, to his rue, by Secretary of State Warren Christopher seventy-two years later.)

Standard English synonyms include *spirited, lively, energetic* and *vigorous.* All those words have the requisite life in their meaning, but only the grand old *peppy* can claim yesteryear's quality of being full o' *pep.*

You quoted Lloyd Cutler as saying, in part, ". . . because I'm married fairly recently. . . ." And I thought, Hot diggity! At last, Safire is going to take off on that appalling New York usage that my wife and others have been assaulting my ears with for years. But, dad gum it! You didn't even mention it. You blew the whole column on stuff like "peppy." Not a word about the abominable garbling of the time relationship between the verb and its modifier.

Could it be that you've been a New Yorker for so long that this usage now seems acceptable? I have heard even well-educated New Yorkers speak such absurdities as, "I'm here twenty years." Could it be that that sounds okay to you? Please, Mr. Safire, put the kibosh on this anti-grammatical obscenity once and for all.

Donald S. Bustany
Los Angeles, California

Downsize That Special Sea Change

"I've just come from a Management Meeting," said one of America's top corporate executives, urgency in her voice. "After the third time somebody used *sea change,* the publisher wanted to know, 'Where the hell does *sea change* come from, and how does it differ from any other change?' "

Was I ready for that! Despite my having set the world straight on this a few years back, the sea-change file was bulging: Norman Lear "criticized the press," a recent *New York Times* report noted, "for ignoring a *sea change* in attitudes." Representative Charles Schumer, the omnipresent Brooklyn Democrat, said of a retailer's decision to halt gun sales, "When Wal-Mart, the family store of Middle America, does this, you know there's a *sea change* under way in the gun-selling business." Jacques Barzun, a member of Olbom—"On Language" 's Board of Octogenarian Mentors—had already alerted me to the torrent of usages of this hoary term, suggesting it was time to brush up my Shakespeare.

"Full fathom five thy father lies," I began the quotation to my caller.

Of his bones are coral made:
Those are pearls that were his eyes:
Nothing of him that doth fade,
But doth suffer a sea-change
Into something rich and strange.

Ariel, the sprite, is singing of the supposed drowning of King Alonso in *The Tempest.* Professor Barzun adds, "A sea change is a miraculous, unexpected transformation, not just any change."

Members of the Gotcha! Gang will surely point out that the Bard erred in "Of his bones are coral made," preferring "is coral made"; immortal writers have to take this carping all the time. Others will note the Shakespearean hyphen—*sea-change*—that has been worn away by the tides of usage.

Four centuries ago, the phrase had freshness, but its recent vogue has made it waterlogged. If every slight shift, permutation or switcheroo is called a *sea change,* what's left to describe major changes? Give a thought to *revolution* or *metamorphosis* for a change.

We have slipped seamlessly into the analysis of vogue words. (Seams, madam? Nay, *seamless* used to mainly modify *hose,* but now the only seam to be worked is the narrow area between two zones in a football defense; this has left *seamless* to be used by a generation of writers who eschew *smooth.*)

Notice how everybody who used to talk about *the politics of [whatever]* is now profoundly discussing *the culture of [whatever]*? When Surgeon General Joycelyn Elders blasted the sale of toy guns as contributing to *the culture of violence,* a columnist, Colin Campbell, exploded at the voguishness of it all, citing book titles from Lewis Mumford's 1938 *The Culture of Cities*—a usage then fresh and appropriate—to the recent *The Culture of Addiction* and *The Culture of Time and Space.*

"They're not talking about the practical cultivation of organisms (*the culture of oysters*)," he wrote in *The Atlanta Journal-Constitution,* "or of real societies (*the culture of ancient Egypt*). The new cliché refers instead to subgroups, problems, values, jobs, notions and statistical abstractions *as if* they were species, tribes and nations. The implication is that they have their own rules, languages, etc."

I would argue (and if I would, then why don't I?)—O.K., I argue that when a subgroup like English teachers or beauty parlor operators or the Mafia has an inside lingo, a set of agreed-upon moorings and a secret handshake, that can be defined as a culture. It describes, as Mr. Campbell notes, a closed system. But the phrase is getting abused by the culture of title-writers.

"Could we deep-six *downsize*?" asks Irv Molotsky, weekend editor of *The New York Times* in Washington. He cites my own 1989 adjuration to Mikhail Gorbachev to "*downsize* the empire"; more recently, corporations describe layoffs to increase productivity as *downsizing.* The Smithsonian Institution, looking around for a euphemism's euphemism, has come up with *rightsizing.*

The good news in the Vogue Word Watch is the decline of *caring*—the word, not necessarily the practice—and the simultaneous slump in its companion, *sharing. Caregiver,* after a fast start, is sinking, and hardly any with-it politician says, "I want to share my thoughts with you tonight."

On the other hand, *special* still has us by the throat. "It is time to contain the spreading ooze of the word *special,*" writes Michael Johnson of London, who is especially turned off by television personalities who sign off with "This evening has been real special."

One sense of the word is "uncommon; unusual"; another sense is "favored, select"; yet another is "particular, individual," and that's only the beginning, with others ranging from "different" to "handicapped." Because the word has so many senses, its vogue use has been drained of meaning; when you use "he's special," he can be "really something," which is really nothing. We ought to downsize it to zero usage; that would be a nice sea change.

Nothing of him that doth fade
But doth suffer a sea = change
Into Something Rich and Strange

After reading your story about the term "sea-change," I recalled this inscription on the grave of Shelley in Rome. It is the first sight of the term in my experience and I thought you may be interested in its existence. As to why the stonemason chose the equal sign as a connector, I can't guess.

The strong generative power of water in general and the sea in particular could be behind the term. From Lucretius, through Boethius to Paracelcus, early writings are filled with references from life arising from the sea as Lucretius witnessed with eels or life being altered by its force as Boethius marveling at the metamorphosis of a goose barnacle into a barnacle goose. Shakespeare lived in this time-line of thought. In this sense "sea-change" does mean a monumental and remarkable event. Maybe the quote was written by Byron or another friend who exhumed Shelley's body from quicklime and cremated it on the beach and who felt the loss was monumental.

Marc Marcussen
Mansfield, Massachusetts

"Dr. Livingstone, I Presume? Assume? Suppose?"

"The assumption here," John Vinocur writes from Paris, "is that Helmut Kohl is an excellent politician." Toward the end of an original analysis of anti-foreigner terrorism in Germany—and the insight that the German Chancellor is driven by a need for national normalcy—the executive editor of the International *Herald Tribune* concludes with "The presumption here is that Helmut Kohl is an excellent politician."

A pundit perusing this piece thinks to himself, "Uh-oh—the writer knows something I don't," and gives it a second, closer reading. That's because the writer has given the reader a clue to the progression of his thinking: He starts with an *assumption* and concludes with a *presumption.* The words overlap in some senses, but they are not synonyms; something is afoot in the choice of first one, then the other.

Climb the ladder of inference: *To suppose* is "to guess"; I suppose you're interested in this stuff, but it could be that your eye is just slopping over from the ad on the facing page. *To assume* is stronger, "to accept tentatively," either as the basis for argument or in the absence of evidence to the contrary; you can assume, for example, that anybody who makes it to Chancellor must be a good politician.

To presume is strongest of all: "to take for granted," not just hypothetically but authoritatively.

Consider *the presumption of innocence;* it gives the accused a lot more protection than a mere *assumption* would. David Mellinkoff, in his *Dictionary of American Legal Usage,* shows how the verb *presume* is converted by stages into a rule of law: "(1) to be convinced that something (A) is a fact; and then (2) to infer from A that something else (B) is also a fact, though you are not certain that it is; and then (3) to conclude as a matter of law that in the absence of sufficient evidence to the contrary, B is a fact." For example, when you send a computer fanatic an E-mail message, you draw a reasonable inference (unless there's been some huge power blowout in that area, with systems crashing and teeth gnashing) that he's received it, and you then *presume* he has.

O.K., then: Was the reporter-explorer Henry Stanley correct when he uttered his immortal line in 1871, upon finding David Livingstone in darkest Africa, "Dr. Livingstone, I presume?" (A question with a question inside it gets only one question mark; I never had that come up before, and just made that decision. I'm not going to look it up anywhere; that's it. If you're not secure in this language dodge, you're dead.)

You have to get inside Stanley's head. You've been trekking around the Congo for months, following rumors of the "lost" Livingstone, and here's this white man who could be him (yes, *him,* not *he*). If you're skeptical, you'd say, "Dr. Livingstone, I suppose?" If you're hopeful but not sure, you would say, "Dr. Livingstone, I assume?" Only if you are fairly certain and want to close the deal would you say, "Dr. Livingstone, I presume?" I think Stanley, eager to get and file his story, was pushing it.

Presume's other sense—"to venture without permission," like presuming to say, "Hi, Helmut" to Chancellor Kohl—reinforces the degree of force in presumption. In the piece by Mr. Vinocur, the point made by the contrasting synonymy is the march from tentative assumption to more conclusive presumption; I am certain that he, acting on the facts at hand, would have said, "Dr. Livingstone, I assume?"

Why did you prefer the more presumptuous-sounding "presume" to the more benign sounding "assume"? Merriam-Webster 2nd Edition *is no help.*

Paul Yager
Metuchen, New Jersey

Assumptions *are beliefs, typically unexpressed and unexamined, formed with little or no evidence.* Presumptions *are positions or rules of intellectual engagement; when we presume something, we act as though it were true, irrespective of whether we believe it. In a criminal trial, nearly no one believes that the defendant is innocent; there would be no trial without "probable cause" and the State would not spend fortunes to prosecute a slight possibility. To "presume innocence" is merely to shift the burden of proof to the prosecution, to oblige the prosecution to make a case before the defense presents its own.*

In philosophical and scientific debates, further, we "grant a presumption to the status quo," forcing the advocate for the new idea or plan to prove its superiority to the old, not the reverse. In many disputes, the issue of contention is a suppressed or untested assumption—perhaps shown to be false. One may refute or disprove assumptions, but one suspends or shifts presumptions.

Edmond H. Weiss
Cherry Hill, New Jersey

The Jan 27, 1943 Montreal Gazette *quotes a then 95-year-old man named George Welsh who was an 18-year-old bodyguard of Henry Stanley while they were searching through Africa for Dr. Livingstone. Welsh claimed that when they found him, Stanley shook hands with him and said, "Dr. Livingstone, I believe?"*

If "I suppose?" would have indicated skepticism, and "I assume?" uncertainty, then a good reporter would have said, "I believe?" don't you think?

Mary Peate
Westlake Village, California

To suppose *isn't "to guess" but to be in the state that results from guessing: you can guess how much money I have in my pocket and you can guess wrong, but you can't suppose how much money I have in my pocket or suppose wrong. There's also the other sense of* suppose, *which often turns up at the beginning of* reductio ad absurdum *arguments: one may say "Suppose the C.I.A. paid Oswald to shoot at Kennedy," then go through some inferences that lead to a contradiction, and then conclude that the C.I.A. didn't pay Oswald to shoot at Kennedy.*

I object to your omitting one of the question marks in the Dr. Livingstone sentence. There's room for both of them (one inside the quotation marks for the question that you're quoting and one outside for the question within which you're quoting it), and there aren't any typographical contexts that normally swallow question marks (the way that the periods at the ends of quoted declaratives or after quotes ending in "?" or "!" get swallowed by their contexts).

*Jim [James D. McCawley]**
Department of Linguistics
University of Chicago
Chicago, Illinois

*Professor McCawley, one of the world's linguistic giants and a treasured Lexicographic Irregular, died on April 10, 1999.

I wonder if you are familiar with the old word game where the answer is given and the question is required. Simple example: The answer is "Chicken Sukiyaki" and the question is "Who is the last surviving Kamikazi pilot?" Another: "9W". Answer: "Do you spell your name with a W, *Mr. Wagner?"*

Well, I suppose you've already figured out my example, or perhaps I assume this. Answer: "Dr. Livingstone, I presume." Question: "What is your full name, Dr. Presume?"

David M. Clarkson
Newfane, Vermont

You are right, of course, about Stanley's words to Livingstone. Furthermore, you are just the right person to whom I want to tell a related story before it is lost to posterity:

I heard it during War II from the late Bob Low, a foreign correspondent turned intelligence officer. In the late summer of 1939 he was in the café of the Hotel Select in Stockholm. Duke Ellington, who had just completed a most successful tour of the Continent, was sitting at an adjacent table, and Bob was bemused by the contrast between the Duke and the almost albino Swedes who filled the room.

Through the door came Paul Robeson, who also had given a series of sellout performances in Europe. He spotted the Duke, broke into a mile-wide smile, walked up to him with an outstretched hand, and said—you guessed it.

I believed Bob when he told the story, particularly when I recalled that, during 1940, my senior year at college, Ellington cut a record to which he gave the title, "Dr. Livingstone, I Presume."

It's too good a story to be lost.

Robert A. Riesman
Providence, Rhode Island

Driven-Driven

"This is a liquidity-*driven* market," opined David Shulman, a long-headed market analyst with Salomon Brothers, suggesting that higher interest rates to come would sop up that desirable liquidity.

A cartoon by J. P. Rini in *The New Yorker* shows a man at a modern-art show opening, staring at the EXIT sign, while another museumgoer explains to a friend, "Roger has always been text-*driven*."

What's driving *-driven*?

Frederick C. Mish of Merriam-Webster points out that "having a compulsive or urgent quality" is the *Tenth Collegiate*'s definition for the past participle *driven.* "This use of *-driven,*" he says, "is a fairly straightforward extension of the long-familiar use in phrases like 'motor-*driven* camera' and 'a water-*driven* clock mechanism.' "

The development of *-driven* has steered the term in new directions. "I find *-driven* most often in technological or business contexts," says Fred Mish. "Probably the most common combination is the computer term *menu-driven.* As computers started to become more and more important in business and indeed all aspects of public and private life, the rest followed."

Less technical citations include Gloria Steinem's description of a TV character as "a career-*driven* woman" and a Texas politician's complaints about "formula-*driven* legislation." The current newsletter for the Modern Language Association refers to a poet's biography that paints its subject as "an excessively egocentric and ambition-*driven* artist."

Psychobabble is what is driving *-driven.* It's the same construction that made voguish compound modifiers out of *-obsessed, -compulsive, -intense* and *-motivated.*

Whatever happened to *-oriented*? In the 1950's, everything was culture-*oriented;* not until some Westerner used "Occident-*oriented* " did other users of this formulation become disoriented. Soon after, David Riesman, writing about "The Lonely Crowd" in 1950, got us high on *-directed;* we were either inner-*directed* or other-*directed.* We had a nice run of *-intensive* for a while; it was better to be *capital-intensive* than *labor-intensive,* unless you were short of money. That was back when children were *-minded;* they became like-*minded* and bloody-*minded.*

Today, *-driven* is in the driver's seat. The ad agency for Nissan Motors was sensitive to the trend: Its slogan, playing somewhat frenetically on what was done to the car and what it did to the people who built it, was "We are driven!" To be *-driven,* of course, is to be *-motivated* to the point of being *-obsessed.* (This trend is being studied by trend-focused lexicographers like Fred Mish.)

"Part of the attractiveness of this *-driven* to those who use it," he explains, "where *-motivated* or *-stimulated* or *-induced* might serve, is that it strikes them as a forceful word.

"Who doesn't want to seem strong and forceful?" he asks rhetorically. "You might say that at least some of the current popularity is *image-driven.*"

I disagree with your correspondent Fred Mish, with regard to the term menu-driven. *He includes the term in the same obsessive/compulsive group as* ambition-driven. *Actually, it's more like* chauffeur-driven.

The use of computer-based information is what has changed all those things that Mr. Mish mentions. Menus are merely one way of getting at that information, and a pretty low-class way, at that.

We grizzled computer jocks consider it infra dig *to use menus, if we can possibly avoid it. Menus are for the* arriviste *techno-babblers. No, we know the incantations underlying the menus. Menus are too slow, and waste our time. We get what we want from computers by issuing the by-God* commands. *Stuff like "http://dinnercoop.cs.cmu.edu/dinnercoop/recipes/subjects/icecream.html." just rolls off our fingers. People like us are said to be* command-driven.

Tom McSloy
Marietta, Georgia

Enclitic's Corner

What a wonderful language; there's a word for everything.

The chancellor of Syracuse University, Kenneth (Buzz) Shaw, was expounding to trustees on plans for the school's 125th anniversary: "halfway between a *centennial* and a *sesquicentennial.*" He looked to me for the right word for "125th"; I flunked.

In my wallet was an ad from Plain Old Pearson's liquor store in Washington pushing "Grand Marnier Centcinquantenaire," which is booze with that 150-year-old French flavor, *de rigueur* for a Latin-rooted *sesquincentennial* celebration every century and a half. But there is no bottle advertised for one and a quarter centuries.

Somebody must have had this problem before. Frank Abate, the dictionary and reference specialist in Old Saybrook, Connecticut, rooted around and came up with the answer in a 1993 *O.E.D.* update, with a citation from a 1962 *New York Times Book Review.*

Seems that back then the people of Delavan, a town in Tazewell County, Illinois, wanted to hold a 125th-anniversary whoop-de-do for the town's founding. Delavan's celebratory group "went to the Funk & Wagnalls dictionary people," according to *The Times.* "From there it received the suggestion of *'Quasquicentennial,'* meaning a hundred plus a fourth." Sure enough, in the next citation from a 1962 copy of the Bloomington (Illinois) *Pantagraph,* there was the coinage in use: "The Delavan Quasquicentennial Celebration doesn't officially begin until noon today."

"The combining form *quasqui-,*" Abate says, "blends parts of Latin *quadrans-,* 'one-fourth,' and *sesqui-,* derived from a blending and modification of Latin *semis,* 'one-half,' plus *-que,* an enclitic meaning 'and.' " (An *enclitic* is an attachable word-element, like a suffix, from the Greek *klit,* "slope." Comparative etymology on this you won't get from me.)

While we're at it, if you're planning celebrations, there is a *novennial* (nine years), as well as *duodecennial* (twelve) and *vigintennial* (twenty); similarly, there is *perennial* (occurring year after year), along with *plurennial* (lasting for many years) and *aeonial* (everlasting).

So, Buzz, I'll see you on the *quad* for Syracuse's *quasquicentennial.* When we get to 175, we'll figure out a new word.

Ethnic Cleansing

Clean words can mask dirty deeds.

The word adopted by the Nazi Reinhard (The Hangman) Heydrich to describe the planned extermination of Jews was *Endlösung,* which was translated into the English phrase "final solution." The language soon endows the bureaucratic euphemism with a sinister overtone that has a greater impact than the phrase it replaces: *Final solution* induced more shudders than the straightforward "mass murder," just as *liquidation* is more sinister than "killing" and the icily bureaucratic *termination with extreme prejudice,* even if fictional, carries a more chilling connotation than "assassination."

This generation's entry in the mass-murder category is *ethnic cleansing.* Because it has become a major coinage, now used without quotation marks or handled without the tongs of *so-called,* the phrase's etymology deserves close examination.

Begin with the word *ethnic.* This came from the Scots, meaning "heathen, pagan," who got it from the Greek *ethnos,* which the *Barnhart Dictionary of Etymology* defines as "a people, nation, Gentiles, a translation of Hebrew *goyim,* plural of *goy.*"

Now to its modern application as *ethnic group.* Julian Sorell Huxley and Alfred Cort Haddon, in their 1935 book, *We Europeans,* coined that phrase with authority: "Nowhere does a human group now exist which corresponds closely to a systematic sub-species in animals. . . . For existing populations, the noncommittal term *ethnic group* should be used." The authors referred later to a "special type of *ethnic grouping* of which the Jews form the best-known example."

Ethnics as a noun referring to members of a group, but along racial lines, was first used by the sociologists W. Lloyd Warner and Paul S. Lunt in 1941; a 1945 study by Warner and Leo Srole applied the noun to groups like the Irish and the Jews. By the time David Riesman used *ethnicity* in 1953, the meaning was "identification with a national and cultural group," especially among second-generation Americans. The power of ethnicity—both racial and national, covering "the

Negroes, Puerto Ricans, Jews, Italians and Irish of New York City"—was explored in *Beyond the Melting Pot,* a 1963 book by Daniel P. Moynihan and Nathan Glazer.

Ethnic as an adjective received its baptism of fire in politics when Jimmy Carter referred to *ethnic purity* in his winning 1976 campaign: His usage was probably intended to refer to the pride of groups within a neighborhood, but got him in hot water with those who saw in *ethnic purity* a veiled reference to support of housing segregation.

Now to *ethnic cleansing.* (It takes etymologists a while to get there, but getting there is half the fun. I will skip the roots of *cleansing,* except to note that this gerund developed from the pre-1200 verb *cleansen,* derived from the Old English root of *clean.*)

In 1988, well before the Soviet Union came apart, clashes broke out between Armenians and Azerbaijanis in the autonomous enclave of Azerbaijan known as Nagorno-Karabakh. According to Sol Steinmetz, executive editor of Random House dictionaries, who cites Serbo-Croatian sources, the attempt by one group to drive out the other was called by Soviet officials *etnicheskoye chishcheniye,* "ethnic cleansing."

On July 9, 1991, a Serbian building supervisor named Zarko Cubrilo told Tim Judah, a *Times* of London reporter: "Many of us have been sacked because they want an *ethnically clean* Croatia." On July 31 of that year, as Orthodox Serbs and Catholic Croats began the conflict that led to the breakup of Yugoslavia, we had the first English use of the phrase in its gerund form: Croatia's Supreme Council was quoted by Donald Forbes, a Reuters reporter in Belgrade, as charging, "The aim of this expulsion is obviously the *ethnic cleansing* of the critical areas . . . to be annexed to Serbia."

A year later, journalists in the battle zone picked up the phrase: John F. Burns, in *The New York Times* on July 26, 1992, described the movement for a "Greater Serbia," observing that "the precondition for its creation lies in the purging—*'ethnic cleansing'* in the perpetrators' lexicon—of wide areas of Bosnia of all but like-minded Serbs."

That's the first take at a big phrase that is likely to be with us for a while. If the practice is not stopped, the term will continue in active use; if the world forces the forcible separation and killing to end, the phrase *ethnic cleansing* will evoke a shudder a generation hence much as *final solution* does today—as a phrase frozen in history, a terrible manifestation of ethnocentrism gone wild.

I would like to draw your attention to an adjectival use of "ethnic" by Sigmund Freud.

Freud coined the expression "ethnic narcissism." It is a (pathological?) condition rampant in our society in the guise of "pride in one's heritage."

Moshe Leshem
Tuckahoe, New York

Etymological Discovery

Whence *root and branch*?

In a political dictionary, credit for coinage is given to Justice William J. Brennan Jr. in *Green* v. *County School Board of New Kent County, Va.* (1968): "In which racial discrimination would be eliminated *root and branch.*"

Comes now Sol Steinmetz, executive editor of Random House dictionaries, who had been dipping into what he calls "that ever-revealing source of English idioms, the Bible."

From Malachi, last of the Prophets, 4:1, in the King James Version: "The day that cometh shall burn them up, saith the Lord of hosts, that it shall leave them neither root nor branch."

Coincidentally, now that I look at Malachi, the verse following this dire warning of destruction contains a phrase used by both Woodrow Wilson and Richard Nixon in stirring perorations: "The Sun of righteousness arise *with healing in his wings.*"

Farewell, My Attractive

In a piece about a high-powered dinner party for the Clintons in the home of Katharine Graham of The Washington Post Company, I referred to the presence of other journalists including "Judy Woodruff of PBS and her attractive husband."

This wording was a feeble effort to align myself with feminist resentment at the longtime putdown of wives in society reporting. In reports and in introductions, it always has been "Joe Blow and his attractive wife" or "Sam Shlump and his attractive bride." He's important; she looks good, as befits a bimbonic arm piece.

Attractive has lost its attraction, especially in Hillary-era Washington. From the Latin *trahere,* "to draw or pull," the word has long been used to describe not just the pulling power of pulchritude, but the indefinable magnetism of a person to the observer of the opposite sex.

You can still assess "an *attractive* candidate" or hail "an *attractive* proposal," but it is no longer socially acceptable to say "an *attractive* woman." In all the coverage of the Attorney General–designate, nowhere could I find a description of the forty-year-old Zoe (Greek for "life") Baird as "attractive." Not even "good-looking"; editors rely on running a picture next to the text profile. Have you seen Dr. Bernadine Healy, director of the National Institutes of Health, described as attractive, much less a knockout? Forget it; reference to looks is sexist, degrading and perhaps actionable.

The incisive Ms Woodruff (*incisive,* applied to a woman, is the new code word for attractive; *brilliant* means she is in Dr. Healy's league) is married to Al Hunt, *The Wall Street Journal*'s Washington bureau chief; evidently she finds him attractive, substantiating my patronizing description. Al got the point, of course, dropping me a note: "It's amazing how often we overlook the little guy's contributions. Next time if you have any interest in what I was wearing, just holler."

Commenting on some of the reporting of the Graham party, the *Washington Post* columnist Richard Harwood quoted something Hillary Clinton said, and then applied the coup de grâce to the word for our time by attributing a subsequent remark to "her attractive husband."

Fashionable Words

At the Pentagon, the vogue word is *win-win,* the strategy of being able to fight two nonnuclear wars at the same time. This supplanted the "win-hold-win" strategy, designed to hold one war on a back burner until the other war is won, then to win the first one. These locutions are based on the "no win" derogation of strategy of a generation ago, which in turn was antedated by a slick "no lose" bet by gamblers.

In academe, the vogue word is *daunting.* A professor may be *intimidated, cowed, appalled* or even *spooked* by the lengthy work of a colleague (which is what a coworker is always called), but the only term to use this year is the present participle of *daunt* (rooted in the Latin for "tame"), as in "The subtext is *daunting.*" (Sighted *subtext;* sank same.)

In politics, *feckless* is still in vogue—the *feck* has the same root as the middle of *ineffective*—though we've been getting a nice run of *parious* lately (better dangerous than feckless). *Seamless* is in, too, meaning "smooth," as in "a seamless presentation of the condition on the ground."

In music, Thomas J. Famularo of Brooklyn signs on with the vogue use of *signature.* Recent *New York Times* articles have commented on the musician Billy Joel "with his piano adding a personal *signature*" and a revival of the musical *On the Town,* with "that exuberant *signature* love song to a town: 'New York, New York.' "

What are the words in fashion in fashion? More than anywhere, that is the field in which *same-old-same-old*—the vogue derogation of anything un-new on campus—is to be avoided. *Life in the fast lane* is for slowpokes; *to live on the cutting edge* has been cut to *living on the edge.* People in the fashion world (which, to their credit, they don't call "the fashion community") wouldn't be caught dead using a word like *seamless* (which originated in the leg community), because the trend is toward taking metaphors from the anti-fashion world.

The linguistic question in fashion is: Have we come at last to the *post-grunge era*?

Grungy is a 1960's adjective defined by Robert K. Barnhart in his etymological dictionary as "bad, inferior or ugly," perhaps a blend of *grubby* and *dingy*. It was picked up (more accurately, *picked up on*) and back-formed into the noun *grunge* by rock musicians in Seattle like Nirvana and Pearl Jam in the late 80's to express their anomie-tooism. In Britain, also afflicted with punk rock, the discordance was translated into clothing: Hobnail boots and bag-lady knits soon appeared on the catwalks of couture, the carefully designed sloppiness racing against the genuine anti-fashion statements of the youth culture. For a time, as the mass culture followed the elite culture following the grunge-rock subculture, frumpiness was next to godliness.

Hegelian antithesis followed. When Donna Karan held her Family of Grunge show in New York, Cathy Horyn of *The Washington Post* wrote: "In the general droop of things, sweaters withered from shoulders, sweat pants slid from waists. . . . Nothing new, and one suspects that grunge is already over and out."

We now have *anti-grunge* and *counter-grunge*—presumably to label any outfit whose components match—and the reaction to *geek chic.* Italian designers "have opted for a safe—just on this side of drab—style for the coming fall and winter," writes Daniela Petroff of the Associated Press, suggesting that the winter woman would wear tattered jeans under a sable coat in an exhibition of *drunge:* "midway between a dandy and a grunge."

With less hemming than hawing, the lexicographer David K. Barnhart has been tracking such new fashion terms as *indie-rock look, street* and *fade.* As a synonym for *grunge look,* the phrase *indie-rock look* points to the flannel shirts of independent rock musicians. *Street* means "appropriate for a street-smart person," according to the *Barnhart Dictionary Companion,* and *fade* is a man's hair style with the hair on the side of the head very closely cut.

Swerving out of the sluggish fast lane and right out to the edge, this department called Alice Morgaine, editor of *Jardin des Modes* in Paris, for her update on *les mots justes* for this fall. Last year, a key French word was *godillots,* for heavy army boots. Her husband, the author Daniel Morgaine—who as foreign correspondent for *France-Soir* was that country's best ambassador to the United States—adds that the fashion word had a double meaning, having been the nickname of followers of General de Gaulle. (Boots are very big over here; a *hob* is a projection, and a *hobnail* is one that projects out to reduce wear on a boot's sole or heel. Now you know the origin of *hobnail boot.* A *clodhopper* is one that enables the wearer to hop over clods of earth, though a heavy boot is hardly conducive to hopping.) Where was I?

In Paris. The *godillots* were accompanied by *le n'importe quoi,* "the anything-goes look," in which the rule has been to mix but not match: long with short, lace or velvet with denim, the patchwork ambience of the confused janitor.

Now, reports Madame Morgaine, Europeans have *la mode réfléchie*—"the thoughtful, reflective look," the opposite of a slapdash or impulsive appearance, in which frugal buyers invest in clothing that helps them on several different occasions.

How to praise the new fashions? *Glamour* magazine's long-running fashion feature—"Dos and Don'ts"—promotes *do* and *don't* as nouns for good and bad styles. Oprah Winfrey's talk show has popularized *fashion do* for any stylish look, while more recent street slang offers the compliment of "That suit is *dope*!"

Neo-puritans may be giving thanks for the return of the Pilgrim look, part of the trend toward religious motifs that has secular women picking up nuns' habits. Alison Moore commented recently in *The New York Times Magazine,* "Imagine how amazed the Pilgrims would be to discover, three centuries later, that their starched white collars and simple black robes were the height of fashion for fall 1993."

My favorite current fashion locution is all-American, snatched with great panache from everyday life. You know those half-automated car-wash emporia that advertise an "all-cloth wash," where machines jiggle gloppy lengths of wet chamois (pronounced "SHAM-ee") against your car as you ride through? I always feel, as those flat fingers of sodden material slop heavily against my windshield, that I am experiencing virtual reality inside a giant's lower intestine. At any rate, lengths of material hanging from the waist, looking like a slit skirt produced by a designer who couldn't stop slitting, now go by the name of a *carwash skirt.* Fashion has a future.

Fly Me to the Zone

Who baked the *no-fly* pie?

At the end of Desert Storm, Saddam Hussein was denied the right to send Iraq's aircraft into the areas over the embryonic Kurdistan above the 36th parallel, or to threaten rebellious Shiites below the 32d parallel. Those areas were promptly dubbed *no-fly zones* by anonymous speakers of Pentagonese, and the curious locution was picked up—uncritically at first—by the media.

When the Iraqi dictator moved surface-to-air missiles into one of the proscribed regions, *no-fly zone* exploded into common usage. But discomfort with the phrase was shown in maps published in *The New York Times:* One called it an *air-exclusion zone,* and a couple of days later, a *no-flight zone.* In the text of articles, the conversational *zone where flights are banned* was tried; ultimately the decision was made to use *no-fly zone* but to put it in quotation marks, thereby noting its slangy or bureaucratic origin.

"*No-fly* is an unusual formation," says Fred Mish, editorial chief at Merriam-Webster. "The verb *fly* is being used as an attributive noun modifying *zone,* in a type of functional shift or perhaps a rare grammatical pattern. Ordinarily you'd expect to see a participle or a gerund there—*flying,* not *fly*—as in *no-parking zone.*"

Nobody, not even the most bureaucratic traffic cop, says *no-park zone.* Other *no- [verb]* constructions use words that can be construed as verbs or nouns, as in *no-knock* authority, or *no-load* mutual funds. Ornithologists have also used the verb *fly* as an attributive-noun modifier: *Fly-way* is a century-old term for the pattern of migrating birds.

Although the molasses-laden *shoo-fly pie* offers an interesting parallel, my guess is that *no-fly* was coined on the analogy of *no-go,* Pentagonese for "not suitable for proceeding"; the verb *go* is treated as a noun, and has even come to draw an article ("O.K., Gridley, *that's a go*"). A similar military usage is *no-fire line,* defined by the *Dictionary of Military Terms* as "a line short of which artillery or ships do not fire on targets except on request of the supported commander, but beyond which they may fire at any time without danger to friendly troops."

Zone has become a popular word, outstripping *region, area, district* or *belt* (the meaning of its Greek root). Baseball has its *strike zone,* football its *zone defense* and *end zone,* basketball its *zone press.* Teachers point to a *drug-free zone,* and students like to *zone out,* or fall asleep. Every *time zone* has its *safety zones.* The military likes *killing zone* and *demilitarized zone,* which is *DMZ* for short; it is inordinately pleased with the *no-fly zone.*

Should we drop the quotation marks and accept the functionally shifty verb as standard usage? Let's wait; although *air-exclusion zone* is pretentious (and misleading—we're not talking about a vacuum), *no-flight zone,* with *flight* doing the usual modifying work of an attributive noun, is readily understandable Standard English. In my book, for the time being at least, *no-fly* is a no-go.

In what now seems to be early days of aviation to many (but not to me, having been professionally and emotionally involved since before 1942) there was a similar phrase "No Step." It was prominently painted or stencilled on fabric surfaces close to strengthened walkways and steps leading to open cockpits. Also later on relatively weak metal surfaces, near such walkways.

Douglas A. King
Riverside, California

Foam Fell on Alabama

For writers, the possibility of error—linguistic or factual—is infinite. We cannot be paralyzed by this. Check, recheck and then go ahead and take a chance; if you wait for absolute certainty, you will never commit a word to paper.

This profundity grips me after a polemic I wrote in another space criticizing the critics of a theme park planned by the Walt Disney Company in Manassas, Virginia. Standing firm for artistic expression, even by Mickey Mouse, I had taken a pop at several columnists opposed to honky-tonk intrusion into the neighborhood of the battles of Bull Run. One of those popped was Jonathan Yardley of *The Washington Post,* a defender of the area's serenity who, I asserted, had written *"foamingly"* on the subject.

In choosing that unfamiliar but readily understandable word to describe excessive vituperation, I intended to call up an exaggerated mental picture of a maddened animal "foaming at the mouth." I rejected *foamily,* which looks too much like "family" and sounds like a dialect rendition of *formerly,* as well as *frothily,* from the expression, less common in America, of "frothing at the mouth."

Mr. Yardley, a veteran book critic unaccustomed to incoming fire, responded with an *ah-hah!* column centered on his discovery of a word error by a professed word maven. (I keep such zingers in my "Uofallpeople" file.)

"*Foamingly?* Hunt as I may, hunt as I might," he modified danglingly, "it is a word nowhere to be found. Not in the *American Heritage Dictionary of the American Language, Third Edition,* that [*sic*] is kept handy to my reading chair, not even in the *Webster's Third New International Dictionary of the English Language, Unabridged,* that [*sic,* again—try "which" when introducing a nonrestrictive clause] sits on a stand beside my desk. *Foamily,* yes, but *foamingly,* no."

Well, then—is there such a word as *foamingly*? To put the question more accurately, has that adverb ever been cited in a reputable lexicon as having been used before?

Yes. Three citations can be found in the *Oxford English Dictionary,* the most famous being the passage from the poet Robert Southey's 1801 narrative poem, *Thalaba the Destroyer,* an epic about an Arabian hero fighting the forces of evil: "The winter torrent rolls/Down the deep-channell'd rain-course, *foamingly*." The revised *Random House Second Unabridged* cites that adverb as well.

The point here is that nobody can be absolutely, 100 percent sure when correcting another person's choice of words. Mr. Yardley checked two reliable sources, enough for an investigative reporter; isn't that enough for a critic?

No, it's not. Even had he tried the current CD-ROM of the *Oxford English Dictionary,* the most thorough language source in the world, and even if that data base did not have any citation (though, as we have seen, it has at least three), that would not allow certainty; some specialized dictionary or publication (*Chemical Foaming Reactions Review,* or whatever) might turn it up.

What to do? You can't check around forever if you're writing for a newspaper. So you take the plunge and hope the pool has been filled, or that nobody cares enough to correct you. In the case of *foamingly,* it wasn't and somebody did. (At this very moment, somebody is searching the *O.E.D.* for *danglingly,* the adverb used above to tease my fellow cultural commentator about a dangling modifier. Relax; it's there, though I may be the first to use it since 1611.) When I called previous usages of *foamingly* to my columnar colleague Yardley's attention, he good-naturedly replied, "I'd always suspected that Southey was a pinko permissivist."

Later on in my diatribe about not stopping Disney from developing its Civil War theme park, I referred to the moment Thomas Jackson, the Confederate general, was given his sobriquet, *Stonewall.* It happened at First Manassas, I wrote with the confidence that comes from a lifetime's Civil War buffery, when an Alabaman shouted to his troops, "There stands Jackson like a stone wall—rally behind the Virginians!" Recognizing that the Nitpickers' League has a large Civil War contingent, I protected myself by adding that some historians think that the Alabaman's comment was not a compliment but a complaint—that the shouting general was sore at Jackson for remaining in position like a damned stone wall, instead of charging the Union troops.

In comes this note from Vic Gold, the author and political adviser: "Re your reference to *Alabaman:* the natives, I have learned to my sorrow, prefer *Alabamian.* Ditto *Louisianian.*"

O.K.; I started to correct that in this space, when another blindsiding letter came in, this from Gotcha! Gangster Bruce Stewart of Chevy Chase, Maryland: "Since Gen. Barnard Elliott Bee died shortly after making his famous remark ('There stands Jackson like a stone wall'), we'll never know for sure whether he was criticizing or commending Jackson. What we do know, however, is that General Bee was from South Carolina, not Alabama."

Be not discouraged; do not freeze at the prospect of possible error. As the fumblerule directs: Learn from misteaks.

Mr. Gold's natives must occupy the state of Alabamia, for my friends and acquaintances next door—the ones who can read, at least—are all Alabamans. *I take as my text the Georgians' view of it from Stephen Vincent Benet's* John Brown's Body:

A girl to be kind to, a girl we're lucky in,
A girl to marry some nice Kentuckian,
Some Alabaman, some Carolinian—
In fact, if you ask me for my opinion,
There are lots of boys in the Northern sections
And some of them have quite good connections—

Clayton H. Farnham
Atlanta, Georgia

Follow-up on *Follow-on*

After the first Whitewater hearings, the Senate Banking Committee Chairman, Don Riegle, predicted "*follow-on* hearings" after the Senate leadership discussed "the scope of a *follow-on* resolution." Everybody nodded as if this word—freshly inserted in most major new dictionaries—were not merely voguish but widely understood.

New it's not. "He toc and wente and folwede on" can be found in biblical exegesis written about 1250, and the compound verb was used in an 1884 book about billiards to explain a stroke "when you cause your ball to *follow on* after the ball it strikes."

But for *follow-on*'s development as a noun and adjective, neither exegetes nor hustlers can claim credit: That belongs to the aerospace industry. "The Bomarc II is a '*follow-on*' air defense weapon for the 200-mile Bomarc missiles" is a citation from *The New York Times* in 1959, supplied to me by Jesse Sheidlower of Random House. A year after this linguistic liftoff, an ad in *Farmer and Stockbreeder* magazine touted "advice about 'follow-on' feeding." With

Pentagonians and farmers using the term, it was soon seized upon by politicians and is now part of Washington's vogue vocabulary.

What's the difference between *follow-up* and *follow-on*? It's roughly analogous to *continual* ("pausing and resuming") and *continuous* ("without pausing"): A *follow-up* is a "re-examination, pursuit, review," and a *follow-on* is a "continuation, succession, development."

Mnemonic: Nothing succeeds like *follow-on.*

Footprints on the Infobahn

Say the word *footprint,* and I immediately think of the Abominable Snowman of the Himalayas. Does this prepare me for a nanosecondary grasp of computer lingo? Not yeti; a generation of hackers, confronted with the old word *footprint,* thinks first of its latest sense, "the desk space taken up by a computer."

Those of us with fat footprints (I am pounding this out on an archaic, thirty-three-megahertz pre-Pentium monster that I have to start with a crank) get the feeling that ours is an *offline* life. I take that new usage from a clipping about *cybersex* sent over by my computer multimentor, Andy Glass of Cox Newspapers. *Cybersex* is defined in *Compuserve Magazine* as " 'adult-oriented' games and CD-ROM's; steamy online 'chats'; people discussing their sex lives and wanton desires with strangers in online forums, even falling in love without having met."

The article quotes Janis O., which is the *nom de ligne* of a person conducting an online Human Sexuality Forum, saying, "There is nobody in my *offline* life that I would feel comfortable exploring sexual submission issues with." Let's not give in: *Online,* in use since the dark ages of 1950, means "available or accessible through computer or telecommunications," with more specific senses of "connected and turned on" or "having a feature that can be used without exiting an application." (As *leaving* leaves, *exiting* enters.)

Offline is not quite the opposite: According to the *New Hacker's Dictionary* by Eric Raymond, it means "not now or not here"; when a person suggests removal to her *offline life,* as in the story of Janis O., she alludes to direct human contact, or at least nonpublic communication through E-mail for those who cannot bear the retrogression of *going postal.*

In the *Courier-Journal* of Louisville, Kentucky, James A. Fussell defines *going postal* as "a euphemism for being totally stressed-out or 'losing it.' " He suggests the derivation is from postal employees who have gone on shooting rampages, while others attribute the phrase's origin to not being online or using an E-mail address.

A sagan of new computer terms (that uses *sagan* as an eponym for "large quantity," from Carl Sagan's use of "billions and billions" on his TV series) includes *cracker,* not a Southern put-down but an unsanctioned hacker; like the *safecracker* who breaks through a security system, the shorter form *cracker* identifies any hacker who breaks into a computer system without authorization.

There's also the noun for a computer complaint: *Gritch,* which sounds like a portmanteau of *grouch* and *glitch.* (Hackers will lodge a gritch if you confuse the honest *hacker* with the dishonest *cracker.*)

Cyberdom's fixation on acronyms continues: The people who brought us DOS (Disk Operating System) and CD-ROM (Compact Disk–Read Only Memory, which means you cannot write on it) have come up with MIDI, not French for "noon" but Musical Instrument Digital Interface: Through this keyboard connection, President Clinton could play his saxophone without ever having to take a deep breath or inflate his cheeks. Initialese is usually a sign of laziness in neologizing, but sometimes shows imagination: GUI stands for Graphical User Interface—the pointing to pictures and symbols called *icons*—and has the advantage of being pronounced "GOO-ey."

Will you find a date in time for the *trackball*? Think of a dead mouse, lying on its back, the tail connected to the computer. This odious extension of the rodent metaphor refers to the ball-bearing on the mouse's stomach, which can be operated by the finger, and is therefore easier when there is little desk space to roll around. The ball-bearing that manipulates the pointer on the screen is known as the *trackball.* (Two-sewer hitters await computerdom's use of *stickball, curb ball* and *punchball.*)

Have you *met Ed*? You don't want to; the weak inflection is a downer. In grammar, words like *rejected* and *disappointed* are examples of weak inflection, with the addition in Old English of the suffix *-ed* to form the past tense and past participle. Strong inflection forms the past tense without a suffix, as in *sang* and *ate;* computer linguists have seized on the weak *-ed* to personalize the past. If you've *met Ed,* you're finished, washed up, history. (This may be an offshoot of *Ralph,* the power booter: Campus beer drinkers know that *talking to Ralph on the big white phone* is to find a commodious receptacle for regurgitation.)

Dump is in. As one who almost went broke paying for what seemed like a Nexis *core dump* when I couldn't follow directions to sign off and stop the cascade of data, I welcome *brain dump,* a useful expression to describe the imparting of everything one knows on a given subject.

Here's the latest jargon dump from *Wired* magazine. I was given a subscription to this electric new publication with an in-your-interface attitude by my son the former software developer (now my son the interactive multimedia producer; nobody treads water in that business). *MorF?* is an interrogatory acronym for "Male or Female?" This is the question posed in the People Connection "rooms" of America Online, "as conversants try to determine the sex of other occupants."

The magazine notes that when a question like "Sandy—*MorF?*" is asked, the answer often includes age and geographical location, as in "F/24/Cleveland," which can lead to perfectly respectable communication and not unsafe cybersex.

Try not to confuse *MorF?* with *morph,* the computer animation technique that allows figures to change from one shape to another.

Magalog, reports *Wired,* is "a mail-order catalog disguised as a magazine in the hope of sucking in its recipients." *Interrupt-driven* describes "someone who moves through a workday responding to a series of interruptions rather than the work goals originally set."

Ah, here's one I was looking for: "The Infobahn Is a Big, Fat Joke." That's the headline over an article by Mark Stahlman predicting "no 500-channel future," "no $3 trillion mother of all industries," "no virtual sex" (now he's getting depressing) and "no *infobahn.*"

Vice President Al Gore's staff claims, without citations, that he called for a national network of *information superhighways* in the early 80's; I predicted two months ago that mouthful would be shortened to *infoway* or *I-way,* but it seems the German word *Autobahn* has provided the combining form for Gore's footprint in the sands of time.

One parallel—and possibly older—use of online *and* offline *is in television.*

An online edit session is the session that produces the final, for-broadcast show. Offline edits are working drafts, or "rough cuts."

Although some mistakenly use the terms to refer to computerized and manually controlled edit equipment (since the more sophisticated computer-controlled devices are routinely used for finished edits,) offline *and* online *correctly refer to the end use, not the means of production. (This confusion may be a corruption from the computer use of* online.*)*

The television use of online *and* offline *comes from the banks of video monitors found in TV control rooms. From the earliest days of broadcast, the monitor that fed the broadcast tower (or network line) has always been labeled "Line." Hence,* online *meant "destined for broadcast."*

Scott Auerbach
Atlanta, Georgia

Being that you are a stickler for the correct use of words, allow me to point out your incorrect use of the words ball bearing.

There are many types of bearings in use today. There are roller bearings, needle bearings, ball bearings, sleeve bearings, journal bearings and more. There is no need to place a hyphen between the two words.

The trackball used as a pointing device on a computer is just that, a ball, not a ball bearing.

I have enclosed a miniature ball bearing for your inspection. As you can see, it has an inner and outer raceway, many balls and a separator. This entire unit is called a ball bearing.

I hope this makes clear the difference between a ball and a ball bearing.

Kenneth Abeles
President
Pioneer Bearing Corporation
West Orange, New Jersey

Frankly Speaking

Federal Reserve Chairman Alan Greenspan and House Banking Chairman Henry Gonzalez are having a classic contretemps over the independence of federal agencies and the public's need for accountability. Leafing through the transcript of this erudite and historic hearing, I came across a citation by Mr. Gonzalez of a passage in a book by Carter Glass, a predecessor who fathered the Federal Reserve Act, titled *Adventures in Constructive Finance.*

Mr. Gonzalez's selection was about President Woodrow Wilson's challenge to bankers about participating in their own regulation. Mr. Greenspan countered with a different interpretation of the same passage in full context.

Barney Frank, a committee member fighting to stay awake through all this, interjected, "Mr. Chairman, doesn't this come down to the question of whether or not Carter Glass was half empty or half full?"

Freaked on Clout

Following a cease-fire in Sarajevo, an Associated Press photographer captured a happy sight: "Bosnian children could return to being children," read the caption in *The New York Times,* "hitching a slippery ride behind a United Nations armored vehicle."

Hitching a ride? To most of us, that means "thumbing a ride," asking a driver to pick you up. The action of the Bosnian children in the snow required a reach into dialect. Earlier that week, Beth Wagner of the A.P. reported from Philadelphia about the same dangerous but frequently engaged-in pastime: "It's called *hopping cars* in Philadelphia, *bumper-hitching* or *shagging* in Detroit, *skitching* along the Eastern Seaboard. In northern Indiana it's *hooky-bobbing.*"

Not to mention *bizzing* in the Northwest and *bum-riding* in Utah; all these denote the action of daring, often foolish, children who grab a ride on the back end of a moving vehicle. All but one of these regionalisms are reported, with careful notation of time and place, in the *Dictionary of American Regional English.* "I couldn't find any examples of *shagging* in this sense," says Joan Hall of *DARE,* "and am especially glad to get this."

Obviously, *hooky-bobbing* is a sport frowned on by parents all over the world, no matter what it is called. But it has a different name everywhere, and probably regionalisms within each major language. Collecting and describing the names, using a system of historical and geographical cross-references, is the work of regional lexicographers and dialectologists. In America, *DARE* at the University of Wisconsin is the best resource, building on earlier dictionaries of Americanisms; Fred Cassidy, its guiding light, scrounges for funds among foundations who do future generations a favor by supporting *DARE*'s scholarly work.

The related field of slang, which is in many instances a national sublanguage, tends to get commercial sponsorship. Dictionaries of slang sell; that's why publishers invest in them. Usually these are glossaries of a special field or subculture, but now Random House is preparing a full-scale dictionary of slang, on historical principles and with detailed citations, which will do for non-Standard English what *DARE* is doing for regionalisms and what the *Oxford English Dictionary* supplement did for the whole language.*

Pick up a current newspaper and see how slang enlivens our lingo. "Before arriving at 7 A.M., he makes calls all along the way . . . ," Meg Cox of *The Wall Street Journal* writes about the media tycoon Rupert Murdoch. "Insiders say he runs his empire by 'phone and clone,' and even he admits to being a 'phone freak.' "

What's a *freak*? The *Historical Dictionary of American Slang,* edited by Jonathan Lighter, shows how the slang word developed along two senses. The first is "a person who is markedly or offensively eccentric in dress or behavior; weirdo." The first citation, earlier than any other dictionary's, is from Finley Peter Dunne's *Mr. Dooley* series in 1895: "The deluded ol' freak . . . had me up all las' month." A year later a fictional character objected to a "swell girl . . . holdin' on to some freak with side whiskers."

That sense cannot be what Rupert Murdoch has in mind in describing himself as a *phone freak.* The second sense, which began developing at the same time, is "an ardent or extreme devotee, practitioner or enthusiast." Aha! A *maven.* A student slang glossary in 1895, as well as a *Dialect Notes* citation the same year, defined the word as a student with high marks; in 1946, Duke Ellington was quoted in a book about jazz as saying, "I'm a train freak."

Now we have some solid data on which to ground our definition of the two senses of the slang term. Synonymists like me can then split hairs: An *enthusiast* is avid but inexpert, as is an *aficionado;* a *connoisseur* is a coolly judgmental expert; a *maven* is a scholarly nonexpert, often self-taught, who delights in the sub-

*The first volume, covering A–G, was published in 1994; the second, H–O, appeared in 1997. Letters P–Z are forthcoming.

ject; a *freak* is someone who gets carried away by the subject beyond all good sense (though the term is less pejorative when used self-mockingly, as I will explain when Murdoch gets me on the phone).

Does the dictionary have *clout*? When I once wrote that this term originated in New York politics, I was sharply taken to task by my colleague in columny Mike Royko, who insisted it was a classic Chicagoism.

The *H.D.A.S.,* as it is known in scholarly circles, defines it as "political influence; (*hence*) power." Jesse Sheidlower, a contributing editor to the slang dictionary, offers a citation that antedates the earliest *DARE* reference by seventy years: "The provenance of the remarkably early 1868 quotation," he notes, "suggests that the term arose in New York; though it is now of national distribution, journalists often associate it with Chicago politics." (He doesn't want to get a blast from Royko.) The citation, earliest of anybody's, is from page 127 of *Dear Walt,* a collection of letters to Walt Whitman; his brother Thomas Jefferson Whitman wrote, "Fellows in Brook[lyn] . . . always think they are going to be deprived of office and *'clout.'* "

And a second sense is presented from police slang: "a politically influential friend or ally." A 1955 usage: "The 'rabbi' in New York police parlance is the 'clout' in Chicago."

For this dictionary, slanguists are itchy, on pins and needles, hot to trot, prepared to be freaked out. . . .

I saw your column on the subject of "skitching."

When I was a lad in Chicago, it was called "dedoing" or to "dedo."

Donald Rumsfeld
Chicago, Illinois

"Hooky-bobbing" reminded me of what that activity was called in S.F. in the 1930s–40s—"nipping." One nipped a streetcar by riding at the back of the car on its upraised cowcatcher (odd term that—in a city).

Don Cunningham
San Francisco, California

Free Lunch

Who coined "There ain't no such thing as a free lunch"?

We know that *free lunch* was advertised in Western bars in the 1840's, meaning that the eats were free to those who bought drinks. But when did the awakening come, encapsulated in the aphorism, that the price of the food was included in the price of the required drink?

The economist Milton Friedman popularized it in the name of a 1975 book, but frequently disclaims coinage. Fans of the science fiction writer Robert A. Heinlein point to his use of the phrase in his 1966 novel *The Moon Is a Harsh Mistress;* it was there that its long acronym was coined, "tanstaafl." But, as Ralph Keyes shows in his icon-busting *Nice Guys Finish Seventh,* the "no free lunch" phrase pops up in the writings of two columnists, Burton Crane and Walter Morrow, dating back to 1949.

George W. Bardes of Cos Cob, Connecticut, noted a passage in Robert A. Caro's 1974 book *The Power Broker,* a biography of Robert Moses, which casts more light on the phrase's introduction into politics. He is writing about the beginning, in 1934, of the mayoralty of Fiorello La Guardia, New York's "Little Flower":

"Bounding up the front steps of City Hall on the morning of his Inauguration Day, he had stopped, a roly-poly figure in a ridiculous black hat and a rumpled black suit," goes the Caro account, "and had shaken his little fist at its white Georgian elegance and shouted, *'E finita la cuccagna!'* ('No more free lunch!'), a phrase which, a friend explained, the Mayor was using to promise 'The party is over! No more graft!' "

This usage provides a nice transition between the early, literal meaning of *free lunch* ("a bartender's spread to entice paying customers") and its present sense of "economic lesson" (you are paying for that so-called free lunch).

All that remains now is to find the first written citation of "There ain't no such thing as a free lunch." The finder won't get the Nobel Prize for economics, but will be fed great heaps of pickles and pretzels at no cost (to him or her) at gatherings of political etymologists.

From April 1946 through December 1951 I was an economist on the staff of the National Industrial Conference Board (now the Conference Board) in New York City. Sometime during that period—and I believe most probably between 1948 and 1950—a communication that referred to the "no free lunch" statement and also used the acronym relating to it *crossed my desk. I still vividly remember the circumstance, although I no longer have a copy of the document in question.*

Lawrence A. Mayer
New York, New York

Phrasedick Find

The Phrasedicks—those intrepid Hawkshaws who track famous phrases back to their sources in antiquity—have finally begun to hit pay dirt with what the novelist Robert Heinlein acronymed Tanstaafl.

"There Ain't No Such Thing as a Free Lunch" has often been attributed to the economist Milton Friedman; he readily admits using it, perhaps popularizing it, but disclaims coinage. Last year, Ralph Keyes in *Nice Guys Finish Seventh* (Leo Durocher did not say they finished "last") cited a usage in a 1949 article in the *San Francisco News.*

Treating that citation as a clue, Fred Shapiro of the Yale Law School library, author of the profoundly researched *Oxford Dictionary of American Legal Quotations,* has turned up the June 1, 1949, copy of the newspaper. In it is "The Fable of the King and All the Wise Men—or Economics in Eight Words," by Walter Morrow.

When a plague of poverty came upon an ancient land, Morrow wrote, the king called in his wisest counselors and demanded a short text on economics. A year later they returned with eighty-seven disputatious volumes; he ordered guards with crossbows to shoot half of them. In subsequent years, they cut it to forty volumes; he kept shooting them until the last economist prostrated himself before the king and said: "Sire, in eight words I will reveal to you all the wisdom that I have distilled through all these years from all the writings of all the economists who once practiced their science in your kingdom. Here is my text: 'There ain't no such thing as free lunch.' "

Note that the original (if nobody finds an earlier citation) lacks an *a* before the *free lunch,* which would conform to the name for customer enticement in saloons. And here is an unexpected phrasedickensian bonanza: The article is preceded by "Here's an editorial we published 11 years ago. In view of all the 'plans' now coming out of Washington, we offer this as a timely reprint."

Mr. Shapiro notes with pride, "The phrase actually dates to at least 11 years earlier than anyone has previously established."

Dear Bill;

*When I used it on the last page of a book of mine (*Alistair Cooke's America, *p. 389), I thought it so familiar that I apologized for using it by writing: "More often than I care to admit, one of the oldest of American chestnuts seemed newly roasted" (I'm winding up by summarizing what I'd seen and felt after roaming round 100,000 miles of the country): "It is that line of the Italian immigrant asked to say what forty years of American life had taught him: 'There is no free lunch.' By now, it is a facetious truism, but it is also a profound truth forgotten by the*

Founding Fathers in the ecstasy of promising everybody life, liberty, and the pursuit of happiness."

That was written in 1973. I can't remember a time when I didn't know the phrase (certainly decades before I'd ever heard of Milton Friedman, who, I must say, is getting to be the Dorothy Parker of economic folklore (having the good things of other wits ascribed to him).

I read *it first in D. W. Brogan's little book,* The American Character, *published here in 1944 by Knopf. I've looked through it now but can't spot the sentence about the Italian shoe-shine man who plied his trade just inside Grand Central Station. I can't spot it offhand. Run your MRI over it and pin it down. I'm quite positive it's Brogan, and it may be that I picked it up from him. But that's fifty years ago, when even you hadn't heard it!*

Alistair Cooke
New York, New York

Function Fish

What Americans call *rubber chicken,* the British call *function fish;* both refer to the food required to be consumed at large gatherings. The use of the noun *function* to mean "event," long a Standard English sense of the word, has been on the increase in the United States. From Bernard E. Ritzinger of Seattle, a part-time bus driver for Gray Line, we have a spotting of a campusism that is catching on.

"On assignment recently to the Kappa Kappa Gamma sorority at the University of Washington," he writes, "I learned a new word." He was waiting in his bus near the sorority house to take his passengers to a dance, and saw many of them visiting a fraternity house across the street. After two hours, he asked about the delay and was told the young people were *pre-functioning.*

"They were socializing before the dance, or function," he explains. "Eventually I took a busload of young people to the function. When it was over, I returned them to the sorority house.

"Presumably," the Lexicographic Irregular driving the bus concludes, "those still able to function then went post-functioning."

The Fuzz and the Wuzz

Waking up the sleepy audience at the Radio-Television News Directors Association, Dan Rather of CBS lit into the "Hollywoodization" of news.

"Thoughtfully written analysis is out, 'live pops' are in," he said. (A *live pop,* also known as a *live stand-up,* refers to the ad-libbing that a broadcast correspondent in the field does on camera after a news anchor introduces the story. When the anchor says, "Now we're going to Charles, who's standing live in the dark where something happened three hours ago, but you can't see it now," the *live pop* is what Charles has to ad-lib because he hasn't come back to the studio to write his stand-up.)

Mr. Rather continued: "Hire lookers, not writers. Do powder puff, not probing, interviews. Stay away from controversial subjects. Kiss [vulgarism], move with the mass [rhymes with that vulgarism], and for heaven and the ratings' sake don't make anybody mad. . . . Make nice, not news."

The pop that enlivened his speech to slanguists was Rather's complaint that "They've got us putting more *fuzz and wuzz* on the air." I was familiar with *fuzz,* defined in Godfrey Irwin's 1931 *American Tramp and Underworld Slang* as "a detective; a prison guard or turnkey. Here it is likely that 'fuzz' was originally 'fuss,' one hard to please or over-particular." But what about *wuzz*? Was this similarly derived from *wuss*? Patricia Ireland, president of the National Organization for Women, in commenting a few months ago about Hillary Clinton jokes, told the *Boston Globe,* "The overall theme is one of Bill Clinton being a *wuss.*" She probably used this term as if it were synonymous with *wimp,* unaware of the etymology of *wuss* as rhyming slang meaning "like a woman" in a derogatory sense.

The CBS co-anchor, obviously drawn to rhyme in oratory, clarified his catchy phrase in a reply to a query from this department. " 'Fuzz and wuzz' refers to police ('fuzz') and dead bodies (was—'wuzz')." In slang, the past tense lives.

Dan Rather refers to "fuzz and wuzz." Godfrey Irwin's 1931 source for "fuzz" is a little skimpy. Maybe there was more which was not cited in your article; there is more to the slang term's history, beyond the Tramps and Cons. I first heard it in the carnival sub-culture, in reference to any law-enforcement presence on the midway: an obvious hazard to any "flat" operator (a concessionaire whose games may be modified in such a way as to take unfair advantage of the player). Any good Carny (and possibly Mr. Irwin, as well) knows who "Mister Fuzzynuts," later elided to "Mr. Fuzz," was.

And any kid . . . my *age . . . can tell you:*

Fuzzy-Wuzzy was a bear.
Fuzzy-Wuzzy had no hair.
Fuzzy-Wuzzy wasn't fuzzy, was he?

Finally, there is/was a society (somewhere in Africa as I recall) known to the general public as Fuzzy-Wuzzies, *and Mr. Rather may rather have been thinking of these people when he took his live pop.*

Paul Strong
Mountain View, California

Get a Life!

"Government by all-nighters is getting tired," *Newsweek* wrote in its "Conventional Wisdom Watch," the sprightliest section of the magazine. It advised the youthful Clinton White House staff, "Go to sleep and *get a life.*"

An *all-nighter,* which only a generation ago described a leisurely arrangement with a prostitute, has changed its meaning to "a nightlong session of studying, or cramming, for an examination." More to the newsworthy point, however, is the growing use of the imperative expression *Get a life!*

"There are those who say that early citations of *Get a life!* might shed light on its origin," writes Michael J. Keyes of Coram, Long Island, "but I doubt it. *Get a life!* is a fine example of language as it is reinvented by children. I first heard the expression, spoken quietly but with the force of an expletive, from a teen-ager several years ago."

Teen-agers, unfortunately, rarely publish their comments. The first citations I can find were published in *U.C.L.A. Slang,* edited by Pamela Munro, reporting in 1989 on research going back to 1983. One read: "Geez, Joe, you're a 27-year-old burger fryer at Big Tommy's. *Get a life!*" The other followed the operative phrase with a series of exclamatory imperatives: "Do something constructive with your time! Stop being such a jerk! . . . Have some ambition!"

An early media usage is found in an October 27, 1989, *Chicago Tribune* movie review by Caitlin Creevy. In *Fat Man and Little Boy* (nicknames for the first two atomic bombs), a character named Kathleen commented on the connotation of an adjective: "Naked—isn't that a beautiful word? Tonight—I want to make love." In panning the picture, the reviewer wrote: "And she was being totally serious. Kathy, baby, *get a life.*" The use of the phrase without explanation suggests common usage at that time in the teen vernacular.

The phrase was picked up and popularized throughout the culture in the fall of 1990 as the title of a Fox Broadcasting situation comedy starring Chris Elliott as a childlike thirty-year-old newspaper boy. About that time, a *Los Angeles Times* writer, Elliott Almond, covering a widely practiced sport, observed: "David Farmer discovered early that not everyone appreciated his obsession with bicycling. In the fifth grade, he was dropped by a girlfriend who told him to *get a life.* More than a decade later, Farmer is one of the United States' leading professional riders."

We can speculate that the expression originated as "Get on with your life," influenced by a comment like "You call that a life?" What we know is that the phrase, like *reality check,* is a young person's way of deriding a preoccupation with superficiality or fixation on fiction. As such, this godsend of a phrase is a with-it way of awakening those who have been too taken with being with-it. It says, "Be sensible; grow up; get real." Underneath that, it says: Stop pretending that imitating the lifestyle of celebrities, or living the life of the dropout, or playing the role of the alienated in a previous generation, or striking the pose of the exhausted savior of political humanity is connected to the need to grow and develop and make plans for the future.

As a vogue phrase, it can be derided, but as a waker-upper, *Get a life!* is conservative, constructive advice. Don't knock it.

Regarding "Get a life!," I contend the first reference was by William Shatner on Saturday Night Live. *"Move out of your parents' basements. Get a life!" he admonished a crowd of Trekkies at a* Star Trek *convention. It was December 20, 1986.*

Charles Kochman
Brooklyn, New York

The people who most often use the expression "Get a life!" are, invariably, the kind of people Henry David Thoreau observed with ample opportunities and finally said: "The mass of men lead lives of quiet desperation."

Eugene Wright
New York, New York

"Get a life" among the workaholics in the publishing industry I know has been used to send obsessive/compulsives (especially those in upper management) home from the office to become more well-rounded and whole. It has meant get a family, get some outside interests, get a pet, even get a significant other, and respect those who already have a life, for starters.

"Get a life" among the teenagers I know has had a similar significance (also suggested by your cyclist example, but with a different twist). When I tell my son, for example, that he should put in several more hours studying and reading, get-

ting focused and even getting ahead on his assignments, his reply is that he "has a life," and only those who don't have a life, among teenagers, would work with the seriousness that I've suggested. So, as in our office example, "get a life" to the various teenagers I know means have outside interests, play sports, be social, and don't simply be a nerd.

Susan Badger
Needham, Massachusetts

As I hear it used around here, and among my son's thirtysomething associates, "Get a life!" seems to mean something like, "abandon that fixation—stop relating everything to the goddamn environment (or human rights, or the capital gains tax, or politics, or even ritual satanic abuse), and get a broader focus—pay attention to ordinary things in which real people are interested."

Frank Mankiewicz
Vice Chairman
Hill and Knowlton
Washington, D.C.

I worked for Forbes *magazine for a number of years. Sometimes when we had put in a 12- or 14-hour day and were totally obsessed with whatever it was that kept us there so late, someone would say, "God, I need to get a life." Overzealous employees were chided: "Get a life." People would comment that Microsoft's Bill Gates, totally involved in his company, should "get a life."*

It would seem that for those of us who have grown up and gotten real, and have developed plans for the future, the "life" we now wish we could "get" is one in which we would be spending more time with family and friends, enjoying experience more and worrying less about the last corporate crisis. The life we aspire to would not be spent racing from one meeting to the next, or living in neon-lighted cubicles eating bad carry-in food, too tired to do more after work than vegetate in front of the television.

I left Forbes *18 months ago and am now a freelance writer (or a "virtual employee" of a number of "virtual corporations") living in a small town in New Mexico. I was talking to a former colleague on the telephone the other day. After detailing how hard she was working, the frustrations of her dealings with management and the like, she suddenly burst out, "I need to get a LIFE." I was sitting there watching the river flow by and the sunlight on the red rocks. I knew exactly what she meant because I "got a life."*

Kathleen Wiegner
Jemez Springs, New Mexico

Get off My Laptop

In my growing file on computer *subnotebooks,* I have this letter on a related subject: "Recently, in speaking to a British friend in London," writes Roni Finkelstein of Colchester, Connecticut, "I referred to my *pocketbook.* When it became obvious that he was totally confused as to my meaning, I pointed to it. 'Oh,' he said, 'your *handbag.*' How and when did the word *pocketbook* come into common American usage?"

That's easy; in 1617, the word first surfaced to denote a small book, now called a *notebook;* it was a book of addresses, or notes, that fit in a pocket. By 1816, women were carrying a book-like case with compartments for papers and knickknacks, and they called it a *purse, handbag* or—extending the old term—*pocketbook.*

Fast-forward to the 1990's. (That's a new verb meaning "press the 'fast-forward' button on your cordless remote control, or zapper, or clicker," to get past the commercials on your videotape.) We have just whizzed past the late 80's, when computers smaller than the original portables, or luggables, were called *laptops.* That word, coined on the analogy of Dashiell Hammett's 1929 *desktop,* has slid off the hacker's scope to land in the laps of the users of archaic machinery. (I like my old laptop. Wish I could still see my old lap.)

Welcome to the new world of *notebooks,* a far cry from the pocketbooks of prehandbag days. "We have a rule of thumb that describes a notebook as five to seven pounds," says Bill Howard, executive editor of *PC Magazine* from Ziff-

Davis, who will stretch it to eight pounds in a pinch. "It must have a battery. It should have a form factor of a sheet of notebook paper or slightly bigger—no more than 9 by 12 inches." *Form factor?* "That's a buzzword meaning 'two-dimensional size or area'; some people say *footprint.*" I prefer *footprint;* his *form factor* is too close to *fudge factory.*

Now how about a newer entry, *subnotebook*? "A subnotebook is a notebook without the floppy disk drive, which was about ten to twelve ounces," says Howard, who predicts the term will extend down to units of two pounds. The ones that do not have a keyboard, instead offering up a screen to a stylus, are called *tablets,* drawing on the experience of Moses in jotting down the Ten Commandments.

You might expect the size smaller to be called *mini-subs,* but you would be wrong. Below two pounds, stuffable in a pocket if you have strong seams, are *palmtops,* an echo of the long-forgotten *laptops.* From the Latin *palma,* "inside of the hand," the noun *palm* appeared in Old English as *folm,* which survives in a word familiar to football fans: When the quarterback does not slap the handoff firmly on the fullback's *folm,* you get a *fumble.*

This botched play draws derision from the guys in the press booth pounding their *palmtops*—unless, of course, they carry P.D.A.'s, initialese for *personal digital assistants.* Those are the subnotebooks that work Moses-style if you are hooked on handwriting, also called *personal communicators* when used for telephoning.

Let's kill P.D.A. P.D.Q. (The last set of initials stands for "pretty damn quick," a racily profane term familiar to those who used the twenty-three-skidoo laptop.) Initialese is confusing. When you decry P.C., are you condemning a personal computer, complaining about your personal communicator, or denouncing political correctness?

Not only do I resist the initials P.D.A., but I also think the term "personal digital assistant" is too close to *masseur.* It evokes a personal trainer for fingers, palmtopping a bribe from a silicon-man. The industry can do better.

Handheld is the umbrella term to describe the palmtop computer, the personal digital assistant and the personal communicator. Perhaps *handholder* is the word, though that has a meaning of "sympathizer." The word *personal* was used to differentiate computers that could fit on desktops from *mainframe* computers; are we now stuck with *personal* to describe anything small? How about a word like *little*? Or, if we could figure out a way to hold off the eavesdroppers, we might try *private.* A last resort: *pocket.*

I think you were misinformed.

Footprint *is, of course, two-dimensional.*

Form factor, *though, I believe is three-dimensional and includes the overall shape of the object, not just its crude dimensions. A table lamp might have the same dimensions as the rectangular cardboard box it's shipped in, but not the same form factor.*

People who discuss brick-shaped objects, like laptops and notebooks, easily confuse footprint *and* form factor*—all the more so if they aren't paying much attention to the third dimension of thickness.*

Peter Norton
Santa Monica, California

When my sister and I were little, and never mind when that was, our mother had three friends in for an informal bridge afternoon, and one of the three mentioned her purse. Guest #2 bridled politely and said that she had been brought up to call it a pocketbook. Guest #3 had a sharp tongue, and Phi Beta Kappa key from Smith, and a British husband; she announced, in a tone of invincible authority, that "purse" and "pocketbook" were, well . . . (the term "non-U" had not yet come to light but it was implied), and the object was called, in civilized company, anyway, a handbag.

At this point Mollie, our County Mayo cook, came in with the tea tray, and Mother, enjoying the brouhaha far more than the by now disintegrating bridge game, said, "Mollie, what do you *call the thing you carry your money, comb, and lipstick in?"*

"I call it my bag," said Mollie promptly.

"Thank you, Mollie. So do I," said Mother with cheerful finality. But the guests were making pursy-mouthed tch-tch-tch noises, and a potentially venomous situation needed a swift, light antidote. "So call the thing a reticule and be done with it!" said Mother, giggling.

The suggestion was not lost upon my sister and me, for we have called the accessory a reticule ever since. In French this becomes, handily for us, un réticule, *which the* Petit Larousse *defines as* un petit sac à main, *which brings us back to handbag and, I suppose, to Square One.*

Lucille B. Gaignault
Princeton, New Jersey

You write: "From the Latin palma, *'inside of the hand,' the noun* palm *appeared in Old English as* folm.*" This suggests that* folm *is the Old English form of* palm *and is therefore derived from Latin* palma, *whereas in fact* folm *and* palma *are cognates,* i.e., *they have a common source in the Indo-European parent language.*

Indo-European initial p *was preserved in Latin but became* f *in the Germanic languages, including English. Thus,* folm *is necessarily a cognate, not a derivative, of* palma. *Similarly, our* paternal *is a derivative (or loan-word) of Latin* pater, *"father," but* father *is a cognate;* pedal *is a derivative of Latin* pes *(stem* ped-*), "foot," but* foot *is a cognate;* plenty *is a derivative of Latin* plenus, *"full," but* full *is a cognate; the prefix* pro- *is a derivative of Latin* pro, *"for," but* for *is a cognate.*

To cite another example, Indo-European initial k *was preserved in Latin (spelled* c*) but became* h *in Germanic, so that the second element in* unicorn *is derived from Latin* cornu, *"horn," but* horn *is a cognate;* canine *is a derivative of Latin* canis, *"dog," but* hound *is a cognate;* century *is a derivative of Latin* centum, *"hundred," but* hundred *is a cognate.*

Louis Jay Herman
New York, New York

Good-Deed Dungeon

"Stuffin' envelopes" is how the name of George Stephanopoulos is remembered. Recently the White House aide who sits in the West Wing office closest to the President's was called upon to defend the actions of two Clinton aides who had left the Administration to take up jobs directing lobbying efforts, despite 1992 campaign oratory from candidate Clinton about how he would "stop the revolving door."

Spin-doctoring into the storm of criticism, George tried to point out that Clinton ethics rules were more stringent than ever before, and that reporters were holding this Administration to higher standards. "This is proof of the old adage," he insisted, "that no good deed goes unpunished."

An *adage,* from the Latin for "to say," is an old saying. Those of us who enjoy living in synonymy know that an *adage* is not quite as graven in collective wisdom as a *proverb* or a *maxim;* it is not as legalistic as a *dictum* or as scientific as an *axiom* or as sentimental as a *homily* or as corny as a *saw,* nor as formalized as a *motto,* but it is more rooted in tradition than an *observation.*

Mr. Stephanopoulos's error was not in synonymy but in redundancy. The essence of an adage is age; *sayings* are coined and adopted all the time (Tip O'Neill: "All politics is local"), but an *adage* is an *old* saying. Any "old *adage*" is redundant and subject to execution before the Squad Squad.

The mistake is often made. In 1933, when Franklin D. Roosevelt was criticized for prolonging the Depression, he replied: "There is an old and somewhat lugubrious adage that says, 'Never speak of rope in the house of a man who has been hanged.' In the same way, if I were a Republican leader speaking to a mixed audience, the last word in the whole dictionary that I think I would use is that word 'depression.' " (Though F.D.R. erred in his redundant use of "old adage," his selection of the unfamiliar word *lugubrious*—"ridiculously mournful"—deftly took the macabre sting out of the old saying.)

All of which is prelude to the point of this item: What is the source of *no good deed goes unpunished*? Is it a saying of recent vintage or an authentic *adage*?

In *Bartlett's Familiar Quotations, Sixteenth Edition,* Justin Kaplan threw up his hands and listed it only as a *saying,* with no attribution or guess at time of origin. Computer data bases pop up with an F.B.I. official in 1978 telling *The Washington Post* of an "old Georgia saying—*no good deed goes unpunished*"; in that same year, it was included in a list of sayings by a *Post* writer, Bill Gold, alongside "Everything costs more than you thought it would" and "It's easier to get into something than out of it." It has been attributed by *Forbes* magazine in 1979 to John P. Grier, an American financier who died in 1939, and by a *New York Times* editorialist in 1980 to a former Treasury Secretary, Andrew W. Mellon, who died in 1937. The person most frequently cited as the source is Clare Boothe Luce, and I kick myself for not asking her about it when she was alive.

In the 1991 book *The Phrase That Launched 1,000 Ships,* Nigel Rees does yeoman service to the Phrasedick Brigade, as the etymological Hawkshaws of modern phrases call themselves. He cites a diary entry of June 13, 1967, by the British playwright Joe Orton: "Very good line George [Greeves] came out with at dinner: 'No good deed ever goes unpunished.' " Less specifically cited is this: "Before opening in Noël Coward's play *Waiting in the Wings* (1960), the actress Marie Lohr went to church and prayed for a good first night. On the way to the theater she slipped and broke her leg. 'No good deed ever goes unpunished' was Coward's comment." To cover himself, etymologist Rees says it has been ascribed to Oscar Wilde as well.

In the absence of help from Lexicographic Irregulars, who have failed miserably to respond to past pleas for specific data on this, that's the best I can do. George Greeves, where are you? Did you pick it up from Noël Coward? Anyone who has the answer can do a good deed for lexicography, and you know what you get for that.

Dear Bill,

A minor footnote to "No good deed," an adage that has fascinated me since I first heard it at the National Gallery. It was in daily circulation when I went to the Gallery in the winter of '69–'70 and was always and reverently attributed to Andrew Mellon. It seemed to go with his dour, Presbyterian face and also served the Gallery's mandarin staff. I also thought it might have reflected Mr. Mellon's reaction to his possible indictment by the new Roosevelt administration at about the time he was planning to create the Gallery. One day I asked Paul (P.M. His sister was A.M. in Gallery code) if he had heard the attribution. He replied that he had but then said, "Of course it's from Oscar Wilde."

Until your piece I had assumed that it was indeed Wilde. I seriously doubt John Walker or anyone else on the staff had ever heard of Joe Orton or his diary entry of 1967. More I deposeth not.

William Henry Adams
Shenandoah Junction,
West Virginia

Good Providers

Dr. Stephen Jones of Rockville, Maryland, calls me his *patient.* I like that word; it makes me feel secure. Dr. Richard Selzer, the surgeon and writer, once told a Mayo Medical School graduating class that the word *patient* comes from the Latin *pati,* "to suffer," adding: "Doctors have patients. This is, above all, what distinguishes us from lawyers, who have clients. . . . We have patients, and they suffer."

Clients suffer, too, at the hands of some lawyers, but the distinction is valid. In recent years, however, a dehumanizing note has crept into the medical language: Patients have become *health care consumers.* Victor Cohn, the former *Washington Post* health columnist, was among the first to deride the trend toward calling doctors *caregivers* and *healthcare* [one word] *producers;* the new terms lump the M.D.'s among less well-trained professionals.

The big word now is *provider,* which has taken care of *caregiver.*

Thanks to the info explosion, it's spreading. I used to be a writer. Now I'm a *content provider.* Don't laugh; it could happen to you.

You discussed the term provider *as applied to physicians. This brought to mind a discussion I had had with my boss in the late 1970s, when I worked for the Blue Cross and Blue Shield Associations. (The final* s *in* Associations *has been recently eliminated.)*

My boss related a conversation with a physician who had objected to seeing the term provider *on claims forms. He wanted insurance companies to call him a* physician. *My boss informed him that, because the "Blues" wanted to avoid an overabundance of forms, they had decided to use* provider *for all independently billing professionals. He added, "After all, Doctor, if we had only one form for 'physicians,' we would have to refer to chiropractors as physicians." This quickly ended the conversation.*

John Gregory
Jouy-Sur-Eure, France

The Gotcha! Gang

To test readers and to pull mail, I occasionally stud my political diatribes with mistakes in English. These studied solecisms not only make me seem human, but also provide the basis for the annual review in this nonpartisan space of the "Uofallpeople" file.

"*Et tu,* Safire?" writes Klaus Perls of New York, adding, "Then, English, die!" What moved my corrector to this Caesarean mock-horror was this rhetorical question I posed in telling the Secretary of State how to deal with North Korea: "Which works best, the promise of reward or the fear of punishment?"

Instantly spotting the misuse of the superlative in place of the comparative, Mr. Perls notes, "I thought that in a comparison of two, the word is better *better*." He is correct, of course, though his parody of the conclusion to Shakespearean Caesar's remark to the stabbing Brutus ("Then fall, Caesar!") calls for the parallel "Then die, English!"

In another case, to illustrate the need for the proper placement of modifiers, I wrote, "After talking to Hillary Clinton, Ms [Margaret] Williams locks the files in a closet in the third-floor family quarters of the White House, to which she had the only key."

Calvin Thompson of New York was induced to write, "Who is the *she*?" Perry Stewart of Yellow Springs, Ohio, added, "I don't remember that in diagramming class." By the rule of proximity, *she* refers to the nearer antecedent, Ms Williams. But it would have been clearer if *to which she had the only key* had followed the word *closet.*

Upon seeing my phrase "our mutual fascination with espionage," Alistair Cooke of New York wrote as if quoting a shocked Conservative leader: "You mean 'our common'—or 'our shared'—fascination with espionage. 'Our mutual fascination' means our fascination *with each other.* 'Our mutual fascination *with*' anything is nonsense, you dummy! And I thought you were the American language wallah!" Mr. Cooke, a member of the "On Language" Board of Octogenarian Mentors, probably took Charles Dickens to task for the title of his novel *Our Mutual Friend.*

When I directed the Keystone Kops investigating the death of the White House lawyer Vincent Foster to "search for a Foster safety deposit box,"

John Gebhardt of New York gotchaed: "The term is *safe deposit box.* There's no *safety* involved; it's just a means of keeping deposits *safe.*" (Over to you, Al D'Amato.)

Not all my "errors" are grammatical. A highly paid lecturer once turned down a request for a freebie with "I could not love thee, Dear, so much/Loved I not honoraria more." This grasping thought comes to mind in reviewing my words: "At the Syracuse University commencement exercises, Robert B. Menschel of Goldman, Sachs accepted his honorary Ph.D." To which William A. Moffett, director of the Huntington Library in San Marino, California, responded: "An *honorary* Ph.D.? An honorary doctorate of laws, perhaps, or doctorate in humane letters, or some such honorific—but Ph.D.'s get their degrees, as the man says, 'the old-fashioned way: they earn it!' "

In tut-tutting about the passing of "The Year of the Woman" in politics, I wrote, "One sign of women voters' political maturity is that the moment of high-heeled shoo-ins has past." Most readers were so enamored of the play on *high-heeled shoe* and *shoo-in* (taken from the fixed horse race in which the winner has been "shooed in" by corrupt jockeys) that they missed the "mistake."

Not so Norman Lindsey of Yardley, Pennsylvania: "Shouldn't *past* be *passed*?" A writer using the pseudonym of Ann/Ed Mirer of Highland Park, New Jersey, composed a poem: "Once *past* is *passed,* only hereafter remains / Notwithstanding, norwithsitting. / The moment *is* past, or the moment *has* passed? / Not to equivocate, but gently elucidate."

Elucidating this "mistake" requires a lucid explanation of the homophones *past* and *passed.* The shorter *past* may be a noun ("in the past"), a preposition ("drove past the house") or a modifier ("a past life"). When forming a verb, however, you need *passed,* the past participle of *pass.* The moment of high-heeled shoo-ins has *passed,* and any attempt to use "has past" should be passed up.

Sometimes a seeming error is a fishhook—a reaching-out for the accurate rendition of an anecdote that the author cannot otherwise find. To illustrate how the election of 1994 was not directed at all incumbents, I wrote: "On a summer's night many decades ago, at the triumphal Carnegie Hall debut of the violin prodigy Yehudi Menuhin, the violinist Mischa Elman said to the pianist Artur Rubinstein: 'Hot in here, isn't it?' To which Rubinstein replied, 'Not for pianists.' "

"Your anecdote is inaccurately populated," writes Erik Tarloff of Washington and Hollywood. "Although Mischa Elman was indeed present that hot summer night, his pianist-interlocutor was not Artur Rubinstein, but rather Leopold (Papa) Godowsky—a legendary wit, and the hero of innumerable musicians' stories—while the violinist making his American debut was Jascha Heifetz, a virtuoso whose uncanny technique was guaranteed to unnerve any fellow-fiddler." The literary critic Alfred Kazin adds: "I once asked Godowsky's son, 'Is the story true?' 'It certainly is,' he replied. 'I was in the box.' "

Some will say that these "errors" are not little devices of pedagogy, but are actual mistakes in English by me, of all people. That's the sort of pervasive, corrosive cynicism that President Clinton has roundly condemned.

A Heads Up on *Fulsome*

Senate investigations churn up testimony that reveals the language not as it is written—with much of the blood and flavor squeezed out—but as it is spoken by real people while squirming. The staff of the Senate Select Committee on Intelligence has given aficionados of colloquial lingo, as well as students of synonymy, a nice bunch of citations in its recent report on the involvement of our spooks in the Iraqgate affair.

The Deputy Director of Central Intelligence, William O. Studeman, went to his boss, Robert M. Gates, to—in Studeman's words—"give the Director a *heads up* that [Attorney General] Barr might be calling him."

Heads up!, as every hard hat knows, is an interjection—the warning cry of construction workers on high scaffolding to anyone who might be strolling by, about to be struck by a dropped hammer. It replaced a longer expression, immortalized in the sobriquet of Look-Out-Below Bernstein, a legendary New York piano mover of the Weissberger Moving and Storage Company.

In most up-to-date dictionaries, *heads up* is listed as an adjective, hyphenated, extending the old shouted warning to a meaning of "alert, resourceful," as in playing *heads-up baseball.*

But the Senate testimony shows it used as a noun, and when native speakers stop to think of it, that's the most frequent current usage. To give someone a *heads up* is to issue something less sinister than a *warning* or a *tip-off*—closer to an *alert* than to an *alarm.*

A memo that was of considerable embarrassment to the Department of Justice was a C.I.A. analysis saying that intelligence sources "confirmed" press reports of the involvement of Bank Lavoro's Rome headquarters in billions of dollars of loans to Iraq from the branch in Atlanta. Justice had been pretending it had no secret intelligence about whether "Rome knew," but here was a document that hinged on the verb *confirmed.*

"What I meant," the C.I.A. analyst explained in the document causing so much heavy sweating in Washington at the Ninth Street Immunity Bathhouse, "was these sources [the intelligence reports] were additional information that indicated that they [BNL-Rome] knew. . . . In retrospect, perhaps I should have said, this 'apparently confirms' or 'appears to confirm' or 'corroborates.' But we in the Intelligence Community regularly use the word *confirm* to mean . . . *corroborate.*"

If that is true, imprecision reigns at our central spookery. Another analyst explained that "*confirmed* only means 'lends credence to' and nothing more than that," to which Laurence Urgenson of Justice retorted that the C.I.A. had "evaded the problem by torturing the language."

Here is some synonymy to affix to the wall of the language-torture chamber of C.I.A.: *Confirm,* rooted in the Latin *firmus,* "strong," means "to sweep away doubt with the addition of some authoritative evidence." *Corroborate,* rooted in another Latin word for "strength," *robur,* has come to mean "to support a statement from some other source." We have other synonyms for affirming accuracy: *substantiate,* "to offer evidence to sustain a statement that needs support"; *authenticate,* "to attest to the truth by an expert," and *verify,* "to establish proof by comparison to an original or an established fact." All these words are in the ball park of attesting to the truth, but the greatest of these is *confirm.* If something has been *corroborated,* it has support, but if it has been *confirmed,* bank on it.

The Senate report itself makes a common error: "The attempt to draft a public statement also proved difficult . . . going through a number of progressively less *fulsome* drafts as the week wore on." The word the context suggests was intended here is *lengthy,* related to *abundant* or *full;* however, the meaning of *fulsome* means "excessive, unctuous, disgusting"; on second thought, perhaps that was what the writers intended.

Among the odd locutions preferred by quoted legal counsel was "That was the entirety of the conversation," meaning "That's all that was said," and one gem by Bruce Cooper, a C.I.A. lawyer, who found a way to sound authoritative while leaving open an escape hatch: "I'm sure I probably did. . . ."

For the last 50 years I have heard and used the expression "Heads up," not as a construction worker but riding to hounds in my kind of hard hat. All this time I (erroneously?) took it originally to be a foxhunting (rather than a "vixen"-chasing) term warning the hounds that a horse is approaching from behind them and that they had better take their noses off the scent of the trail and raise their heads to see what is going on and get out of the way.

Benkt Wennberg
Wyncote, Pennsylvania

Health Care Provider, Heal Thyself

"As a physician, I am somewhat distressed at being called a *health care provider,*" writes David A. Worth, M.D., P.A., of Union, New Jersey, "rather than a doctor, a physician or a professional." He suspects he knows why the new nomenclature is being adopted: "It is easy to regulate *providers* but more difficult to regulate *doctors,* as people have a mental picture of their own doctors' care. Let us not devalue our physicians by terming them *providers.* This is just one step away from limiting what they say and depriving them of their ability to make professional decisions."

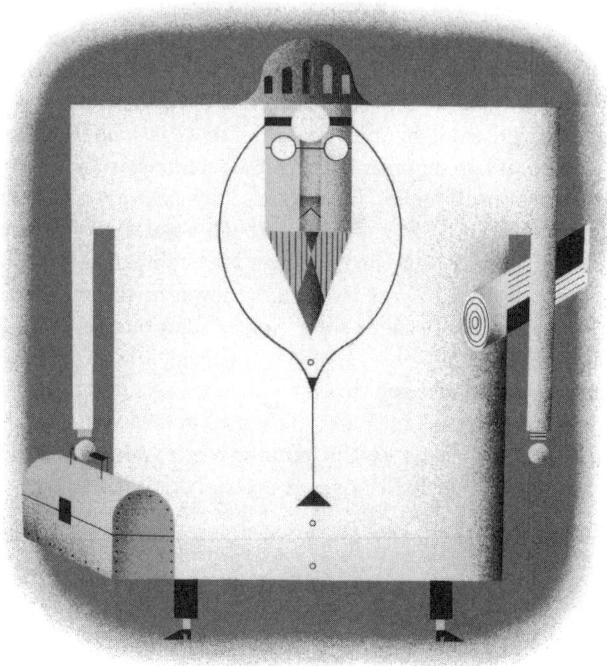

This language department, Olympian as always in its detachment from political controversy, is resolved to be irresolute on the issue of health care, formerly medical care. But on the linguistic issue of the term *health care provider,* hand me that scalpel and forceps.

The earliest citation I can find of the now-famous phrase is in a *New York Times* article of February 24, 1972, about a study to improve the city's much-criticized Medicaid program. "The project will bring about better medical service to the poor," said Jule M. Sugarman, Human Resources Administrator, adding that "improved operational methods and prompt payment will encourage more physicians and other *health-care providers* to participate in the program."

Note that Mr. Sugarman spoke first of physicians; his use of the word *other* suggested that *health-care providers* subsumed physicians, including them as a component element in the broader category.

Reached in Washington at the Center on Effective Services for Children, Mr. Sugarman scratches his head and says, "I don't recall coining *health-care provider.* Didn't the original legislation contain the term? Title 19 of the Social Security Act was the law that authorized Medicare and Medicaid; it was passed in the late 60's. I think that's where you'll find it."

Risking bureaucratic suffocation, an ailment reaching epidemic proportions uncovered by insurance, I waded through Title 19, passed by Congress in July 1965; *provide* is surely the operative word, appearing twenty-one times in the legislation, and the phrase *home health care services* (unhyphenated) appears once, but nary a single *health-care provider.* That coinage awaits further research, in which people who can call themselves "lexicographic aid facilitators" are invited to help; for the time being, it's Sugarman's baby.

The verb *provide,* originally linked to the noun phrase *health care* by the legislation, has become fused to that phrase because a synonym, *give,* has been taken up by the noun *care:* We now have *caregiver,* a term originating in hospices about 1980, its primary sense defined in the new *American Heritage Dictionary* (which favors a solid word) as "an individual, such as a physician, nurse or social worker, who assists in the identification, prevention or treatment of an illness or disability." The second sense of *caregiver*—a parent attending to the needs of dependents or a kid taking care of the old folks, which still happens in some areas—is, I think, taking over.

A *health care provider* encompasses (sighted *subsume;* sank same) *caregiver.* The *Los Angeles Times* reported that President Clinton "suggested that consumers as well as *health care providers* [the noun phrase is no longer hyphenated even when used as a modifier] must brace themselves for sacrifice—with the general public adopting healthier lifestyles, and [here come examples of health care providers] doctors, hospitals, drug makers and insurers accepting lower profits."

Thus, a doctor with all those years of pre-med, the costly postgraduate education, the dreary internship and the years of getting up in the middle of the night to make a house call—there must be a couple of doctors like that left—is miffed at being lumped together with insurance salesmen and bedpan bandits. No wonder they're fuming at the subsuming. A close student of the vernacular can offer only this paraphrase of a comforting Americanism: Take a couple of euphemisms and call me in the morning.

Which brings us to the hot phrase in the world of health care (which is usually illness care, but who wants to check into an illness center?): *managed competition.*

A "White House Interagency Health Care Task Force," a thundering herd headed by Hillary Rodham Clinton, is considering ways to set up and enforce a national medical policy. "The task force work group addressing global budgeting issues," burbles the Bureau of National Affairs daily report for not-too-busy executives, "suggests that additional incentives and enforcement tools are needed to control health spending beyond the savings that would result from a system of *managed competition.*" (*Work group,* by the way, is coined on the analogy of *play group;* a *working group,* formerly called a committee, is not to be confused with a *playing group.*)

The phrase began in business lingo. In 1975, James F. Atkins, president of Bell Helicopter, objected to the award of government contracts to firms on the basis of who most needed the business: "I don't want to see managed competitions like that." Reached in retirement in Fort Worth, Mr. Atkins says this is what he meant: "Evidently the government could manage competitions in a way to award contracts, perhaps unfairly, to somebody basically who had low business volume in order to help a company to survive."

The phrase in its present context was coined in the title of an article in *Health Care Financing Review*'s 1986 annual supplement: "Managed Competition in Health Care and the Unfinished Agenda," by Professor Alain C. Enthoven of the Stanford University Graduate School of Business. In that study, he cited a proposal, made during the Nixon Administration by Scott Fleming, called *structured competition.* Professor Enthoven started calling his own approach to creating sponsors who act as collective purchasing agents for large numbers of people *regulated competition* in 1977, but I presume he discovered that *regulated* had a nasty government sound and *structured* was unoriginal while *managed* had a businesslike air.

Is *managed competition* an oxymoron, a juxtaposition of opposites like *cruel kindness* provided by heartless caregivers or *thunderous silence* coming from famously anonymous task force work groups?

No. If the noun *competition* may be modified by jarring adjectives—*cutthroat* comes to mind—why not such restraining modifiers as *structured, regulated* or *managed*? You might think that conservatives would come up with a plan named *healthy competition,* with its built-in sell; surely that would be better than the jocular slogan supposedly behind their approach: "Don't Get Sick."

Today's tract comes to you from a work group on supervised food fighting in the task force of linguistic counsel providers.

Did David A. Worth, M.D., P.A., really write the lines you quoted in "Health Care Provider, Heal Thyself"? My suspicions are that David A. Worth, M.D., P.A., is a professional corporation, as is Howard M. Shapiro, M.D., P.C., and that David A. Worth, M.D., did the writing.

P.A.'s (for "Professional Association") and P.C.'s (for "Professional Corporation") were stirred into the lexicographic alphabet soup after state laws granted doctors, lawyers, and other professionals some benefits of incorporation while retaining practitioners' personal liability for malpractice.

The Main Street Medical Group, P.C., might include among its employees John Doe, M.D., F.A.C.P. (Fellow of the American College of Physicians, an organization of specialists in internal medicine) and Mary Roe, M.D., F.A.C.S. (Fellow of the American College of Surgeons), neither of whom should object to being identified by surname with six appended initials. Fellowship in one American College or another is a status symbol, and people who identify Joseph Bloe, M.D., an employee of Joseph Bloe, M.D., P.C., as Joseph Bloe, M.D., P.C., are probably assuming that the P.C. is a mark of distinction and trying to be nice.

I keep telling people that I am neither a professional corporation nor a personal computer nor politically correct, and reminding them that P.A. and P.C. are just an invisible Inc.

Howard M. Shapiro, M.D.
West Newton, Massachusetts

With respect to health care providers *and to* caregivers, *the problem is that* functions *have changed so rapidly that new terms have to be invented and used before anyone is comfortable with them. There was a day when physicians did the healing and the rest of the heavy work in medicine, and everybody else (including nurses and other helpers) did the (presumably) lesser job of caring. Today, lesser mortals than the hallowed physicians of old, including nurse-practitioners and an array of other professionals, are now trained to participate in healing. And since there are and will be a lot written about what they can and cannot do, and how they will or will not be paid, we need those new generic terms. I think if your correspondent, Dr. Worth, were satisfied with being called a health care professional, he might wage a successful campaign, but he will have to come to terms with the fact that physicians are no longer all alone on the top of the mountain, and that the generic terms reflect a real-world change, not just (dare I say* just*?) a usage change.*

Lisbeth B. Schorr
Washington, D.C.

The first use of health care provider *that I found was in a March 1976 decision of our board. In that decision there is a quote from an obsolete section of the Provider Reimbursement Manual, issued by the Medicare Bureau of the Social Security Administration (the organization responsible for Medicare at that time). Section 232 stated in part: "(On May 29, 1973, Medicare regulations were revised to eliminate . . . from the Medicare principles of reimbursement to* health care providers. . . ." *(My emphasis.) Thus the first usage of this term appears to be sometime earlier than 1976, perhaps even in the late 1960's, coined by a federal bureaucrat in an instruction on Medicare reimbursement.*

Lester Cohen
Baltimore, Maryland

You ask, "Is managed competition *an oxymoron, a juxtaposition of opposites like* cruel kindness *provided by heartless caregivers or* thunderous silence *coming from famously anonymous task force work groups?" Although the two examples you provide partially redeem you, I cannot suffer such an inadequate definition of* oxymoron *in silence.*

An oxymoron is certainly not simply a "juxtaposition of opposites." According to Webster's Third New International Dictionary, *an oxymoron is "a combination for* epigrammatic effect *of contradictory or incongruous words" (italics mine). The authors of the* Oxford *dictionary, unconstrained by the salubrious discipline of the single volume, go on at considerably greater length, but to the same effect: "A rhetorical figure by which contradictory or incongruous terms are conjoined* so as to give point *to the statement or expression; an expression, in its superficial or literal meaning self-contradictory or absurd,* but involving a point*" (italics mine). The explicit part of your definition lacked these crucial italicized qualifications.*

I was at first willing to give you the benefit of the doubt. The phrase "like cruel kindness*" might be taken to be restrictive, after all, and thus part of your definition. However, you then go on to give a negative answer to your question merely on the grounds that* managed competition *is not a contradiction, without regard to its rhetorical merits. Under the circumstances,* contradiction *would have served your purposes better than* oxymoron.

Please, please, let us not vitiate this fine old word. Keep oxymorons ὀξυ—sharp—as well as μωρός—dull, stupid, or foolish. In other cases, one might argue that common usage determines meaning, but here, I think, stouthearted lexicographers must stand firm. After all, contradiction, *with its roots meaning* speaking against, *is a perfectly good term for* juxtaposition of opposites. *But were we to lose* oxymoron, *how would we concisely contract* a combination for epigrammatic effect of contradictory or incongruous words*?*

My feelings on this particular word are in part a reaction to questionable motives I attribute to its abusers (present company excepted, of course). Their purposes would be fulfilled by contradiction, *but of course they would then miss the opportunity to respond to questions along the lines of "What is an oxywhatchamacallit?" and to have the pleasure of exhibiting the sizes of their vocabularies. To those in the know, such practices can backfire. A few years ago, for example, one of our San Francisco papers placed the following message on billboards, with nary an italic or quotation mark in sight: "A television newswriter is an oxymoron." One presumes this was a dig at the literary quality of a rival medium. If so, it was an unfortunate attempt; not only does it contain a misuse of* oxymoron, *but a confusion of use with mention as well. They meant to say, "*Television newswriter *[the phrase, that is, not its referent] is a contradiction."*

Paul N. Hilfinger
Berkeley, California

As a sociologist who studies medicine and nutrition, I have seen the term "health care provider" rise in use as a political tool in the battle between professions for control of health care turf. Physicians were traditionally the dominant profession for providing medical care, and would prefer to continue to claim that they are exclusively the profession in charge of medicine and have ultimate authority. By generalizing the term from "physician" to "health care provider," it becomes more inclusive. Use of "health care provider" implies that nurses, psychologists, social workers, nutritionists, etc. have a claim to providing care. You would expect a physician to mount claims against the new term, but other health care professionals continue to use the broader wording to show they have a legitimate stake in the area.

Jeffery Sobal, Ph.D., M.P.H.
Associate Professor
Cornell University
Ithaca, New York

The *Horny* Dilemma

Toward the end of *Meet the Press,* where I occasionally come on to shoot the wounded, we were discussing Whitewatergate. David Broder of *The Washington Post* took issue with my suspicions of heavy financial scandal ahead. "If you told me that Bill Clinton was very horny or very ambitious," Mr. Broder opined over the NBC network, "I would have no trouble believing it. If you told me that he was money-hungry and was cutting corners for money, I'd say that doesn't sound like the Bill Clinton I know."

When the show ended, the Pulitzer Prize–winning reporter and columnist looked around and innocently asked, "Can you use a word like *horny* on television?" The only answer was yes, because he already had. But has *horny* crossed the line from slang to colloquialism, from mild vulgarity to acceptable informal usage?

First, to the roots. *Horn* can be traced to the Latin *cornu.* The proto-Germanic *horna* bloomed in Old English, in *Beowulf,* around the year 725. (This scholarly material is being larded in to reassure nervous editors.) The original meaning referred to the hard protuberances growing from the head of ungulate mammals or mythic creatures like the satyr, a bestial being combining a goat (undeservedly vilified as a lecherous beast) and a human.

The poet James Russell Lowell, extolling the virtues of hard work, wrote in 1843, "Blessed are the horny hands of toil!" Hardworking fishermen today prize as bait the North American *hornyhead chub.*

Now to the point. A horn is hard; it is shaft-shaped; since the fifteenth century, it has been used as a symbol for the male's erect sex organ. "No horn could be stiffer," John Cleland wrote in *Fanny Hill* in 1749; earlier, Shakespeare used the term *horn-mad* in *Much Ado About Nothing* and other plays to mean both "lecherous" and "cuckolded." The nose "horn" of the rhinoceros has long been believed to possess aphrodisiac qualities, which led to the endangerment of the species.

"*Hornie* is an 18th-century Scottish term for 'devil,' " reports Alan Richter, author of the 1993 *Dictionary of Sexual Slang,* "which itself is another old term for penis, dating back to Boccaccio. Robert Burns refers to *auld hornie,* meaning the devil, and *old horny* is also a 19th-century term for penis. But plain old *horny,* meaning 'sexually aroused,' only makes its debut at the end of the 19th century, originally applied exclusively to males." Henry Miller, in his 1949 *Sexus,* turned it into an equal-opportunity word with "Her thick, gurgling voice saying . . . [raunchy bit deleted] 'I'm horny.' "

That brings us to today: Do we use *horny* in everyday speech, along with its Scottish synonym *randy,* to mean "sexually aroused"? Yes; it's common usage, and it has lost much of its taboo.

Next question: Should we use the term in family newspapers or on television talk shows? In my opinion, no; common usage is not necessarily good usage, and *horny* has not lost all its taboo. My colleague Broder caught himself, and asked about it. What is natural in dramatic dialogue can be jarring in more formal discourse.

Instead of "if you told me he was horny," try "if you told me he played around a lot." (In formal newspaper writing, of course, you could not use *play around,* except in a quotation; you would have to use terms like *promiscuous* or the fuzzier, less judgmental *sexually active,* or if referring to a specific state, *sexually aroused.*)

Relatedly, the word *penis* appeared a few paragraphs back, and it did not bother you. That Standard English word has been thrust into everyday speech by the trials of John and Lorena Bobbitt.

"Her crime," the *New York Times* editorialist wrote, ". . . serves as permission to say a bald anatomical word in newscasts that Howard Stern only recently appropriated for talk radio." The writer didn't need to use the word, but *penis* was used in the paper twelve times in the opening weeks of the year, compared with no uses in the same period the previous year.

Once more unto the breach, dear friends: Because I cannot be sure that this piece separating horniness from godliness is going to make it through the shrieks, groans, hoo-boys and tut-tuts that are part of "the editing process," I might as well go all the way. Here comes more than you need to know about the part of the body that daring novelists used to refer to as "his *manhood.*"

The word *penis,* according to the *Barnhart Dictionary of Etymology,* is from the Latin *penis* for "tail" and is cognate with the Greek *peos* and Sanskrit *pasas,* from the Indo-European *pes-/pos-*.

Penis surfaced in 1992 in our living rooms in the Clarence Thomas hearings during Anita Hill's testimony, which also necessitated exhaustive etymological research into the slang synonym *dong* in this space. The word *penis* resurfaced in Michael Jackson's videotape statement defending himself from charges of child molestation, and became part of life's daily language in the avid coverage of Lorena Bobbitt's trial.

Don't blame the messenger; the clear, standard, direct way of describing what happened was "she cut off his penis"; only on second reference could it be "an act of sexual mutilation" or "her attempt to remove his manhood."

We have come a long way in a short time, thanks to television, in removing a sense of shame in using the right word. Time was, a few courageous parents would eschew all baby-talk terms and accurately identify the part to their children, only to blush furiously when their kids freely used the "clinical" word to other adults.

We've come a ways in journalism, too. In his book *My Times,* John Corry wrote about a *New York Times* article on the subject of sex: "It had been decided that my story could remain as it was except for one word. That was *penis. Vagina* was acceptable, but *penis* had to be replaced by 'male sex organ.' "

The times, they are a-changin'. July 13, 1993, will be remembered as the day the word *penis* appeared in thirty-point type in *The New York Times.*

Standard English has no dirty words. The word *penis*—severed or reattached, flaccid or erect—is as innocent, and as usable in polite company, as the hornyhead chub.

I thought you might be interested in a further history of "penis" on television. I was the NBC censor on Saturday Night Live, *a job most people believe doesn't even exist.*

On December 15, 1979, Al Franken and Tom Davis used the word in a comedy routine that drew all of 24 negative telephone calls. But on October 15, 1988, we telecast a sketch called "Nude Beach" in which the word was used about fifty times! In it, a bunch of nude guys, delicately covered by furniture, shrubbery, and even a guitar, gathered at a beachside bar and discussed their penises in a gossipy way, much as women might sit around yakking about hairdos. It was casual, conversational, and matter-of-fact. Thus the word was spoken in a non-sexual, harmless, clinical way—which was the point of the sketch.

We debated hotly within the Broadcast Standards Department, finally deciding to consider the material less than tasteful, perhaps, but not obscene. And certainly within the parameters of Saturday Night Live *acceptability at 11:30 P.M.*

Predictably, Reverend Donald Wildmon, the self-appointed guardian of America's morals, saw otherwise, as he generated a negative postcard campaign that eventually totaled over 46,000 pieces! Gosh, I wonder what he must be think-

ing as he watches the Bobbitt trial, the Thomas hearings, and the Buttafuoco/Amy Fisher confessions?

In any event, our friends at Saturday Night Live, *always proud to be on the cutting edge of progressive humor, were once again a step ahead of popular opinion. And, while we had some monumental disagreements, I've always been comfortable with having approved "Nude Beach."*

William G. Clotworthy
Westport, Connecticut

As a former resident of Florence and an ardent Italophile, I have long wondered about the obvious kinship between the English adjective "horny" and the Italian word cornuto.

While literally meaning "horned," or "wearing horns," cornuto *is a vulgarism that is commonly accompanied by a hand gesture of an upraised index and little finger. The understanding of the insult is that the (male) recipient has been cuckolded, i.e., his wife is playing around. The result of the situation, read as a great insult to the macho Mediterranean male, is the raising of "horns." One assumes that the "horn," or erect member, is a constant companion for the Italian male, who, when he is cuckolded, has no way to get rid of it.*

Thanks to you, and to Meet the Press, *for raising this issue.*

J. William Shank
San Francisco, California

Use of "horny" yields some delightful scenes in a delightful movie, Coal Miner's Daughter. *Doolittle Lynn tells his wife, Loretta, "Baloney makes you horny. Everybody knows that." (Quote perhaps inexact.) He refuses to tell her what "horny" means, and she then uses it during a radio interview, causing the station manager to respond with fear and fury.*

Judith S. Stix
St. Louis, Missouri

You implied that the use of the word "horny" is now correct. Perhaps so, but innocent creatures may be maligned. We live in an age of political sensitivity. Think of the vanishing owl. In the night an owl signals for a mate; hoo-hoo-hoing is what he's doing. It's his way of wooing. To call him horny is corny.

Marjorie Killeen
Berkeley, California

Hundred Days

On a visit to George Stephanopoulos, the Clinton communications director, I wondered idly when the date of the *hundred days* would be. Without missing a beat, he said, "April 30, 1993."

(Those of us who have confused his name with that of another prominent Greek-American in Washington, Arianna Stassinopoulos Huffington, have a pronunciation mnemonic for Stephanopoulos: "stuffin' envelopes.")

In a few days, we will be inundated with thumb-suckers assessing the "first hundred days of the Clinton Administration." For historical perspective, it should be noted here that the phrase did not begin in Franklin D. Roosevelt's time, though it was popularized at the time of the 1933 special session of Congress he called to combat the Depression.

Louis XVIII (that's the Eighteenth, as those of us who watched the Redskins trounced in the Super Bowl by the Raiders will never forget), noting the triumphant return to France of Napoleon from exile on the island of Elba, got out of Paris in a hurry. After the Napoleonic tide was turned back at Waterloo, the prefect of Paris, Louis de Chabrol de Volvic, told the returning King, "A hundred days, sire, have elapsed since the fatal moment when Your Majesty was forced to quit your capital in the midst of tears."

Mark your calendar: The subsequent assessment of the Clinton era will be made on October 17, 1995. That will be *a thousand days,* the title of a memoir by the historian Arthur Schlesinger Jr., based on John F. Kennedy's remark to Ted Sorensen during the preparation of the inaugural address: "I'm sick of reading how we're planning another 'hundred days' of miracles. Let's put in that this won't all be finished in a hundred days or a thousand." That was done, in a passage ending "But let us begin"; the thousand-days phrase gained poignance when it measured the approximate length of the Kennedy Administration.

It's hundred-days time. Let us begin, assignment editors, and let us get it over with.

The Hunt for *Near Abroad*

The most ominous phrase in diplomatese these days is *near abroad.* It means "people of Russian ethnic background who now live in states that broke away from the Soviet Union." If Russia and Ukraine go to war over Crimea, until 1954 a part of Russia and with a mostly Russian-speaking population, it will be over Russia's reach to bring back in its *near abroad.*

The earliest citation turned up by the Dialog retrieval system is this letter to the *Washington Times* of April 21, 1993: "Mr. Bodie criticized Russia's proclaimed interest in the '*near abroad.*' He said that Russia's belief that it must resurrect its presence in the near abroad is 'the opiate of the political classes' and does not serve the Russian democratization movement.' "

The earliest Nexis citation is not until November 30, 1993, in the English-language *Moscow News,* describing a competition of hairdressers "from different cities of Russia and the '*near abroad.*' "

The meaning is usually "Russian ethnics living in neighboring states, but near Russia's border and under a claimed Russian protection." In Britain, the *Oxford English Dictionary* editors tell me their earliest citation is from a British publication, the *Art Newspaper,* dated April 1993, and defines the phrase more by territory than population: "Russia's new borders with the so-called '*near abroad*' (the republics of the former U.S.S.R.) are becoming a reality." In October 1993, the *Boston Globe* also defined it by territory and hyphenated the phrase: "the new nations along the Russian periphery—a swath of territory that Russians call 'the near-abroad.' "

We're missing something big. I'm speculating, but usage must have begun soon after the breakup of the Soviet Union in August 1991, probably by the Russian press in quoting Russian officials.

Who coined *near abroad*—in Russian *blizhneye zarubezhye,* I'm informed by Celestine Bohlen, the *Times* Moscow bureau chief—and who first translated it into English?

The Near Abroad

Who are, or what is, the *near abroad*? Who coined the phrase in Russian, and who first translated it into this English phrase? What does it mean, and is it important?

The answer to the last is: You bet it's important, because the words deal with the new relationship between Russia and the other republics of the former Soviet Union. Tension on the border of Ukraine and Russia, for example—with Moscow claiming influence over ethnic Russian brethren within Ukraine—cannot be reported without the use of this big diplomatic term.

A fishhook in this space, citing a few not-so-early uses of *near abroad*—the best translation of the Russian *blizhneye zarubezhye*—drew some nibbles from sources more adept than me at the use of data bases.

The earliest use in Nexis, Fred Shapiro of New Haven writes, is an article in *The Russian Press Digest* of June 9, 1992, titled "*Near Abroad* Wants to Be Far"; by December 7 of that year, Strobe Talbott—then a *Time* magazine columnist, now Deputy Secretary of State—had picked up the troublesome phrase: "Many Russians have not yet been able to accept the idea that the 14 non-Russian republics of the U.S.S.R. are today independent foreign countries. Russian politicians have even coined a new phrase—the *near abroad*—to distinguish between the former republics and the rest of the world."

Meanwhile, Mary V. McGlynn of Brussels was searching News Retrieval, a Dow Jones product, and scorning that service's discouraging word that *near* was a linking word used in searching and not usable as a keyword. She found: "With regard to conflict situations in countries of the *near abroad,*" wrote Sovinfolink, *The Soviet Press Digest,* on August 20, 1992, summarizing in English a piece in *Nezavisimaya Gazeta,* "[Russian Foreign Minister Andrei] Kozyrev is critical about attempts to threaten neighbors."

An earlier Kozyrev use was found by Paul Brock, a consultant for Dialog, Knight-Ridder's data retrieval service: "Foreign Minister Kozyrev warns that every Russian gesture of 'heroic patriotism' will trigger Russophobia in Ukraine," Mark Frankland wrote in *The Observer* on April 26, 1992, "and the rest of what Moscow now calls 'the *near abroad,*' that is the old Soviet Union."

That's the printed-citation winner so far of that phrase in English. Other translators in early 1992 were reaching for the best way to handle the Russian idea. Roger Donway, managing editor of *Orbis* magazine in Philadelphia, culled the Foreign Broadcast Information Service for its translations of the Russian phrase. On January 15, 1992, Izvestiya referred to "the concept of 'abroad close at hand,'" putting the phrase in quotation marks. Tass, on April 9, 1992, used "nearby foreign lands"; three days later, the Moscow Russian Television Network spoke of what the broadcast information service reported as "countries not far abroad, as they call it." Later that month, Interfax, in English, wrote of "the emergence of a new geopolitical entity, which is often referred to as the Near Foreign Countries."

The seminal phrase, *blizhneye zarubezhye,* was obviously giving translators a hard time. *Blizhneye* is the neuter of *blizhniy,* an adjective meaning "near" (Near East is *Blizhniy Vostok*), but "*zarubezhye* is a noun with no English equivalent," writes Kenneth Katzner of Washington, author of the *English-Russian, Russian-English Dictionary,* based on American English. "It is built around *rubezh,* a word meaning 'border.' The prefix *za* means 'beyond.' "

Mr. Katzner thinks that the translation *near abroad,* with or without capitals, is an abomination because *abroad* is essentially an adverb that should not be preceded by a modifier, and that the translator is someone "we should string up by his heels," apparently an old authoritarian custom.

This position is countered by Christian Caryl of Berlin, who writes: "Both German and Russian routinely and naturally use *abroad* as a noun. When confronted with *near abroad* for the first time, I remember wondering how I'd translate it into English, where *abroad* is so strictly adjectival—the 'nearby foreign countries'? Imagine my delight when I began to see others blithely breaking the rules. Now *abroad* has entered English as a noun."

My Berlin correspondent says he noted in his diary on June 7, 1991, this explanation of the concept in Russian: " 'The term originally had an ironic nuance,' said the historian Ivan Ivanovich. 'People spoke of *nastoyashchyeye zarubezhye,* "the present-day abroad." But now the words have acquired a purely informational meaning, in order to distinguish the new states of the C.I.S. [Commonwealth of Independent States, a title now in the dustbin of history] from the "original" abroad.' "

To follow up the history of the phrase in Russian, without citations: "*Near abroad* was used extensively by Soviet dissidents in the 1970's and 80's," notes Terry Thompson of Ellicott City, Maryland. "Russians under Brezhnev used the expression in either ironic or wistful tones. The serious connotation of the phrase was that the Russian people had to sacrifice a higher standard of living to support their 'socialist comrades' everywhere."

William Bodie of Los Angeles first heard the expression in January 1992 from Paul Goble of the Carnegie Endowment as a term in use throughout political Moscow referring to the non-Russian republics of the recently defunct U.S.S.R. He sees the phrase as political rather than geographical or demographic.

"Rightly or wrongly," Mr. Bodie writes, "Russia's political classes have difficulty viewing the republics on its periphery as fully sovereign entities; use of the term *near abroad,* in addition to qualifying their independence, signifies to the 'far abroad' that Russia claims certain rights in the region that transcend traditional diplomatic conventions."

Many of the people in those adjacent countries, especially the non-Russians, reject this heavy-handed Russian version of the Monroe Doctrine that some Moscow officials call a "hen gathering up its chicks."

Mr. Bodie notes, "In Riga, Kiyiv and a dozen other capitals, the chicks consider Russian policy to be the Roosevelt Corollary as interpreted by Ivan the Terrible."

Thus, what we know so far about this most significant diplomatic coinage since the popularization of *détente* in the early 70's is that it made the jump into English in early 1992, and that *near abroad* means "the claim by Russia of political interest and influence in states adjacent to it that were once part of the Soviet Union." Some political lexicographers (namely, me) insist that it has a second sense of "ethnic Russians living as a minority, sometimes supposedly oppressed, outside the borders of Russia."

I've been an avid reader of your column ever since I came to this country from Russia almost 20 years ago. Never in my wildest dreams could I imagine that I would be writing to you with a correction! However, when you speak of "nastoyashcheye zarubezhye," *you (or the historian Ivan Ivanovich) translate it as "the present-day abroad" and insist it has an ironic nuance. The translation doesn't make any sense, and certainly does not sound ironic.*

The thing is that the word "nastoyashcheye" *has two meanings in Russian: one is, indeed, "the present day," and the other one, "real." People were talking of the "real abroad," i.e., countries that were always considered "abroad" (Britain, France, etc.) as opposed to the newly formed independent republics that used to be part of the U.S.S.R. In its second meaning, the phrase can be used ironically.*

Natalie Meerovich
Philadelphia, Pennsylvania

Impassioned Executive

Not just the Chief Executive gets corrected here; his sub-execs deserve their fair share. Lexicographic Irregulars, cruelly seeking to embarrass members of the new Administration, have been sending in citations of language lapses. I comment on them here not to show hostility to honeymooning government officials, but to provide a gathering place for members of the Gotcha! Gang when they are not after me.

At his confirmation hearings after designation as Secretary of Commerce, Ron Brown* skillfully slipped around conflict-of-interest questions but may have tripped up on the meaning of a modifier. He promised "*vehement* enforcement" of United States trade laws, especially regarding our anti-dumping statute that so troubles our European allies, some of whom like to dump.

The word usually wedded to *enforcement* is *vigorous*. Departure from cliché is to be commended, but is *vehement* what Mr. Brown meant? One sense of the word is "powerful," so he can find support in the dictionaries, but most of us take *vehement* to mean "fervent, impassioned," even to the point of "red-faced, heated, angry."

The policing of political rhetoric in this space is *active, dynamic, energetic* and *spirited,* but not *vehement.*

For example, let us look with amused concern at the mixture of metaphor put forward by Jim Sasser, Senator from Tennessee, about William Jefferson Clinton's command of domestic issues: "This guy knows his oats."

As noted by Louis Jay Herman, the late consigliere of the Gotcha! Gangsters, "Mr. Clinton may be *feeling* his *oats,* but he *knows* his *onions.*"

The mangling of metaphors may become a mark of membership in the Clinton Administration, reports Cy Liberman of Arden, Delaware. Samuel R. Berger, the Deputy National Security Adviser, emerged from the basement of the White House to appear on *This Week with David Brinkley* and answer a question with "We ought to put our shoulder to the grindstone on that one."

Well, they promised us change. The rest of us have our noses to the wheel.

*Secretary of Commerce Ron Brown died in an airplane crash in Bosnia on April 3, 1996.

The Imperious Imperative

"Get over whatever personal hang-ups you got," said Marion Barry, re-elected Mayor of Washington, after having been brought low four years before on a cocaine charge. To those who did not vote for him, he repeated, "Get over it."

This imperious imperative caused a small furor in politics' hometown. The satirist Mark Russell hailed *get over it* as "the city's new motto," adding cruelly about Mayor Barry that "his will be the most watched nose since Cyrano de Bergerac's."

Curiously, only a few months before, the media-harassed Supreme Court Justice Clarence Thomas was reported to have told a group of black officials in his chambers: "I'm going to be here for forty years. For those who don't like it, get over it."

A disk jockey on WMZQ, a country music station in the nation's capital, reported that a turkey rights group had suggested people eat tofu for Thanksgiving, and asked listeners for appropriate songs to respond. Among them were Travis Tritt's "Here's a Quarter, Call Someone Who Cares" (theme music for *How the Gingrinch Stole Christmas*); Pam Tillis's "Don't Tell Me What to Do," a favorite of libertarians, and—here we go—a tune recorded in the summer by the Eagles, reunited after fourteen years, titled "Get Over It."

And where did the rock group pick up the phrase? A bumper sticker after the 1992 presidential election read: BUSH LOST. GET OVER IT. Shortly after that, when the Buffalo Bills won their divisional championship and returned to the Super Bowl, their motto was "We're Back, America. Get Over It." (They lost again, and they still can't get over it in upstate New York.)

This phrase, first used in 1839 in *Thirty-Six Years of Seafaring Life,* has evidently achieved its voguish pinnacle today. Without the *it,* the infinitive phrase *to get over* has century-old slang meanings of "to improve one's status" and "to seduce." In its modern vogue sense, *get over it* has shouldered aside *let's move on,* last year's triumphant brushoff, and is in one sense challenging the ever-popular imperative exclamation *forget it!*

As an exhortation, *get over it* means "surmount your self-created obstacle; cure your self-induced debilitation." A related sense, more of a put-down, is "it's your problem, not mine" (sung to the tune of "Here's a Quarter, Call Someone Who Cares"). It overlaps *forget it* in the narrow sense of "don't bother me with that nonsense."

Sidney Harman, of Harman International Industries of New York and Washington, writes: "On the way into the city this morning, I asked the cabbie to wait for me a few minutes at my house. He said it would be difficult to park there because 'this city is crazy with politics—forget it!' What did he mean by *forget it*? Did he mean 'this city has gone to the dogs—nothing works'?"

The meaning of *forget it* in this context is "don't ask," its root meaning "I am facing a situation of such stress that it will be impossible to cope." ("Ask me how I feel." "How do you feel?" *"Don't ask."*)

Do not confuse this with the more common meaning of the same phrase, "it will never happen," usually pronounced without the *r* and as a single word. (Asked if the Palestinians would make Jerusalem the capital of their state, Israel's Prime Minister, Yitzhak Rabin,* replied for the record, "Fuggeddit.")

Even as command economics is waning, command linguistics is waxing. Grouchoism: "There's a man outside waxing wroth." "Let Roth wax him for a while." The late Leo Rosten told me that this old gag may have come from the playwright George S. Kaufman, who wrote *The Cocoanuts* for the Marx Brothers in the 1920's. Mr. Rosten's book *Carnival of Wits* draws a fine line between a *wisecrack* (wordplay for a specific situation) and a *witticism* (true wit that's universal); he once received a backhanded compliment from Groucho: "From the moment I picked up your new book, I was convulsed with laughter. Someday I intend to read it."

"Lighten up!" say the kidders to the gloomers, which is what I am trying to do to this scholarly analysis with classic old gags. DO IT NOW was the sign over the rolltop desk of George Merriam, a founder of Merriam-Webster. *Just do it* is the Nike slogan, and *Just say no* was the imperative promoted by Nancy Reagan.

In Contradistinction to Jejune

"I'm glad you asked that question," President Clinton said at a news conference, "in *contradistinction* to the one you asked right afterward."

What's the difference between *distinction* and *contradistinction*? The Latin *distinguere* means "to make distinguishable to the eye as something discrete, separate." A *distinction* is a separating; a *contradistinction* is a sharper separation, using *contra,* "against," as an emphasizer. However, a native speaker does not say "in distinction to"; that thought would be expressed as "as distinguished from."

"*Contradistinction* is a convenient and emphatic way," Jacques Barzun says, "of pointing out the difference one has in mind when using words that are close in meaning or commonly confused: 'I mean knowledge in contradistinction to information.' *Distinction* by itself does not permit the use of *to* and, requiring *between* instead, it seems to call for an explanation of what the difference actually is: 'I have in mind the distinction between knowledge and information.' All right, tell us what it is. The other construction, using *contradistinction,* needs no accounting on the speaker's part."

Contradistinction is *distinction* by means of contrast. President Clinton used

*Prime Minister Yitzhak Rabin of Israel was assassinated on November 4, 1995.

the word correctly and, by using a forty-dollar word (where's that from?), elevated the public discourse. However, politicians seeking the common touch might prefer *in contrast to* or *which is much different from,* and critics of the foreign policy of past Administrations should steer clear of *contra* constructions.

While I had Professor Barzun's attention (as a member of the "On Language" Board of Octogenarian Mentors, he feels an obligation to respond), I asked about the word *nubile:* Why does this word for "marriageable" apply only to females? The sex is deep-rooted: The Latin *nubere* means "to take as a husband," not to take as a wife, and Professor Barzun traces the etymology a step further.

"The historical reason *nubile* applies only to girls," he says, "is that only they wore a veil at the marriage ceremony: *Nubes* equals *cloud.* The practical, linguistic reason is that the connotation has always been 'capable of bearing a child.' The word marks the point, at any age, where physical development is perceived as adequate to that purpose. It follows that *nubile boys* sounds facetious; nubility carries an essentially passive aura."

While he had my attention, the great usagist took issue with a political comment in my Mr. Hyde role about the President's *jejune jitters.* "The meaning 'youthful, childish' for *jejune,*" Barzun noted, "has got into the dictionaries only as a concession to the misusers."

The original meaning of *jejune*—"empty of food, meager"—led to its modern sense of "dull, insipid." Probably because the word sounded like *juvenile,* it picked up a meaning of "puerile, childish," which is the way it is most commonly used today.

Should we stand with the prescriptivists, as Barzun suggests, and hold fast to the "proper" meaning? Or do we go along with the language slobs, adopting as "correct" a mistake merely because it is so frequently made?

At a certain point, what people mean when they use a word becomes its meaning. We should resist its adoption, pointing out the error, for years; mockery helps; if the meaning persists, though, it is senseless to ignore the new sense. I say *jejune* means *puerile* now. And, besides, it goes with *jitters.*

In the Deep Heart's Core

"We have to first create a language," said Hillary R. Clinton to Michael Kelly of *The New York Times* in one of those eye-popping, seminal magaziners, "that would better communicate what we are trying to say, and the policies would flow from that language."

Language first, policy second; there's a woman who has her priorities straight. Language mavens across the land are prepared to take a crash course in

Hillaryese, centered on what the writer Michael Lerner has named "the politics of meaning."

The key noun, as I interpret it, is *core.* "The problem with the language," wrote Mr. Kelly, troubled by the gushy jargon, "goes right to the *core* of the question of what it all means." He asked, "Is there one unifying idea that is at the heart of the politics of meaning?"

"I don't think there is one *core thing,*" replied the First Lady, urging that the politics of meaning be thought through on "a variety of planes."

I have since been flying US Air, Delta and United, thinking about *core values, core ideas* and the whole *core thing.*

David Wilhelm, Chairman of the Democratic National Committee, used the magic word on *Meet the Press* to define Bill Clinton's plan as including "the *core idea* that we need to improve the economic chances of hardworking, middle-income families."

Senator Edward M. Kennedy showed how he could get with the program: "I think that all of us understand that one of the fundamental *core values* of our society is voluntary service."

Secretary of Education Richard Riley was confronted by the Hillaryese vocabulary as well, when he hosted a satellite town meeting. (A meeting in a satellite town, or suburb? No; a town meeting via satellite.) During the program, an educator said, "The *core idea* is that the workplace becomes a learning environment for young people."

The *core thing,* as against the *vision thing* from a previous Administration, is directed inward. "Cohorts are generations of people with the same birth years and core values," wrote Natalie Perkins in *Advertising Age.* Philip Gailey, a columnist for the *St. Petersburg Times* (must be Florida; the paper in Russia is the *Sankt-Peterburgskiye Vedomosti*) found "continuing signs that [Clinton] is what his critics have long said he was: a politician with squishy *core values.*"

To a previous generation, *core*—from the very middle of Middle English—was the acronym for the Congress of Racial Equality. To tomorrow's generation, a *core dump* is a copy of the data stored in the *core memory* of a computer, usually transferred to an external disk. (I'd better hit the "save" button before all this slips into cloud-cuckoo-land.)

In a sense, the current generation of boomers is participating in a cohortwide core dump, downloading the word *core* as an attributive noun on all our heads. That may fall short of the meaning of life, but it gives us a leg up on the meaning of the politics of meaning.

An aging General Douglas MacArthur, bidding farewell to the corps of cadets at his beloved West Point, presaged this plunge into the politics of meaning with his immortal closing line: "Today marks my final roll call with you. But I want you to know that when I cross the river, my last conscious thoughts will be of the core, and the core, and the core." (That's how it sounded, anyway.)

Grand Allusions

This is the only place in the whole global media where subtle, sensitive souls can find explanations of poetic allusions in current hardball political discourse.

Members of the Poetic Allusion Watch (PAW), however, have endured a dismaying year. Politicians using poetry are stooping to identify their allusions as they make them, taking out the fun and insulting the electorate.

Representative Henry Hyde, Republican of Illinois, the thinking man's right-winger, was taking a pop at the special prosecutor in the Iran-contra case, whose prosecutions were blocked by President Bush's eleventh-hour pardons.

"Lawrence Walsh's term has now gone on for more than six years and nearly forty million taxpayer dollars have been spent," said the white-maned solon. "Like Tennyson's brook, it runs on and on and on."

This was no allusion; it was a direct citation of "The Brook's Song," by Alfred, Lord Tennyson, a verse of which goes:

I chatter, chatter, as I flow
To join the brimming river,
For men may come and men may go
But I go on for ever.

No fun in that; too cut and dried. However, above a *New York Times* editorial hailing President Clinton's speech commemorating Earth Day (and a few of us hawks are touting Mars Day), there appeared this headline: "A Greener, Cleaner President."

"Do you still solicit contributions to PAW?" asked Donald Marks of New York. "I enclose an example, perhaps by a 'group journalist' with a yearning to send a message."

The allusion, he grudgingly told me, was to Rudyard Kipling's "Mandalay," a poem by the writer beloved by Tories for his stiff-upper-lip, white-man's-burden support of the British Empah: "I've a neater, sweeter maiden in a cleaner, greener land."

I called the editorial department of *The Times,* which is indeed peopled by groupies—journalists who preserve their anonymity to speak for the institution as a whole—and reached Robert Semple, who was hanging around late that day.

"Allusion to Kipling?" he responded. "Us? This is *The New York Times*. We do Yeats." Without revealing the author of the headline or the editorial, he flatly denied any allusion at all. The writer, whoever it may have been—and Semple is big on the environment—merely liked the rhyme of *greener* and *cleaner*. No, he didn't get Kipling backward, inverting the word order—that was just the way the pair of words tumbled out. Great poetic minds don't think exactly alike.

What a pity. Ever since being disappointed at the paucity of PAW, I'm a fleeter, beater writer with a leaner, meaner mind. We'll come back to this study when subtlety can again be heard in the deep heart's core.

Yes, of course; some of us old-timers (over 50) remember "deep heart's core" from Yeats's "Lake Isle of Innisfree."

It's the kind of thing we read in high school (and his own reading of the poem is memorable). Thanks to The Times *for reminding us of all the good things we have in some way retained.*

Robert Fitzgerald
State College, Pennsylvania

In the Mist, In the Dust

In his debate with Vice President Al Gore on Nafta, Ross Perot lashed out in this manner: "See, again, he throws up propaganda. He throws guerrilla dust. It makes no sense."

That's how the spoken words were transcribed by the Federal News Service, a private firm that supplies texts to news organizations. (It assures us it "is not affiliated with the Federal Government." So why does it pick a confusing name?)

A *guerrilla,* from the diminutive of *guerra,* which is Spanish for "war" and comes from Germanic roots, is a member of an irregular military force. (A *terrorist* calls himself a *guerrilla;* a *guerrilla* calls himself a *freedom fighter.*) Although the word is often used as an attributive noun—modifying *tactics* and *warfare*—I had never heard it hit the *dust.*

Plugging a book on Conan O'Brien's late-night talk show, I wondered aloud about Mr. Perot's figure of speech; sure enough, an insomniac named Randall Ravitz of Livingston, New Jersey, supplied this zoological data: "When a gorilla (not guerrilla) feels threatened and is forced to assume a defensive posture, it will throw up dust or dirt in order to distract or blind its opponent."

Thus, *gorilla dust* is what we used to call a *smokescreen* that has been inhaled with a *giant sucking sound.*

Inaugural Nitpicks

Working under the deadline pressure experienced only by drama critics on opening nights, this former presidential speechwriter raced back from the inaugural oath-taking at the Capitol to review what Democrats hope will be "Clinton's First inaugural address."

Because I did not have a seat on the aisle, I was delayed by the exiting crowd. (The Rev. Jesse Jackson, also eager to get out, inveigled a medical worker to push a stretcher through the mob, crying, "Medic coming through!" and followed in his wake. Mr. Jackson did not make a lot of friends with that maneuver, but certainly displayed his resourcefulness.)

Back at the office, pounding my processor at fever pitch, my literary voice like thin ice breaking, I graded the new President on speechifying: nicely thematic ("renewal" or "renew" seven times), suitably metaphoric (seasonality, "forced spring") and blessedly short (fourteen minutes, J.F.K. length). That rated a B, but because his delivery was so good and the day was sunny and hope contagious, I gave it a B+ in my political essay. (I would give my own critique an A– because I used *anaphora* for "repeated endings" instead of "repeated beginnings"; the correct term is *epistrophe.*)

Now, as Woodrow Wilson put it, the time for sober second thought: nitpicking about grammar in the language column.

Subject-verb disagreement. In dumping on the Washington influentials so eager to embrace him, the new President hailed "those people whose toil and sweat sends us here and pays our way." *Toil and sweat,* like *blood, toil, tears and sweat,* its Churchillian predecessor, is a plural subject; it should take the plural verbs *send* and *pay.*

Later, in one of the politically pregnant phrases of his speech, he pledged to act not only when vital national interests were at stake but also when "the will and conscience of the international community is defied." In my white-heat review, I wished that he had said "will *or* conscience," because that would have meant he would not be constrained by the will of other nations, but would act on his own reading of their conscience. Now that I think about it, the *or* would have made it grammatically correct, too, because *will and conscience* is a plural phrase, requiring a plural verb: *are,* not *is.* Mr. Clinton should note on his cuff before the next exam: "Presidents who seek international agreements and agreements with Congress should first set an example with subject-verb agreement."

Pronoun-antecedent disagreement. "And now each in our own way," began a line of the peroration. Wrong. *Each* is singular and *our* is plural, and trying to force them together is like trying to make an agreement between nations whose interests are fundamentally antagonistic. I presume he was avoiding the sexist "each in his own way" and trying to save words by avoiding "each in his or her own way," but he would have been better off with "all of us in our own way."

It wasn't as if William Jefferson Clinton (fitting use of his formal name for the formal occasion—I winced at "I, Jimmy Carter") were rebelling against the rules of grammar. He is a confirmed whomnik, properly using that noxious pronoun in "The world for whom we hold our ideals, from whom . . . to whom. . . ." Generations of Miss Thistlebottoms yet unborn will point with pride to his *whom* behavior, beyond the call of usage. But they will shudder at:

Raised for *reared.* "Raised in unrivaled prosperity, we inherit. . . ." He inherits a mistake: You *raise* cattle; you *rear* children. This distinction is breaking down, but the purist vote is not to be ignored.

Each other for *one another.* "It is time to break the bad habit of expecting something for nothing from our Government or from each other." *Each other* is limited to two; *one another* is for more than two. He used both in the peroration and batted .500: "We need *each other* [incorrect] and we must care for *one another* [correct]." (H. W. Fowler doesn't consider this distinction important, but the style manual of *The New York Times* rightly holds the line.)

Double negative. Don't use *nor* when *or* is called for. "While America rebuilds at home, we will not shrink from the challenges *nor* fail." The negative *not* does not go with the negative *nor;* it creates a double negative, which is a no-no. Substitute *neither* for the *not* or change the *nor* to *or.*

I am all for reducing the size of the White House staff by 25 percent, as candidate Clinton promised, but maybe he should leave unfilled a couple of national security slots and hire one good copy editor.

In correcting Clinton on "each in our own way," didn't you mean to say "all of us in our own ways?"

Raymond K. Price, Jr.
New York, New York

Jericho, Trumpets, Walls, Etc.

That signing of a peace agreement on the White House lawn—will it be remembered as a historical moment?

No. *Historical* refers generally to history, as in "a historical fact"; the shorter *historic,* however, means "a moment or event of great significance, to be long remembered."

A second problem: What article belongs before *historic, a* or *an*?

H is a beginning consonant that sometimes vanishes completely, as the heirs of honest hours will tell you; in those cases, it takes an *an,* as do all words beginning with a vowel sound; Norma Loquendi, Ms Native Speaker, would never say or write "a honest man." At other times, *h*'s *huh* sound leads forthrightly, as in *hope,* the aspiring aspirant, calling for the *a* without the *n.* The question arises when the *h* is there, but weakly stressed, as in Yasir Arafat's words, "this historic event." Here's my answer: The noun *history,* with its emphasis on the first syllable, emphasizes the *h;* that takes a preceding vowel, *a,* "a history." The adjectives *historic* and *historical* put the emphasis on the second syllable, turning the initial *h* into a wimp, requiring a consonant to firm it up: *An historian* covering *an historic event.*

Now, in sober retrospect, we can examine the rhetoric used on the South Lawn of the White House at the handshake that shook the world.

Big day for Scripture. President Clinton, I am reliably informed, rose at 3 A.M., unable to sleep, and picked up a King James translation of the Bible to read the chapter on Joshua, who fought (*fit* is the dialect term, from the song "Joshua Fit the Battle of Jericho") a battle in which "the walls came tumblin' down." I was not alone in being so informed; every White House aide called his assigned press contact to pass that bit of color along. Maureen Dowd of *The New York Times* was the only one who had the detail about the President's tie; it had trumpets on it, surely more appropriate than going tieless in Gaza. The drafter of the President's tasteful, eloquent short speech was Jeremy Rosner, a hitherto unsung National Security Council speechwriter, with a contribution from Fouad Ajami, America's most perceptive writer on Islamic and Arab affairs.

Clinton's speech, the longest of the day, rose to the occasion. It was studded with half-concealed messages: "A peace of the brave is within our reach" alluded to the Syrian dictator Assad's reference this spring to a peace of the brave, and with Henry Kissinger sitting in the front row, Clinton used "within our reach" rather than "at hand." There was alliterative eloquence in comparing "the easy habits of hatred to the hard labors of reconciliation" and in the "defining dramas" of history. The phrase "a great yearning for the quiet miracle of a normal life" was beautiful, though followed by a banal "We know a difficult road lies ahead." He has a jarring habit of soaring and then dipping, as in the Lincolnesque "Let us resolve" followed by "will be a continuing process."

But above all, the cadences of the King James Version: The word *happen* was eschewed for "come to pass"; Clinton used "when the word went forth" (a biblical construction favored by Isaiah and also by President Kennedy in his inaugural), and also spoke of "the season of peace," an allusion to Ecclesiastes 3:1–8, which the Israeli Prime Minister, Yitzhak Rabin, quoted specifically: "To everything there is a season. . . . A time to love and a time to hate, a time of war and a time of peace."

The President also alluded to Isaiah 60:18 with "that the cry of violence shall no more be heard in your land, nor wrack nor ruin within your borders" (so that's where "wrack and ruin" comes from) and to Isaiah 57:19, quoting the Lord on peace, chosen to be read in Hebrew by Foreign Minister Shimon Peres.

Lest he be accused of tilting toward the Hebrew and Christian Scripture, the President's writers turned to the Saudi Ambassador, Prince Bandar bin Sultan, to find a suitable passage from the Koran: "If the enemy inclines toward peace, do thou also incline toward peace." Arafat's opening words were from the opening lines of the Koran: "In the name of God the most merciful, the compassionate." (The English translation "passionate" was an error.)

Clinton closed the ceremony with a direct reference to ancient Jericho, which will soon become a P.L.O. headquarters, using its walls as a metaphor: "The sound we heard today . . . was of trumpets toppling walls, the walls of anger and suspicion between Israeli and Palestinian, between Arab and Jew." A nice touch was added at the end with the key word spoken in three languages: "Shalom. Salaam. Peace."

Chairman Arafat taught the other speakers a lesson in oratorical delivery in an outdoor setting: His voice rang out, his pronunciation sounded lyrical to even those who understood no Arabic. On reading the text, however, a rhetorician searches in vain for a memorable phrase or original figure of speech; the speech seems produced by a cautious committee. Its high point was to repeat a phrase used by Rabin earlier, taking up the slogan of Israel's Peace Now movement, which was based on the 1969 John Lennon song title "Give Peace a Chance"; he strained for emphasis by adding the word *real:* "Our two peoples . . . want to give peace a real chance."

Rabin's speech not only stole the show but also advanced the "process." From its anguished opening—"it's not so easy"—the Israeli Prime Minister drove across the impression of a man overcoming his most grievous doubts. The speaker's purpose was to identify with and reassure the Israeli doubters in the reliability of the P.L.O. rather than to further satisfy the triumphant believers. The reluctant handshake, a picture carefully planned, reinforced this message of determined hope over grim experience.

The speech was drafted by Rabin's longtime press spokesman, Eitan Haber, and hewed to the style of the plain soldier. Former General Rabin's central message of the imperative of war's exhaustion was set up with "We who have fought against you, the Palestinians—we say to you today, in a loud and a clear voice" and encapsulated by the words that made headlines, sound bites and perhaps history: "Enough of blood and tears! Enough!"

Most of his vast television audience, and many on the White House lawn, did not grasp the significance of his choice of Hebrew prayers, which he introduced as "the prayer recited by Jews daily" and later translated as "May He who brings peace to His universe bring peace to us and to all Israel." Most observant Jews recognized it instantly as also the conclusion of the Kaddish, the prayer of mourning, words spoken at graveside and repeated regularly by the bereaved in remembrance of the dead. But that prayer itself makes no mention of death; instead, it affirms faith even in the midst of death. As such, the Kaddish was a powerfully fitting choice for the speaker's pained affirmation of peace in the midst of bloodshed—for never forgetting the sacrifice of lives in an effort to bury the past.

The first man to translate the Bible into English from the original Hebrew and Greek was William Tyndale. He Englished part of the Old Testament and all of the New Testament. His translation from the Hebrew was published in 1530, and the final edition of his New Testament appeared in 1535.

He was also the first Bible translator to use "it came to pass." But he did it only seven times in Genesis, whereas the men of the King James Version employed it 63 times to translate the Hebrew "hayah," *which occurs 101 times in Genesis.*

Another KJV phrase which I especially like is from Luke's Christmas Gospel. It speaks of Mary "being great with child." That was taken from the Bishops' Bible of 1602.

Father Edmond Bliven
Church of St. Michael the Archangel
Portland, Oregon

In my estimation you made an horrendous mistake.

I've made it an habit to read your articles and follow your gospel, but not in this instance. I would consider it a honor if you would reconsider so that I will not be an hysterical person.

If an "h" is pronounced, "a" is sufficient; if "h" is silent, "an" is appropriate. I do not have A holier than you attitude.

Beverly E. Wender
Riverdale, New York

Of course, I respect your right to disagree with the first item in the New York Times Manual of Style, *but I, the puny David, must rise to its defense against you, the mighty maven, when it comes to words beginning with* h *where the emphasis is on the second syllable. The manual says nothing about the wimpitude of the* h, *and who is to decide whether any given* h *is wimpish or not? I pronounce the* h *in "historical" with as much force as in "hat," as no doubt do millions of others. If you are going to put an* an *before every* h *word that stresses the second syllable, should we say*

an horrific explosion?
an horrendous crime?
an holistic theory?
an hallucinatory vision?
an Hamitic language?
an harangue?
an harmonious group?
an Helvetian native?
an herbarium?
an hendiadys?

an harmonica?
an herbivorous animal?
an herculean task?

It will be an heroic achievement if I can persuade an Hibernian friend to cook you an humongous meal on an hibachi, as an humane deed, if you ever come to Tucson.

Leonard Rosenthal
Tucson, Arizona

Maybe it was a subliminal slip of the pen (or word processor, as the case may be) or maybe it was an intentional attempt to see if any of your readers are paying attention, but your reference to being "tieless in Gaza" alludes to John Milton's "Samson Agonistes," who is "eyeless in Gaza, at the mill, among slaves."

My question is this: Does a pun disqualify an allusion from meeting the criteria of a true literary allusion? There's no question about this sort of wisecrack being an allusion; but what kind? For lack of a more specific term, I suggest calling figures of speech like this one allusive puns. *Can you improve on that, or is there already a term for this sort of construction?*

Dwayne Viergutz
Heidelberg, Germany

Kakistocracy

In a recent polemic in another space, I zapped Russia's "rump kakistocracy." Readers caught the allusion to the *rump Parliament,* the remainder left in England's Parliament after gutting by Oliver Cromwell, but some queried *kakistocracy,* defined in the *American Heritage Third* but not yet picked up by other leading dictionaries.

The Greek-rooted word was used in adjectival form more than three centuries ago and has been cooking along steadily ever since, filling a need that has not diminished. It means "government by the worst people."

Keep Your Eye upon the Bagel

"As you ramble on through life, brother," goes the profound poem in the Mayflower coffee shops, "whatever be your goal, keep your eye upon the doughnut, and not upon the hole."

Sage advice, lightly sugared; however, it now appears that doughnuts may be what worried marketers call "a mature product." And the notion of dunking a doughnut into a cup of coffee is so mature as to be decrepit.

What is the essence of a *doughnut,* sometimes spelled *donut*? Its circularity, you may say, or similarity to a ring; your geometry teacher would say a doughnut is *toroidal,* and if pressed for an explanation, would describe the surface generated by a nonintersecting line and closed curve rotating about it in the same plane as *doughnut-shaped.*

It's made of dough, but why is it called a dough*nut*? Nuts don't come with holes in the middle, like lifesavers. (Life Savers, the brand name for a doughnut-shaped mint, took the name of the circular device designed to keep swimmers afloat, thereby saving their lives; when the product was offered to airline passengers by flight attendants, then called stewardesses, some nervous passengers panicked, thinking that the plane was ditching in the ocean; for that reason, the flight attendant now offers "mints.")

Where was I? Yes: Where is the toroidal quality in a nut? (Only a few moments ago, you would not have understood that question.) The answer is that a nut has no such quality; as you ramble on through life, you will never come across a nut with a hole in the middle.

The earliest reference to a *doughnut* was Washington Irving's 1809 description of "an enormous dish of balls of sweetened dough, fried in hog's fat, and called doughnuts, or olykoeks." In 1851, Herman Melville was evenhanded in *Moby-Dick* in referring to "old Amsterdam housewives' doughnuts or oly-cooks"; in the nomenclature competition, though, the Dutch "oilcake" lost out to the American "dough-nut," because the little brownish bomb of chloresterol was originally shaped like a large nut—spherical, but without a hole in the middle. In the early nineteenth century, the Pennsylvania Dutch (from Germany, *Deutschland,* not from Holland) got fed up with the soggy centers in their *fastnacht* cakes (a Shrove Tuesday treat), and created the hole in the doughnut.

What makes this background necessary to news junkies (consumers of junk food for thought) is the item in *USA Today* that consumption of doughnuts, sweet rolls and Danish pastry has increased only slightly in the past decade: from eleven per person in two weeks in 1984 to twelve per person in two weeks last year. According to my projections based on personal sweet-roll and Danish wolf-downs, that amounts to about one doughnut per person every three days.

Meanwhile, Nanci Hellmich writes in that Gannett publication, "Bagels are the fastest-growing food on the menu. People ate an average of 7 bagels per person [in a two-week period] in 1993, up from 2.6 in 1984."

What does that tell us about toroidal food consumption today? That's one bagel every other day, compared to one doughnut every third day. Bagels have already outstripped doughnuts, and are pulling away in popularity with each passing day.

Linguistically, this means that Merriam-Webster must soon stop defining *bagel* as "a hard glazed doughnut-shaped roll" and start defining a *doughnut* as "a bagel-shaped cake fried in fat."

The bagel, according to the Yiddishist Leo Rosten, was first cited in the community regulations of Cracow, Poland, in 1610; the toroidal roll was said to be a gift to women in childbirth. (That strikes me as apocryphal; next we'll hear that the Civil War expression about bearing pain, *to bite the bullet,* was rooted in *to bite the bagel.* Not so.)

The word for the medieval jawbreaker was imported into English from the Yiddish *beygl,* which in 1919 was spelled *beigel* and in 1932 was shortened to *bagel.* According to the *Barnhart Dictionary of Etymology,* it is rooted in the Old High German *boug,* related to *biogan* "to bend," from the Proto-Germanic *biuzanan* and the Indo-European *bheugh-,* the pronunciation of which is a melancholy exhalation.

If the leavened dough has not been dipped or poached in nearly boiling water for at least a long moment before baking, the toroidal product cannot be defined as a *bagel,* but is more properly considered an uncrumble-able *doughnut.* (Some will wonder why I hyphenated *uncrumble-able;* that's to make easily pronounceable a word that may never have been used before. *Uncrumbleable* looks funny because, unlike *unpronounceable,* it is unfamiliar. People who are unwilling to try new words are the type who refrain from dunking doughnuts.) A threat exists that cold warriors used to call "convergence"; will doughnuts become more chewy while bagels become more crumbly, until there is no clear differentiation between them? Perish forbid.

Dunk, a word even more closely associated with doughnuts than *glazed,* is from the Pennsylvania Dutch *dunke,* "to dip, to immerse in liquid," from an earlier German root. The famous Dunkard Church (known as Dunker Church in many histories), a Maryland landmark in the Battle of Antietam, was the house of worship of German-American Baptists who practiced total immersion in baptism. The dismay of doughnut dunkers who lost control of their pastry during the process of dunking led to the term *sinkers.*

Dunking is proper for doughnuts; it is barbaric for bagels.

I bagel your pardon, but I doughnut know what to make of the statement you attribute to the Barnhart Dictionary of Etymology *that Old High German* biogan *"to bend" is derived from Proto-Germanic* biuzanan. *(In fact, I can bialy believe my eyes.) The Indo-European aspirated consonants* bh *and* gh, *as in the root* bheugh-, *lose their aspiration in Germanic and become simply* b *and* g. *Thus, the correct form in this case is* biuganan. *Perhaps the* z *is just a typo. Well, that about lox it up. Please forgive my tart comment.*

Louis Jay Herman
New York, New York

Since a considerable number of the Pennsylvania Dutch (Deutsch) came from Switzerland, as well as Rhineland Germany, the term "Dutch" refers not to their country of origin, but to the language *spoken. Hence, they are not the Pennsylvania Germans, but the German*-speaking *people of Pennsylvania. If I read them correctly, the Swiss no more appreciate being referred to as Germans than do the Belgians appreciate being classified as French.*

Carl Bowman
New York, New York

The approximately toroidal (albeit inedible) thing that goes on the end of a bolt is also called a nut. According to the O.E.D., *the word for it had been around for 200 years by 1809. Moreover I would venture that the early bolts came in sizes mostly larger than* $\frac{1}{8}$*", and may possibly have been made of wood; thus, the early doughnuts may have resembled "nuts" in size as well as shape, and perhaps even in texture.*

James H. Lee
Fairfield, Connecticut

"Perish forbid*"?!? Heaven the thought, sir!*

Frederic C. Marston
Whitefish Bay, Wisconsin

I can't tell you how much I enjoyed "as you ramble on through life, brother, whatever be your goal, keep your eye upon the doughnut and not upon the hole." I'm reminded of so many things, practically a whole lifetime growing up in the shadow of the doughnut.

Remembering my father who started "Mayflower Coffee Shops" and opening up in the upscale Savoy Plaza and being told the decor had to adhere to its new-

found elegance. There sat the coffee mugs with their familiar motto on a marble counter. I learned and laughed about the researched history about the doughnut and am happy to be so informed. I've felt bitter and angry about the bagel moving in on the doughnut. In a way the idea of the bagel is on a different plateau than its rival—it being a more proletarian upstart. The doughnut is a sweet reward with coffee. And in Pop's day it was far superior to what it is today. We eschew anything deep fried today, but I remember when we had two shops on 45th Street during the war watching people salivate as they bet on the moving trays how many doughnuts would fall into the hot grease. The aroma I remember hearing was useful in attracting customers.

Pop was a back-slapping, hand-shaking friendly guy whose interest in his "fellow man" contributed to his success.

I'm grateful to you for nudging these palatable fond memories, and thanks to you, others will be reminded of how delicious a doughnut can be.

Dorothy Beskind
New York, New York

Incorrections

Beware of *incorrections,* a word coined by my chief language associate, Jeffrey McQuain, to denote those false settings-straight by the inexpert or too-expert.

When I referred to *one on one* as "a basketball defense," the incorrections dribbled in. Larry Lesser of Washington pointed out that what I meant was *man to man:* "*One on one* is a variant basketball game for two people." Larry Craig of Huntsville, Alabama, agreed that *one on one* is "the title of a two-person basketball game in which one player plays against another."

That's one meaning, but in current usage, *one on one* also refers to defensive maneuvering by a basketball team, perhaps developed from *man to man* and influenced by the general replacement of *man* by *person* ("one person, one vote"; "person of the week," etc.). *The Language of Sport* by Tim Considine lists the two-player game as a secondary meaning, with the primary sense "a situation in which a player offensively or defensively . . . is confronted by a single opponent" and an extended meaning of letting one person interact with another unbothered by interlopers. The term also appears in football. An undated citation in *Merriam-Webster's Sports Dictionary* quotes O. J. Simpson, in his playing days: "If we at least clear enough of their guys out to leave me *one on one* with the last tackler, that's cool, because *one on one* is my game."

Another incorrection: "The world of transportation shaves words and phrases," I wrote, "like no other." Isabelle Loughlin of New York gently objects: "I'd correct *like* to *as.* Maybe I'm not with it and the rule has been changed." Nope: *Like* is correct as a preposition taking an object ("no other"). Had I added a verb ("like no other can" or "like no other has"), then *like* would be replaced by the conjunction *as.* The rule is as it was (not *like* it was); when a verb follows, the clause requires a conjunction *as,* not the preposition *like.*"

In the same way, the great horde known as the Gotcha! Gang descended on me for writing about "sources more adept than me."

"You used *me* where the nominative was called for," snorted Dr. and Mrs. Darwin Prockop of Philadelphia, in unison. Sorry, all you staunch nominatarians: I treat *than* as a preposition, calling for the objective *me.* You can zig with your old ways, but the world has zagged.

All this is a surly way of introducing a real double-damning correction, from Manfred Kroger, professor of food science at PennState (that's the snazzy way the Pennsylvania State University styles itself).

In a piece about the triumph of bagels over doughnuts in the toroidal-pastry war, I described the latter as "little brownish bombs of chloresterol." I must have been inhaling chloroform. "You doubly misspelled *cholesterol,*" Dr. Kroger writes. (And I have been pronouncing it wrong all my life, too; no longer will I snicker at those who say "nukular.") "Second, there is no cholesterol in doughnuts from frying in oil, though there is a little from the milk and eggs used. Only animal fats contain cholesterol, and doughnuts are no longer fried in the 'hog's fat' as they were when Washington Irving first mentioned them in 1809."

The PennState FoodSciProf suggests that I should have stressed the fat content of doughnuts (ten grams of fat vs. one or two grams in the average bagel). Bagels have gone one on one with doughnuts like no other pastry, but nobody could have been more mistaken about their cholesterol content than me.

I read with interest your item on "incorrections." Mr. McQuain is to be congratulated on this ingenious coinage.

There is already a word for a correction that is itself incorrect, however; I found it last year in O.E.D. *in the process of looking up something else, as one finds so many good things. The word is positively gorgeous:* paradiorthosis. *One doesn't often run across such delights. I committed it to memory on the spot, and I take great pleasure in sharing it with you now. It's an obscure word, to be sure, but then it addresses a situation that is also obscure, except possibly in the life of a language columnist. Besides, what a splendid way to disconcert your opponent!*

Thomas W. Parsons
Brooklyn, New York

I have played basketball at such bastions of linguistic correctness (LC), as the University of Chicago and Duke University. I grew up "shooting the rock" on the linguistically free-form streets of the South Side of Chicago. But in all of my varied experiences, I have never heard the term "one-on-one" used to describe a basketball defense. It is always and everywhere used to describe basketball offense. Chet Walker, star forward of the Philadelphia 76ers and Chicago Bulls in the 1960's and 1970's, was often called "the greatest one-on-one player in the game," a phrase universally understood to describe his offensive skills.

Charles K. Bobrinskoy
Chicago, Illinois

You wrote, "I treat than *as a preposition, calling for the objective* me."

I find this to be a rather cavalier statement. The choice of the pronoun I/me *following* than *can drastically affect the meaning of the sentence. Consider, for example, the following two sentences, which have quite different meanings:*

1) Alice likes Betty more than I.
2) Alice likes Betty more than me.

Geoffrey A. Kandall
Hamden, Connecticut

Kubla's Comeback

"In Xanadu," wrote the poet Coleridge, transcribing an interrupted dream, "did Kubla Khan/A stately pleasure dome decree."

Pleasure used to be a powerful word. Rooted in the Old French *plaisir,* it came into English and developed that sensual *zh* sound in the middle, similar to the pleasing *azure,* favorite of romantic poets. As a verb, it means "to give sexual satisfaction to"; as a noun, it is not so lively as *delight* or *gladness,* not so rapturous as *joy, bliss* or *ecstasy,* and not so amusing as *delectation. Pleasure* is an emotion that suffuses one who has been gratified or stroked; it's a good feeling, whether physical or intellectual.

It is also a semantically endangered species. Kathie Wellde, the Washington lecture agent who heads Speakers of the Times, sends in this disturbing heads up: "Instead of saying *Have a nice day,* people are ending their conversations with *My pleasure.*"

Come to think of it, I've noticed that, too, especially at high-class hotels: The phrase is used not merely to mean "I'd be glad to," or even "It's a thrill just to be asked," but with the added sense of "O.K. and so long." Example: "I'll be checking out at noon." "My pleasure."

Where is this coming from? European responses to thanks range from the French *je vous en prie,* using "I pray of you" to mean "you're welcome," to the German *bitteschön,* literally a combination of "please" and "beautiful," and the Spanish *de nada,* "for nothing." In Chinese, the Mandarin dialect response is *bu keqi* (pronounced "boo KUH-chee"), and is used for "Don't mention it." But the impetus in our vocabulary has to come from closer to home.

Ellie Peters at the Ritz-Carlton hotel in New York informs me that Horst Schulze, president of the chain of twenty-eight hotels, distributed a credo as part of the employee orientation that includes this as Point 12: "Maintain positive eye contact. Use the proper vocabulary with our guests. Use words like . . . 'I'll be happy to' and '*My pleasure.*' "

I don't hear too many *I'll be happy to*s in the Phoenix Ritz-Carlton, but *My pleasure* has grabbed hold at Laguna Niguel and Naples. And the fond farewell is in vogue not just in hotels; as Ms Wellde reports, the soothing phrase is spreading like wildfire. (Like most urban Americans, I have never seen wildfire with my own eyes, but presume it to be a conflagration that spreads quickly.)

Some people (along with *others,* joined by the dopey *those who*) hate to see a lush word like *pleasure* made part of a routine parting or a cheery telephone operator's sign-off, but it beats *Have a nice day,* originally a happy thought but now one very tired phrase. A more exasperated conversation concluder is *Get a life!* (see page 73).

At this point, a with-it sign-off comes all too readily to mind.

You say that pleasure *contains a sound* similar to *the medial consonant in* azure. *This sound, which you describe as* zh *and which linguists may represent as [ž] or* [ʒ], *is the* same *in both words.*

Ellen Measday
Livingston, New Jersey

The Latest Issue

The economy is a *bread-and-butter issue,* at least among pundits not worried about cholesterol; abortion and gun control are *hot-button issues;* Nafta, causing splits within each party, is a *wedge issue.* What kind of issue is health care reform?

It's a *kitchen-table issue.* Talk-show hosts (*host* now covers both sexes; I am still waiting for the hostess to be seated) and news-magazine writers covering health reform have glommed on to this locution.

For its provenance, I turned to Dialog Information Services in Iselin, New

Jersey, the Knight-Ridder computer library that provides access to some four hundred data bases—newspapers and magazines, outfits that cover radio and television shows, texts of vital and not-so-vital speeches, and far-out technical publications. (It marks the searched-for term with crosshatches, a timesaver.)

In a *Boston Globe* poll reported on July 15, 1984, a category of likely voters was described thus: "Understands and cares about *kitchen table issues,*" and that phrase was defined as "the problems that everyday working people face in trying to make ends meet." In 1988, Judy Mann of *The Washington Post* wrote that Sarah Harder, president of the American Association of University Women, believed that "women will be voting *kitchen table issues* in the 1988 election. Not women's issues, not bread and butter issues, but *kitchen table issues.* 'They come,' said Harder, 'from the center of family life.' " The writer cited care-giving as one example of the issue; others are education, use of leisure time and, of course, health.

A *bread-and-butter issue* focuses exclusively on economics: "Can we afford this or not?" A *kitchen-table issue* asks, more broadly, "What's best for the family, and how can we work it out?" The locution covers a sociopolitical as well as an economic range, and fulfills a linguistic need; with the first two words hyphenated as befits a compound adjective modifying the noun *issue,* it should be part of the comprehensive basic issue package that cannot be taken away.

Hyphen Hype

"Who is it in the press that calls on me?" asks Julius Caesar in the second scene of the first act of Shakespeare's play.

It is Paul R. Martin, assistant managing editor of *The Wall Street Journal,* known to his colleagues as the Great Hyphenator. He commends me for defending the use of the hyphen in *kitchen-table issue* "as befits a compound adjective modifying the noun *issue,*" but then takes me to task for using *health care reform* with the compound adjective *health care* naked of hyphenation.

All Americans deserve health care, but does all adjectival *health care* deserve a hyphen? Usagists disagree.

Mr. Martin does a sprightly flier on usage for the *Journal,* called "Style & Substance," along the lines of the occasional "Winners & Sinners" that used to be put out by usageers at *The New York Times.* (I'm just trying out *usageer,* as an alternative to *usagist;* it has a three-musketeers quality, and usage diktats take courage and loyalty to a tight little band.)

In it, he asks us which of the following compound-modifier constructions (thereby using *compound-modifier* as a compound modifier for the first time in the history of grammar) should be hyphenated.

Mr. Martin's brain-teasing list: *"mutual fund manager; hard line faction; health care program* [we know that one]; *fast food chain; drug price increases; credit card operations; page one article; variable annuity buyers; tax deferred annuities* [you can tell what paper he works for]; *real estate agent; high school student; natural gas pipeline."*

His answer: "All of the above."

He's a hyphenation purist; I'm not. With *health care reform,* I'll go along with *New York Times* style that calls for no hyphens, as in *sales tax bill,* when the meaning is clear without them. I disagree with the tendency of many *Times* editors to forgo the hyphen whenever nouns are used together as a compound modifier. Use no hyphen in *health care reform,* but because it adds to clarity, put a hyphen in *kitchen-table issue.* A hyphen is a tool. We own the tools; the tools don't own us.

But what about Mr. Martin's title, assistant managing editor? Should that have a hyphen? He says no: "I assist the managing editor; I don't assistant-manage the editor."

You were prescient in suggesting that WSJ *staff people call me the Great Hyphenator. They didn't . . . but they do.*

I would, of course, take issue with your apparent conclusion that a hyphen in kitchen-table issue *"adds to clarity" while a hyphen in* health-care reform *doesn't.*

In my view, it is well and good for a book editor to decide on a case-by-case basis when a hyphen adds to clarity. But on a daily newspaper, with its squadrons of copy editors, one editor's addition to clarity is another editor's superfluous hyphen, so the tighter the rule the better. Moreover, the hyphen in compound modifiers always helps the reader, I feel, even when it isn't absolutely necessary for clarity or for avoiding ambiguity.

Paul R. Martin
The Wall Street Journal
New York, New York

On the occasional indispensability of the hyphen: Personals ads seem to be a goldmine of casual usage—never proofread and seldom submitted to grammarians for grading. One gem was from a man who started describing himself as a BIG FIRM ATTORNEY.

W. W. Keen James
Providence, Rhode Island

Mr. Martin's "brain-teasing list" contains mostly adjective-noun combinations (except for tax-deferred, *which is a noun-participle combination, and* page-one, *which is a noun-adjective combination). Of those modifiers that are adjective-noun combinations, a number are compound nouns that represent a well-established concept or institution (*mutual fund, health care, credit card, variable annuity, real estate, high school, *and* natural gas*). I would argue that when such well-established compound nouns are used as compound adjectives before a noun, no hyphen is necessary.*

I would, however, hyphenate fast-food *and* kitchen-table *as compound adjectives because in the context in which they are used, they don't conjure up a concept or an institution. They are more like* short-term, long-distance, *and* high-level *than* mutual fund, health care, *or* credit card.

Drug price increases *is tricky. If this phrase signifies:* increases in drug prices, *one could justify* drug-price. *However, if the phrase is taken to refer to* price increases *for drugs, no hyphen would be used. Because of the ambiguous syntax here, I would leave the expression unhyphenated.*

William A. Sabin
Author, The Gregg Reference Manual
Bristol, Maine

About hyphens, we technical editors have a particular problem because we are caught in the middle between the engineers, who hate hyphens, and the keyboarders, who view them as an essential part of "the rules."

As you know, hyphens are often compared to measles, and company-style-manual compilers and computer-software publishers may be carriers. But, unlike the Wall-Street *(?)* Journal, *technical writers are not likely to use* wind-tunnel test, dry-cell battery, high-school graduate, third-base umpire, ice-cream cone, *or* 8-in.-diameter-by-10-ft.-length pipe. *It may be because we spawn so many more compound adjectives than newspapers. For example, a recent technical newsletter freely used an open style on* nose barrel extension, work release order, night attack capabilities, performance appraisal form, *and* merit review process. *This didn't seem to offend our* technical writing sensibilities.

Most style manuals have lists of common compounds. But, as you intimated, hyphens are most needed in "temporary compounds" that are not *common, like your* kitchen-table issue. *You may have seen a recent* Wall Street Journal *headline about a Russian pretender that poked fun at* Used-Czar Shopping. Used car *is a common modifier and may not need a hyphen (*used car sales, used car lot*), but* used-czar, *tovarich, demands one.*

Horace Teall, writing in The Compounding of English Words *(N.Y.: John Ireland, 1891), suggested using hyphens after nouns that were used attributively (*brick-yard*) but not after true adjectives (*brick house*). He noted the heavy accent* *on the former, and viewed that as a discriminator. He thus embraced hyphens in* book-shelves *and* thunder-cloud, *which have since become one word, and also in* freight-train, apple-tree, entrance-hall, *and* cider-mill, *which have not.*

One young technical editor hit upon this same solution recently, but ran into the wrenching problem of having to give a hyphen to steel-guitar players *while denying it to* french horn virtuosi.

Why didn't King Alfred straighten all this out once and for all? To quote John Benbow in the style book of the Oxford University Press, "If you take hyphens seriously, you will surely go mad."

Don Bush
San Diego, California

Someone—perhaps Mr. Martin—seems to have been asleep at the switch here. An "assistant-managing editor" would be an editor who manages an assistant. Compare a "name-dropping columnist," for example. People are already confused about hyphens—no need to add to the murk.

Jessie Howland
Jamaica Plain, Massachusetts

Leaping the Rhetorical Gap

At a meeting with the President in the Cabinet Room, with mouth-filling words like *multilateral* and *multinational* flying around, a Senator wondered if they weren't losing touch with the words that real people use in everyday life.

That off-the-record remark about our language was promptly leaked to this department. At a subsequent interview with President Clinton, I used it to form the basis for a penetrating question. (Actually, my question was a not overly harsh "Can you give me a little more on that?" but even so, it penetrated.)

"Today I think that we still don't speak in a language that ordinary Americans can understand," Mr. Clinton replied. He believed that the diplomatic lingo we now use fails to "support the kind of bipartisan engagement that I'm convinced the United States has to have." In this President's phrase (bottomed on "the missile gap" charge by candidate John Kennedy in 1960), the nation has been presented with the problem of "a rhetorical gap."

Apparently this presidential discontent registered on his staff. The need to reject the no-longer-pertinent language of the cold war—from Lenin's *peaceful coexistence* to Churchill's *iron curtain* to George Kennan's *containment*—reached the writers in the White House basement who are working on national security affairs. How do you go about building a new vocabulary? You start with a single word.

The chosen word is *enlargement.* In a seminal speech to the School of Advanced International Studies of the Johns Hopkins University, Anthony Lake, national security adviser to the President, used the noun *enlargement* or the verb *enlarge* twenty times. I take that to be a subtle signal that the word is intended to be associated with the approach the Clinton Administration is taking to foreign affairs. Here are two of the twenty drumbeats: "The successor to a doctrine of containment must be a strategy of *enlargement,* the *enlargement* of the world's free community of market democracies."

Within forty-eight hours, the word reverberated in the speech of the chief delegate to the United Nations, Madeleine K. Albright. She enumerated the "four overarching goals"—bond-strengthening, emerging-democracy aid, rogue-state isolation, chaos-containment—in a strategy that "looks to the *enlargement* of democracy and markets abroad."

Secretary of State Warren Christopher, however, in a speech the same week, resisted *enlargement,* preferring *engagement,* a word put forward in the 80's by Gary Hart and later by James Baker. In "the latest round in a century-old debate between engagement and isolationism," the Secretary said, "the United States chooses *engagement.*"

The choice was once posed as between *intervention* and isolation; however, interventionists were able to shuck that label, with its hawkish and jingoistic connotations, in favor of *internationalist.* Meanwhile, isolationists remained with

their heads in the sand; the slogan "America first" carries too much pre–World War II baggage. Anti-interventionists have failed to choose a label for themselves, so they are stuck with *isolationist,* chosen by their adversaries.

The intervention crowd, having had success in the containment era, and alert to the pejorative nature of *involvement* or *entanglement,* has long been leery of *interventionist* and worries that *internationalist* sounds too U.N.-y.

Should it choose *engagement* or *enlargement*? This question is evidently roiling the waters between the White House basement and Foggy Bottom; though the Christopher-Lake-Albright speeches were policy-coordinated, what Mr. Clinton called the "rhetorical gap" was not closed.

I'm all for a new word to describe America's role in the world, but somehow *enlargement* doesn't do it for me. First, there is the connotation of swelling: Enlargement of the spleen or the prostate comes to mind. Then we have the photographic sense, with its synonym of "blowup"; surely that is not what diplomats seek. Mr. Clinton may want to grow the economy, as he says frequently, but are we metaphorically ready to grow democracy? Is a generation that celebrates Robert Browning's "less is more" ready for a new *enlargement* policy?

No; let us eschew this slapsy *maxi.* As a card-carrying intervenor (my preference as a human-rights hawk), I vote for *engagement*—not only because of its dim naval-battle origin, with inherent rules, but also for its previous commercial association with the loveliness and success derived from cleansing cream: "She's lovely; she's engaged; she uses Pond's."

The President is undecided. In his United Nations speech, he said the United States "plans to remain *engaged*" and also "we seek to *enlarge* the circle of nations" with free institutions.

The Battle of Rhetorical Gap continues to rage.

Left Is Not Right

"Does it bother you as much as it does me," writes Ray Bradbury, "to hear former Communist groups in Russia described as *right-wingers* or *conservatives*?"

Yeah, it does; where do those old-line radicals, loony lefties and die-hard pinkos get off trying to climb into my post-modern political lifeboat?

The problem is that the left-right spectrum no longer works. The bird metaphor began in 1707 in descriptions of the right and left wings of an army; in the French National Assembly, the radicals were seated at the President's *côté gauche,* or left side, with the conservative nobles on the right and the moderates in front. But confusion reigns today in the republics of the former Soviet Union, because the forces of change toward conservative market economies are described as being on the left, while the old radicals—who long for a return to the discredited statist command economies—are said to be on the right. What a halftime this has been!

Some newscasters, sensitive to the anger of American right-wingers at being lumped in with the apparatchiks of the Evil Empire they helped defeat, prefer a spectrum different from left-right. Sam Donaldson of ABC, for example, uses a variation of hard-soft, describing the former Communist leaders as *hard-liners.* However, this leaves only *soft-liners* to denote the reformers, and nobody likes to be called a softie. (This contrast began with the Hard Shells vs. Soft Shells, also known as Barnburners, fighting over slavery policy at the 1848 Democratic convention in Baltimore.)

Metaphorically, where does that leave us? It's the *reformers* vs. the *hard-liners,* which is no metaphor at all. Worse, the hard-liners want to change the current Yeltsin Government, not the usual goal of a hard line, while the reformers want to keep the executive in power, not the usual goal of reform.

Somebody is going to make a big reputation, maybe even a fortune, coming up with a new metaphor to describe the clash between returners to the old way and keepers of the new way. Lites and Heavies? Ups and Downs? Suggestions will be entertained.

There's an obvious answer to Ray Bradbury's question about what to say instead of "left" and "right" for the factions in Russia. (I avoid "left" and "right" as political designations: they misleadingly make political ideology appear to be one-dimensional.) Yeltsin and his supporters are progressives *and his communist opponents are* reactionaries.

Jim [James D. McCawley]
Department of Linguistics
University of Chicago
Chicago, Illinois

Let 'Er Rip

"There's a lot of money in the health care system," President Clinton said in criticism of the insurance industry, "that doesn't have a *rip* to do with health care."

What's a *rip*?

To most of us, a *rip* is a tear in a piece of clothing. The noun is formed from the verb *to rip,* from the Middle English and Flemish *rippen,* "to strip off vigorously."

The word bears tearing apart. To an aviator, a *rip cord* is a device to release a parachute by tearing its container; to a carpenter, a *ripsaw* is a tool with coarse teeth to cut with the wood's grain. The word has an affinity with water: To a swimmer, a *rip tide* is a strong current that pulls you away from the shore, and to a sailor, a *rip* is a stretch of water made choppy by crosscurrents. Latin *ripa* means "riverbank," leading to riparian rights, like the right to fish (though the word has no connection with *R.I.P., requiescat in pace,* "rest in peace").

Not all current uses of the word stem from the verb meaning "to pull apart." *Rip* once also meant "a dissolute fellow; a rake," possibly from *rep,* short for *reprobate;* from that sense of boisterous behavior, we get the current *riproaring* and *ripsnorting.*

In 1904, an anonymous prison inmate wrote in *Life in Sing Sing* that the verb *rip* meant "to steal with impunity," probably in the sense of separating, or ripping apart, a piece of property from its owner. In 1967, that was stretched to *rip off,* and as a noun that colorful word picture *rip-off* has become a permanent synonym for *theft* and *swindle.*

Separation is the essence of the meaning. John Bartlett, in his 1857 *Dictionary of Americanisms,* spotted *let her rip,* which he defined as "let her go," an indication that some device was about to be allowed to leave at some great rate. Returning to the noun form, and the idea of an item torn away, in Scottish dialect, a *rip* is "a shred, rag, tatter," leading to the Scottish and English dialect sense of "rubbish; anything worthless." Similarly, in both British and early American slang, a rip was "an old, broken-down horse."

Which brings us, meaning no disrespect, to the President and "that doesn't have a *rip* to do with health care." Joan Hall, associate editor of the *Dictionary of American Regional English,* provides me with a couple of citations to show how this sense of worthlessness in this versatile word "has also developed into a general euphemism that allows one to avoid *hell* or *damn.*" From a story by Southern author James Still in *The American Mercury* in 1940: "I hate like rip to call him down." From a 1942 pamphlet called "Dialect of Grant County, Ind.": "I don't give a rip."

When *DARE*'s field workers asked its interviewees, "If you don't care what a person does, you might say, 'Go ahead, I don't give a ——,' the word *rip* was offered, especially in the South and South Midland states.

"Clinton's use fits this basic pattern," Ms Hall says. " 'That doesn't have *the slightest thing* to do with health care,' or 'That doesn't have *a damn thing* to do with health care.' And Clinton, of course, comes from the South Midland, so he's being true to his roots."

Some readers will wonder why I am making such a big deal out of a little word, using valuable space that could be devoted to something important, like a slashing attack on the misuse of predicate nominatives. Ah, but *rip* is a diamond of a word, buried deep in the earliest Indo-European languages, cut into different meanings by various trades and faceted further by thieves' argot and by creative plain folks.

To follow its permutations back into the roots of our tongue is to delight in etymology, dialectology and the study of modern slang. Meanings of simple old words separate into a variety of senses and often, after decades or centuries, come together in unexpected ways; you cannot study language without a sense of family.

The next time you see a sports headline like "Skins Rip Cowboys," or thrill to a movie about Jack the Ripper, or hear the President of the United States profess not to give a rip about his reputation—think about this little word's long journey. It can hook you into language mavenhood.

Linguaclip

Language is speeding up.

It began with initialese, that deliberate shortening of names and phrases by way of initial caps (a clip of "initial capital letters"; there is no clipping penalty in professional writing). Government agencies known by their initials were attacked in the 1936 Alf Landon campaign: "Up with Alf, Down with the Alphabet" was a slogan that went nowhere, as F.D.R.—whose initials are better known than his whole name—swamped the G.O.P., which most new Republicans don't know stands for "Grand Old Party."

To the question "What is PMS?" the answer is sometimes "Why the hell are you asking me that!" but that question is more coolly answered, "Premenstrual syndrome," a periodic manifestation of irritability or sensitivity; many users of the initials have half-forgotten the full term. Similarly, a generation ago, some complained of "PCR," or post-coital remorse, but now nobody remembers the initials or the phrase or even the feeling.

Troubled by P.D.A.? Nancy Evans, insightful editor in chief of the new magazine *Family Life,* features a column of Family Facts that includes this caution to unrestrained huggers: "The worst thing parents can do to embarrass eleven-year-olds is to engage in P.D.A.'s," which the magazine usefully defines as "public displays of affection."

Whether initials are used to save space or to exhibit insiderhood, they soon gain a life, or meaning, of their own. Consider how the word *cow,* which is just a few letters on a page, comes to be treated as the referent—the mooing, often discontented animal itself. But just as the word is not the referent, as Alfred Korzybski taught semanticists, the initials are not the phrase. The representative is not the thing.

If the F.B.I. believes in a defector code-named Fedora and the C.I.A. credits Top Hat, those code names may reflect the differences that the letter *I* stands for—*investigation* in the first instance, *intelligence* in the C.I.A.'s case. The initials "F.B.I." have connotations and resonances that the full name does not have; an arresting agent could get himself killed by shouting the full "Federal Bureau of Investigation—*freeze!*"

Condensation can lead to confusion when initials form an acronym, or pronounceable word. Members of the Squad Squad, shock troops of RARE—Readers Against Redundant Error—have complained about the "VAT tax." (Mostly they fulminate about *safe haven*—there are no unsafe havens—but the "Value Added Tax tax" comes in second.) "How much is the VAT?" can inquire about the tax on an item or the price of a container in which to boil missionaries.

Another cause of accelerated language shortening, or linguaclip, is highway signage. We no longer slowly tootle along the road reading the series of rhyming Burma-Shave signs (Whatever happened to *Burma-Shave*? For that matter, whatever happened to *Burma*?) Now we zip along at a minimum of fifty-five m.p.h. (those initials stand for "miles per hour" but for some obscure reason are not capitalized) and have to snatch our information from signs at a glance. Ever try to read a roadside historical marker? Driving into Martinsburg, West Virginia, I start to read a roadside sign about the home of "Belle Boyd, Confederate Spy," whose father had something to do with the founding of the place, originally Boydsville, but I never get to the next line because, if I slow down, the guy behind me will plow me into the Blue Ridge Factory Outlet.

As a result, we have linguaclipped highway messages. I have two inflatable dummies to set up in the back seat when the "H.O.V. lane" is activated. That's because I have independently learned that H.O.V. stands for "high occupancy vehicle," and a lane is reserved for these civic-minded, traffic-reducing car poolers.

"While driving to Baltimore for a meeting of the American Society of Neurophysiologic Monitoring," writes Dr. Alan D. Legatt of the Montefiore Medical Center in the Bronx, "I passed a road sign with the message NO HAZMATS on the approach to a bridge. I briefly wondered whether this was a harbinger of a new type of ethnic cleansing, but then I realized that *hazmats* was an abbreviation for 'hazardous materials.' "

Having returned from A.S.N.M.—we all know what that outfit is—Dr. Legatt observes: "Many abbreviations have been used to fit messages onto road signs with as few characters as possible, so that the letters will be large and legible from a distance. Some of these are less comprehensible than others, and the results can be humorous or misleading."

That is surely a problem with highway signs. Signs on approaches to bridges have always been disconcerting, shortened or not; I recall a despairing sign on the Triborough Bridge in New York in the 50's: "In event of nuclear attack, drive off bridge," which not every driver interpreted as meaning "drive to the end of the bridge."

Just the other day, I heard one of the dummies in the back saying to the other, "No *hazmats* in the H.O.V. lane," to which I responded, "Cut out the P.D.A., it leads to PCR." We understand one another. Saves precious time.

At least we linguaclippers communicate verbally, relying on the signs and sounds of the English language. We are not in the same league with the semioticians who have introduced global sign language to signs and universally understood icons to computer users.

No is no longer an answer; *no* is now a circle with a line through it, accompanied by a little picture of a truck, or a honking horn, or the symbol for whatever activity is proscribed. We are in the grip of a little-picture trend, closer to Chinese calligraphy than to Western writing.

I will now send this copy to my editor by modem. I am calling up my Windows menu. Lo! I am offered a screenful of little pictures, icons understandable to any child in any country. "File Manager" is a two-drawer file; the fax modem symbol is a rural mailbox. Words? Feh! Pictures are all. Speeded-up discourse is progress of a sort, but presents a danger: A people speaking in initialese, and—silent as mice—pointing to things rather than using representational sounds. Think about it; if necessary, point to a picture of a person with furrowed brow, known to the cognoscenti as a P.W.F.B.

No doubt you'll smile with nostalgia to be reminded that the phrase "post-coital remorse" is the English translation of Ovid's wistful: Omnia animalia post coitus tristram est.

Bonni M. Weinstein
Carmel, California

Dear Bill:

One obvious respect in which the what ever *of "What ever happened to* Burma-Shave*?" behaves like two words and the* whatever *of "Do whatever he tells you to do" like one is that one says "What the hell ever happened to* Burma-Shave*?" and not "What ever the hell happened to* Burma-Shave*?" but "Do whatever the hell he tells you to do" and not "Do what the hell ever he tells you to do."*

Jim [James D. McCawley]
Department of Linguistics
University of Chicago
Chicago, Illinois

Linguaclips

John Horne Tooke, the radical English politician and cleric of the eighteenth century, should be a hero to Americans, especially the fast-talking. With anti-colonist feeling at its height, he tried to raise money for the relief of Americans "murdered by the king's troops at Lexington and Concord"; for this activity he was prosecuted, jailed for a year, forced into retirement in a country house known as Purley. There, I am informed by Pat Winter of New York, he turned from politics in 1786 to write a treatise on language, *The Diversions of Purley,* which offered his world and ours an insight into abbreviations.

"Words have been called *winged,* and well they deserve that name," Tooke wrote, ". . . but compared with the rapidity of thought, they have not the smallest claim to that title. Philosophers have calculated the difference of velocity between sound and light: But who will attempt to calculate the difference between speech and thought! What wonder then . . . the stretch to add such wings to their conversation as might enable it . . . to keep pace in some measure with their minds."

That stretch was the technique of abbreviation, of clipping long words into short ones, and more lately of using initials, which sometimes take the form of acronyms, to quicken our speech.

Tooke! thou shouldst be living at this hour: Never has the shortening been so hotly in the fire. As the pace of life increases and as time becomes more valuable, linguaclipping is rampant.

Acronyms abound in the race for brevity. Some are patterned after existing words: "Physicists argue whether the universe's missing mass is in WIMP's," writes Norman Olsen of Peekskill, New York, "which stands for 'weakly interacting massive particles,' or in Machos, 'massive, compact halo objects.' " Donald Marks of Kew Gardens, Queens, who recently underwent heart surgery, notes that coronary artery bypass surgery has been initialed as CABG, pronounced like *cabbage.*

Initialese without any relation to existing words has been accelerating. Did the F.B.I. tell the C.I.A. what the K.G.B. was doing? Will the I.R.A. (Irish Republican Army) offer its members I.R.A.'s (individual retirement accounts)?

The frequency with which the points are dropped in these initialed agencies, a.k.a. "alphabet agencies," causes great teeth-gnashing among copy editors. (The initials *a.k.a.,* for "also known as," have replaced *alias* in the civilian adoption of police lingo.) *N.Y.T.* style is to include the points except in cases when people pronounce the initials as an acronym—HUD, for example—though that principled position collapses in the face of NBC, CBS, ABC and CNN. (If the acronym is five letters or more, only the first letter is uppercased, as critics of Nafta know.)

This practice sometimes gets out of hand. Morton Zalutsky, a tax lawyer in Portland, Oregon, notes that he told a colleague, "The 401(k) passed the A.D.P. because the N.H.C.E.'s received a Q.N.E.C." He would never take the time to say, "The 401(k) plan passed the Average Deferral Percentage because the Non-Highly Compensated Employees received a Qualified Non-Elective Contribution."

To a sophisticated layman—I suppose I should change that to *lay reader*—he might say, "The 401(k) plan passed the nondiscrimination test of the I.R.S."—assuming the listener would know he was referring to the Internal Revenue Service, known to linguaclipping moonshiners defending their stills with shotguns as "the revenooers." To an unsophisticated audience? "The client," Mr. Zalutsky says, "would be told, 'The plan is O.K. this year.' "

F.Y.I.: In health reform, Bill Clinton wants H.H.S. to get H.M.O.'s operational A.S.A.P. (For your information, if you cannot make sense of that sentence about Health and Human Services, you are living in the past and need help from your health maintenance organization as soon as possible.) Better stay away from N.P.R., as it could stand for National Performance Review, New Production Reactor, Naval Petroleum Reserves or National Public Radio.

In the old days—B.C., which to structural linguists is "before Chomsky"—abbreviations would use a period to chop off a word, as in *abbr.* That's still in vogue (like *inc.* and *etc.*), and many new clips are introduced without explanation. Macy's advertised two-ply cashmere sweaters: "Sale $99.99 Form. $160." Do you have to fill out Form 160 to buy the sweater? No; the *erly* has been dropped from *formerly.* In upscale stores, that would be *prev.,* getting rid of the excess baggage of the *iously.*

You want to slim down a phrase by jamming it all together and seeing what stands up? I am sending this copy by a modulator-demodulator. We computer whizzes, flipping through *Wired* (which can be construed as a magazine, a movie title or a highly agitated state of mind), call it a *modem.* Steve Deyo, in *The Puget Sound Computer User* (I read everything), headlines an article "Morph Me, Baby!" *Morphing* is a trend in TV ads that shifts shapes to catch the eye; the word comes from the Greek root *morph,* "shape, form," source of *metamorphosis,* which is what the language is going through. (*TV,* sometimes lowercased "tv," is a linguaclip of the word *television,* in case today's column is placed in a time capsule and found by an alien civilization.)

The world of transportation shaves words and phrases like no other. Look out your airplane window: See the words *no step* on the wing. Not "Do not step here" and certainly not "If you stomp your big foot on this delicate spot, you'll break the wing in half, dummy!" In the same way, crates in cargo holds have stenciled neatly on them *no push.* Why not "Do not push"? No reason.

On the Merritt Parkway in Connecticut, a route apparently taken by psychiatrists, the sign appears: DEPRESSED STORM DRAINS. In addition, reports Karen Rockow of Cambridge, Massachusetts, signs in Vermont boast SCARIFIED PAVEMENT. In San Francisco, the Metropolitan Transportation Commission cheerily describes its "acronym zone" in a pamphlet for motorists: As you zip down the familiar H.O.V. lane, for "high occupancy vehicle," note the signs for *Travinfo* on your way from the TIC (Transportation Information Center) to the TOC (Traffic Operations Center).

Drivers ask: How do you pronounce PKY? What's a CYN? (Parkway, and Canyon.) And what's the meaning of the cryptic TRAFFIC REVISION AHEAD? (I don't know; I have enough trouble with my own revisions.)

Compression is all. Allan Metcalf, executive secretary of the American Dialect Society, reports the group's choice for the phrase that best typified 1993 was *information superhighway.* This expression is, of course, a mouthful, taking a full second to get out. In a few months, it is sure to be called the *infohighway,* since both *tainment* and *super* are expendable. Then, in a few years, as we all look back fondly at antiquated fiber optics, it will be the *infoway.* The next snip will lead to *I-way.* Next century, the phrase that fills our mouths today will zip by in the blink of an *I.*

I regretted that you did not, while making reference to abbreviations, mention contractions ("ass'n" for "association," "don't" for "do not," "dep't" for "department," etc.). The difference between the two, as I have understood the rule, is that an abbreviation is created by excising the latter part of a word and substituting a period (e.g., "inc." for incorporated"). A contraction, on the other hand, involves elimination of letters in mid-word, the absence of which is signalled by an apostrophe (ass'n, don't, dep't, supra*).*

Confusion seems to exist, though, and it is not unusual to see a contraction with no apostrophe and followed by a period. Denville, New Jersey, when viewed a while back, proudly announced its "Police Dept." on a building facing busy Route 46. "Is this *the image the people of Denville want to project to the world, day after day?" muttered a concerned passenger of mine. "Doesn't* anyone *here know it should be 'Dep't'?"*

If the above correctly states the rule, the matter might have been worth a passing reference. It would at least have reduced confusion and, more important, brightened the spirits of said passenger, who still growls about the matter from time to time.

James G. Starkey
Justice, Supreme Court of the State of New York
Brooklyn, New York

You mentioned the Merritt Parkway sign, DEPRESSED STORM DRAINS. *This reminded me of two signs that I saw in England last year:*

1) DISABLED PUBLIC TOILETS, *and*

2) (in a store that sells electronic equipment) ALARMED CABINETS.

Paul Nix
Summit, New Jersey

Long Word's Return

"I am . . . a firm defender of the establishment of the Church of England," said John Habgood, Archbishop of York. The word *establishment,* in that context, means the government's recognition of that church as the "official" ecclesiastical body, whose head, the Archbishop of Canterbury, anoints the sovereign.

Certain shenanigans by members of the Royal Family, however, as well as a decline in churchgoing by the Church of England's parishioners, led *The Times* of London to suggest a breaking of the chain of establishment; one columnist, Simon Jenkins, called it anachronistic. The centuries-old name for that idea is *disestablishment.*

Such talk infuriates the defenders of establishment. "The American dream of an 'ideologically neutral state,' " wrote George Curry of St. Stephen's Vicarage in Newcastle-Upon-Tyne, "is proving to be a nightmare in which religious values are replaced by a new political 'orthodoxy' that exalts reason, experience and personal preference above revelation. . . . Disestablishment would hasten it."

We are now approaching what used to be known as "the longest word in the dictionary," despite the presence since 1741 of the twenty-nine-lettered *floccinaucinihilipilification,* which means "the habit of estimating as worthless," as Daniel Patrick Moynihan keeps reminding the Senate.

The name for the espousal of opposition to those who would cut the Church of England loose from the crown? You remember it: the twenty-eight-letter *antidisestablishmentarianism.* It's alive and well and flourishing in the Mother Country.

The Longest Bumper

"We were trying to think of what our bumper sticker would be," said the President at a luncheon, seeking to change the Administration line from "less shock, more therapy," a formulation of a Strobe Talbott aide that had not played well.

"I think our slogan would be there needs to be more reform and more social service support," Mr. Clinton said, "more attempts to build a safety net to deal with the consequences of reform, but not an attempt to slow down the reform effort."

Some slogan. The longer he rolled on, the more eyes rolled heavenward, until he realized the bind he had gotten himself into. He interrupted himself to say, "No, no: 'more reform, more support.' I should have said when the bumper sticker stops."

Slogan is from the Scottish Gaelic *sluagh,* "army," and *gairm,* "cry," which combined to form the word denoting the battle cry of the Scottish Highland clans. A battle cry, or slogan, should be short enough to fit on a bumper sticker. The President recovered with "That would be the newest rap on me: 'Clinton endorses wraparound bumper stickers.' "

Maid Service

Where are the fair *maidens* of yesteryear? The noun, developed from an Old English word dating from the year 950, long ago acquired a poetic or archaic air; a *maiden* was defined as "an unmarried woman," with the particular expectation of virginity. The *maidenhead* was the hymen, a membrane unbroken in many women who had not had sexual intercourse. A *maidservant,* first used in the 1382 Wycliffe Bible, was a young woman who served a master or mistress; a half-millennium later, Thursday became *maid's night out.*

In today's language, the *maidservant* has been euphemized; if you want maid service at a hotel, you punch "housekeeper," and if you want to hire a maid, you look in the classified ads under *domestic servant;* only in casual speech do you wish you could afford to hire a maid. The noun hangs on in *maid of honor,* the chief unmarried attendant to the bride at a wedding; the association with "honor" may be preserving the usage, as nobody has yet demanded to be called *bride's chief female attendant.*

Maiden, as an adjective meaning "first," rooted in the metaphoric loss of virginity, is also falling into disuse. A ship's first venture by the owner after delivery by the builder is still called the *maiden voyage,* but how many cruise ships are being launched these days? In Britain, the first speech by a newly elected Member of Parliament is still a *maiden speech,* a vestige of the days when new members were expected to be shy and demure; when Sir Alan Herbert's first address in the House of Commons was unusually forthright, Winston Churchill evoked the early meaning of *maiden* by calling it "a brazen hussy of a speech." In America, nobody calls a Congressman's first harangue for benefit of C-Span a *maiden speech.*

The latest assault on the adjectival *maiden* is in its use defining an unmarried woman's name. The French have long used *née* to identify the last name of a woman before her marriage, but we have since 1689 preferred *maiden name.* Now we are beginning to hear *birth name,* as if *maiden* were somehow pejorative or sexist, like *girl.* Writers of bureaucratic forms are likely to seize on the anti-maidenhood trend as linguistically inoffensive.

Paradoxically, maiden names—I'll stick with the untried and true—have never been so respected. Many women, especially those who have established their names in careers before marriage, include their new middle names in their married names. Length is not considered an obstacle; on the contrary, a mouth-filling or column-long moniker has a nice ring to it.

A Time Warner executive, Edward Bleier, longs for the day he can make the following introduction: "Arianna Stassinopoulos Huffington, meet Barbaralee Diamonstein-Spielvogel."

For the horseperson, a maiden is a horse which has yet to win its first race. A race comprised of maidens is called a maiden race, and the winner is said to have "broken its maiden" or to have "lost" its maiden condition. Most interestingly, the term "maiden" in this context applies equally to male or female horses.

Elysabeth Kleinhans
New York, New York

Mangled Metaphors

"Perot is a good fellow," Lee Iacocca said about Ross Perot (the former H. Ross Perot) in preparing to challenge the billionaire's anti-Nafta campaign, ". . . but he's on the wrong side of the angels here."

In reporting this comment, *Newsweek* said the former Chrysler boss was "gearing up for his role" as Administration anti-protectionist spokesman. *Gearing up* was a suitable figure of speech to describe the action of an automobile executive.

If he is to shift into high to catch up with Mr. Perot—whose *giant sucking sound* of jobs supposedly moving to Mexico is the metaphoric powerhouse of the year—Mr. Iacocca had better get on the right side of the side of the angels.

There is no "wrong" side of the angels. There is the side of the angels, and the side of the apes. This phrase was coined in England in 1864, at the height of the controversy about Charles Darwin's theory of evolution. At the Oxford Diocesan Conference, Benjamin Disraeli, who had been a leader of the Tory protectionists, and who was eager to be the fittest to survive in his climb up the greasy pole to the prime ministry, took what is now seen to be a reactionary stand:

"Is man an ape or an angel?" he asked rhetorically, oversimplifying the debate. "I, my lord, I am on the side of the angels. I repudiate with indignation and abhorrence those newfangled theories." Disraeli is remembered with fondness now by political lexicographers for his coinage of *dark horse,* which fitted Mr. Iacocca a few elections ago. But the Detroit free-trader cannot put the angels in the middle, as if they were the issue. Before engaging ol' Sucking Sound himself, the Michigan mauler needs to get right with the angels.

Iacocca's metaphoric mangling was quickly topped by James Baker, former Secretary of State, who was reaching for some homespun trope in which to wrap criticism of Clinton policy toward Somalia. "At first it was all about helping the starving," he said, referring to the mission to Mogadishu that he and President Bush authorized. "Suddenly, it was supposed to be about building a nation, whatever that means, or chasing some chieftain." Baker characterized this change of purpose as "Someone somewhere *widened the goal posts.*" He locked in the sports metaphor with "That was never the original goal."

But Mr. Baker was reading from the wrong hymnbook. "*Widening* the goal posts makes the job easier," writes Mark Thompson, a Washington correspondent for Knight-Ridder newspapers. "*Moving the goal posts* (the standard metaphor) makes it more difficult (assuming, of course, they're moved away from the kicker)."

Gotta be careful with metaphors. Before we leave the subject of metaphors and Somalia, a word about the origin of *cut and run.*

The earliest citation the lexicographer Cynthia Barnhart can find is from a 1704 Boston newsletter: "Captain Vaughn rode by said ship, but *cut and run.*" This nautical metaphor was defined in the 1794 *Elements and Practice of Rigging and Seamanship:* "*To Cut and run,* to cut the cable and make sail instantly, without waiting to weigh anchor." Its nonnautical use is always pejorative, implying panic, synonymous with the military's *bug out;* proponents of immediate withdrawal prefer a noun phrase that might have originated in computerese, suggesting profound planning in heading for the escape hatch: *exit strategy.*

Marley's Ghost Rides the Trolley

In a political harangue far from the nonpartisan confines of this space, I disparaged some action of the First Lady with this metaphor: "The *clank* of falsity goes to the top."

This criticism elicited a spirited response, which I enjoyed reading, from the Clintons' private attorney, David Kendall of Williams & Connolly. Then, a few days later, in an interview with *The Wall Street Journal,* Mr. Kendall denied another accusation from another source, charging it had "the unmistakable and *clanging* ring of falsity."

A *clang* is not a *clank.* Mr. Kendall, said to charge clients four hundred dollars an hour, is meticulous in his choice of words. I called him, quickly dispensed with the nonlinguistic matters covered in his response to me as the horrendous Mr. Hyde, then assumed my natural Dr. Jekyll identity: Why did he change the *k* in *clank* to the *g* of *clang*?

"I had in mind a counterfeit coin," Mr. Kendall said. "In my aural sense, gongs and cymbals *clang,* while chains—the ghost of Marley comes to mind—*clank.* To me, the false ring of a fake coin is a *clang.*"

Presuming his time was billable to the President's legal defense fund and the clock was running, I hung up quickly. But his carefully considered change of my *clank* deserves examination.

Clang is rooted in the Latin *clangere,* "to resound," and was used in ancient times to describe the reverberating sound of a trumpet. Some etymologists think it is akin to the Greek *klazein,* "to scream or bark," and the Old English *hliehhan,* "laugh." (One thinks of a pre-Chaucerian muckraker sneering to King Ælfred's attorney, "It is to *hliehhan.*") In modern English, the verb made its debut in 1576 in *A Panoplie of Epistles* by Abraham Fleming: "By the clanging trump of swift report, proclaimed." It became a noun twenty years later, defined as "a loud ringing metallic sound" with a second sense of "a harsh cry of a bird (as a crane or goose)."

Contrariwise, *clank* can claim no proud Latin lineage. First sighted in 1656 (when the poet Abraham Cowley wrote, "No clanck of Chains was known"), it is probably imitative in origin, like the onomatopoeic *zap* or the echoic *hiss.* An *Oxford English Dictionary* lexicographer—Sir James Murray or one of his successors—anticipated the contretemps I would have with Mr. Kendall, defining *clank* in contradistinction (to use one of President Clinton's favorite locutions) to *clang.* According to the *O.E.D., clank* is "a sharp, abrupt sound, as of heavy pieces of metal (e.g., links of a heavy chain) struck together; differing from *clang* in ending abruptly with the effect of a knock."

Mr. Kendall's reference to Jacob Marley, who wore chains in his ghostly visit to Ebenezer Scrooge in *A Christmas Carol* by Charles Dickens, is therefore correct: Those chains *clanked.* The *O.E.D.* also suggests that *clank* is the offspring of *clang* crossed with *clink,* "to express a sound intermediate to the two, which has the quality of a 'clang,' but is abruptly shortened like a 'clink.' "

However, the sound of a counterfeit coin's being tested by being dropped on a hard surface would not be the pure, bell-like ring of silver or gold, but would be brief and off-key—closer to *clink* than *clang.* Therefore, in using a metaphor of a metal with a false or discordant ring, I prefer *clank*—the *clank* of falsity.

Mr. Clinton's entire legal team may choose *clang,* but the *ng* sound—as the comedian Bert Lahr demonstrated frequently in parodying an opera singer—lends itself to length. If "Trust is the coin of the realm," as attested by another lawyer, the former White House Counsel Lloyd Cutler, then that coin, when tested, should never *clank.*

If Barbra Streisand, on the other hand, revisited the White House and sang a song popularized by Judy Garland in *Meet Me in St. Louis,* she would make the rafters ring with the sweetly reverberating "*Clang, clang, clang,* went the trolley. . . ."

Masterful Meltdown

"She does a *masterful* job of analyzing the evolution of the international monetary system," *Library Journal* writes of Judy Shelton's *Money Meltdown: Restoring Order to the Global Currency System.*

The word the reviewing librarian intended is *masterly,* "expert, with the skill of a master"; *masterful,* according to *Webster's New World Dictionary, Third College Edition,* means "fond of acting the part of a master; domineering; imperious." The Simon & Schuster lexicographer includes, as a second sense, "having or showing the ability of a master; expert; skillful; masterly." It adds ominously to this second, sloppy sense: "usage objected to by some."

I'm one of the "some." *Merriam-Webster's Tenth Collegiate* goes further in its usage note some-ing up: "Some commentators insist that use of *masterful* should be limited to sense 1 [inclined to play the master] in order to preserve a distinction between it and *masterly.* The distinction is a modern one, excogitated by a 20th-century pundit in disregard of the history of the word." Using *masterful* to mean "skillful," Merriam-Webster insists, "cannot rationally be called an error."

The pundit being sneered at by the roundheeled upstarts led by E. Ward Gilman in Springfield, Massachusetts (none of the usual academic deference from us lexies; we like to slug it out), was Henry Fowler, the super-usagist. "The 'domineering' sense of *masterly* dropped into disuse around the end of the 18th century," Mr. Gilman notes in the masterly but determinedly unmasterful *Merriam-Webster's Dictionary of English Usage.* "Fowler seems to have thought the world of English usage would be a tidier place if *masterful* too were limited to one sense. He therefore declared the differentiation between the two words to be complete," which was "only wishful thinking in the first place."

Fowler! thou shouldst be living at this hour to excoriate the excessive excogitation of the "turn 'em loose, Bruce" school of lexicography. Here were a couple of words that cried out for separation; the language for centuries drove a wedge between the two, and a great usagist, on the side of clarity and precision, issued his useful guidance to a waiting world.

This was not a case of Bishop Lowth's cooking up a "rule" of grammar (never using *who* as an object) to force English into Latin ways, nor was this an instance of language snobs looking down their noses at *ain't.* This was a sensible prescription by a man of authority to help English speakers stamp out confusion between two similar modifiers.

Call me irrational, but I say anybody who uses *masterful,* "imperious," to mean the same as *masterly,* "skilled," is in error. Thus, we have the masterly writer Meg Greenfield, correctly observing in *Newsweek* how President Clinton in his news conference mode "deliberately walks into the lion's den and is seen to take on all comers . . . to show himself as *masterful* and in charge."

Meanwhile, Back at *Revanche*

"I believe the Western world and Western countries did not understand the reality of *revanchism,*" said Boris Yeltsin, standing at the side of the French President, François Mitterrand. He defined the term in the next sentence: "a serious attempt to restore the Communist regime of the Soviets."

Mitterrand could have told him that *revanche* is the French word for "revenge," usually meaning the retaking of lost territory or return to old regimes. For generations, Soviet leaders complained of West German revanchist aims toward East Germany; now the term, evidently a Russian favorite, will be popping up at summits, directed at the Communist apparatchiks seeking to make a comeback in Moscow.

The word is always used pejoratively; if you are for economic revanchism, you eschew that word and say instead you favor retaliatory democracy or you're a reciprocitist. *Revanche,* in diplomacy, is never admitted to be sweet.

Mind Games

"I decided not to play any *mind games* with myself," Nancy Kerrigan told reporters after winning the Olympic silver medal for figure skating, "to question myself, because I knew I was capable of this."

She probably took that locution from the cover of *U.S. News* the week before. "Mind Games" was the newsmagazine's cover title, alongside a picture of the skater; the subhead was "Nancy Kerrigan's mental struggle. . . . How champions steel themselves to win."

Only a couple of months before, the political campaign consultant Ed Rollins was explaining his fiction about paying ministers in a New Jersey campaign as merely "playing *mind games* with Jim Carville," his opposite number in the race.

On the CBS soap opera *The Young and the Restless,* watched mainly by the old and rested, one character says of his business rival: "He is a master of *mind games.* You zig, he zags. . . . You never know where you stand with the man."

And this postcard came in from Joan Macey in Binghamton, New York: "We were discussing personal ads, and didn't know what 'no *mind games*' or 'no *head games*' meant. Perhaps you could elucidate."

Ever the slave to primary sources, I went through the personal ads in my *Village Voice.* Under "Men Seeking Women," this ad stood out: "SWM [single white male], 27, 5-10, brown hair, blue eyes, muscular build, hot blooded [apparently too passionate to hyphenate], seeking SF [single female], no kids, who is voluptuous and who has good morals and manners. No *head games.*" In many other ads, the hot-bloodedness is ignored, and the mind-gameless "commitment" and "honesty" are stressed.

What is this game that is so universally derogated? The lexicographer Anne Soukhanov, after a brief study of the language of manipulation as it relates to personal ads, reports that the ratio of ads with the header of *games* ran three female to one male. That suggests women are more conscious of, and resistant to, the dread game.

"The use of *mind game* and *head game,*" Ms Soukhanov says, "reflects the writer's perception of having been victimized or manipulated mentally and emotionally in the past. In my opinion, the increase of usage therefore is a semantic indicator of the culture of perceived victims." She adds that some feminists note that too much introspection along these lines is self-defeating.

Head gained a sense of drugginess in the 60's: To go on a *head trip,* you went to a *head shop* and bought a *head drug.* In this sense, the head was not the skull with hair on top, but the thinking that went on within; this intercourse with introspection also was expressed in the heavy use of the word *mind,* as in the lyric "The Windmills of Your Mind" by Marilyn Bergman (Ascap's new president) and Alan Bergman, and the description of some drugs as *mind-altering* and *mind-bending.* The 50's verb "to brainwash" was replaced by a hyphenated term suggesting copulation with the mind. In 1973, John Lennon wrote "Mind Games," taking this sense of *mind* into game theory.

The Soukhanov theory is that we have come full circle: The resentment at *mind games,* as well as the desire for "honesty . . . ready to settle down . . . commitment" in many personal ads, suggests that the American Family Dream of the 50's has been recast into 90's expressions derived from the counterculture of the 60's.

Playing games, without the head or *mind,* has long had a slang sense of deceptiveness, evasion or manipulation; the addition of the counterculture favorites underscores the resentment of the psyched-out marionette toward the puppet master.

Your delightful column about the origin of the current use of "games" as in mind games etc. reminded me of two people whose contributions are so much part of our consciousness that we've almost totally forgotten them!

First, the Dutch philosopher Huizinga, whose seminal book, Homo Ludens: A Study of the Play Element in Culture, *was published in 1939. Then Eric Berne, whose* Games People Play: The Psychology of Human Relationships *(1964) was a huge bestseller. He invented transactional analysis, which interestingly by the way was the origin of the now very popular Inner Child work.*

People operate from varying states of consciousness often from moment to moment, which he named, the Parent (two kinds, Punitive and Nurturing), the Adult (the objective, non-emotional state), and the Child. (Adapted, which conforms to the demands of the Punitive Parent and the Free, which is the spontaneous and creative). Berne wrote that "child rearing may be regarded as an educational process in which the child is taught what games to play and how to play them".

Doe Lang
New York, New York

Morphin' Time

"Investigate the use of the word *morph* as a verb," urges Rabbi Carl M. Perkins of Needham, Massachusetts. "In the phrase 'It's morphin' time,' used by the characters on the 'Power Rangers' television program, I have the sense that it means 'to transform.' "

Morphe, in Greek, means "form"; preceded by *meta-,* denoting "change," we had *metamorphosis,* which means "change of physical form," a word the first-century Latin poet Ovid used in its plural form as the title of his legendary work, *Metamorphoses.*

Ovid also celebrated Morpheus, the god of dreams (not to be confused with Orpheus, a poetic character who knocked about the underworld). Morpheus, in Greek mythology the son of the sleep god Hypnos (you are getting drowsy), led us to *morphology,* a branch of linguistics that dissects words: A *morpheme* is the smallest meaningful unit in a language. In the word *words,* for example, *word* is a free morpheme and *-s* is a bound morpheme. (Hypnos wins; you are now under my control, heh-heh; have a shot of morphine.)

A *morph,* still a noun, was used by science writers in the 1950's to mean "a variant form of an animal species," like a resident of the Planet of the Apes. But along came the computer, and the word was transformed into a verb meaning "transform from one shape to another by computer graphics," in the definition given by John and Adele Algeo in *American Speech.* Citation: "There are flashes of the special effect known as *'morphing,'* " *The Atlanta Constitution* wrote in 1992, "in which Mr. [Michael] Jackson—who arises from a pile of magic dust—materializes and dematerializes."

Characters also *morph* in the popular children's television series *Mighty Morphin Power Rangers;* in this live-action fantasy, teen-agers are transformed into superheroes empowered with the strength of prehistoric creatures.

The technique is also becoming a force in advertising: A recent *Washington Post* article on the use of computer imaging in commercials was headlined "*Morph* for the Money," which plays in the elision fields.

The god of dreams is not finished with this word. Extending the computer graphics sense of the verb, Roxanne Roberts, covering the Miss America pageant in Atlantic City for *The Washington Post,* wrote, "Now in its 74th year, this contest has *morphed* into part political nominating convention, part triathlon and part 'Star Search.' "

Computer literati, so far ahead of the rest of us that they are prepared to pun on senses unfamiliar to the cyberstupids, will occasionally ask Internettled anonymous correspondents *MorF?* That means "Male or Female?" but is surely a play on *morph.*

Motherese

On guard, Mothers! The Chomskians are after you.

You know that language you talk to your toddler? Not *baby talk,* accompanying a tickle with *itchy-gitchy-goo!*—that's the use of nonsensical singsong sounds to amuse or reassure babies, puppies, kittens and hungry gerbils.

We're talking here about *Motherese,* a nonjudgmental coinage by Dr. Henry Gleitman first cited in a 1977 paper from a doctoral dissertation by Elissa Newport. "The older literature used *baby talk,*" recalls Dr. Newport, now profes-

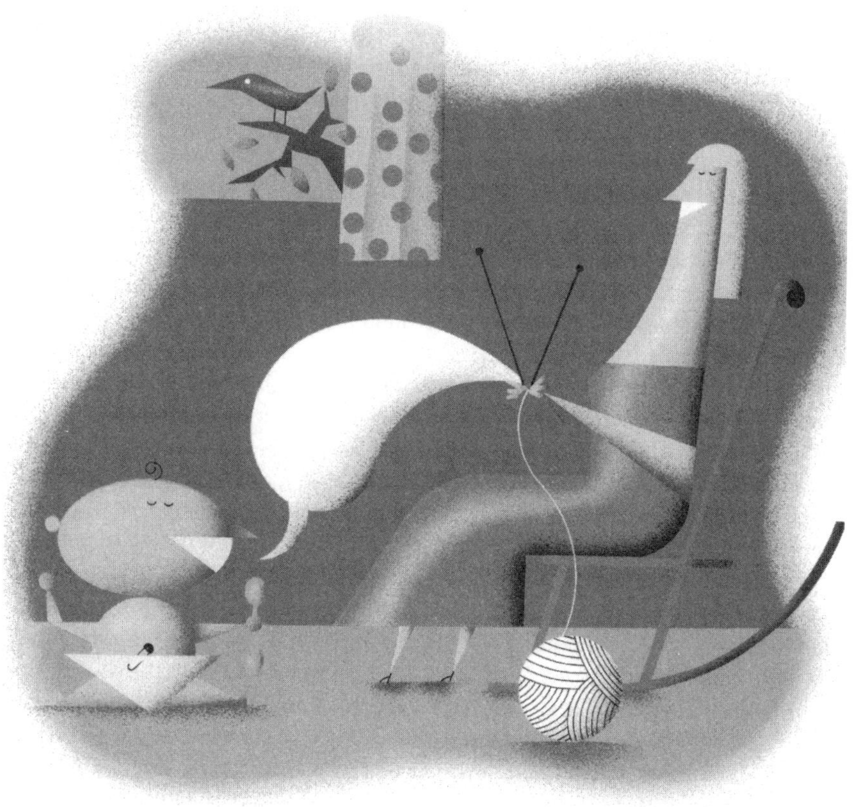

sor of psychology at the University of Rochester, "but our focus was on how mothers talk to girls. Newer terms take into account that fathers and others influence the child's language. I've heard *caretaker talk* and *child-directed speech* but no single word is as effective as *Motherese.*"

In *Motherese,* words and sentences are short and simple; the mother consciously tries to make her meaning easy for the child to understand. Most mothers, since time immemorial, have assumed this helps the kid learn language.

Forget all that, the Chomskians say. In a new book, *The Language Instinct,* blurbed on the front cover by Professor Noam Chomsky of M.I.T., Professor Steven Pinker gives *Motherese* a hard time.

"First, let us do away with the folklore that parents teach their children language," asserts the Chomskian Pinker, director of the Center for Cognitive Neuroscience at M.I.T. ". . . Many parents (and some child psychologists who should know better) think that mothers provide children with implicit lessons. These lessons take the form of a special speech variety called *Motherese* (or, as the French call it, Mamanaise): intensive sessions of conversational give-and-take, with repetitive drills and simplified grammar. ('Look at the *doggie*! See the *doggie*? There's a *doggie*!')" He argues that "children deserve most of the credit for the language they acquire" and scorns as yuppie-esque "the belief that Motherese is essential to language development."

What does a doctor (one of those who ought to know better) think of this Chomskian blast at Motherese?

"That's baloney," says Dr. James Egan, clinical professor of psychiatry at the George Washington University and former head of Psychiatry at Children's Hospital in Washington. "The very underpinnings of the Head Start program are predicated on early language interaction between parent and child. Studies of immigrants in New York City have shown that the child's developing language is directly related to the sophistication of language spoken to the child. Also, classic studies have shown that you can reliably tell the difference in babble between middle-class and lower-class children by six to seven months of age. Those 'new' ideas," Dr. Egan argues, "are uninformed and contrary to virtually all the developmental data."

We have a difference of opinion here reminiscent of the classic heredity-environment debate. Does a child learn language from others, or is there an innate grammar programmed into the head at birth, like the software that comes free with a computer? For an answer, let's turn to the *wugs*.

Professor Pinker cites the "*wug* test" to demonstrate that "normal children do not learn language by imitating their parents." A kid is shown a picture of a creature called a *wug*, a nonsense word the child cannot have heard before in Motherese. Asked what to call two of them, the child will say *wugs* because something deep in the brain says the plural is formed by adding *s*. A normal kid knows; a language-impaired adult does not.

I ran this past Dr. Jean Berko Gleason of the Boston University Department of Psychology, who dreamed up the wug test back in 1958. She agrees with the Chomskians that grammar is an innate capacity—something that people have and chimpanzees don't—but parts company with the Chomskians on this: "Dr. Pinker tends to restrict the understanding of language to grammar, but language is more than grammar. There's also vocabulary, and if parents aren't teaching that, does that mean we're born with English in our head? No; we learn from people around us. Explicit vocabulary is taught, along with a pragmatic system of politeness; often the first words babies speak are 'bye-bye,' polite words that help them function in society."

Let's stipulate that in acquiring language, the human brain has an innate, instinctive edge on all other creatures. (Tell that to a dolphin and watch him smile.) There may well be, as Chomskians postulate, a deep structure of rules in babies' heads, enabling them to learn a language faster than they're taught it or even to cook up a new language from scratch, in isolation. But in pressing home their exciting theory, the Chomskians may be going overboard. "For many years, in the wake of the innateness hypothesis," David Crystal writes in the *Cambridge Encyclopedia of Language,* "the importance of the language used by adults (especially mothers) to children was minimized. But studies of 'Motherese' . . . showed that maternal input . . . can no longer be neglected in devising theories of language acquisition."

At this point, common sense rears its ugly head. If parents talk to their children intelligently, perhaps even encouraging them to use Standard English, the kids will be more likely to speak and write intelligently and do better in life. Just as a lack of education stymies a brilliant mind, a lack of Motherese limits the realization of the potential of our inborn linguistic power.

This makes some Chomskians grumpy because it mars the purity of their "language is not imitative" argument. Language mavens irritate Professor Pinker, too: Who are we to "correct" English with the imposition of all sorts of grammar rules and usage diktats not grounded in loosey-goosey deep structure?

About grammar rules, he thunders, "If they were ever followed they would force writers into fuzzy, clumsy, incomprehensible prose." (That sentence needs a comma after "followed"; the comma would separate the dependent "if" clause from the independent clause that follows, thereby making the sentence clear, graceful and comprehensible.)

Pinker is the first Chomskian to write understandably, even entertainingly. By dumping on mothers and mavens, he reaches for the controversy that widens his audience, and I'm not one to knock controversialists. Nor do I take offense at his headline writer, for a *New Republic* excerpt from his new book, who calls me a "pompous know-all" (the compound is *know-it-all*). But when you get into this arena, you have to expect a pop back from a pop grammarian willing to stoop to defending Motherese on Mother's Day.

Mouthing On

Mouth to mouth is a form of resuscitation; *Mouth 2 Mouth* is a magazine from *Time* aimed at teenagers of both sexes and is described by its editor, Angela Janklow Harrington, as "a cross between *Vanity Fair* and *Mad.*"

I have plunked down fifteen dollars for a year's subscription because it has a feature titled "Words We Hate" by Evie Shapiro, damning the "subtle and insidious" words "that pollute a conversation."

Ample is out: "a fancy way of saying you're fat." Youthful resistance to euphemism is a hopeful sign, but *moolah* and *ointment* are also taboo in speech for an odd reason: "Notice how your face has to scrunch up unattractively. . . . Plus, they sound like you're making barnyard noises."

Nite, kwik, e-z, thru—"flat-out lazy. Why do advertisers think misspelling is such a consumer draw?" Can't kid the kids.

"If we've saved just one person from the crushing shame," Ms Shapiro writes, "of using, say, *brouhaha* in a casual conversation, we can consider our job done."

Gee, I'm sorry to see *brouhaha*—"hullabaloo"—vanish from the teen scene. It's a peppy word.

Movin' On

In announcing his pardons for many of those convicted or charged in the Iran-contra scandal, George Bush cited the precedents of James Madison and Lafitte's pirates, and several general amnesties (pardons to a whole class of people) like Andrew Johnson's to the Confederate soldiers, and Harry Truman's and Jimmy Carter's to draft evaders in two wars. "Notwithstanding the seriousness of these issues and the passions they aroused," President Bush stated, "my predecessors acted because it was time for the country to *move on.*"

This locution has become one of the most useful and frequently employed in the modern language.

"One of the things about Hillary," said Ruth Harkin, a Washington lawyer, whose husband, Tom, was a Democratic primary opponent of Bill Clinton, "is she *moves on.*"

When the Republican insurgent Pat Buchanan rejected calls to apologize to groups he had offended, he concluded with a defiant "We're *movin' on.*"

The meaning of *move on* is not the same as that in the *Oxford English Dictionary:* "The order given by a policeman to a pedestrian who is standing too long in one place so as to cause obstruction." Nor is it the same as the order, in American dialect first cited in 1888, to *get a move on,* or hurry up. Nor should it be confused with the current *to make a move on,* "to make a pass at." Its sense is closest to the "I'll be *movin' along*" or "I'm *a-movin' on*" in cowboy lingo, meaning to pull up stakes in all its figurative extensions.

Although it seems to be a clip of *move on to [something else],* the expression *move on* without the following preposition *to* has a meaning subtly different from "to proceed to" or "to move forward to." The *move on* in "move on to something else" (meaning "change the subject") has a sense quite different from the free-standing *move on* in "Let's move on."

The prepositionless *move on* is a well-understood way of expressing impatience at the difficulty of quick resolution: "We can argue about this forever and get nowhere, so let's have done with it and leave it unsettled and maybe the whole issue will go away." It can also have an escape-from-quagmire emphasis, perhaps derived from usage by folk singers leaving their loved ones: "I cannot let this bog me down and ruin my life, so I'm outta here."

In both the earlier *get a move on* and the policeman's imperative *move on,* the *on* was deemphasized or neutral; in the new argument-is-unrewarding or lemme-outta-here senses, the emphasis is on the *on.* In its participle form, the *g* in *moving on* is clipped in pronunciation and, reflecting that slangy sound, in written form: *movin' on.*

Sociologists have much to ponder in the rise of a locution that suggests a weary resignation at a problem's insolubility. Some will see a lack of courage in confronting a conflict; others will find pragmatic a cool willingness to recognize an impasse and walk away from it.

Ellen Goodman, writing about "graceful exits" in the 80's before the *g* in *moving* was clipped, offered a more upbeat definition: "It begins with the vision to recognize when a job, a life stage, a relationship is over—and let it go. It means leaving what's over without denying its validity or its past importance to our lives. It involves a sense of future, a belief that every exit line is an entry, that we are *moving on,* rather than out."

Enough about this already; the time has come, as they say, and you know what they say.

You reminded me of the Stephen Sondheim musical Sunday in the Park with George. *The next to last song in the second act is "Move On" (track 15 on the CD). It was written in 1984 and describes an artist's need to find new ways to express new ideas.*

Charles F. Hruska
Brooklyn, New York

My Old Flame

In David Ignatius's bone-chilling post–cold-war suspense novel, *The Bank of Fear,* one character in the search for Saddam Hussein's hidden wealth is a computer guru. "Her idea of fun," the reader is told, "was roaming the Internet bulletin boards and *flaming* people she didn't like."

The author, an editor steeped in the lore of the Middle East, has evidently spent long hours in the company of creative hackers researching the techniques of computer-directed heists. Among that set of nervous netties, *flaming* is a hot word.

Though some hackers claim the verb (and its noun, *flamage*) was coined in the early 1970's, the earliest use on the Dialog retrieval system is from a June 1987 issue of *PC Week:* "The quickness of response available with E-mail may lead to *flaming,*" Robert Kelley noted, "where people impulsively react to a message and send uncensored, emotionally laden and often derogatory return messages—a practice that is almost nonexistent in paper writing."

The earliest Nexis citation, from *MacWeek* in June 1989, reinforces the hurried connotation: "E-mail sent in anger, and usually in haste, is called *flaming.*"

We've all written a furious letter, looked it over, then decided not to send it at all. Writing unsent letters is a fine way to ventilate hot feelings without triggering nuclear exchanges, but it requires the planned use of "snail mail."

The net set has no such fail-safe system. "Rapid-fire wordmeisters often prefer to communicate via E-mail," Stephen Wilbers wrote in the Minneapolis *Star Tribune* recently, ". . . and their inflammatory messages have been nicknamed 'flame mail.' " He later identified one letter to himself as the "most searing flame mail," which called him a "self-serving, arrogant windbag." (What does he know about reader heat? I would put that in my "generally supportive" stack.)

The word is in global use, as befits the network. In Britain, Clancy Sigal in *The Guardian* observes the "heady frontier freedom that is remarkably democratic if you don't mind brushing elbows with the unseen post-pubescent sixth-formers . . . and the *flame-out* artists who specialize in joyful adolescent invective." (*Flame-out,* a 1950 term for jet engine failure, preceded the hacker verb *to flame* by two decades.)

"Netiquette frowns on *flaming,*" says Jack Cushman of *The New York Times,* my in-house Internet expert. He equates the use of all capital letters (sometimes used in flaming) with shouting, and finds it the sign of the *clueless newbie,* one new to the net. Another breach of netiquette: excessive cross-posting, asking for information in a number of forums, which sometimes brings a flaming response. And before asking a basic question, the polite nettie "FAQ-checks"; that's looking up "Frequently Asked Questions" before posting a query. It's computer communications courtesy, and Judith Martin—Miss Manners—had better do a column on it before some cyberboor flames her out.

Far be it from me, a professional vituperator during the week, to decry the use of invective; yet I have to admit that the old system of "paper writing," to use the new retronym, had an advantage over instantaneous E-mail. Rather than look back to the old, slow days, let us look ahead: The trick will be to develop software that builds in a delay to your E-mail when it spots a flame word. Type "blithering idiot" and the machine automatically freezes, while a soothing multimedia voice asks, "Do you really mean that? As the Ghost of Hamlet's father said, 'Leave her to heaven.' "

I have two nostalgic names for the software: *Flame Thrower* or *My Old Flame.*

N.M.I.

The classic case of the Law of Unintended Consequences was the decision by the War Department in the early 1940's to require all personnel without middle names or initials to declare that inadequacy on documents. A corporal named Joe Sadsack would become Corporal Joe N.M.I. Sadsack, the initials standing for "No Middle Initial"—thereby defeating the intent of Joe's parents to avoid the letters between given name and surname.

We have come full circle: Middle initials are regaining popularity, and whole middle names are in fashion, especially among women. A generation ago, some militant feminists refused to adopt the surname of their husbands; in time, a compromise was found in the use of both names, like Josephine Jones Sadsack, sometimes hyphenated in the British style, Josephine Jones-Sadsack.

Recently, the preference expressed by the First Lady to include her maiden name in her identification pushed this usage to the fore. Hillary Rodham Clinton is the name accepted by most publications on first reference, with "Mrs. Clinton" (rather than "Ms Rodham Clinton") on subsequent references.

This is a good idea. A name is intended to supply information about a person, and the more background a name offers, the better. Names of males used to add "son" or, in Hebrew and Arabic, be preceded by "ben"; it helped put a person in the context of a family.

For example, as Louis Jay Herman of New York notes, the current fashion, if applied a few generations ago, would have asserted the relationships of a presidential family: "If Eleanor Roosevelt were alive today, she would be known as Eleanor Roosevelt Roosevelt." (To be painstakingly accurate, her maiden name was Anna Eleanor Roosevelt; her married name was Anna Eleanor Roosevelt Roosevelt.)

Newtonian Linguistics

"It is hardly news that Newt Gingrich is not Mr. Nice Guy in politics," wrote my Op-Ed colleague Anthony Lewis. "But his signals that he is going to stick to the Rottweiler game matter a lot."

Although television pundits happily wrestle each other to the ground and join in furious food fights, newspaper sages—especially at *The New York Times*—are expected to, and do, conduct their communications with a collegiality bordering on outright civility. Though Tony and I disagree on almost everything, we alert each other to potential misreadings of our works. In this case, we have what hypersensitive dog lovers could take to be a pejorative reference to the Rottweiler, a large black-and-tan dog named after a town in southwest Germany. Because of their fearsome aspect (though not because of any vicious trait in the breed), these dogs have become the second most popular breed in America, and are panting hard after the most popular, Labrador retrievers.

This is not the place to draw a political parallel to the rise of the pugnacious pups from twenty-fourth only a decade ago to their recent overtaking of seemingly kinder, gentler breeds. But liberal critics of draconian social policy can hardly afford to lose the support of 104,160 registered Rottweiler owners, so I sent Tony this fax: "What have you got against Rottweilers?"

In a return fax from Boston, he dismissed my concern about his impolitic allusion with a brief "arf!" and added, "I thought you'd like the Shakespeare."

As a founder of the Poetic Allusion Watch (its acronym, PAW, is not intended to be a canine slur), I combed through the Lewis column looking for some play on a Shakespearean phrase. Finally, my glance lighted on the headline, where the clue lay like a purloined letter: "Eye of Newt."

Of course: the witches of *Macbeth.* A concordance guided me swiftly to Act IV, Scene 1, as the second witch stirs the pot and recites the recipe:

> *Fillet of a fenny snake,*
> *In the cauldron boil and bake;*
> Eye of newt, *and toe of frog.*

A *newt* is a small lizard related to the salamander and sometimes confused with a spotted eft. In Washington these days, however, Newt is the shortened form of the first name of Newton Leroy Gingrich of Georgia.

Newt will be elected Speaker of the House of Representatives when the 104th Congress assembles in January, because Republicans will form the majority.* However, because that election has not yet been held, journalists have struggled with a title. *Speaker-to-be* is a popular choice, though the jocular *Speaker-in-waiting*, a play on the royal *lady-in-waiting,* is sometimes used. *Speaker-designate* is sometimes heard on television, but no official designator can be named. *Putative* is a more standard usage, meaning "supposed"; other choices are *likely, all-but-certain* and the simple but not provable *next*. Some writers have drawn on royal usage for *Speaker-presumptive;* Adam Clymer of *The New York Times* slipped me *Speaker-presumptuous*.

The noun phrase most often tossed at Newt is *bomb thrower.* "People who dismissed Gingrich as a cartoonish *bomb thrower* underestimated him," William Sternberg wrote in the June 1993 *Atlantic.* Though this phrase is still applied to him in most profiles, the role and the title are moving on to the next House majority leader, Richard Armey of Texas, identified by *Newsweek* as "second in command to Newt and the designated *bomb thrower* when Gingrich is forced to play statesman."

* This column originally appeared on December 4, 1994.

The phrase in a quasi-literal sense was applied in politics to anarchists early in the century, shown by cartoonists as bearded men with large bombs in their hands. The figurative sense—"a divisive or disruptive radical"—seems to have taken hold in the 80's, but earlier citations would be welcomed.

The linguistic bomb tossed by Newt Gingrich was the distinction he drew between *cooperate* and *compromise.* "On everything on which we can find agreement, I will *cooperate,*" the man of the hour said after the Republican sweep. "On those things that are at the core of our philosophy . . . there will be no *compromise.*"

Cooperate, no longer hyphenated, comes from the Latin *operari,* "to work," and the preceding *co-,* "together." Oliver Goldsmith wrote in *The Citizen of the World* in 1762 that "It is . . . difficult to induce a number of free beings to co-operate for their mutual benefit," an observation being made again in the White House.

Compromise is a word with both a positive and a negative connotation. The Latin *com-,* like *co-,* means "together"; the end *promise* is, of course, a pledge; the Latin *compromittere* means "to promise mutually."

The positive sense is "to come to agreement through mutual concession." But a second, more sinister sense has long been with us: "To speak truth, I compromised matters," confessed a character in Charlotte Brontë's novel *Villette:* "I served two masters." That usage led to the definition "to agree by the partial surrender of position or principles." And to be caught in an embarrassing position is to be *compromised.*

The meaning is not so much in the dictionaries as in the mind of the user: To the tender-minded, *compromise* is a necessary *accommodation* leading to agreement; to the tough-minded, the synonym for *compromise* is *sellout,* leading to betrayal of values. In carefully differentiating, Professor Gingrich was saying he would work together with Democrats to pass conservative legislation, but would not make concessions to pass or preserve liberal legislation.

In a related example of connotational *Fingerspitzengefühl,* when Newt said he expected to "grow" into the role of Speaker, a half-dozen of his conservative allies remonstrated with him: The Speaker-presumptuous told *Time* magazine he was informed that *grow* was "a code word for selling out."

That same sensitivity to synonymy was apparent in the Newtonian rejection of *transition* (from the Latin *transitus,* "passing across") to describe the period between Speakerships, and in his embrace of *transformation,* "beyond the present structure, to change in character."

I cannot specify the origin of *Mr. Nice Guy,* cited above, but a 1960's joke popularized it in a punch line: Some neo-Nazis appealed to Hitler, hiding in South America, to lead them into a new takeover of the world, to which Der Führer replied, "O.K., but this time—no more Mr. Nice Guy."

A politician of any stripe who welcomes controversy and splits hairs over words is sure to be a lexicographer's delight. After the "eye of Newt" is added to the steaming brew, all the witches sing: "Double, double, toil and trouble;/Fire burn, and cauldron bubble."

No Ifs or Ands, Either

"She glues her swimsuit to her *butt,*" Roxanne Roberts wrote in *The Washington Post* about a contestant in the Miss America pageant.

"Purposeful debasement of the language," a *Post* reader objected. "*Butt* used this way is gutter language," Thomas Parker Jr. continued, ". . . not acceptable in polite conversation."

Another reader, Donald P. McEwan, countered, "This commonplace and inoffensive word is not identified as a vulgar usage in *Webster's New World,*" adding that the dictionary includes "a synonym for *butt* that I imagine Parker would be even less pleased to see in print."

Butt is a clip of *buttock,* a Standard English word rooted in German for the fleshy back of the hip on which a person sits, as acceptable in polite modern discourse as *foot* or *penis.* The slang expression *to kick butt* is also inoffensive to most people, and *butt-head* long ago lost its taboo.

Butt-head uses the verb *butt* based on a Germanic verb for "to thrust or beat," and the noun, with a lowercase *h,* names one of MTV's cartoon characters Beavis and *Butt-head.* A recent Federal District Court decision in California tossed out a libel suit by the astronomer Carl Sagan on the use of the word. He'd sued Apple Computer after insisting that Apple stop using *Carl Sagan* as the code name on its personal computer; the company complied, changing the code name to *Butt-Head Astronomer.* In dismissing the case, Judge Lourdes G. Baird wrote, "One does not seriously attack the expertise of a scientist using the undefined phrase *butt-head.*" (Another root leads to the French *but,* meaning "target," and is the source of "the butt of jokes.")

As Mr. McEwan suggests, *butt* is a euphemism for *ass,* a word not permitted in *The New York Times* unless referring to a donkey. Editors have lifted this restriction when quoting Presidents, as in some usages on the Nixon tapes and in George Bush's remark (intended to be private) after a debate that he "really kicked ass."

Horses are the genus *equus;* a donkey is an *equus asinus,* source of *ass* and the adjective *asinine.* (A *jackass* is a male donkey; to call a woman a *jackass* is a solecism.) In "The law is a ass," Charles Dickens was using the sense of "donkey," an animal that is thought to be dull-witted.

The other *ass,* the absence of which is not a major loss to any medium, is a variant of a different etymon, *arse;* the *r* was dropped in common usage, just as *parcel* became *passel* and *curse* became *cuss.*

Though the vulgarism is in frequent street use, and is overused by screenwriters in a reach for realism, it retains some taboo; hence, the use of a euphemism by President Reagan in "I've had it up to my *keister*" (reportedly a Yiddishism for a collapsible display case used by con men, sometimes sat or fallen upon); the choice of "cover your *rear end*" to define *C.Y.A.* by Senators; the recent popularity of the word *buns* in fashion magazines, and the inclination of some editors to seize upon the word *butt.*

A butt is also a keg or barrel and it gives us another word for gossip.

Sailing ships had a barrel of water opened midship for drinking. It served the same purpose as a water fountain in a modern office; people hung around it and talked; and we received another word for gossip or rumor—scuttlebutt.

John J. Howley
Rockaway Park, New York

Now Overhear This

The language of penetrated privacy has a new noun.

The verb *to overhear,* "to hear what is not intended by the speaker to be heard," has been used by snoopers since 1549, when a man on the gallows murmured a message meant for a lieutenant, but—according to a sermon by Bishop Hugh Latimer—"the worde was over heard."

The word *over* is used in this verb not in the sense of "above" but with the meaning of "beyond," as in "to hear beyond the intended reach of the voice."

But what shall we call the overheard remark itself? *Eavesdrop* is a verb, rarely used as a noun. When my telephone was wiretapped, the content of that eavesdropping activity was called the *tap,* or when recorded in written form, the "tap transcript." No noun existed for the overheard conversation itself.

The language vacuum has been filled. The other day I called Joseph diGenova, a Washington lawyer who serves as an independent counsel investigating the unlawful disclosure of the Clinton passport files during the campaign of 1992. My purpose was to find out the status of the investigation, which has been delayed by the tainting of evidence by some illegal eavesdropping (euphemized as "monitoring") within the Department of State.

"Can't talk about the *overhears,*" he said.

Switching to a linguistic mode, I asked what an *overhear* is. Long pause, during which I presume the prosecutor was mentally reviewing Rule 6 (e) of the Federal Rules of Criminal Procedure, forbidding the disclosure of grand jury proceedings. Assured of the query's exclusively lexicographic thrust, the lawyer promised to get back to me by fax.

Which he did. An *overhear,* in law-enforcement circles, is defined by Mr.

diGenova as "surreptitious interception (usually electronically) of oral communications."

Eavesdropping has a nice etymology. The eaves of a house are the ends of the roof that overhang the windows. The *eavesdrop* is the water that drops from the eaves. An intrusive person who wants to overhear what is going on inside stands next to the window, close up against the wall, within the eavesdrop.

What the eavesdropper is getting is an *overhear.*

Off Of

Do you get angry at people who get angry with you? Do you get *off* on zapping people for getting *off of* the subject?

If so, you are a preposition freak. Judy Stoffman of Toronto sends a photocopy of a page from Calvin Trillin's book *Remembering Denny,* containing a passage about "the extracurricular part of Yale that Griswold had warned us off of from the start." Cries Ms Stoffman: "Calvin, how could you? Off of with your head!" And Ruth Fretts of Brooklyn notes the Hallmark ad: "Just ask for your certificate, worth $5 off of birthday cards purchased in June."

Even a single *off* can stir consternation among preposition freaks. Ann Harty of Pittsburgh sends this ad from A.T.&T. and wonders if she has to retrain her ear

for language: "Now there's a way to save off A.T.&T.'s basic rates," goes the ad, repeating the curious usage with "Save off direct-dialed, A.T.&T. Long Distance." Not *off of,* just the single preposition *off*—but back when Alexander Graham Bell was operating, the expression was *save on,* as in "Mr. Watson, come here, I want you. We can save *on* long-distance rates!"

I say *save on* (just as I achieve a *saving* at the Blue Ridge Factory Outlet Center in Martinsburg, West Virginia, which allows me to add to my *savings* in the bank; I'm cheap but consistent). *Save off* may be in use, but not common use; for a copywriter, it's a wrong number.

And *off of,* though much more common and usually pronounced "off-uh"—as in "get your feet off-uh the couch"—is a case for the Squad Squad, the redundundancy watchers. Yes, it can be found in Shakespeare, in *Henry VI, Part II,* when Simpcox is asked by the Cardinal, "What, art thou lame?" The Duke of Suffolk asks, "How cam'st thou so?" and Simpcox replies, "A fall off of a tree." But use it only if you like to affect dialect; if you prefer Standard English, get off it, not off of it. To *sign off on* is neither dialect nor slang, but bureaucratic gibberish.

Finally, to *angry at* vs. *angry with.* "A commentator noted that President Clinton was 'angry *at* his aide,' " writes Sam Berliner of Sea Cliff, Long Island. "Isn't proper usage *angry with*? One may be *angry over* a deed or *angry with* the doer, but not *angry at,* or is this mere pedantry?"

Pedantry is a good word for it. "The present meaning of *with,*" says William A. Kretzschmar Jr. of the University of Georgia Linguistic Atlas Project, "is one of inclusion (you go *with* somebody, coffee *with* cream), but there are many words in English that testify that it used to mean just the reverse: *Withstand* means 'stand against,' *withhold* means 'hold back,' and *withdraw* means 'draw away from.' Modern variation in usage, such as *angry with . . . angry at,* occurs because speakers are looking for a particular shade of meaning."

That would explain the current academic vogue use of *speak to a question,* which is more direct than *speak about,* even though *speak to* seems to turn an abstract question into a sentient human being. Undermining *angry with,* Professor Kretzschmar asks, "Doesn't anger set people *at* odds, rather than *with* each other in feeling?"

Either is correct. Better not to get angry with or at anybody, least of all preposition freaks.

Off Those Ramparts

On Looking into the Abyss is the title of a book of politically incorrect essays—she calls them "untimely thoughts"—by Gertrude Himmelfarb. The title piece derides Derrida and historical deconstructionists who look at "history from below," ignoring heroes and villains. "If it cannot take the measure of greatness," she writes, "neither can it appreciate the enormity of evil."

Note the use of *enormity* in the way generations of usagists have considered correct: "huge wickedness." They have held that *enormity* should be limited to descriptions of evil, and that *enormousness* or some other noun like *immensity* be used for good as well as bad things of great size.

Now consider this line in one of President Clinton's State of the Union addresses: "Our support of reform must combine patience for the *enormity* of the task and vigilance for our fundamental interests and values."

Barbara Balph of New York, who is as well-trained and conservative as Bea Kristol (Gertrude Himmelfarb's nonliterary name) in proper English usage, objects: "If it were an *enormity,* my patience would be short-lived. The President subverted his meaning."

I think not. A dozen years ago I abandoned the ramparts on the limitation of *enormity* to wickedness. The phrase "enormity of the task" is familiar enough to be a cliché (and for that reason might well be eschewed by presidential speechwriters), which brings it easily to the mental tongue of Norma Loquendi. It would be nice for linguistic precision to be able to direct the English-speaking world to restrict *enormity* to big evil and to use *enormousness* for big good, but the world doesn't always follow orders.

What Norma wants, Norma gets; I know that sounds loosey-goosey, but if the native speakers want to use a word in a new or broader sense, and persistently ignore all authoritarian strictures to the contrary, then that usage becomes "correct." Consider the sage advice of Claude Swanson, F.D.R.'s Secretary of the Navy, on the subject of acquiescence to the inevitable: "When the water reaches the upper level, follow the rats."

Or, as the First Law of Language Mavenhood directs, "Know when to hold 'em and know when to fold 'em." The unrestricted use of *enormity* is no huge deal.

I'm sorry to see you cite that faithless strumpet Norma Loquendi as authority for cutting the word enormity *loose from its traditional association with wickedness. I think the lady should be renamed Norma Errandi, since so much linguistic change results from the confusion of less-than-literate people who can't quite get the hang of what words actually mean. Incidentally, if you broaden the application of* enormity, *you can no longer use it in a concrete sense,* i.e., *employ an* enormity *as an elegant synonym for* an atrocity *or* an abomination.

*Further on, you say that "if the native speakers want to use a word in a new or broader sense, and persistently ignore all authoritarian strictures [*sic*] to the contrary, then that usage becomes 'correct.' " Here you seem to be striking a blow for traditionalism, since, unless I miss my guess, you are using* stricture *in the older sense of "sharp criticism, censure" rather than as a neologistic (and completely unneeded) synonym for* restriction. *In such cases, there is a kind of lin-*

guistic Gresham's Law that causes the new meaning to supplant the old one instead of settling down comfortably alongside it, thus impoverishing the language. For years now, Norma and her tone-deaf cohorts have been confusing fortuitous *with* fortunate, *with the result that practically nobody remembers that the traditional (and etymologically correct) meaning of* fortuitous *is "happening by chance." The people who think that* reticent *means "reluctant" are well on their way to killing that word, and I was glad to see that you recently took a prescriptive stance on the matter.*

Louis Jay Herman
New York, New York

On the Edge

Elizabeth Drew's highly insidery book about the Clinton presidency is titled *On the Edge,* from a quote attributed to a close friend of the Clintons: "Bill has always been someone who has lived *on the edge,* politically and personally." The reporter treats it to mean "in the aura of danger."

On the edge is where it's at, metaphorically speaking. A blurb for Mark Olshaker's novel *The Edge,* reads: "a thriller that stretches the limits of the genre [?] and takes readers to the terrifying edge of human behavior and medical science."

Edge—from the Middle English *egge,* based on the Old English *ecg,* meaning "corner, point"—came to mean "border, margin, rim," a place that lends itself to a pyrotechnic display of metaphors. What, for example, does *on the edge* mean?

One sense is "at the dividing line," as on the cutting edge of a blade; the lexicographer Anne Soukhanov traces it to the 1718 Alexander Pope translation of Homer's *Iliad,* where each Greek "stands on the sharpest edge of death or life." W. Somerset Maugham used this sense in his 1944 title *The Razor's Edge.*

Another sense is "poised, ready," as to be on the edge of a major decision; an 1884 biography of Francis Bacon recounts, "He was now on the very edge of losing his office," a position familiar to many current candidates. This is more frequently expressed as *on the verge of.*

Yet another sense is "about to go crazy" or, in more clinical terms, "bordering on mental instability" or "losing control." The King James Version of Jeremiah says, "The fathers have eaten a sour grape, and the children's teeth are set on edge." Since 1837, *edgy* has been synonymous with "testy, irritable"; the closer we get to the edge, the more nervous the meaning. *Time* magazine recently titled an article about cops who committed suicide. "Officers on the Edge." This usage is related to *over the edge,* which since 1929 has meant "insane."

Now we come to the sense of *on the edge* taking over at the moment: "in a precarious position," calling to mind standing on the edge of a precipice. That's Ms Drew's "aura of danger." In a 1985 novel, Nelson DeMille wrote of "the excitement of combat, of living *on the edge,*" and CBS promotes its emergency-response series, *Rescue 911,* as "the one television show that will take you to the edge."

To live *on the edge,* in its latest meaning, is to court danger, to experience the thrilling state of always nearly getting caught.

Of course, that does not begin to explore the varied uses of *edge.* "Advantage" is another meaning: Rhett Butler, in Margaret Mitchell's novel *Gone with the Wind,* compares the madam Belle Watling with Scarlett O'Hara: "Belle's got the edge on you . . . because she's a kind-hearted, good-natured soul." Headline writers on sports pages use that sense in "Caps Edge Rangers, 3–2." And a drunk is happy to *have an edge on,* considered a state of advantage over sobriety: "We'll drink to Fred Sloane," says an F. Scott Fitzgerald character in a 1920 novel, "who has a fine, distinguished edge." The *cutting edge* replaced *state of the art* as a description of *avant-garde* (though it now seems stale to those *on the cusp*).

Tracking *edge* has taken us from the sharp side of a cutting instrument, to a perilous path on a narrow ridge, to shades of mental instability, to constant stimulation by an existential romance with danger. Why have I inflicted this on you? Because it is an instructive example of semantic development, not to put too fine an edge on it.

The late Lawrence Alloway (1926–1990), the influential British art critic who spearheaded the Pop Art movement in New York back in the 1960s, became chief curator at the Guggenheim Museum. When to mostly everyone's shock and surprise, and apparently to his, he was abruptly fired, The Times *quoted him as saying, brightly, "I've gained in stature, but lost in edge."*

Stanton L. Catlin
Research Professor, Fine Arts
Syracuse University
Syracuse, New York

W. Somerset Maugham's The Razor's Edge *comes originally, I believe, from the Indian* Kathopanisad *(Chapter 3, verse 14): "Arise! Awake! Approach the great and learn. Like the sharp edge of a razor is that path, so the wise say—hard to tread and difficult to cross."*

M. K. Gandhi subsequently expressed the same idea in My Religion: *"I know the path: it is straight and narrow. It is like the edge of a sword. I rejoice to walk on it. I weep when I slip. God's word is: He who strives never perishes. I have implicit faith in that promise. Though, therefore, from my weakness I fail a thousand times, I will not lose faith."*

Although Pope's translation of The Iliad *makes allusion to the "sharpest edge of death or life," Maugham's "razor's edge" has more of a moral spin, referring to the sharp path one treads between spiritual life or death, and owes more to the Hindu image of the painful and arduous approach to the supreme good.*

Virginia Hunter
New York, New York

Only the Factoids

Can a little group of willful newscasters, representing no opinion but their own, render the common understanding of the meaning of a word helpless and contemptible?

"What on earth is a *factoid*?" demands Jane Duggan, M.D., of Atlanta. "I have seen this word on CNN as a heading for a few lines of quasi-truthful information. I cannot locate it in my computer's spell-checker. Does a factoid resemble a fact as a deltoid resembles a delt, or as a sesmoid (a bone in the wrist) resembles a sesm?"

Barry Osborne gets a bone in the wrist about this word, too: "*CNN Headline News* from time to time prints *factoid* on the top of the screen," he writes from Santa Barbara, California, "followed by some bit of arcane trivia. I think they mean *factlet,* 'a brief fact,' because the ending *-oid* implies only 'similar to' or 'like' the foregoing element." He adds ominously: "*Psychology Today* used to similarly misuse *factoid.* I wrote 'em about it, and shortly after, they went bust." (The magazine resumed publication in 1992.)

At CNN headquarters in Atlanta, Bob Cain, an anchor who laboriously looks up words in a dictionary, rather than relying on the lightning action of a spell-checker, is plainly concerned about the distance between the word's meaning as used all over CNN and the one supplied in the latest dictionaries. "*Factoid* is almost universally used to denote some relatively obscure, mildly interesting fact," he asserts, using *universally* to mean "all of us here at CNN," adding in a troubled tone, "a usage clearly at variance with the enclosed definition."

The definition, from the *Random House College Dictionary,* is "a lie or half-truth, devised especially to gain publicity and accepted as a fact because of constant repetition in print, conversation, etc."

That's a far cry from "factlet," or a "little bit of arcana," which is the CNN meaning. Which is correct?

The earliest use turned up by Dialog, the wide-ranging data base, is in this 1985

Los Angeles Times article by Paul Simon: "A few months ago, I read a whole story about barbecuing in *USA Today* that was packed with what a friend of mine calls 'factoids.' " Simon then gave this definition: "A *factoid* is something that is probably true, but even if it isn't, who cares?" That's halfway between the two definitions.

The pundit George Will used the word in its sense of being misleading: "One often-repeated statistic of suffering is that one in four college women is a victim of rape or attempted rape. One study that popularized that *factoid* has interesting flaws: 73 percent of the women categorized as rape victims did not themselves define their experiences as rape." To Will, a *factoid* is deceptive, not a whole truth—the dictionary definition.

An Orlando *Sentinel* feature writer, however, cites an "interesting *factoid*" as small but revealing, and a *Washington Post* columnist, Steve Twomey, profiling a teacher, agrees: "She won't share one *factoid,* her age." They go with CNN in the sense of "factlet."

So what to do? The Greek suffix *-oid,* long used in mathematics and astronomy (*rhomboid, asteroid*), usually means "similar but not the same" when applied to a noun; an *android,* as Mr. Spock's fans know, is very like a human being but is an automaton.* On that analogy, the noun *factoid* would mean "like a fact, but not quite a fact."

Let's see what the word's coiner intended. Norman Mailer, writing a biography of Marilyn Monroe in 1973, derided the work of a previous biographer, who "develops a book with facts embellished by factoids (to join the hungry ranks of those who coin a word)." Having established in that backhanded way his coinage, the novelist-turned-biographer defined the term: "that is, facts which have no existence before appearing in a magazine or newspaper, creations which [*sic*] are not so much lies as a product to manipulate emotion in the Silent Majority." (I threw that gratuitous *sic* in there because Mailer went on with a gratuitous parenthetical sentence: "It is possible, for example, that Richard Nixon has spoken in nothing but factoids during his public life.")

But not even the word's coiner has the final word on its meaning. Here's my judgment: *Factoid,* which seems with us to stay, has three senses. The first is accusatory: "misinformation purporting to be factual; or, a phony statistic." The second is neutral: "seemingly though not necessarily factual"; the third is the CNN version: "a little-known bit of information; trivial but interesting data."

I would use it in its first sense: a phony or at least challengeable assertion masquerading as an indisputable fact. But there goes *CNN Headline News,* every day, pounding away with the "factlet" sense. Who will prevail? Stay tuned.

* For a follow-up on this misstatement, see "Zero Misteaks," page 281.

Sesmoid *should be written* sesamoid. *It is a bone that is completely encapsulated. The best example of a sesamoid bone is the patella, the bone in front of the knee. There is occasionally a bone in the wrist of that nature but not in the normal.*

Heskel M. Haddad, M.D.
New York, New York

Out of Control

Under a cartoon of a man in underpants with a drink in hand racing along a tropical beach, *The Economist* headlined, "Don't you just love being *out of control*?" The cartoon character in the London-based magazine represented the recently privatized British utilities, freed from government's heavy hand, but the phrase is the latest extension of the psychological cliché of the year.

To be *in control,* as in "As of now, I am in control here in the White House," a phrase used in 1981 by Secretary of State Alexander Haig when Ronald Reagan was wounded, is to be boss. To have a blaze *under control* is what every firefighter hopes to announce. To be *beyond control,* as in "circumstances beyond my individual control," was a cop-out first used by Mr. Micawber in Charles Dickens's novel *David Copperfield.* But to be *out of control* is to be damnably difficult in every field of endeavor.

Students are susceptible: "The campus is *out of control,*" declared a Republican Assemblyman in 1969, as students rioted at the Berkeley campus of the University of California. Workers, too: A year later, the railroad union leader William Winpisinger testified that workers were "running right on the ragged edge of being *out of control.*" And deficits lend themselves to the phrase: Representative Barber B. Conable Jr. of New York worried in 1981 about "keeping the budget deficit from getting *out of control.*" A copywriter for Hefty lawn bags noted the phrase's power: "Lawn *out of control*? Better get a Hefty."

The familiar phrase lends itself to use as a compound modifier: An editorial in *The New York Times* in 1990 commented on a bill by the Senate majority leader, George Mitchell, "to put a lid on *out-of-control* campaign spending." In a recent *TV Guide* profile of the actress Loni Anderson, its writer, Mary Murphy, asked, "What about the stories branding Loni as a mercenary, an *out-of-control* shopper?" (A friend denied that, but only made things worse with "Once we went shopping for twelve hours and came back with nothing.")

The phrase was popularized by psychiatry. "The ego is in charge of feelings, actions and perceptions," explains Dr. E. Michael Ehlers of Bethesda, Maryland. "*Out of control* refers to any sort of ego failure. The phrase cuts across many types of disorders, from explosive behavior in psychotic disorders to compulsions and hysteria. The term probably predates psychiatry, but the use of ego functioning in relation to control dates from the late 1800's, the beginning of modern psychiatry."

Has the time come for this weary phrase to be consigned to the cemetery of stereotype? Ordinarily that order would issue from this department, but I don't want to be accused of being a *control freak.*

Ozarks on the Potomac

In his conscious selection of colorful phrases, Bill Clinton often turns to popular music: "On this last day of the campaign," he said before his election, "we should take it to the limit one more time." That was an evocation of "Take It to the Limit," a song by the Eagles, the rock band (not the football team or the Republican fund-raising group).

Sometimes, also consciously, he will point to his roots by selecting a down-home proverb. After losing a game of hearts, he wrote on a reporter's scorecard, "Even a blind hog can find an acorn." This is *Ozark* lingo. Ozark, the name of a mountain range in Missouri, Arkansas and Oklahoma, is derived from the French *aux Arcs,* "to the (region of the) Arc (Arkansa) Indians," according to *Webster's New World* etymologists.

More interesting, and less a product of image-manipulation, is President Clinton's unconscious use of Ozarkian speech. In Tulsa recently, in one of the many launches of his health reform campaign, he said, "The only thing I can tell you is that everything I ever *suspicioned* about the way the federal government operates turned out to be true, plus some." (*The New York Times* has a style rule against using *launches* to mean "kickoffs"; I use it here for illustrative purposes. You are allowed to do anything for illustrative purposes.)

I ran *suspicion* as a verb past Frederic G. Cassidy, professor emeritus and editor of the *Dictionary of American Regional English* at the University of Wisconsin. "Two hundred years ago, to *suspicion* something or someone appeared in Britain, took root in the American colonies both north and south, and spread westward with them," says Professor Cassidy, eighty-five and going strong. "*Suspect* was there and could have done everything necessary, but *suspicion* is a good mouth-filling word, a word to say rather than to write. Both words have notable short forms: I *'spect* and I *'spicion* so.

"In American English, to *suspicion* was once used 'even by genteel people,' as Madame Sarah Kemble Knight wrote in 1704. It is still in use throughout the country as a spoken word," Professor Cassidy says, "though it would be out of place in print or in formal speech. It has less prestige than *to suspect* but perhaps stronger emotional resonance. It holds on better in the linguistically more conservative South. That includes Arkansaw." (He likes to use the dialect spelling.)

In *The Adventures of Tom Sawyer,* Mark Twain used the noun-turned-verb: "Anybody would *suspicion* us that saw us." I suspicion that President Clinton's use of the term popped out of his native lingo.

The *plus some* at the end of his sentence, in lieu of the more familiar *and then some,* was probably influenced by modern advertising, which popularized *plus* as a big timesaver over *and what's more.*

Packagers

"Every program or proposal president Clinton makes is described as a *package,*" complains Richard L. Bacon of Potomac, Maryland. "We recently had a *stimulus package;* now we have a *tax package.* Waiting in the wings is Mrs. Clinton's *health care package* and a *Russian aid package.*"

True, every day is Christmas, packages piled under the tree. What's become of plans, proposals, strategies, bills, agendas? All wrapped up and bundled in a single vogue word: *package.* "The contents of a package are not the package itself," Mr. Bacon points out. "Don't we know the difference anymore between the wrapper and the contents?" That's arguable; the contents remain a package until separated. But it's hard to argue with "I don't recall F.D.R. sending a New Deal Package to Congress. Would today's journalists call his program a New Package, or better, a Package Deal?"

That phrase caused a mild furor when used by "Engine Charlie" Wilson in an Eisenhower Cabinet meeting. When conservatives resisted a negotiated peace in Korea because they feared it might lead to recognition of "Red China," Defense Secretary Wilson asked innocently, "Is there any possibility for a package deal?" Sherman Adams recalled later, "Eisenhower managed to control himself."

We might well give the overworked, neatly tied word a rest; a *set of proposals* might be worth a try. But that will not be easy with Laura D'Andrea Tyson, chairman of the Council of Economic Advisers, telling *Barron's,* "The *stimulus package* was just one part of a *multi-part package.*"

Paw

Don't beat up on headline writers; they may be more literate than you think. A recent headline in *The New York Times* read, "Dog Shows: None Dare Call Them Tranquil." A reader in La Jolla, California, circled the *none* as if it were a mistake.

Fortunately, the Poetic Allusion Watch is on the job. Here is a passage from Sir John Harington's collection *Epigrams* (published posthumously in 1618), which goes not only for dog shows but also for moles and coup plotters:

Treason doth never prosper; what's the reason?
For if it prosper, none dare call it treason.

Pencil Pushing

Tom Brokaw reports a new sense of the verb *to pencil,* as in "I'll have my banker pencil it." The new meaning differs from the traditional verb's "to draw or mark with a pencil," and should not be confused with *to pencil in,* "to schedule tentatively," as in "I'll pencil you in for a meeting with the secretary, but we'll see if he can't do better." It has nothing to do with the meaning of *pencil* as metonymy in media slang, "a member of the writing press," as in a press secretary's order, "Cameras up front, then net bigfeet, then pencils in back."

The new jargon verb *pencil,* without *in,* means "to work out the details" or "examine closely," quite different from the tentativeness of *to pencil in.* I'm speculating, but it is presumably rooted in the old phrase "to take a sharp pencil to it"—that is, to cross out extraneous expenditures in a budget.

It's good to see this word for an old but ergonomic hand-held word processor gaining new popularity. As *pencel,* it was used by Chaucer in *The Canterbury Tales* and derived from the Latin *penicillus,* "paintbrush," a diminutive of *penis* in its sense of "little tail."

Two days before I read your item on "Pencil Pushing" I attended a meeting at which one of our local casino types used pencil *in much the same way as reported to you by Tom Brokaw. Speaking about bringing big-name entertainers to the lake, he said that the basic cost for an outdoor concert was $150,000 and commented that without some advance guarantee of that amount, there was no point in "penciling it." At first, I thought he must have said "penciling it out," but I knew he hadn't.*

Thus, I was happy to read in your column that my ears hadn't betrayed me and that at Lake Tahoe we're not entirely out of the lexicographic loop. My guess is, however, that pencil *is just a short form of* pencil out, *which I believe I have heard used more than once to mean "work out the details (or a detailed estimate) informally" as you suggested.*

Jerome Evans
Zephyr Cove, Nevada

My mother was Oscar Hammerstein II's assistant for the last ten years of his life and I remember her talking about "having a pencil." When a Broadway-bound show was out of town in those days, most members of the production had to pay their own expenses. The exceptions were the producers and their staff, whose expenses were picked up as part of the production costs. Since Rodgers and Hammerstein produced their own shows (those guys knew a bottom line when they saw one), my mother's expenses were paid by R&H and thus she was one of the people in the show who "had a pencil."

John Steele Gordon
North Salem, New York

Pinchbeck

In an editorial encomium to the late actress Lillian Gish, *The New York Times* recalled one of her less memorable roles and commented, "The movie is *pinchbeck;* Gish's evocation of horror, pure gold."

That was the eponym of the month. Eponyms, as fans of Amelia Bloomer and Captain Boycott know, are words based on names. Christopher Pinchbeck, a London watchmaker, invented an alloy—five parts copper, one part zinc—that looked somewhat like gold, and was used in making cheap jewelry.

In 1734, two years after Pinchbeck died, the novelist Henry Fielding helped preserve his name in the comedic play *The Intriguing Chambermaid:* a character selling genuine gold watches is said to have complained "that the nobility and gentry run so much into *Pinchbeck,* that he had not dispos'd of two gold watches this month." By 1859, William Makepeace Thackeray, in his novel *The Virginians,* was using the term in derision: "Those golden locks were only *pinchbeck.*"

The meaning: "sham, bogus, counterfeit, ersatz." A word worthy of resuscitation.

All of my many dictionaries say that eponyms are names on which words are based, not *words based on names. Are my dictionaries wrong? Should I throw them out and buy new ones?*

Barbara Thorburn
Newton, Massachusetts

***Pinchbeck:** one further citation, from Meredith Wilson's* Music Man. *In the "Trouble" song, Professor Harold Hill (not to be confused with Professor Henry Higgins) speaks of River City youth playing pool for money while dressed up in a "pinchbeck suit," listening to some out-of-town jasper.*

Gary Muldoon
Rochester, New York

Your "Pinchbeck" comments brought back a flood of youthful memories. I recalled my father who only handled the finest of antique jewelery saying "Oh, it's only pinchbeck" when I admired a pair of long earrings shaped like ears of barley. Shamefacedly I said that I liked the earrings anyway, and much to my surprise, he gave them to me. Of course I didn't value them as I should as they were only pinchbeck.

Many years later, here in New York, the moving company packed up my belongings as I slowly made my way uptown. On arrival at the new apartment I discovered the unvalued earrings were gone! Of course I had been stupid to leave them in a drawer for Weissburgers(!) to move, but then they were only pinchbeck. After mourning their loss for some months I did see them again. On the ears of the elderly English actress Margaret Lockwood in a movie! I was thunderstruck. They were definitely my *earrings as one of the sides was slightly uneven due to a careless impact when my book fell on them. I considered getting in touch with the producers, but realized it was all pretty futile.*

I'm glad the earrings found their way home to London, and I hope whoever owns them now values them the way I should have, even though they are not gold . . . but only pinchbeck.

Thank you for bringing back a touch of my careless youth.

Janise Bogard
(Mrs. Howard Bogard)
New York, New York

Pinpricks

We have a new type of bombing.

Bombardiers of yore spoke of *saturation bombing,* which was followed by *carpet bombing,* the laying down of bombs as if laying a carpet. Because these attacks in a total war included nonmilitary targets, they came to be derogated in limited war.

We then had *precision bombing,* sometimes called *area bombing,* but soon given the metaphoric moniker *pinpoint bombing,* taken from a previous generation's *pinpoint accuracy.*

In 1989, a Reuters dispatch from Istanbul coined a new term: "Spates of leftist *'pinprick' bombings* have punctuated Turkish political life." A *pinprick* is a minor irritation, hardly noticeable.

When NATO planes dropped six bombs (two of them duds) on Serb forces attacking the Muslim town Gorazde, the meager nature of the allied response was immediately characterized as *pinprick bombing* by Zbigniew Brzezinski on *One on One* (John McLaughlin's television-interview program that has the title of a basketball defense). Dozens of other commentators promptly picked up the phrase.

Pinpoint is praiseworthy bombing, evoking admiration for a *surgical strike;* it now has an antonym, *pinprick bombing,* the hallmark of contempt for feckless response from the air.

You refer to "precision bombing, *sometimes called* area bombing. . . ." *In fact, as the enclosed London* Times *review of my monograph indicates, the two terms were opposites in British usage during World War II. Area bombing denoted the targeting of large urban areas, often entire cities. Saturation and carpet bombing target areas, but not necessarily urban areas; the British never used these terms.*

Harvey B. Tress
Albany, New York

Post Card

A pitch came in from the Third Millennium, an outfit describing itself as "the new *post-partisan* advocacy group." This on top of hearing myself described as a "post–cold-warrior," and seeing determinedly *au courant* critics reduced to tears after having been outdated by *post-post-modernism.*

Wherefore this posting with such dexterity? To David K. Barnhart, general editor of *The Barnhart Dictionary Companion,* who has compiled a list of recent *post* usages from *post–Anita Hill-stress-syndrome* to *post-yuppie:* "People attempt to place important events in recent history by adopting terms such as *post-Chernobyl, post-Watergate* and *post-Communism,*" Barnhart notes. "And the passing of a prominent person is exhibited in such terms as *post-Khomeini* and *post-Gorbachev.*"

Among terms recently leaving the post are *post-emergent herbicide, post-*

feminism, post-natal depression, post-punk, post-structuralism and (without a hyphen) *postvention,* which is what happens at the tail end of a convention.

One item listed caught my eye: *post-consumer.* Is consumerism dead already, before I had a chance to join a class action against some predatory producer? No; the earliest citation was from *Fortune* magazine in August 1989: "Markets for recycled plastic garbage—euphemistically called *'post-consumer'* plastics—generally are so modest that vast investments in recycling don't make economic sense."

So what does *post-consumer* mean? An item tossed away after a consumer is finished with it? An avid reader of *The Washington* or *New York Post*? Or—as in "this age of post-consumerism," by Sharon Stangenes in the *Chicago Tribune* last year—the era when consumers are so smart they reject the old consumers' movement?

Post is too much in vogue; it identifies a time only by what preceded it. If originality fails, and you cannot name the time or place you are in, take a leap with the prefix *pre.* Welcome to the pre-millennial era.

Presenting: OLBWS

"Another highly recognizable name in Washington retailing will soon be history," Kara Swisher wrote, with heavy heart, in *The Washington Post,* "when the owners of Peoples Drug Stores drop a name that has been around for almost 90 years."

"Peoples" is a warmly populist name, from the Latin *populus.* Mao Zedong recognized this when he named his regime the People's Republic of China, differentiating it from the plain Republic of China when Kuomintang leaders were driven to Taiwan. Lyndon Johnson once satirically spelled it out in a burst of oratory: "the people—*p-e-e-p-u-l.*" Abraham Lincoln drew on the phrase making of the Rev. Theodore Parker for his "of the people, by the people, for the people" in the Gettysburg Address. Further back, the framers of the United States Constitution led their document with "We, the people," a democratic phrase that drew a strenuous objection from Patrick Henry of Virginia, who preferred "We, the States."

Building on that great tradition for nearly a century, Peoples Drug Stores invested millions of ad dollars in the firm's name. Its 270 stores proudly proclaim the populist message. What terrific idea for a name could account for the scrapping of the familiar old "Peoples"?

Answer: CVS Stores. In case CVS does not instantly grab you, consider this: CVS is the name of the corporate parent, which already operates nine hundred drugstores in the Northeast under that name, and which bought the Peoples chain a few years ago. Its president, Thomas Ryan, fixed up the old stores and is obliterating the old name "to show more clearly who was behind these changes."

CVS does not stand for Columbia Voadcasting System, as many assume. The initials stand for "convenience, value, service," though these three words do not leap readily to mind when the initials appear. "Why isn't CVS referred to as Consumer Value Stores if that's the image the company wants to convey?" asks David Metcalf, an advertising copywriter for a Detroit bank. "If that's too long, why not choose a more presentable name? There seems to be a serious lack of form following function here."

Another question arises: Why change any familiar name to a set of unfamiliar initials? First National City Bank picks up a certain swiftness by shortening itself to Citibank, but does the Farmers and Merchants Bank attract new customers by becoming F&M? Mr. Metcalf writes copy for NBD, which used to take a whole two seconds to say as National Bank of Detroit.

Some initials are identifiable because the corporate names were famous; AT&T and IBM stand for words that people know. (MCI does not; it was Microwave Communications Inc.)

Some name-happy companies are moving in the opposite direction, from initials with forgotten antecedents to whole words: the Great Atlantic and Pacific Tea Company was able to identify itself as A&P, though when the chain wants to get away from its old image, it chooses the name of Super Fresh. (How soon S&F?) Similarly, "C&P Telephone is changing its name to Bell Atlantic" is the proclamation of an initialized entity that few remember was the Chesapeake and Potomac phone company; it's nice to have that communications company back in the world of words.

Another, more understandable trend in corporate nomenclature is the run-on name. TelePrompTer led the way a generation ago—hyphenless, with internal letters capitalized instead. (*The New York Times* generally lowercases internal capitals. Nobody pushes us around.) Others created a single word out of two: name-blends include Ameritech, Microsoft, Unisys. Which brings us to the MashreqBank.

"Notice of Name Change" is the direct, even catchy headline of a tombstone ad in *The New York Times,* "MashreqBank (Formerly Bank of Oman Limited)." What was the matter with the friendly neighborhood "Bank of Oman," which we used to run into before going shopping at Peoples Drug? Only this: "It is incorporated in the United Arab Emirates and not in Oman." Good reason! There is probably an equally good reason for it to be known as MashreqBank, or the Bank of Mashreq, rather than, say, as EmiratesBank, though the ad does not say.

Jed Rothwell of Cold Fusion Research Advocates in Chamblee, Georgia, has a theory for "a fad in which NamesAreRunTogetherLikeThis." He thinks it was started, or at least popularized by, Niklaus Wirth, a computer scientist and designer of programming languages. "When you tell a computer to add up your lunch bill with a 15 percent tip plus tax," Mr. Rothwell writes, "you write something like this: TOTAL = LUNCH + (LUNCH * .15) + TAX." But if you have both federal and state or local taxes, you would have to write FEDERAL TAX, which would confuse the computer because it could discern no operator (like + or – or * or /) between the words as two variables.

To lump the words together into a single variable, Wirth wrote it as FederalTax. "Many of us programmer types have been doing it that way ever since," says Mr. Rothwell, whose theory will be received with suspicion from scientists who greet cold fusion advocacy with angry shouts and great hoots. He adds, "We started calling our products FastFormatter and TaxTime; other people noticed and began imitating that style and, as they say, TheRestIsHistory."

It may be that computer programmers influenced capital infixation; the main influence is mergermania. Jamming names together without a hyphen, or even a virgule, seems an affectation; I see no advantage in styling this column "OnLanguageByWilliamSafire," or saving even more space with "OLBWS."

Spread out. Slow down. Use words in your names. Eschew faddish nomenclature; promote humanification. Maybe we can work out a compromise with CVS: ConValServe Drugs, the chain that is itself a division of Melville Corporation. Here's a thought for the Melville brass who bought CVS, and who are undoubtedly thinking about a voguish change to *Melvicorp* or *MelCo:* How about plain old "Peoples"?

Not that you asked, but just in case you're wondering, here's what Mashreq *means.*

Mashreq *is "Orient" in Arabic, so MashreqBank is Oriental Bank and Bank of Mashreq is Bank of Orient.*

To the Arabs, the Orient is not the Far East but the eastern Arab countries. The western Arab countries—Morocco, Algeria, and Tunisia—are known as Maghreb *("Occident"); Libya is usually—but not always—regarded as part of the* Maghreb.

Of course, both the United Arab Emirates and Oman are in the Mashreq*—in fact, they are the Arab world's easternmost countries.*

As a footnote, Mashreq *is closely related to* mizrah *(Hebrew for "east") and* Maghreb *to* ma'arav *(Hebrew for "west").*

Raphael Danziger
Editor
Near East Report
Washington, D.C.

At Lippincott & Margulies, our corporate identity professionals have lived through and participated in almost every type of naming challenge imaginable, and have developed corporate names in all of the categories you mentioned: "Initials" (RCA), "Jammed Together" (PacifiCorp), "Blends" (Amtrak), and some you didn't mention such as "Coined" (Humana) and "Bridge" (Harcourt General).

It has generally been our experience that, when legally feasible, a communicative name is often the best option. That's why "People's" does feel better than CVS. It may be that when initials are "acquired" after a long relationship (e.g., AT&T, RCA, IBM, 3M, etc.), they feel comfortable—a shorthand that springs from familiarity and perhaps even respect and affection. These "alphabet soup" icons are also capitalizing on the brevity and memorability that their shortened names provide.

On the other hand, brand-new initials with no apparent rationale or history are unfamiliar, impersonal and uncomfortable. Like a soldier's stripes, initials must be earned.

Kate Moran
Principal
Lippincott & Margulies Inc.
New York, New York

I wanted to respond ASAP to William Safire's column on CVS, so I'm sending this letter by fax rather than FedEx or U.S. Mail.

Why the objection to CVS? FYI. We operate stores from ME to DE. In CVS you can find VO5 shampoo; M&M's; GE light bulbs; Haley's MO; ept pregnancy test kits; K2r spot remover; STP gas treatment; vitamins A through E; and CVS brand products. In our Rx department, you can obtain prescriptions from a courteous, professional RPh. For our employees, CVS offers an ESOP and a 401(k).

I never imagined that changing the Peoples Drug name to CVS would attract the attention of a distinguished columnist. Certainly, this event isn't as newsworthy as the NATO maneuvers in the former USSR, the CIA scandal, or even the NCAA basketball tournament. But I guess any attention is OK as long as they get your name right.

F. J. McGrail
Dir., Corp. Comm.
CVS
Woonsocket, Rhode Island

A Prevent Defense

O.K., you health care–reform advocates, are you for *preventative* medicine or *preventive* medicine?

Cyril Mazansky, M.D., chairman of the strategic planning committee of Carney

Hospital in Boston, wants to know: "As we train our future primary care physicians to concentrate on *preventive* (*?preventative*) medicine, will they prescribe *preventive* drugs, and during their afternoon off, take their car into the dealer for *preventative* (*?preventive*) maintenance?"

Although a tad upfront with his question marks for my taste, Dr. Mazansky poses a question that embarrasses usagists, who are all over the lot on this one. When everything is correct, nobody's comfortable.

Here's my suggestion: Use *preventive* as an adjective and *preventative* as a noun. Thus, as you practice *preventive medicine* and give your car *preventive maintenance,* you take a flu shot in your arm—and slap a coat of wax on your car—as a *preventative.*

I know I'm being prescriptive, but it's better than being prescriptative.

To my ever-oversimplifying (simplisticizing?) mind, preventative *is a fatherless child, one large level in dignity and respectability below a bastard. Since there is no recognized verb* preventate, *there can be no recognized word* preventative, *whether as adjective or noun. A pound of cure is not kept idle on the shelf by an ounce of* preventation. Preventative *has no more legitimacy than* corrective, inventative, *or* reproductative *would have. It is a misinflation used only, present company excepted, by ignorant, pretentious people, who also say things like "irregardless" and "irrevelant" without thereby making them into real words. Back off! Take it back! Recant! Repent! Or, perhaps, Repentate!*

John Strother
Princeton, New Jersey

Whether you construe it as an adjective or a noun, there is no valid etymological basis for the word preventative, *even though the misbegotten little critter has been skulking about in lexicographic back alleys for many, many years; in the words of* Webster II, *the last dictionary with guts, it is "an irregularly formed doublet" of* preventive. *The point is that* preventive *makes a pair with* prevention *(from Latin* praeventio*); if the correct adjective was* preventative, *there would be a noun* preventation *(which there ain't).*

There's more to it than that, however. Latin verbs of the second, third and fourth conjugations have infinitives ending respectively in -ēre, -ere -īre, *and they accordingly cannot produce derivatives with suffixes containing an* a. *On the other hand, first-conjugation verbs have an infinitive ending in* -āre, *and their derivatives do contain an* a. *Thus,* admonēre *(2nd)* > admonition *and* admonitory; prohibēre *(2nd)* > prohibition *and* prohibitive; praescrībere *(3rd)* > prescription *and* prescriptive; prodūcere *(3rd)* > production *and* productive; praevenīre *(4th)* >

prevention *and* preventive; audīre *(4th)* > audition *and* auditory. *By contrast,* declarāre *(1st)* > declaration *and* declarative; consultāre *(1st)* > consultation *and* consultative.

Louis Jay Herman
New York, New York

The Process Process

We never heard the long hoo-ha threatening an invasion of Haiti described as a *war process.* Why not? Certainly every other procedure and proceeding—all from the Latin *procedere,* "to go forward"—in today's diplomacy has been so expressed. *Negotiation* is out; *process* is in.

We have, of course, the *peace process,* an alliterative outgrowth of the 1789 *peace talk* that's now applied mainly to the Middle East. In Peter Rodman's behind-the-scenes history of the cold war, *More Precious Than Peace,* we have a reference to *the negotiating process* in Angola, as if this longtime Kissinger aide does not want to overdo the phrase made famous by his former boss in 1974. According to another of Henry's helpers, Harold Saunders, the shorthand expression *peace process* was chosen then because it "encompasses a full range of political, psychological, economic, diplomatic and military actions woven together into a comprehensive effort to establish peace between Israel and its neighbors."

The pull of *process* is powerful in other disciplines as well. The literary scholar Helen Vendler, commenting on Shakespeare in a recent report to the American Academy of Arts and Sciences, observed, "I *processed* the sonnets differently from most other people." (Most of us read those sonnets along a "static axis of similarity," but she hangs them together "along a dynamic curve of inner emotional evolution," which I suppose in the sessions of sweet silent thought beats comparison to a summer's day.)

In context, her use of the verb *to process* suggests the meaning of putting the information through a mental process, or "to work it out in your head." In this sense of putting something through a kind of grinder or mixer, it is also possible to *process* meat and cheese. In *processed cheese,* the food is heated and blended, often with other cheeses and flavorings; in the usage process, the *-ed* was clipped, and we now have *process cheese.*

Copywriters for bank advertising are part of the process process: "Our investment consultants simplify the often mystifying process of allocating your assets," says Chemical Bank's demystifiers, while Nation's Bank, styling itself

NationsBank, advertises classes to "help you understand the approval process." ("How do you do, I'm a fishy-eyed approval processor.")

The noun has a grand history. "Without *process* of law" (leading to *due process*) made its debut in a political song before 1325, and Shakespearean analysts have long processed how in *Hamlet* Polonius tells King Claudius, "Behind the arras I'll convey myself/To hear the process."

A later verb sense of "to treat or handle by procedure" led to the modern sense of developing pictures as *film processing.* Art that concerns itself with acts—like spreading a floor with sawdust to be disturbed by the viewer's feet—was called *process art* in the 60's. In the same sort of way, a computer's ability to examine or analyze what passes through was called in 1970 *processing data.*

If it's such a hot word, why do we have such trouble with its pronunciation? More Americans say "PRAH-sess" than "PROH-sess"; the Brits prefer the latter, which is more logical, considering the spelling. The plural gives some people a tough time: It should be "PRAH-sess-iz," but there is a determined young bunch that mistakenly sees an analogy with the plurals of *basis* and *thesis*—"BAY-seez" and "THEE-seez"—and afflicts *processes* on us as "PRAH-sess-eez." It's an affectation, like pronouncing "controvershul" "con-tro-VER-si-ul." Stick with "PRAH-sess-iz."

Those who expect a snapper of an ending to this item using *word processor* will be let down: I did it with a quill pen.

As part of Vice President Gore's effort to reinvent government, the U.S. Customs Service has heartily embraced Total Quality Management and its accompanying ritual and jargon.

At a meeting in Washington a couple of weeks ago, we were introduced to personnel, each of whom was assigned a particular task in order to help reorganize Customs.

Each individual was designated a "process owner."

M. Sigmund Shapiro
Baltimore, Maryland

Pun Jab

"Miss Bhutto has Punjab in her grasp, but Sind remains a problem." So goes a line farther back in *The Economist,* which I am reading because it has a new editor and is going through a news-magazine identity crisis, much as *Time* is doing here. (If it gets out of control, chaps, see Dr. Ehlers.)

Sind is the home province of Benazir Bhutto, who recently regained power in Pakistan. Though married and a mother, she is known by her maiden name, as befits the daughter of a slain Prime Minister, which is why *The Economist* calls her "Miss" Bhutto. *The New York Times* uses "Ms." Bhutto; at least it doesn't assert that she is single.

It's good to see Sind back in the news because it recalls the play on words that so delighted diplomats and linguists of a previous century.

Sir Charles James Napier was the British general sent to quell agitation in India in the early 1840's, and in 1843—some say without imperial orders—moved to take the province of Sind, now part of Pakistan. Nervous diplomats in Westminster awaited the results of the battle of Hyderabad, key to the province. Then came the telegraphed message from Napier: the single Latin word *peccavi.* The Foreign Office broke into cheers because a knowledge of Latin was the mark of a good education in those days, and because Catholic rites used that word from the penitent seeking absolution from the confessor. *Peccavi* means "I have sinned."

Napier's message meant, of course, that he had taken the province of Sind. The historical scholar Mark Burnyeat of New York suggested that the general was sending yet another message: Because he proceeded on his own initiative, risking overextension of his logistical lines, Napier was both boasting of his victory and mock-apologizing for going beyond his orders with "I have sinned."

You don't get generals using multilingual puns in their messages like that these days.

I was delighted to read your account in The New York Times Magazine *of Sir Charles Napier's conquest of Sind. Since my roots are in Sind, I was impressed by your erudite recapitulation of a climactic event in 19th century Sind.*

Benazir Bhutto
Prime Minister
Islamic Republic of Pakistan
(1993–1996)

RE: General Napier's famous message, "Peccavi."

But he didn't telegraph it at all, and certainly not from the back of beyond to the center of the world in 1843. Samuel F. B. Morse only telegraphed his *famous message, "What hath God wrought?" from Washington to Baltimore on May 12, 1844.*

John Steele Gordon
North Salem, New York

You conclude the section "Pun Jab" (clever enough) with the assertion: "You don't get generals using multilingual puns in their messages like that these days." However, at least one American general is well skilled at the use of multilingual puns in his own diplomatic practice.

I have in mind General Vernon Walters (USA, Ret.), a distinguished soldier, diplomat and linguist. While on a visit to Cuba as a special envoy of the U.S. President (I believe during the administration with which you were associated), the revolutionary leader remarked that the two men were both members of the Roman Catholic Church. To this the general responded in Spanish: "Yes, but I have remained Fidel*!"*

James W. Davis, Jr.
President's Fellow
Institute of War and Peace Studies
Columbia University
New York, New York

Apropos of the "Peccavi" quotation of Sir Charles Napier, I have enclosed another wonderful pun—this one dating from the fall of Lucknow during the Indian Mutiny—which I hope will amuse you. It's from Christopher Hibbert's The Great Mutiny, India, 1857:

"On entering Lucknow one of Sir Colin Campbell's aides-de-camp—in imitation of Sir Charles Napier's message 'Peccavi' 'I have sinned'), announcing the annexation of the province of Sind—issued in his master's name the proclamation, 'Nunc fortunatus sum' *('I am in luck now'). But although Lucknow was certainly in British hands again, the rebellion was far from being suppressed."*

Linda Wheeler
Stanford, California

Purportedly

"Because the [Weinberger] notes were withheld from investigators for years," went the response of the independent counsel, Lawrence Walsh, to the Bush pardons, ". . . key witnesses had *purportedly* forgotten what was said and done."

Purport is a useful word for a prosecutor. The verb is rooted in the Latin for "to carry an argument forward," and has come to mean "profess." But in the adjectival and adverbial forms, *purported* and *purportedly* mean "supposed" and "supposedly"—seeming to be so, but not necessarily. As time goes by, a more larcenous connotation is being added to *purported,* as actions are revealed to be not what they *purport* to be.

Qualifiers

Note the way congressional hearings have focused attention on qualifiers, those weaseling words that provide the speaker with a way out.

"At this point," the presidential press secretary, Dee Dee Myers, told reporters circling the Treasury Department like vultures, "the President has full confidence in his team." She later realized that her qualifying phrase, *at this point,* was taken as a broad hint (much as "no *present* plans" means "soon we'll tell you the plans"). She then said: "I should not qualify it. The President has full confidence."

A poignant example of unacceptable qualifying was set forth in the questioning of Joshua Steiner, the Treasury aide whose subpoenaed diary—written in the expectation of privacy—was a source of embarrassment for the Clinton White House.

When a Democratic Senator, Paul Sarbanes, asked if he had any conversations about a disagreement between Treasury officials over who had initiated a controversial White House briefing, Mr. Steiner replied, "I don't believe I've had any specific conversations."

"Strike the word *specific,*" Senator Sarbanes said to the witness.

"I can't recall any conversations directly—" Mr. Steiner began again.

"Strike the word *directly,*" said the Senator, again going for the qualifier urged on witnesses by legal counsel.

"Senator," said the disqualifiered witness, flushed out at last, "I have heard conversations. . . ."

What is a springtime without sunshine? What is testimony without qualifiers?

Ragtag Modalities

Before President Clinton put military muscle behind his negotiations in Haiti, his attempted intimidations, exhortations and dire warnings aimed at the local junta were summed up as *huffing and puffing.*

"Heralded by the *huffing and puffing* of a spin doctorate gone wild" were the words of one hawkish polemicist in *The New York Times,* while *The Washington*

Post headline over a Mary McGrory column was "*Huffing and Puffing* Over Haiti."

Puff is the older word, from Old English *pyffan,* of imitative origin, meaning "to blow in short gusts" or, metaphorically, "to inflate; make proud or conceited." Richard Brinsley Sheridan, in a 1779 play, wrote of "a practitioner in panegyric, or, to speak more plainly, a professor of the art of puffing." From the *powder puff,* a soft and fluffy pad for dispensing talc and other cosmetics, came the *puff piece,* or "adoring article."

In the scruffy 60's, "Puff (the Magic Dragon)" was a children's song popularized by Peter, Paul and Mary with what some suspected to be a subtext of smoking dope.

Huff—"to bluster, to emit puffs of breath in anger"—gained a meaning in 1599 of "a short spell of anger," as in "to leave in a *huff.*" In this century, it was automicized as "a six-cylindered Huff."

The two verbs were combined in the nursery tale of "The Three Little Pigs," as the wolf warned, "I'll *huff* and I'll *puff* and I'll blow your house in." (Other versions use "blow your house *down,*" but the 1933 Disney movie version helped immortalize "blow your house *in*" as a rhyme for each pig's refusal to give entry: "Not by the hair of my chinny-chin-chin!") Thus the combination of *huff* and *puff* came to mean "bombastic threats" to be derided.

Another old word leaped into vogue during the huff-puff period: "The American military will make quick work of Haiti's *ragtag* army," Jim Hoagland wrote in *The Washington Post. The Economist* agreed: "America's 20,000 troops . . . can make short work of the *raggle-taggle* Haitian forces on shore."

The expression began as *tag and rag* in the sixteenth century; the rags conjured an image of *motley,* a woolen fabric of mixed colors worn by jesters; hence, *ragtag* became "a motley, or variegated, crowd of misfits." By the 1820's, it evolved in the world of politics as *ragtag and bobtail,* an aristocrat's contemptuous term for "rabble." As a rhyming modifier, *ragtag* is being used outside of Haiti discussions. Asked on *60 Minutes* about his inner-city childhood, Kweisi Mfume, the Maryland Representative who is chairman of the Congressional Black Caucus, said, "I was a *ragtag* kid in the streets."

A snippet of bureaucratese also made its way to the forefront. Asked whether high-level emissaries were on their way to the junta, Dee Dee Myers, the White House press secretary, noted that "the time has long passed for negotiations" but added, "If the dictators were willing to leave, we'd be willing to discuss the specific *modalities* of their departure."

Ms Myers is not the sort to dip naturally into diplolingo; that word, a favorite of the Kissinger era, was drilled into her by a foreign-policy wonk. *Modalities* means "means," as opposed to ends; structure, not substance; the trappings rather than the essence. It is often a sneer word, akin to "technical details," unless you are in charge of the communications or security of a negotiation.

"The last time *modalities* was on center stage," comments the lexicographer

Anne Soukhanov, "was during the 1970's when the Vietnam War peace talks were going on." She traces the diplomatic sense of *modalities* back to 1957 and points out that its use in negotiating is almost invariably as a plural. "If usage of *modalities* transcends diplomacy and seeps into the general parlance, it, like *methodology,* may become an abusage issue," Ms Soukhanov adds.

"Clinton, Advisers Consider 'Endgame' Plans on Haiti," read a *Washington Post* headline, based on an unattributed quote from an official talking about "endgame planning." *End game* began more than a century ago as a chess term, like the older *gambit* ("opening gambit" is redundant, as is "final endgame"). By 1964, the novelist Vladimir Nabokov was using it as a single word: "We'll simply take the endgame position at the point it was interrupted today." In diplolingo, *endgame* is usually followed by *exit strategy,* first used in business in the late 1970's.

Foreign-policy crises can often produce new diplolingo. Just as the Cuban missile crisis in 1962 produced *hawks and doves,* an early American metaphor recoined by the columnists Charles Bartlett and Stewart Alsop, and *eyeball to eyeball,* a popularization of an Army phrase by Secretary of State Dean Rusk, the Haitian occupation produced the noun *de factos,* used repeatedly by Secretary of State Warren Christopher. In a White House briefing he referred to "factors that conjoined to convince the *de factos* that the time had come for them definitely to go" and "it became apparent to the *de factos* that they were going to be taken out in other ways."

This was taken from the Latin words for "in fact," often contrasted to *de jure,* "in law." The two Latin phrases became familiar to most Americans in the 60's to describe forms of segregation in education, when *de jure* segregation was struck down while *de facto* segregation was still tolerated, not deliberately caused by public policy. *De jure* can be used pejoratively, to mean "in name only": A slashing vituperator in Washington often titled Janet Reno "Attorney General *de jure,*" suggesting that her then-deputy, Friend of Bill Webster Hubbell, was Attorney General *de facto.*

In the Haitian case, Secretary Christopher, after a thousand mentions of the Raoul Cédras junta as "the *de facto* government," began shorthanding his reference by calling the generals "the *de factos.*" (If you don't think *shorthand* can be used as a verb, *longhand* me a postcard.) The columnist Richard Cohen doesn't think the coinage will last: "Sounds too much like 'mobster Joey DiFacto and his gang.' "

In the eyeball-to-eyeball moments of the crisis, a curious usage began to be heard around Foggy Bottom: "We're on *spilkes* here." This was a mispronunciation of the Yiddish term *shpilkes,* "pins," metaphorically extended to the American dialect term "pins and needles"—the prickly feeling accompanying nervous apprehension—similar to the stretched-out, vulnerable feeling of being "on tenterhooks."

"End game *began more than a century ago as a chess term, like the older* gambit *('opening gambit' is redundant, as is 'final endgame')."*

Nyet! *A* gambit *is a variety of opening in which a man (usually a pawn, rarely a piece) is sacrificed (sometimes only temporarily) early on so as to obtain a positional or tactical advantage. Openings without this sacrificial motif are* not *gambits, so "opening gambit" is not redundant, at least when referring to chess. "Final endgame" is indeed redundant. (That's a basic fundamental.)*

Franklyn J. Davenport
Bellevue, Washington

"Opening gambit" is not redundant, may a chess player inform you. "Gambit" simply means the offer of material (usually a pawn) for a long-term advantage. This often happens in an opening, but can happen in the middle game or the endgame. "Gambit" is often misused just to mean maneuver or tactic: The essence should be that something is offered. ("Final endgame" is redundant.)

Another chess misuse may interest you. "Stalemate" is often used to describe something that goes on and on and is boring. In chess, it means something sudden and exciting: No legal move is possible and the game ends in a draw. This is often a triumph for a player who would otherwise lose.

The French for a stalemate, incidentally, is "un pat," *which is expressive. The post-revolutionary French, incidentally again, call the piece that is a "bishop" in English a* "fou," *or clown.*

Ken Mackenzie
Paris, France

REGO **Is a MEGO**

REGO—a word formed from the first syllables of "reinventing government," the title of a 1992 book by David Osborne and Ted Gaebler—burst on the national scene recently, propelled by a photo of the President and Vice President denouncing government waste and standing in front of forklift trucks holding obfuscatory regulations.

"From Red Tape to Results" was the selling line above the report of the National Performance Review, signed by Vice President Al Gore. *Red tape* was popularized by Thomas Carlyle in 1850, describing himself as "little other than a redtape Talking-machine, and unhappy Bag of Parliamentary Eloquence." A decade earlier, Washington Irving had derided a politician with "His brain was little better than red tape and parchment"; both references were to the red ribbon used to bind official documents and court briefs.

(*Results,* from the Latin for "to leap back," entered English in 1432, filling the need for a word to express the effects of an action.)

The REGO report (not to be confused with MEGO, an acronym for "my eyes glaze over") was written and edited by gnomes determined to reinvent grammar and usage.

In the reinvention of spelling, we have *should* spelled *shoud;* there is a case for dropping the *l* if you believe in simplified spelling, but the word would then be better spelled *shood.* Mr. Gore, in his transmittal letter, hailed government workers with "This report benefitted greatly from their involvement"; in old-style, unreinvented spelling, that would be *benefited.* He quotes himself as saying that these dedicated bureaucrats "cannot be treated like automatons or children bound up in straightjackets." Dedicated child-binders usually spell that *straitjacket;* the jacket is not *straight,* meaning "free of curves" or "following strictly" or "without exceptions," as in "The gay man voted a straight ticket," but *strait,* meaning "narrow" and "confining," as in the poet's "It matters not how strait the gate."

I will give a pass to "Reeingeering Through Information Technology" in the appendix, because that word is spelled *reengineering* in the main body of the report, and typos are to be expected in a document written without the help of spelling checkers or other information technology. However, I would put a hyphen between the double vowels as an aid to pronunciation: *re-engineering.*

In the reinvented language, modifiers are placed by whim. In "the intensive, six-month study of the federal government that you requested," it was the study, not the "federal government," that was requested; that phrase would have benefited (one *t*) from recasting (no hyphen). Also, the *United States Government Printing Office Style Manual* calls for capitalizing *Federal Government* and writing out numbers from one to nine, then using numerals, except for units of time; thus, *6-month* is right, but the report's "savings in four years" is inconsistent.

Mr. Gore is of two minds about capitalizing *federal:* "Make it a felony," he urges, "to knowingly lie on an application for benefits under the federal Employees' Compensation Act and amend Federal law." Pick one and stick to it, Al, especially in the same sentence (and all lies are knowing, though not all untruths are). He's inconsistent about capitalizing *Congressional* in "Congressional appropriations" and "congressional budgets" (I say keep it lowercase in general references, and this strange style manual agrees with me), and he spells his own regime both up and down: Better to stick with the Clinton *Administration.*

REGOspeak features an odd choice of words. *Most importantly* doesn't really need that *ly. Increasingly tiny* sounds funny. "Consistency of agency actions—with each other and with the President's program" suggests more than two, calling for *one another,* not *each other.* A sentence that reads, in its entirety, "The time is ripe" sort of sits there, getting rotten, calling out for an extension of the cliché to "The time is ripe for (whatever)." And when recommending a biennial budget, to be issued "each even-numbered year," note that the year in between is not one of the "off years," as the report states, but an "odd-numbered year." The President may be having an off year, but a biennium does not.

A favorite REGOspeak word emerges: "Hamstrung by rules and regulations. . . ." "Fifth, we will eliminate thousands of other regulations that hamstring federal employees." "O.M.B. will simplify the apportionment process, which hamstrings agencies." What is this collection of pieces of hamstring? The word begins with *ham,* the thigh of an animal's hind leg, or the back of the thigh of the human leg; the *hamstrings* are the tendons behind the knee, attached to the ham. When the hamstrings are cut or damaged, the person is crippled, handicapped, impaired, challenged or differently abled; the metaphor is extended to the verb *to hamstring,* to frustrate, cripple or curtail.

Beware noun cluster bombs: In this report, *comprehensive health and welfare reform task forces* abound, and *its 13 fiscal year 1995 appropriations bills* lurk.

And when is the new Administration (cap *A*) going to adopt a comma policy? *Over the next five years* is followed by a comma, but *Within 18 months* is not. And then we have "In addition to savings from the agencies and savings in personnel we expect that. . . ." A comma is desperately needed after *personnel.*

The report could save space, time and—in my projection, assuming no change in interest rates—twelve billion commas during the biennium's next off year by simply doing away with the serial comma, which is the comma in a series before a conjunction. The time is ripe for a comma cap. By taking REGOspeak's *fraud, waste, and abuse*—with its unnecessary comma after the second word—and reforming it to *fraud, waste and abuse,* we could release a huge pile of commas for shipment to hamstrung grammars abroad. (That phrase is more widely expressed now as *waste, fraud and abuse.*)

Al Gore takes these criticisms in good humor; when he asked what I thought of his reforms and I replied that a linguistic analysis would be forthcoming, he gave a little moan.

We were wolfing down the great spread that NBC provides guests and panelists after *Meet the Press,* and I tried out the brain teaser that had cost me a quarter: For twenty-five cents, in sixty seconds—name the six living former Vice Presidents. (This quiz has nothing to do with language, but I have a couple of graphs to fill.)

David Broder, Robert Novak, Tim Russert and Al Gore came up with five: Quayle, Mondale, Ford, Agnew and Nixon. They forgot about Bush, but I couldn't crow: The day before, I lost the bet by forgetting Vice President Nixon.

"The president may be having an off year, but a biennium does not." This sentence was grating to read silently as well as aloud. Are you not transgressing even slightly along lines of parallel structure? Thus, does not the "may be having" re-

quire "is not [having an off year" being understood]" at the end of the sentence? Or, did you mean to write "Presidents may have an off year, but bienniums [biennia?] cannot."

S. Robert Lehr
San Francisco, California

Saving those billions of commas can lead to confusion, no?

- *The (four?) table markers were for Oedipus's daughter, son, mother and wife.*
- *The (three?) table markers were for Oedipus's son, Oedipus's daughter, Oedipus's mother and wife.*
- *Who remembers Tom and Jerry, Chaplin, Laurel and Hardy?*
- *Remind me to pay the rent to my landlord, Aunt Mabel and Uncle Joe.*
- *Here comes Hillary, Bill, the Vice President and Speaker of the House.*

Warren Allen Smith Jr.
New York, New York

I see that your adulteries committed with the linguistic zeitgeist have finally ended in a divorce from clarity. I was alarmed when you gave up on "hopefully" and predicate nominatives (and what else, final prepositions, split infinitives?). But I cannot sit idly by and allow the serial comma to be abandoned.

I submit to you that there is a difference between these two series:

W. C. Fields, Laurel and Hardy

and

W. C. Fields, Laurel, and Hardy.

And between these two:

pears, apples and oranges

and

pears, apples, and oranges.

When two terms that form a single common phrase are included in a longer series, it is important to indicate whether the phrase itself or each term of the phrase is being serialized. With the surrender of the serial comma, this subtle difference in meaning will be lost. I hope that you can live with yourself.

William M. Klimon
Phoenix, Maryland

Commas separate; conjunctions bind, I wrote you once. Omission of the serial comma often impedes comprehension. I cited a sentence written by Leslie Gelb: "Banana-republichood is attained when political, business and community leaders do things. . . ." Not much of a slowdown there, I wrote, but some. In another Times *news item, around the same time, I read: "In a Europe of returning demons of racism, ultranationalism and ethnic violence, this depressing. . . ." I see the comma after racism and, naturally I think, pause, expecting a verb after "violence." Then I see I should go on.*

As a longtime editor at major book publishers in New York, I know that the serial comma is the style for textbooks at McGraw-Hill, HarperCollins, and Macmillan. Editors at these and other book publishers favor the serial comma because it enhances reading comprehension. The Chicago Manual of Style *favors it. Please reconsider your stand. Your suggestion to "release a huge pile of [serial] commas" may contribute to hamstringing comprehension.*

Milton Horowitz
Jackson Heights, New York

Return of the Mondegreens

"To my horror and embarrassment," writes Yisroel Epstein of New York, "I was informed recently—and in public—that the phrase I had always thought was *for all intensive purposes* was, in fact, *for all intents and purposes.* After the revelation, of course, the phrase began to make some sense."

In an account of a football game between Cornell and Penn, Jack Cavanaugh wrote in *The New York Times,* "And it was altogether fitting that today's game ended, to all extents and purposes, with a dramatic defensive effort." James Weidner of Merchantville, New Jersey, clipped this usage and sent it in with the comment: "Granted, *extents* could conceivably fit the context of the article, but just what is the usual expression after all?"

The expression is *to* (sometimes *for*) *all intents and purposes.* This mondegreen was spoofed on the literate NBC sitcom (or litcom) *The John Larroquette Show.* One character uses the phrase correctly and is "corrected" by another, who claims the phrase is *for all intensive purposes;* a third authority then makes swimming motions and argues it is *for all intensive porpoises.*

The humor columnist Dave Barry, making sport of word mavenhood, began a column with "It's Mister Language Person, for all intense and purposes." Evidently this solecism is widespread enough to rate delighted satiric treatment in many media; it is my job, as a straight-ahead language person, to trace its true etymology before exploring the cause of its confusion.

Off with its head: It was Henry VIII, in an act promulgated in 1546, who included the prepositional phrase "to all intents, constructions and purposes." After Members of Parliament made it their own, Joseph Addison shortened it in a 1709 edition of *The Tatler:* "Whoever resides in the World without having any Business in it . . . is to me a Dead Man to all Intents and Purposes."

As in much archaic legalese, the synonyms were married in a phrase to cover all shadings of an aim to accomplish, much as "null and void" and "devise and bequeath" gave lawyers a comfortable feeling of nailing down a meaning. (O.K.; ancient attorneys will hold that you devise real estate and you bequeath other items; sue me.) In today's synonymy, *intent* is more specific, as in "legislative intent," while *purpose* is general, like "purpose in life."

In his *Dictionary of Modern Legal Usage,* Bryan Garner derides terms like *to all intents and purposes* and *at all relevant times* as often being "flotsam phrases." (Some say *flotsam* is what floats and *jetsam* is what sinks. Most authorities hold, however, that *flotsam* is wreckage of a ship or its cargo that floats on the surface of the water, and *jetsam* is what is jettisoned or tossed overboard. Someday, somebody will ask you that and you will be ready.) I disagree; the intent of *to all intents and purposes* is to denote practicality, as if to say "when it comes right down to it."

To come right down to it, then, why do some people say "to all intensive purposes"?

It's the Mondegreen Factor. A mondegreen is a word that is construed as it is actually heard, not as the speaker intends it to be heard. It was noted in this space long ago that the most saluted man in America was Richard Stans: Allegiance is pledged every day by millions of kids "to the republic for Richard Stans." Some begin the pledge with "I led the pigeons to the flag." Remember that phrase in "The Star-Spangled Banner" about "grapefruit through the night"? And the ever-good Mrs. Murphy of the Twenty-third Psalm? "Shirley, good Mrs. Murphy, shall follow me all the days of my life."

Although some linguists have called this stumblepunning "unwitting paronomasia," the better word is *mondegreen.* Coiner is the writer Sylvia Wright, who noted in a 1954 *Harper's* article that some children happily sang in church of "Gladly, the cross-eyed bear," when the hymn was "Gladly the cross I'd bear." She remembered the Scottish ballad "The Bonny Earl of Murray" and how she had recited it as a child: "They hae slain the Earl Amurray,/And Lady Mondegreen." The damsel bleeding loyally beside the slain Earl was in her romantic imagination, of course; the last line was written *and laid him on the green.*

In a 1987 essay in *Time* magazine, Gregory Jaynes found a way of surviving the stress of New York City: He recalled a pastor's asking him in his youth to "rise and sing Hymn No. 508, 'Lead On, O Kinky Turtle.' " Later, he found it intended as "Lead On, O King Eternal," but "in the days since, the phrase *lead on, o kinky turtle* has assumed a profound significance in the course of my wanderings. I use it in a kind of incantatory fashion, muttering 'lead on, o kinky turtle' whenever I feel shorted, stiffed, put upon by outside forces."

There are those who claim the word *intensive* to be wholly unnecessary, since it means the same as *intense.* But if it leads to mondegreens like "all intensive purposes," I say leave it in.

With regard to my Sunday School experience while growing up in the New York area, the name of God was no mystery to a little girl in our class. His name was Harold.

Doesn't it say, after all, in the second line of the Lord's Prayer, "Harold be thy name"?

Lee Chadeayne
Acton, Massachusetts

Lately I have also heard another irritating mondegreen.

I have often been hesitant to correct my colleagues for fear of sounding too pedantic. But last night I heard it in the movie The Pelican Brief, *and I knew that it had entered the popular culture.*

In the movie the reporter asks the law student how she was able to "hone in on" the key to the mystery. Now, homing pigeons "home in on" their coops, and guided missiles "home in on" their targets, but one hones a knife in sharpening it.

With the usage in the film it may be too late and speakers of English may have as difficult a time using home *and* hone *correctly as they have in distinguishing between duct tape and duck tape.*

James P. Pfiffner
Fairfax, Virginia

Back in the Depression era when I was a teenager I was pressed into service suddenly to take over a Sunday School class when the regular instructor was ill. Rather than try to conduct a formal class, I had the children pass the time by writing *some well-known, memorized prayers.*

In the Lord's Prayer one youngster wrote "Our Father, who art in Heaven, Harold *be thy name." Another, who chose the "Ave Maria," wrote "Hail Mary, full of grace, the Lord is with Thee! Blessed art thou* a monk swimmin' "

But the one I recall with fondness was a poem that my aunt would recite every time she came to visit:

I have no mother, for she died
When I was very young.

But still her memory 'round my heart
Like morning mist has clung.

Early on I had memorized the last line as "Good morning, Mrs. Klung." Even the Bonny Earl of Murray might have liked that!

James M. Connolly
New York, New York

Your recent column on "mondegreens" reminded me of a tour we were on years ago for the New York Shakespeare Festival. My husband and I were playing in Macbeth *and we took along on that tour our three small children, aged two, three and four years.*

One day, after a matinee performance, I overheard our kids playing the three witches in the opening scene of the play. In their high, young voices and with full seriousness and conviction, they shrilled, "Bubble, bubble, toilet trouble."

Genie Zust
Richmond, Massachusetts

In regard to the Mondegreen Factor: I teach ESOL (English for Speakers of Other Languages). The perpetual challenge is to teach students to understand and then to speak the language they hear—not the language they see.

My Latin students enjoy learning the patriotic song beginning, "José, can you? Sí!" Non-Christians prefer practicing Christmas music with alternative (thus easier) lines, particularly the description of the gentle old monk in the nativity scene, "Round John Virgin."

Sue Sandeen
Gainesville, Florida

My oldest brother long ago came home from kindergarten in Minetto, N.Y. (five miles south of Oswego), and sang a song he had learned: "Minetto Union School, forever mishymoo." He insisted on that, and not until the first PTA meeting did my parents learn the disappointing truth: "Minetto Union School, forever may she rule."

For years I thought there existed in the English language the noble word "forespacious." "Oh, beautiful! Forespacious skies!" As I recall, it meant something like bodaciously spacious.

Of course it's not just children who do mondegreens (or mishymoos, my preference). In college writing classes we come across things like windshield factors of minus 30, people who live next store to the church, and men who put the woman they adore on a pedalstool.

Robert E. McCarty, S.J.
Associate Professor of Inlishlit
Saint Peter's College
Jersey City, New Jersey

Many years ago my niece, then in her early twenties, was writing a letter. She turned to me and asked, "How do you spell 'unsundry'?" Seeing my puzzled look, she added, "You know, 'various unsundry things'."

Since then, we have found the phrase perfectly suited to imply darksome doings, as in "I think they are plotting various unsundry things."

Joan D. Ensor
West Redding, Connecticut

Your mention of the ballad "The Bonnie Earl of Murray" rang a few bells. This ballad refers to an actual historical incident.

As you may recall, the marriage of Mary Stuart to her third husband, the Earl of Bothwell, produced so great an uproar that Mary abdicated and later fled to England (1567–58). Her natural half-brother, James Stuart, Earl of Moray (originally so spelled), became Regent of Scotland for the infant King James VI. His stern, able rule soon made many powerful enemies.

On February 23, 1570, as Moray and his retinue were passing through the little town of Bothwellhough, between Stirling and Edinburgh, he was shot and killed from ambush. The assassin, speedily apprehended, proved to be one James Hamilton. On being "put to the question," he readily implicated his clan chief, John Hamilton, the Earl of Arran, who promptly took refuge in England.

Moray's death plunged Scotland into chaos, so much so that on two occasions (1582, 1600), James VI was actually kidnapped by the Earl of Gowrie of the powerful Ruthven clan! Well might the balladeer lament,

Ye Highlands and ye Lowlands,
O where hae ya been?
They hae slain the Earl O'Murray
And hae laid him on the green!

Lewis B. Shrady
Irvington, New York

Lead us not into Penn Station.
Open, sez me!

Alice Squires
Hampton Bays, New York

You discuss archaic legalese with an explanation that does not include the impact of the Norman Conquest of England on the native language.

When French became the official language of England, the courts were conducted in French, written and spoken. At the start of the 15th century, when English once again became the official language, the legal profession was fortuitously left with two words for everything—one French and one English—so they used them both: for example. "intents" and "purposes." Rather than cover all shadings of meaning as you state, the French and English synonyms are the same meaning. There is really no difference between "null" and "void."

Some others that come to mind are "last will and testament," "rules and regulations," "lawful and legal," "give and devise," "rest, residue and remainder." There are more.

Betty S. Bergen
Cranford, New Jersey

My sister says she was about 30 before she realized that the Andrews sisters were not *singing to: My Dear Mr. Shane. Another child of the 50's recalls that lovely song from* Gigi, *"Laugh and turn blue, dilly dilly, laugh and turn green."*

Nancy Senter
Los Angeles, California

Right Away

"My wife asked me to do something or other yesterday," writes E. J. Kahn Jr. of *The New Yorker,* "and when I replied 'Right away' she was flabbergasted. That got us both to thinking about the phrase and its origin. Why should *right* and *away* have anything to do with 'immediately' or 'pronto'?"

First to Fred Cassidy, chief editor of the *Dictionary of American Regional English:* He notes that *right* means "straight" and is cognate with the Latin *rec-*

tus, meaning "stretched out like a cord" and the source of *rectitude,* the course of those on the straight and narrow. Our curious expression about speedy action *right away* exists in Britain as *straight away.*

But what's the basis for *right away,* which was coined in 1818 as *slick right away*? (No presidential slur intended.) It's an idiom, which means that its meanings are not predictable from those of its parts, but we can break it down with the help of John Algeo, the neologistician of *American Speech* quarterly, now doing his research in Wheaton, Illinois:

Right has a long history as an emphasizer: *rihht affterr* can be found in a document dated 1200, which was soon followed by other intensifiers of time: *right in* (the dawning of a day) and *right now.* The temporal use of this adverb for emphasis was transferred to expressions of place: *right down, right up, right with you.*

What about *away,* in its curious sense of immediacy? An early English translation of the Bible has a line with that sense: "Ye can not beare it *awaye,*" which the *Oxford English Dictionary* interprets as "forthwith, directly, without hesitation or delay; chiefly colloquial in imperative sentences, as *Fire away!* = proceed at once to fire."

Charles Dickens noticed this as an Americanism on a visit here: " 'Dinner, if you please,' said I to the waiter. 'Right away?' said the waiter. I saw now that 'Right away' and 'Directly' were one and the same thing."

Let Professor Algeo sum up the development of the phrase: "*Right away* 'immediately' developed in American English by combining a common, ancient and frequent use of *right* as an intensifier with a limited, old and infrequent use of *away* to mean 'immediately' (as also in *Fire away!*). *Right away* is now in use throughout the English-speaking world, though mainly in less formal language."

That does it; sorry I couldn't get around to this sooner.

If Charles Dickens had been a Southerner he would not have equated directly *with* right away. *I learned, growing up in Kentucky in the 30's, that* directly *(pronounced "drekly") meant "after a while."*

T. W. Havely
Houston, Texas

Dear Bill:

I was surprised that you should follow Mr. Kahn in thinking right away *an instance of arbitrary idiom, that is, divorced from the ordinary meaning of the component words. Surely* right *is the common intensive based on the idea of "absence of hindrance"*—right now, right glad, *etc. The English say* straight away, *which makes the point. As for the* away *in both forms of the idiom, its sense is* off, *indicating the speaker's readiness to go and do whatever is the subject of discourse. The two words together quite naturally mean* immediately.

What is harder to explain is presently, *with its now disappearing meaning of "in a few moments." For the solution, see our next installment (possibly).*

Yours,

Jacques [Barzun]
New York, New York

E. J. Kahn Jr.

One of the most graceful and productive writers around, E. J. Kahn Jr. of *The New Yorker,* died after an auto accident recently.

He had a good habit of tossing observations and gripes about English usage my way over the years. Mr. Kahn had a writer's ear, picking up usages that others missed: "I've noticed that more people are using *amongst* instead of *among,*" he wrote me recently. "And also *amidst.* (I don't believe I've ever read or heard *alongst.*)"

Another illustrative observation of significant detail: "More and more people, when they want to describe somebody's life span, instead of coming up with the plain 'Bill Safire is 37 years old,' are inflicting on us a 'Bill Safire is 37 years *of age.*' Can't you put a halt to this?"

No, nor can I be thirty-seven again. He was picking up a tendency of some writers to shy away from the word *old,* using the slightly more formal *of age* as a semi-euphemism. I was working on this, though; a CD-ROM count of the *O.E.D.* found 459 instances of *years old* and 222 instances of *years of age.* Although historical usage of *years old* is twice as frequent as *years of age,* people who think *old* is a harsh word may be changing that.

Ely Jacques Kahn Jr. was seventy-seven years old.

One of Jack Kahn's delights during his last years of considerable disgruntlement over The New Yorker *was sitting down to write you. A channel in the air opened between his head and yours, in his mind anyway—a pure communication between lovers of the language. When you responded as you occasionally did by dragging his thoughts into your column, he shone with pleasure. Your passage about him recently brought just that kind of pleasure to his whole family—the feeling that he, Jack, has been fully understood and savored. We all thank you.*

Eleanor Munro
(Mrs. E. J. Kahn, Jr.)
Truro, Massachusetts

Satan's Hometown

What's got into Senator Daniel Patrick Moynihan—doesn't he know how to spell? Doesn't Oxford University Press have a proofreader?

Pandaemonium is the title of his sixteenth book; this one, about the ethicity of ethnicity, argues that self-determination is undermining the harmony of mixed cultures. *Pandemonium*—the word, not the Moynihan title—is a word that takes tumult and uproar to their outer limits, a condition of all hell breaking loose. It should be spelled, of course, *pandemonium,* without the *a* before the *e.*

But wait: The very thought of the breaking-loose of hell gives us a clue to the author's intention. *Pandaemonium* is a place. *Pan-* is a Greek combining form meaning "all"; *demonium* is a gathering of demons. John Milton, in his 1667 masterpiece, *Paradise Lost,* coined the word, writing of "the walls of *Pandaemonium,* Citie and proud seate of Lucifer." The Devil called for "A solemn Councel forthwith to be held/At Pandaemonium, the high Capital/Of Satan and his Peers."

The *ae* lasted until Thomas Carlyle, in his 1831 *Sartor Resartus,* wrote of those who "in this hag-ridden dream, mistake God's fair living world for a pallid, vacant Hades and extinct Pandemonium."

The senior Senator from New York is harking back to Milton's meaning—the capital of Hell—in his study of ethnicity in global politics, and can thus get away with the archaic spelling. The rest of us, in using the word to denote "wild disorder, noisy confusion, bedlam," should stick with the capitalization, just as we capitalize *Hell* when referring to the place. (I'll feel like hell when Hell freezes over.) But we should adopt the modern spelling because Carlyle was a respectable writer and *ae* is hard to figure out how to pronounce. Pat should remember that when he writes his encyclopaedia.

Save Our *Zoo* from Language Predators

The Greens, language snobs and political-correctness prescriptivists have gone too far this time.

Lovers of short and simple words were shocked this month by a story properly given front-page attention by *The New York Times:* William Conway, president of the New York Zoological Society, announced with savage glee that he and the other elitists of his board of directors had banned the word *zoo* from such institutions as the Bronx Zoo and the Central Park Zoo. Henceforth, the elephants therein will have to memorize the name "Wildlife Conservation Park."

As the reporter, Francis X. Clines, made clear, the social climbers of the monkey house were tired of being thought of as mere zookeepers. He quoted Mr. Conway's defense of his new nomenclature: "They're highfalutin words for a highfalutin objective," namely, to call attention to the society's holdings and projects from Patagonia to Tibet. Calling the domain of these distinguished executives a *zoo* was demeaning. In that regard, the name "Bronx" would also be dropped, as it does not have the upscale connotation of the International Wildlife Conservation Park. (As carpetbagging candidate Robert Kennedy never said, "Where are the Bronx?")

I know Frankie Clines. He is a careful reporter, sticks to the facts, takes no position, but he belongs to the breed of journalists known as "classy writers" who can kill a subject by quoting him accurately.

"It's short and snappy—*zoo*—and we know we created a problem," said the Wildlifeconservationkeeper, "but in the *American Heritage Dictionary* the word *zoo* has a secondary meaning of a situation or place marked by rampant 'confusion or disorder.' We are not confused or disordered. . . . We need a sea change."

For people desperate to be on the cutting edge, every change is a *sea change;* this trope, coined by Shakespeare in *The Tempest,* is a vogue term as overused as *cutting edge.* Mr. Conway is abandoning the noun backformed from *zoological,* first used in the name of the Zoological Gardens in Regent's Park in London. Why? Not because of the longtime pronunciation problem—the first syllable of "zo-OL-o-gy" is pronounced "zoh," while the clip picked up the second *o* to make it "zoo"—but because he and his Bronxophobe ilk feel sullied by the second sense of the word.

That sense, indeed, connotes disorder, as first used by John Galsworthy in a 1924 novel: "You won't keep me in your Zoo, my dear." Its meaning was illustrated by the classic George Price cartoon in *The New Yorker* of a zookeeper helplessly trying to get his cap back from the monkeys while a matron outside the cage taps her cane and asks, "Who's in charge here?"

Political reporters are aware of the derogatory usage: The *zoo plane* is the aircraft that follows the press plane that follows *Air Force One;* it is so named because it carries the noisy, scruffy television technicians scorned by the blown-dry, bigfoot correspondents and pundits. I first heard this locution in 1970, as the presidential press secretary, Ron Ziegler, told a reporter, "Shape up, or it's the zoo plane for you."

But does the second sense of a word necessarily kill its first sense? In some cases, it has; nobody claims his heart is young and *gay* anymore lest he be taken as asserting homosexuality. And as Daniel Schorr, senior commentator on National Public Radio, points out about the use of *politically correct:* "It is not correct to steal the word *correct* from me."

In this case, however, the power and simplicity of *zoo* ought not to be lightly overturned by the whim of an unconservative conservationist with multisyllabic pretensions. Guardians of the welfare of children should consider the effect of the proposed change to "Wildlife Conservation Park" on little kids who now express themselves clearly with "Wanna go tu-duh zoo."

I am a proud graduate of the Bronx High School of Science, not the Secondary Scientific Education Center of the New York City Borough Attached to the North American Mainland.

The next linguistic sea change in the works, if this bureaucratic monkey business is allowed to stand, is the Respect-Payment Center and Global Remains Repository of Ulysses S. Grant (until recently known all too familiarly as Grant's Tomb) and the International Ruth-Gehrig-Steinbrenner Memorial Athletic and Recreational Facility that used to be a stadium known by what some Southerners treat as a regional slur.

The sound that is being directed at our with-it wildlife's high society is sometimes called a *raspberry,* based on "raspberry tart," which was scatological Cockney rhyming slang, and is known locally as an "inarticulated derisive fricative," formerly *Bronx cheer.*

I thought the reason for the change of "zoo" to "wildlife conservation park" was less of being politically correct but more not to associate with the inner city. The residents of East Detroit, a suburb, voted to change its name to East Pointe.

Ralph Slovenko
Professor of Law and Psychiatry
Wayne State University
Detroit, Michigan

Scalia v. *Merriam-Webster*

In a 1924 dissent, Justice Louis D. Brandeis wrote: "Modification implies growth. It is the life of the law." The law got pretty lively recently on the meaning of the word *modify.*

Justice Antonin Scalia, the Supreme Court's conservative dynamo and frequent dissenter, found himself writing the majority's decision in the case of *MCI* v. *AT&T.* This case, pitting two of the nation's info-age giants against each other, hinged on the reach of the Federal Communications Commission's power to "modify any requirement" in a section of the law. MCI argued that this meant the F.C.C. could make basic changes in that section, which it had made over AT&T's objections.

"We disagree," Scalia wrote for the Court. "The word 'modify'—like a number of other English words employing the root 'mod-' (deriving from the Latin word for 'measure'), such as 'moderate,' 'modulate,' 'modest,' and 'modicum'—has a connotation of increment or limitation."

Having plunged into the language dodge (I would have used the past participle, *derived,* rather than the present participle, *deriving,* in his parenthetical etymology), Justice Scalia cited several dictionaries in support of his definition, including the 1976 edition of *Merriam-Webster's Third New International Dictionary, Unabridged:* "to make minor changes in the form or structure of: alter without transforming."

But the petitioning MCI had found one sense for *modify* among the seven variations in meaning listed in *Webster's Third Unabridged* (similarly set forth in its current abridgement, *Merriam-Webster's Tenth Collegiate*): "to make a basic or important change in." Quite a stretch of meaning, but in a previous Court case involving railroads in which the verb *required* was seen to have "alternative dictionary definitions," the Court had allowed the broader interpretation; on that analogy of a loose *required,* MCI argued for the stretched sense of *modify.*

The conservative Scalia wasn't having any of that. He refused to accept an ambiguity created by a single dictionary "which not only *supplements* the meaning contained in all other dictionaries, but *contradicts* one of the meanings contained in virtually all other dictionaries." (I think he means *merely* rather than *only.*) "When the word 'modify' has come to mean *both* 'to change in some respects' *and* 'to change fundamentally,' " he thunders, "it will in fact mean *neither* of those things. It will simply mean 'to change,' and some adverb will have to be called into service to indicate the great or small degree of the change."

Having delivered himself of the opinion that *modify* "connotes moderate change," the jurist went on to opine acidly that "it might be unsurprising to discover a 1972 White House press release saying that 'the Administration is modifying its position with regard to prosecution of the war in Vietnam'—but only because press agents tend to impart what is nowadays called 'spin.' Such intentional distortions, or simply careless or ignorant misuse, must have formed the basis for the usage that *Webster's Third,* and *Webster's Third* alone, reported."

This high-court double late hit (both at the 1961 lexicographer, Philip B. Gove, and the 1972 press secretary, Ron Ziegler, who distributed some Nixon releases I wrote) required (in the broad meaning of *required,* as construed in *National Railroad Passenger Corporation* v. *Boston and Maine Corporation*) the attention of a full Court press. Accordingly, I contacted Merriam-Webster's editor in chief (not hyphenated), Frederick C. Mish.

"I regret having to say that Judge Scalia is in error on this matter," responded the lexicographer, on whom the judicial assault has not had a chilling effect, "but at least he has the satisfaction of knowing that his error is not reversible by a higher court."

The problem is that sense 4*b* of the *Third Unabridged*—"to make a basic or important change in: alter"—seems to contradict 4*a,* which is "to make minor changes in the form or structure of." Come on, Fred—how can it mean both?

"In lexicography, as in biological taxonomy," explains Dr. Mish, "there are splitters and there are lumpers. The editor who worked on *modify* for the *Third* was evidently a splitter, who came upon the work of an earlier lumper and thought it would be useful if we acknowledged explicitly that when one speaks of modifying something, the changes involved are not always minor. Most often they are, of course, as is recognized in sense 4*a,* but sometimes not."

Were the users of the contradictory sense cited by the dictionary a bunch of kooks and language slobs? "One of the authors quoted is T. S. Eliot, a Nobel laureate in literature," notes Mish. "Another is Edward Sapir, a distinguished and influential scholar in linguistics." (Sapir wrote about a weakening of geography in social organization that would "profoundly modify" attitudes toward personal relations.) "If Justice Scalia wants to call this 'careless or ignorant misuse,' " ripostes Mish, "well, it's a free country."

So who's right? When someone who's writing for the majority of the Supreme Court becomes embroiled in a no-holds-barred linguistic dispute with one of the language's leading lexicographers, who could possibly have the temerity—the unalloyed chutzpah—to presume to adjudicate?

Here is your faithful maven, doing his duty.

I think the dictionary's splitter went a hair too far. In the citation of Edward Sapir, the linguist's use of *profoundly* to modify *modify* indicates his understanding of the meaning of that verb to be "change," neither major nor minor. That is neither the historical nor the common meaning; in fact, the fuzziness of that usage created the need for an adverb—*profoundly*—just as Scalia predicted would happen if the meaning got muddled. A dictionary is duty-bound to report what's out there, but need not report every misuse as a possible sense. *Modify* means "minor change," as in "modified limited hangout," a Watergate phrase that got no credit for its correctness.

"It is perhaps gilding the lily to add this," wrote Justice Scalia in piling on another point. The jurist erred: the Earl of Salisbury in Shakespeare's *King John* deplored redundancy with "To be possess'd with double pomp, . . . to gild refined gold, to *paint* the lily."

Is Scalia's usage a misquotation of the Bard? Yes, but common usage has worn down the accurate quotation, and—thanks to its use in a Supreme Court decision—confirms our acceptance of what was once a mistake.

Shebang

In Shirley Lord's novel *My Sister's Keeper,* the scion of a cosmetics empire on the trail of an anti-wrinkle cream, which I presume is the Holy Grail of skin care, says, "I can't see how I could ever take over from Dad and run the whole *shebang.*"

In a *New York Times* book review of Michael Crichton's reverse-sexist novel, *Disclosure,* Maureen Dowd wrote, "When you merely switch the roles, making a woman act exactly like a man, you give up the most intriguing element of the whole *megillah.*"

We deal here with the language's attempt to cope with totality. *The whole* is evidently never enough; colorful speech demands a whole something.

A *shebang,* in novelist Lord's usage, is an entire corporation. As the late etymologist William Morris once recorded, a possible source is the Irish word *shebeen,* a lowly tavern that sold drinks without a license; from this, the word became associated with cheap real estate, giving rise to an offer of a pittance "for the whole *shebang.*"

Megillah is the Hebrew word for "scroll" (though you do not often hear "the Dead Sea Megillahs"). The Book of Esther is one of the detailed megillahs, which drew yawns from some scholars, whose irreverent friends expanded the term's coverage to prolix prose and ultimately to anything too long and complicated: The Yiddish *gontzeh megillah* is "the whole megillah," now ensconced in English and sometimes used by impatient readers of this column to describe its exhaustive research.

Wait—we're not finished! There's *the whole shootin' match,* beginning as a test of marksmanship, its extension recorded in an 1896 *Dialect Notes* to "any kind of meeting, from a church service to a dance," and in this century to any large social gathering.

Then there's the *whole kit and caboodle,* with *kit* meaning "set of equipment" and *-boodle* possibly from the Dutch *boedel,* "estate, possessions." And Madison Avenue's *whole ball of wax,* the construction industry's *whole nine yards* and California's *whole enchilada.* Pass the anti-wrinkle cream; a lexie could grow old running down the *whole bit.*

Shmush

"Elegant lady enters and carefully lays dress bag on baggage rack," writes Jacob M. Abel of Washington, dramatically setting up the use of a verb unremarked by lexicographers. "Enter older lady, small, much jewelry and heavy suitcase, struggling to get suitcase up onto rack. It rests on dress bag of first lady, who bolts out of her seat to move the suitcase, explaining to the air, 'I don't want my gown *shmushed*!' "

Mr. Abel notes that the German verb *schmeissen* is sometimes used to mean "flatten, demolish," and that's a good long-shot possibility of the origin. The closest English verb is *smash,* probably a blend of *smack* and *mash,* according to *Merriam-Webster's Tenth New Collegiate Dictionary,* but it does not begin with the *sh* sound, which is so essential to *shmush.*

Sol Steinmetz of Random House thinks *shmush* is a variant not of *smash,* as I had guessed, but of the Scottish dialectal *smush,* meaning "to crush." Sure enough, here it is in *Wright's English Dialect Dictionary:* "smush," its first sense "to mash; to crush; to reduce to powder." The citation shows how dairy maids, squeezing the curd through their fingers, are said to be *"smushin' the crud"* (which may also direct us to an origin of *crud*).

But what about that beginning *sh*? "The initial *sh-* variant," says Sol, in his special argot, "is probably due to assimilation to the final *-sh.*" Say wha'? "For example, *spaceship* is often pronounced, by assimilation, as *spash ship* or *spaship.*" The *sh* sound is picked up and used earlier in the word. (Drunken astronauts take it even further, with *shpaceship.*)

No, *shmush*—"to crush, to press down," as in "I can tell the dog slept on the couch because every one of the cushions is all *shmushed*"—is not a Yiddishism. It is an old Scotticism, and its frequency of use should make it a candidate for inclusion in modern dictionaries. Pronunciation: to rhyme with *bush,* not *brush.* (And get that mutt off the couch.)

I have an addenda for the "shmush" section. I have always loved, when talking to a German-speaking person, to ask him what the word Flugelschmeisser *means. When they can't figure it out, I then tell them it is simply a fly swatter and the answer is always "Yah, yah, of course it is a fly swatter." I have always found the Germans have some very descriptive but long and involved words and this is typical.*

Norman Beck
St. Louis, Missouri

Shoulda-Coulda-Woulda

A hard-edged question was posed to Hillary Rodham Clinton at a Whitewater news conference: What about "the suggestion in the R.T.C. memorandum . . . you and your husband knew or should have known that Whitewater was not cash-flowing and that notes or debts should have been paid"?

"Shoulda, coulda, woulda," the First Lady replied. "We didn't."

Some journalists narrowed their eyes at this airy dismissal of financial responsibility in land speculation at the place Mrs. Clinton prefers to refer to as "northern Arkansas." My own investigative lust was instantly replaced, however, by linguistic curiosity: Whence the reduplication *shoulda, coulda, woulda*?

The order of words in this delicious morsel of dialect varies with the user. On the sports pages of *The Washington Post* of December 7, 1978, Gerald Strine wrote about the New England Patriots football team: "The Pats *coulda, shoulda and woulda* been ahead of the Cowboys by at least 16–3 at halftime . . . but three field goals were blown."

Eleven years later, in a United Press International account of another football game, the phrase again led with *coulda,* as a shamefaced kicker was quoted: "I should have kicked the extra point, but *coulda, shoulda, woulda* doesn't do it."

By the 90's, football players were fumbling the order. Said a Notre Dame tackle, Aaron Taylor, offside on his subject-verb agreement: "There's no excuses. *Woulda, shoulda, coulda* is not going to cut it."

During the last two decades, an author told Vernon Scott of *The Hollywood Reporter* he planned a "*Shoulda, Coulda, Woulda* book"; a retailer opined to *Investor's Business Daily* about the decline of Carter Hawley stores: "There are *shoulda-beens, coulda-beens, woulda-beens,* but the fact is they didn't meet the retail revolution that happened in the past five years."

We have here an elision field. *Elide,* rooted in the Latin for "to strike out," means "to omit"; in speech, an elision is the omission of letters and sounds to produce compressions like *don't* and *couldn't,* or as the would-be boxer played by Marlon Brando in *On the Waterfront* said, "I coulda been a contender."

In this rhyming compound, a triple elision does the hat trick: Although each elision expresses something different, when taken together, the trio conveys a unified meaning. *Shoulda,* short for *should have* (and not *should of,* which lexies call a variant but I call a mistake), carries a sense of correctness or obligation; *coulda* implies a possibility, and *woulda* denotes conditional certainty, an oxymoron: the stated intent to have taken an action if only something had not intervened.

Lexicographers have been tracking the individual elisions for decades. First came *woulda,* translated into Standard English in *Dialect Notes* in 1913: "*Would a went,* would have gone." Theodore Dreiser introduced *coulda* and the solid *woulda* in his 1925 novel, *An American Tragedy:* "I coulda chucked my job, and I woulda." A 1933 book on crime used the third elision: "You shouldda seen him."

Taken together, the term means "Spare me the useless excuses." I reached Mrs. Clinton through her aides, each of whom was surprised at the good-natured nature of my follow-up question, to get her definition. Mrs. Clinton passes the word that she heard the expression often in Arkansas, and interprets it to mean: "People can tell you that you should have, or could have, or would have, but the question is: Did you or didn't you?"

In this way, all problematical or ethical fine points are overridden in what the Hollywood set would call "cutting to the chase." A related term, though not synonymous, was used often by Franklin Roosevelt to deflect the entrapping queries of journalists: *iffy question.* Hypothetical questions, using the subjunctive "if . . . would" construction, can draw a political figure into deep water; this can be escaped by the politician with F.D.R.'s "That's an *iffy question.*" In early 1964, when

Robert Kennedy was asked if he would accept a vice presidential nomination on President Johnson's ticket, he played on its speculative basis with "The question reminds me of my brother. When he was posed with such a question, he used to say that is like asking a girl if she would marry that man if he proposed."

The *shoulda, coulda, woulda* phrase (accepting Mrs. Clinton's order as standard) has a wistfully resigned connotation that was evoked in 1854 by the poet John Greenleaf Whittier in "Maud Muller":

For of all sad words of tongue or pen,
The saddest are these: "It might have been!"

A friend of mine who worked in the Pentagon during the Kennedy/Johnson years told me the following. One day a group of secretaries were making plans to go out to lunch, and asked another secretary (from West Virginia) if she'd like to go. She declined. When they returned they were talking about what a good meal they'd had. "Where'd you go?" the West Virginian asked. They named a well-known restaurant. "How'd you get there?" They'd driven, she was told. "Oh," she said. "If I'd knowed I coulda rode I woulda went."

Bruce C. Netschert
Falls Church, Virginia

Sic 'Em

Bob Dole's title was Senate Republican Leader. The sign over his door used to read, MINORITY LEADER, a tradition Senator Everett Dirksen preserved, but Senator Hugh Scott changed it in the late 1960's when he was leader because it struck him as down-putting.

The Senate Republican Leader (going against *Times* style, I capitalize the letter *l* because it is part of a title) called one day and, before passing along a hot news tip, observed, "Those guys in the White House just don't know *sic 'em.*"

I asked what he meant; Dole seemed taken aback, as if surprised to find that I didn't know *sic 'em,* either. "It means 'anything,' " he said. He thought I'd been inside the Beltway too long.

A quick call to *DARE*—the *Dictionary of American Regional English,* at the University of Wisconsin in Madison—turned up the geographic dispersion of the dialect term: a few spottings in the Midwest, explaining Kansan Dole's usage, but heaviest in the Pacific Northwest.

Question JJ156 on the *DARE* questionnaire, skillfully designed to elicit re-

gionalisms, is "Sayings about a person who seems to you very stupid: 'He doesn't know ——.' " Although some would respond with a brief expletive, *DARE*'s query drew twenty-seven answers of *Sic 'em,* along with these more detailed responses: " 'Here' from *sic 'em,*" "*Sic 'em* from 'come here' " and "*Sic 'em* from 'go get 'em.' "

When *American Speech* magazine queried readers about *sic 'em* in 1961, one observed that his mother heard it from Arkansas friends who owned hound dogs. Another reader, the great San Francisco dialexicographer Peter Tamony, replied: "The remark describes an unresponsive, indolent, shiftless person. He is like a dog that shows no courageous and instant reaction to the command *'sic 'em.'* " Mr. Tamony gave an etymological insight by adding that *sic 'em* is "merely a pronunciation modification of *seek 'em* or *seek 'im.*"

The earliest citations are from Stewart Edward White's 1907 *Arizona Nights:* "You see, for all their plumb nerve in comin' so far, the most of them didn't know sic 'em. . . . I didn't know sic 'em about minin'." In Ramon Adams's 1968 *Western Words,* the term is defined as "a cowboy's expression meaning 'ignorant.' I have heard many unique references to ignorance, like 'He don't know 'nough to pack guts to a bear,' 'He don't know dung from wild honey' and many others. Ted Logan referred to a man with 'His head's so hollow he's got to talk with his hands to get away from the echo.' "

The key is the unspoken *from.* Not to know *sic 'em* (sometimes spelled *sickum*) means not to distinguish the master's command to his dog to attack *from* the entirely different command "come here." (This is not a canine slur; either the master or the dog can be the stupid party. Or both can be: When I say *sic 'em!* to James, my Bernese mountain dog, he snarls ferociously and comes at me.)

Modern dialect users are more familiar with *not knowing from beans,* which probably originated in "not knowing split beans from coffee beans," or "not knowing beans from barley," "beans from bullfrogs," etc. The key *from* is found in "not knowing cow chips from kumquats," a fine double alliteration; indeed, alliteration is frequent in this trope of comparison, as the makers of Shinola shoe polish learned to their rue. Today, the *from* is usually dropped, and "He don't know *beans*" is all that remains.

I am indebted to Republican Leader Dole for this lead, if that's what he called about.

Your picture of the stupid dog not responding to the command "sic 'em" reminds me of the corresponding cat story of the man who had made three holes in the bottom of his door so that his cats could come and go when the door was closed. An efficiency-minded neighbor asked him, Couldn't all your cats use a single hole? "No!" he glared. "When I say scat I mean scat!*"*

Fred [Frederic G. Cassidy]
Chief Editor
Dictionary of American
Regional English
Madison, Wisconsin

You quote Peter Tamony as saying that sic 'em *is "merely a pronunciation modification of* seek 'em *or* seek 'im.*" Although the* O.E.D. *supports Tamony's etymology, I am dubious. I believe the expression derives from the Latin word* sic, *meaning "thus." The dog's owner points to the person or animal he wants the dog to attack and says "sic," meaning in effect, "there—that's the one you should bite."*

Before you dismiss my theory as fanciful, consider that the proverbial names for dogs, Rex *and* Fido, *are Latin. The expressions people use with animals, like those we use between children and adults, are among the oldest in our culture. When I was a teen-aged farmhand in Wisconsin, we called pigs for feeding by their Latin name,* Sui, *and called cows to be milked with their Greek name,* Bos *(normally in the bilingual English-Greek construction, "Here, Bos!").*

John H. O'Neill
Leavenworth Professor of English
Hamilton College
Clinton, New York

Simpsonese

Watching NBC's live coverage of the O. J. Simpson pretrial proceedings, I was startled to hear one witness identify himself as having worked "for sixteen years as a *criminalist* in the city of Los Angeles." I asked myself: When is Tom Brokaw, with the vast research facilities at his disposal, going to tell us how to differentiate among a *criminal,* a *criminalist* and a *criminologist*?

The phone rang. It was Tom Brokaw. "You're the word maven. What's a *criminalist*?"

To the epistemologist studying the knowledge of knowledge, this is called circularity. However, I owe Brokaw an answer because he is a faithful Lexicographic Irregular, Jargoneer Group.

Crimen is the Latin word for "accusation, reproach"; a *criminal* thus began as "one accused," and is now "one who has been convicted of a crime."

No word is an island: John Donne wrote in 1631 that "I have read in some of the *criminalists.* . . ." At that time the word meant "one versed in criminal law." In 1892, the *New York Nation* reported on "the theories advanced by the anthropological school of *criminalists.*" *Black's Law Dictionary* also defined it as "a psychiatrist dealing with criminality."

But by 1857, *criminologist* had crept upon the scene. The suffix *-ology* means "study of," and the new study was defined in the *Oxford English Dictionary* as "the science of crime; that part of anthropology which treats of crime and criminals."

When I put the question "When did *criminologist* return to the old *criminalist*?" to David Gascon, commanding officer of L.A.P.D. community information, he replied: "They are two separate terms. *Criminologist* is somebody who studies the sociology of crime; a *criminalist,* on the other hand, is a technician or evidence gatherer."

What caused the split? *The Encyclopedia of Crime and Justice* has the answer under *Criminalistics:* "With the expansion of scientific knowledge, the term *criminalist* was redefined in the 20th century to mean a specialist in empirical knowledge relating to crime. The earlier definition survives . . . to describe the criminal law scholar."

Jerome Skolnick, professor of law at the University of California at Berkeley, differentiates for us: "*Criminalists,* sometimes called forensic scientists, apply knowledge from the natural sciences—chemistry, physics and biology—to analyze such physical evidence as blood, hair, semen and fiber in criminal and civil cases. *Criminologists,* by contrast, are social scientists. They study the causes of crime, the effects of measures to reduce crime and the criminal-justice system itself." That's from the horse's mouth: Professor Skolnick is president of the American Society of Criminology.

Relatedly, a reader noted a mistake in the description of evidence in the

Simpson case. "One of the items found at the homicide scene was a knit cap," declared Deputy District Attorney Marcia Clark, in writing. "Inside the cap black curly hairs were detected which have been determined to be of African-American origin."

Jonathan Balsam of Lawrence, Long Island, sent that in. "Quite startling," he wrote, "that forensic science has advanced to the point where analysis of a suspect's hair can determine not only his race but also his nationality."

That's an example of substituting *African-American* for *black* without thinking. An *African-American* is a citizen of the United States who is a member of the black, formerly Negro, race. Not every black everywhere is an African-American, and no hair anywhere is African-American, as every criminalist knows.

This department will continue to cover the celebrity murder trial of the century from its unique perspective, because the English language is on trial every day.

Skinny Marink

"While reading *After All These Years* by Susan Isaacs," writes Steven Zalben of Sands Point, Long Island, "I came across 'Who's that *skinny marink* . . . ?' Where does it come from?"

From *skinny malink,* in a comic song on the London stage around 1870. The *Scottish National Dictionary* has *skinnymalink(ie),* for an emaciated person or animal. Joan Hall of the *Dictionary of American Regional English* thinks it is rooted in *skinny as the links of a crook,* the chain and hook that hold a pot over a fire. "The *ma-* is probably an infix," she tells me, "a rhythmic syllable added to make the phrase more euphonious."

In 1924, Eddie Cantor popularized the song "Skin-a-Ma-Rink," written by Al Dubin, Jimmy McHugh and Irving Mills.

I'm sure that the origin of "skinny malinky" (a person of slight build) is Russian. In Russian malenky *means little, diminutive or slight. It is the opposite of* bolshoi, *which is well known for the ballet company and means "big" or "grand."*

"Skinny malinky" is a term used by Jews of Eastern European descent who are familiar with Yiddish and Russian.

I am not a scholarly source. My mother has always used the phrase and told me it was Russian.

Barbara Kram
Titusville, New Jersey

Slur Patrol I

I refuse to be a patsy for the Slur Patrol.

In a recent political harangue, I noted that *focus* had become the vogue word in criticism, including self-criticism, of the Clinton White House. Everybody from pundits to politicians to press agents was into focusing. To put a pin into the ballooning usage, I found a reduplicating rhyme and headlined the essay "Focus Hocus-Pocus."

This usage brought a blindsiding objection from the Rev. John P. Mahoney of Providence College in Rhode Island. "The term *hocus-pocus* has an origin arising from English Protestantism as an attack on Catholic doctrine," he asserts. "*Hocus-pocus* was a shortening of the phrase *'Hoc est enim corpus meum,'* the essential formula used in the sacrament of the eucharist. Implied here was that the Catholic doctrine of transubstantiation, abominated by Low-Church Anglicans, was absurd nonsense."

Hocus-pocus may or may not have derived from the Latin words for "This is my body"; etymologists differ on the origins of what is now taken to be a term for a conjurer's quackery, and currently means "sleight of hand" or "a sham used to conceal deception." But even if this reduplication were to be rooted in centuries-old religious controversy, does that mean it must be exorcised from our vocabulary?

"I do think one ought to avoid prejudicial terms," Father Mahoney writes, "such as this one and *Jesuitical.*"

There is such a thing as digging too deep for prejudice. A rabbi wrote me not long ago to complain about my use of *talmudic* to mean "exceedingly scholarly; concentrating on a close reading and interpretation of text." As a native speaker, I know this to be one modern sense of *talmudic,* synonymous with the Greek-based "hermeneutic," and it does not worry me that this sense is not yet in most dictionaries; it'll get there. Hebrew scholars may dispute this, holding instead that *talmudic* means only "relating to the Talmud, a body of literature comprising the Mishnah and Gemara," but I think they are missing an example of the growth of the English language.

Jesuitical is in the same boat. Nobody doubts that it refers to the society founded by Saint Ignatius Loyola in 1540, but it has another sense as well—accurately reported in the tenth edition of the *Merriam-Webster Collegiate Dictionary* as "given to intrigue or equivocation." The *Webster's New World Dictionary, Third Edition,* notes that this crafty, duplicitous sense is a "hostile and offensive term, as used by anti-Jesuits." I think it has developed a third sense, in current use not yet reported but useful: "subtle, intricate moralistic reasoning, informed by a rigorous logic." (When I interrupted Mario Cuomo one day with "That's too Jesuitical for me," he responded, "You mean Vincentian, not Jesuitical," which I am still trying to figure out.)

Because good people do not want to give offense, we have to think about slurs; at the same time, we do not want to let our language be taken hostage by those who too quickly take offense.

Take the verb *to welsh,* for example, an old dialect term meaning "to refuse to pay a debt." This is a clear and unmistakable slur on a nationality—people from Wales—as many of whom pay their debts as thee or me. Same with *Jew down,* meaning "to bargain"; it has a long history in the language, but it is a stereotypical slur. Don't use either one. But what about *to gyp,* meaning "to cheat"? It is rooted in *Gypsy,* a much-maligned tribe; should we strike from the language the traditional mutter, "I wuz gypped"? That's a tougher call; if the verb were *gypsied,* it would be a clear slur, but the clip of the first syllable fuzzes the case. I still use *to be gypped* to mean "to be deceived in trade," but I'm beginning to be sensitized; let's give that another look in a few years.

What about retro-slurs? These are terms that were formerly acceptable but now are considered slurs by those who offer—indeed, demand—a replacement. *American Indian* is one; an undetermined number of members of tribes ranging from the Cherokee and Algonquin to the Seminole prefer *Native American.* If words have meaning, all those born in America, regardless of ethnicity or color, are "native American" (as against "naturalized American"), but the seizure of the phrase by American Indians conveys a political statement that "we were here first" or even "we came from here and you came from there." They can fairly claim to be *aboriginal Americans,* but cannot claim to be exclusively *native Americans.*

When Syracuse University chose the Onondaga Nation chief, Oren R. Lyons, to be its commencement speaker, the draft news release read "the first native American to deliver the commencement address at Syracuse." Chief Lyons, explaining that anyone born on this continent was a native American, asked that it be changed to "the first American Indian to deliver the commencement address at Syracuse."

The press office gulped and made the change, feeling better about it after consulting the *Associated Press Stylebook:* "Avoid the use of *Native American* except in quotations." A.P. then tossed in a kind of anthropological explanation: "American Indians migrated to the continent over a land bridge from Asia." However, an A.P. dispatch came to the attention of John Harvith, the university's national media relations director, that used *native American* freely; because I am a Syracuse dropout and occasional emergency commencement speaker, Mr. Harvith asked my usage opinion.

Stick with the proud title of American Indian, Syracuse, as the Onondaga Nation chief suggests, and do not be drawn into retro-slurs or inaccurate exclusions. Prepare for objections; hold fast to the A.P. stylebook, even if A.P. does not.

The Slur Patrol, when it goes overboard, is a brigade of the Thought Police, to be resisted in the name of robust discourse. For example, I'll get mail objecting to my refusal to be a *patsy,* meaning "one easily fooled or intimidated"; the name *Patsy* is an Irish endearment, and the hypersensitive may take offense. But I'm ready: A case can be made that *patsy* is probably from *pazzo,* Italian for "fool." And when I want to be a patsy, I'll be one.

You confused the issue by using both "native American" and "Native American" interchangeably. The proper noun designed by some to replace "American Indian" may have some slight justification if both words are capitalized, but when the modifier is not capitalized then "native American" loses not only its stature as a proper noun but its possible validity as a modernized substitute for "American Indian."

While you were on the subject of Indians, you should have taken the opportunity to mention "Indian Summer" as a slur term. The way I understand it, the term for that welcome gift of nice weather after the summer season has passed stems from the belief that Indians in America have a reputation from earliest days of taking back gifts they present to European settlers and rival tribes. The gift of nice weather in autumn is snatched back by wintry blasts just as an Indian chief in New England snatched back the hunting knife he gave a visitor in a moment of generosity that he quickly regretted.

Richard Patrick Wilson
Mobile, Alabama

Like you and Onondaga Chief Lyons, as a native American I have always deplored the "politically correct" term Native American. *I have suggested as alternatives* Mohawk American, Onondaga American, aboriginal American *or, if that be considered pejorative,* original, *or* first American. *Hooray for you!*

Marshall A. Mundheim, M.D.
New York, New York

You accept "gyp," from "Gypsy," at least for the nonce, as an acceptable verb. Random House II *confirms my recollection that the noun is rooted in "Egypt," where Gypsies were once believed to have originated. Why is this epithet not as politically and ethnically incorrect as "welsh"?*

William J. McKeough
Greenvale, New York

Patsy, *which you describe as an Irish endearment, is listed in my Collins dictionary with a definition similar to yours, but with origin unknown.*

George Washington used it as a nickname for his wife, Martha. It was not that unusual a usage, and I am told that Patsy as a nickname for Martha persists in various parts of the country even today.

It's not easy to trace the course of the change from Martha to Patsy, but it goes something like this: Martha, Marty, Matty, Patty, Patsy.

In a letter on his appointment as Commander-in-Chief of the American Revolutionary Army, Washington wrote: "You may believe me, my dear Patsy, that so far from seeking this appointment, I have used every endeavor in my power to avoid it. . . ."

And the letter touchingly ends: "I am with the most unfeigned regard, my dear Patsy, Your affectionate George Washington."

The letter is dated, "Philadelphia, 18th June, 1775."

*Arthur J. Morgan**
New York, New York

The Slur Patrol also oppresses cartoonists.

A cartoon of mine in The New Yorker, *showing a couple of mice pursued by a cat and captioned "Two Rodent-Americans pursued by a Feline-American"—obviously to ridicule the vogue of appointing everybody some kind of hyphenated American—evoked an angry letter from a reader, protesting that although she was "not a politically correct person" (no, not much), she was offended by the supposed insinuation that "African-Americans" and "Native-Americans" were no more than animals. Proceeding from that assumption, I was found guilty of promoting slavery and genocide.*

Another cartoon, "We can be proud of our little Attila. He has totally absorbed the Hun ethic," elicited a phone call from a woman who claimed that it denigrated Huns. (And I suppose we should be careful about using the word "denigrate," to blacken.)

J. B. Handelsman
Hampton Bays, New York

Not all current Jesuits are necessarily crafty or equivocal—though I've heard it said you can't ask a Jesuit a question without having him make a distinction.

Q: When you ask a Jesuit a question, does he always answer with a distinction?
A: That depends.

Edward J. Mattimoe, S.J.
Chicago, Illinois

*Arthur J. Morgan, one of "On Language"'s most valued correspondents, died on September 28, 1996.

You can stop trying to figure out the meaning of Governor Cuomo's characterization of his thoughts as "Vincentian" rather than "Jesuitical."

Saint John's University in New York City, from which the governor earned undergraduate and law degrees, was founded by priests of the Congregation of the Missions. The members of that order are referred to as Vicentians in honor of the founder of the order.

During the early 1950's, when Governor Cuomo was a student at St. John's, he must have taken theology courses, which were required for all students in the university's two liberal arts colleges. These courses were frequently taught by Vicentian priests.

Frank Boucher
Washington, D.C.

To relieve you of puzzlement over Mario Cuomo's response to your use of the word "Jesuitical," I call your attention to his alma mater, St. John's University, which is operated by the Vincentian order of priests (as opposed to the Jesuits running Fordham, Georgetown, etc.).

This is not to say, of course, that a Vincentian cannot be lower-case jesuitical, nor their students, one in particular. I accept your third definition of the word; however, given the more widely understood meaning of duplicity, intrigue and equivocation, it is understandable why the governor would prefer "Vincentian," which, if ever used as an adjective, would always be benign.

John M. Dunleavy
Plainview, New York

Poor Fr. Mahoney! His objection to your use of the term hocus-pocus *may be, as you suggest, "digging too deep for prejudice."*

*I wonder whether the good Father also will object to the new film from Disney Studios entitled—what else?—*Hocus Pocus. *Disney guilty of using "prejudicial terms"? I don't think so.*

As for your own declaration, "When I want to be a patsy, I'll be one," I reply, "OK by me." I hope, however, that if you should run afoul of the Slur Patrol, and get hauled off to the slammer, you never (ever!) write about being transported in a paddy wagon.

The dictionary may plead ignorance on the origin of this term, but my Irish ancestors and their relatives and neighbors knew very well whence came this moniker. And they—we!—did not like it one bit. Write, instead, patrol wagon, police van, whatever. Paddy wagon *definitely is a no-no and cannot be traced to an Italian expression for "fool."*

I'm no patsy*—or* Patsy, *either. Nor am I a "Mick," if it comes to that, despite my name.*

Michael F. McCauley
The Catholic Health Association of the United States
St. Louis, Missouri

You discuss the origin of the term "hocus-pocus."

The best explanation I have read for the origin of the term "hocus-pocus" appears on page 28 of Milbourne Christopher's delightful book, The Illustrated History of Magic *(Thomas Y. Crowell Company, 1973, ISBN 0-690-43165-1).*

Mr. Christopher writes: "Hocus pocus was common parlance in England [during the 14th and 15th centuries] to describe both a magician and his tricks. Some writers thought the phrase came into the language after it became customary for Italian performers to appeal to 'Ochus Bochus,' a long-dead wizard, to assist them in their conjuring." He goes on to state that "Some members of the clergy later accused the magicians of profaning 'Hoc est enim Corpus meum.' . . . *This is unlikely considering the difficulties conjurers had had with the church in the past."*

Mr. Christopher also tells us that "Thomas Ady, a British writer, says in A Candle in the Dark *(1655) that the best performer in King James' day . . . 'called himself the King's Majesty's most excellent Hocus Pocus' and used the words in his patter."*

James Royce
Holmdel, New Jersey

With regard to talmudic, *I suggest that it be used only to mean "relating to the Talmud." For the meaning "exceedingly scholarly; concentrating on a close reading and interpretation of text" I suggest* talmudistic; *i.e., like a talmudist, one who studies the Talmud. Likewise, I use* historic *to mean important or memorable, and* historical *to mean pertaining to the study or commemoration of history.*

Howard J. Wilk
Philadelphia, Pennsylvania

I well remember being taught that Vincentian philosophy was based on Aristotelian-Thomastic teachings. The implication was that this was a far stronger foundation than that on which Jesuit philosophy was based.

Teresa Iusi Martinis
Valley Stream, New York

How very clever of Gov. Cuomo to clearly identify his background and training as Vincention. The governor is a graduate of three Vincention institutions, St. John's Prep, St. John University and St. John's University School of Law.

St. Vincent and his successors were not "Jesuitical" in a very important way. Although not anti-intellectual in any sense, St. Vincent, again according to Fr. Poole, was suspicious of intellectual pursuits which did not serve the apostolic needs of faithful or the overall goals of his community. Thus, one might interpret the governor's distinction of Vincention, as opposed to Jesuitical, as his embracing a form of intellectual enquiry rooted in the need for practical solutions for human problems instead of the singularity involved with intellectual pursuits for scholarly purposes alone.

*Anthony J. Scanlon**
St. John's Prep '69
New York, New York

Slur Patrol II

Here comes the Slur Patrol, spraying suppressing fire. Let's take a meeting on taking offense.

"Use of the term *philistinism,*" writes Daniel J. Booser of Houston, "to denote 'smug, ignorant . . . antagonistic to artistic and cultural values' (*American Heritage Dictionary*) is offensive." He objects to this "derogatory ethnic term" that appeared in *The New York Times Book Review;* he equates "Philistines" with "Palestinians."

Philistine—one from Philistia, an ancient region from Jaffa to the Egyptian desert south of Gaza—is an adjective and noun from the Assyrian word *Palastu,* according to the *Encyclopedia Britannica*'s eleventh edition; in Greek and Latin, this term became *Palaestina,* and in English *Palestine.*

The term *Philistine* was first used in English as a term of hostility in the early seventeenth century, meaning "the enemy" and later applied to bailiffs or sheriff's officers. Students in German universities called local townspeople *Philister* after a violent "town vs. gown" clash in Jena in 1693, and a local minister preached on the text "The Philistines be upon you, Samson." The poet and critic Matthew Arnold popularized the word in his essay on Heinrich Heine's poetry in 1865, signifying "inaccessible to and impatient of ideas."

The term *Palestinian* appeared first in 1875, used as an adjective, as in "Palestinian Arab," or as a noun describing Zionists wishing to return to Palestine, the political title of the land west of the Jordan mandated to Britain in

*Anthony J. Scanlon died on January 10, 1998.

1920. The name was officially superseded by *Israel* in 1948, when Jews established a state, but remained in use to describe a region by Arabs who remained, or who left and demanded resettlement. Israelis preferred "Palestinian Arabs" rather than "Palestinians," because the use of the noun suggested nationhood, but that distinction has broken down.

Because *Palestinian* shares a root with *Philistine,* it's easy to see why Palestinians take offense at the sense of the related word as "cultural inferior" or even "barbarian." I usually resist the language police, and surely this is an unintended slur, but it is a slur nevertheless; cultural elitists will just have to come up with a new word.

Now to *fatties,* a term with a two-century history that has come under heavy fire from those who would substitute a euphemism. On the sitcom *Murphy Brown,* a heavyset woman announces, "I prefer to think of myself as a *person of size.*"

Karen Stimson, director of Largesse, a group that fights *sizism,* weighed in with this comment to the A.P.: "Being fat has always meant being downwardly mobile, especially for women. Society discriminates against *people of size.*"

The phrase is bottomed on *people of color,* an eighteenth-century term for "nonwhites" enjoying new popularity among those not pigmentally deprived. The related noun *sizism* or its variant *weightism* has been patterned on *racism, sexism* and *ageism.* The lexicographer Anne Soukhanov offers a 1991 variant reported in the *Chicago Tribune: shapeism,* the charge made against anyone who calls anyone else *shapely.* (Like *ageism,* the noun *shapeism* keeps its *e* before the suffix *-ism.*)

This latest twist of P.C. patois is defined under an entry in Sid Lerner and Gary S. Belkin's 1993 dictionary of current terms, *Trash Cash, Fizzbos and Flatliners.* The adjective *nonsizist* refers to "language that seeks to be nonjudgmental in referring to a person's relative physical bulk. Words such as *thin, svelte, large* and *fat* can be regarded as undesirable in nonsizist language." (I doubt, though, that their suggested use of *generously cut* for "being overweight" will lumber off the ground.)

Fat is a description, not a slur. After Teddy Roosevelt broke up the trusts, his presidential successor, William Howard Taft, softened the attack on big business with his most famous dictum: "Mere size is no sin." The remark was widely noted because Mr. Taft, at three hundred pounds, was our largest President.

Smearing It On, Rubbing It In

"Romance with *commitment.* That's what today's woman wants."

Those were the words of Calvin Klein, introducing a floral-scented fragrance named Eternity. That's when *commitment* was in, a word that has gone from connoting entrance into a mental institution to its modern meaning of "permanent relationship" or perhaps a mutual understanding to date steadily at least through New Year's Eve. If you want a word to stand for a long-range commitment, *eternity* cannot be topped. (*Forever* must have been considered, but the diamond people have a lock on that word; *forever* is expensive.)

Mr. Klein's commitment to *commitment* followed his mid-80's passion for Obsession, which he defined poetically at the time as "passion beyond reason." Times and public moods change, and people in the cosmetics, fragrance and fashion industry like to be right out there on the cusp with the words that reverberate with customers. We can observe some key changes in the public discourse by tracking the latest hot buttons in that multibillion-dollar industry.

In billboard and magazine advertising for his current line of underwear, Calvin Klein is using as his male model a rapper named Marky Mark, who wears a distressed expression that seems to reflect his difficulty in adjusting the zipper on his pants, but the theme of much of the cosmetics and fragrance advertising is behind the product line of Escape; it speaks of having "time to be alone" and being "free." Thus, we have come from the uninhibited passion of Obsession ("Grab her!") to the commitment of Eternity ("Hold her") to the freedom of Escape ("Let her go, and lemme outta here").

Chanel, on the contrary, has delivered a consistent underlying message: the realization of elegant dreams. The advertising slogans play with rhymes ("Every Woman Alive Wants Chanel No. 5" and "The Spell of Chanel"), and the dream-come-true theme is updated. "As the man appeared with the spritzing of No. 5 in the air," I am informed by a Chanel copywriter, Sheila White, "that was a mere statement of wish-fulfillment. In the new campaign, 'Share the Fantasy' invites participation in the dream."

Now to the lingo of *skin care,* a phrase that seems to have replaced *makeup,* suggesting a trend away from painting the face toward preserving it.

"As women have become more demanding of performance from their treatment products," Ms White says, "Chanel has become more explicit in the language of its claims. The old way: 'The Clockstopper' was the headline for an 'anti-aging' product. The new way: 'Up to 45 Percent Reduction in the Appearance of Wrinkles,' but lightened by the fillip 'We don't say it's a miracle. You may think otherwise.' " (That is an example of the rhetorical technique called aporia, in which you feign doubt about where to begin, or make a statement by saying you will not be able to make that statement.)

Skin care copy is pulsating proof that we are in the Anti-Age Age. "Gray hair lies," charges Miss Clairol, with the adjuration to "keep it healthy-looking, young and vibrant." In the old days, Clairol stressed naturalness, asking, "Does she . . . or doesn't she?" with its double-entendre, and asserting that "only her hairdresser knows for sure."

This classic ad was replaced by a forerunner of the escapist school, "If I've only one life . . . let me live it as a *blonde*!" That formulation would not be used today; *blonde* is a color, not a person, and feminists believe—with good reason—that the use of the adjective as a noun demeans the person. "She is blonde" is

O.K., though "her hair is blonde" is better; "she is *a* blonde" is out, though she is perfectly free to live her life like one. The distinction is not trivial; "he is a blond" is rare; "he is blond" more common; "he has blond hair" most common. (*New York Times* style uses the spelling *blonde* only as a noun for a woman.)

In anti-ageism, the enemy is the wrinkle; the defense is high-technology cosmetics. Estée Lauder offers Lucidity, based on *lucid,* "clear," now with the sense of "intelligible" but originally "suffused with light"; the product is described as "Light-diffusing makeup SPF 8." (Deep-penetrating research reveals that *SPF 8* means "Sun Protection Factor 8.") Sun hats off to Estée Lauder for calling it forthrightly *makeup,* but what's this notion of light diffusion?

Color and Light from Max Factor is lightheaded, too: "We discovered a way to make color pigments transparent." Sentence fragments follow in shards: "To let light in. Use light, so skin looks naturally flawless. For sheer impact. In any light. Anywhere."

Just as Prescriptives and Clinique assumed the nomenclature of a clinical, health-care approach, other companies embraced sciencese: Timeless Essence from Charles of the Ritz eschews romance to describe "a new patented molecule that . . . penetrates within the upper epidermal layers" and "helps minimize dead cell buildup."

L'Oréal now offers Technicare, which is not Medicare for aging technicians but "Advanced Technology Color Care." That company's Lightnesse—described as "an original liposome-based cream-gel formula"—stresses the word *natural,* which seems to be the key word in the Anti-Age Age. (A *liposome* is a microscopic sac containing fatty substances. In any light. Anywhere.) Another product, Plénitude, "reduces the signs of aging"; the name is based on the word meaning "abundance," from the Latin *plenus,* "full"; maybe it means that it has plenty of moisturizing "hydra-renewal cream."

Note the spelling of the word *cream.* Time was, regulations required some dairy product to be present in anything labeled "cream"; cosmetics copywriters got around that butter-lobby's obstacle by changing the spelling to *creme,* the French way, but without the accent. ("Beyond the luxury of a silky *creme*" is Rénergie by Lancôme, carefully advertising "the appearance of diminished wrinkles.") I called three different cosmetics outfits to find out why *cream* was now O.K. in their shops, and am still awaiting calls back from Washington law firms.

Do the words of advertising copy really sell these products? You bet they do; that's why they are so carefully attuned to the shifting public moods. What comes after Escape? Try La Safire's Recapture, or wait for my unforgettable (Revlon's favorite adjective) Commitment. (I see the unisex Commitment in a square bottle, with a tiny golden ball and chain around its neck.)

Smilin' *Thru*?

Congress is trying to pull a fast one on tax policy. No, this is not a diatribe about VAT—for "value added tax," wrongly called the "VAT tax" by the Redundance Kids—but a shot across the bow of Senator Dale Bumpers and Representative Robert T. Matsui, authors of a tax bill that would enshrine in law the informal spelling of *through* as *thru.*

Comes now (a fine legal archaism) Anne Heausler of the firm of Fulbright & Jaworski, L.L.P. (short for Limited Liability Partnership, which I assume combines the protection of a corporation with the camaraderie of a partnership) with a fax of a bill to amend the Internal Revenue Code. Our linguistically swinging legislators hope to provide capital gains savings for investors "who make high-risk, long-term, growth-oriented venture and seed capital investments in start-up and other small enterprises," a practice known on the Street as taking a flier on little cats and dogs.

Our solons want to create what they call a "pass-*thru* entity," which they define as "any partnership, any S corporation, any regulated investment company and any common trust fund." To drive home their enthusiasm for clipping the old-fashioned *ough* off *through* and substituting a zingy, with-it *u,* the would-be law-makers add a section on a "look-*thru* in case of subsidiaries," which is defined incomprehensibly but I think is intended to mean "disregard," as in "That snooty White House legislative aide looked right thru me."

This practice is known as lite legislating, which occurs in Washington every nite. Simplified spelling is an enterprise that was undertaken with fervent dedication by no less a language maven than Noah Webster, and carried on with passion by George Bernard Shaw and later by Colonel Robert McCormick, the *Chicago Tribune*'s publisher, but never caught on, no matter how authoritatively or resolutely presented. Certainly usage tends to simplify spelling (alright, already), but native speakers hate to be told by philologists, advertising copywriters and other brisk neatness freaks how to fix the old lingo. We'll make it easier in our own time, the public seems to say—just don't push us.

Merriam-Webster's Tenth New Collegiate Dictionary treats *thru* as an unstigmatized variant of *through,* but not even that publisher's anything-goes *Dictionary of English Usage* greenlites the spelling in noting, "*Thru* was on the first list of reformed spellings issued by the American Philological Association in 1876," adding, "As the organized interest in spelling reform waned, however, the use of *thru* in publications also shrank. . . . It remains a distant second choice in print."

The only place the hapless reform zips along at high speed is on the New York State Thruway, a thoroughfare that is not spelled *throughway.* The "reform" may make it into general speech one day; it's nice to see the old, unsimplified spelling hanging in there, tho.

Incidentally, many lawyers, even those who do not limit their liability, send faxes with a "confidentiality notice" boxed in funereal black. It goes: "The documents accompanying this telecopy transmission may contain confidential information belonging to the sender which [*sic*] is legally privileged. . . . If you are not the intended recipient, you are hereby notified that any disclosure, copying, distribution or the taking of any action in reliance on the contents of this telecopied information is strictly prohibited."

Henceforth, when I get such foolish attempts at unsolicited solicitations from solicitors on the cover sheet of a fax, I will automatically blaze back with the following: "Your attempt to burden this machine, which is my personal property, with your unwanted and demonstrably unconfidential information is summarily rejected; my fax machine is programmed to spew out telecopies of whatever it receives, whenever it gets the urge, with happy abandon to all and sundry, and if you find such dissemination objectionable, you may cease and desist from further unsought importunings and stick your information printed on my paper in your ear."

Have I gotten thru?

I must call your attention to a distressing category confusion that you engage in when you erroneously write (not speak!) of the reform (viz., the thru *spelling) possibly making "it into general speech one day." The issue has nothing to do with speech, but only with conventions of spelling!*

*Peter A. Schreiber**
Professor, English and Linguistics
University of Wisconsin
Madison, Wisconsin

After reading your piece on "thru," I would like to offer another impending casualty, fully to be as lamented as, in this case, ". . . ough." Specifically, I offer the world "until." This is more and more frequently being supplanted by "till." Not 'til, *which carries the legitimacy of the conversational apostrophe, but "till," which, to me, has the verbal meaning:* stir the dirt for food, *or the nominal meaning of* cash drawer *as in* cashier.

Hagen S. Morris
Greens Farms, Connecticut

*Professor Schreiber died on May 27, 1996.

Would that the insertion of the term "pass-thru" in the Internal Revenue Code were only a threat! In fact, the virus has long since entered the Code and spread to its farthest reaches, obliterating the more benign "pass-through" usage in nearly all precincts. Lexis this morning reports that 38 separate sections of the Code (ranging from Section 29—"Credit for Producing Fuel from a Nonconventional Source"—to Section 7701—"Definitions") already contain the mutant form; only one (Section 172—"Net Operating Loss Deduction") stubbornly insists on "pass-through." While I have not undertaken exhaustive research on the topic, the first infection occurred no later than 1986, when "pass-thru" was used in Section 168 ("Accelerated Cost Recovery System").

In other words, those who draft tax legislation seem to have tired of "-through" quite some time ago. Enuf!

Carl M. Jenks
Cleveland, Ohio

After forty-three years working in *Wall Street, I may have become a victim of my own jargon. In reading your column "Smilin' Thru?" I was jolted by the line, ". . . a practice known* on *the Street as taking a flier on little cats and dogs."*

The jolt came from your use of "on the Street" rather than "in the Street." Although I have been employed by the same firm all those years, I have worked at a number of different locations. I have worked on *Madison Avenue,* on *Hanover Street,* on *Third Avenue and even* on *Wall Street itself—three times.*

To my knowledge, my colleagues in San Francisco who have never set foot on *Wall Street still think of themselves as working* in *the Street.*

Robert J. Florentino
Newport, Rhode Island

Spectacular Hair Day

In the old days, newspapers were fairly straightforward about their weather predictions: "Tomorrow: cloudy, likelihood of thundershowers in late afternoon" was typical, or "Tomorrow: mostly sunny, hot and humid." In the heat of competition from handsome, giggling weathercasters on television, however—with their "Boyoboy, is tomorrow gonna be a scorcher!" and "Get out those galoshes, Charlie and Joan, it'll be pouring down cats and dogs"—the too-dignified print medium has had to enliven its prose.

Here is a recent forecast in the upper right hand corner of the front page of *The New York Times:* "Tomorrow, sunny, spectacular."

We all know what kind of weather *spectacular* is: two degrees lower than, and one wispy cloud short of, *glorious.* This sprightly editorialization of the weather news will surely lead to "Tomorrow, unseasonably cold, bone-chilling," perhaps all the way to "Tomorrow, overcast, drizzly, suicidal."

One kind of day that everyone dreads, however, has something to do with the humidity and the wind speed: It is the widely known and feared *bad hair day.* "For the past year or two," writes David A. Florman of Bayside, Queens, "the expression *bad hair day* has been used by my teen-age daughter and her friends. This week I noticed the expression on the cover of *Glamour.* Where was this first used?"

Here's my theory of the origin. Irritated with his coverage by *Us* magazine, the comedian Garry Shandling (who used to begin his routine with "Is my hair all right?") told the *Seattle Times* in January 1991: "I was at a celebrity screening of *Misery* and they made up a quote for me. They said I told them I was having a *bad hair day.* They didn't even talk to me!"

Us was doing Mr. Shandling a big favor, if his claim of misquotation is true: That was the first Nexis citation of a phrase that is upsweeping the country.

"There are good-hair days," wrote Margo Kaufman in the *Los Angeles Times* a month later, "when every curl bounces into place unbidden and I feel as if I can conquer the world. And there are *bad-hair days,* when each tress becomes possessed and I feel powerless and out of control."

A month later, it appeared in *The Toronto Star:* "Did Robert De Niro get caught in a crosswind or was he just having a *bad hair day*?" The following year, Mary Ann Hogan of the *Los Angeles Times* quoted Richard Denaro, a hairstylist: "Bad hair is like the 'check engine' light going off in your car. It's a sign that tells you: Do not proceed. You should just go back to bed."

The phrase crossed over from the style page to the front page with President Clinton's famous two-hundred-dollar haircut. "*Bad hair day* for Codename Elvis" was *Brandweek*'s lead; Jill Dougherty of CNN repeated *The Washington Post*'s headline about "Hair Force One" and added, "Back at the White House, it was a *bad hair day.*"

Since the phrase *bad hair* is being used as a compound adjective modifying *day,* it should have a hyphen, but in almost all the citations does not, and we might as well accept the mistake as idiomatic. Because it has lasted longer than the usual nonce expression, it deserves definition: specifically, "time when humidity leads to terminal frizzies or wind ruins a careful coiffure," but more profoundly, "a sense of frustration at a time when one seems to lose control of the ordinarily manageable details of life."

Cheer up, badhairdaytimers: After the wind and the mugginess muss up and depress us, the clouds roll by and the hairdo of our mind-set becomes nothing short of spectacular.

Squad Squad Report

Have you ever called a toll-free 800 number? If so, you have committed a redundancy: All 800 numbers are toll-free. You either make a toll-free call or call an 800 number, not both.

Does this mean the call is for free? Aha! I have just committed a joculism, which is a word or phrase intended to be an amusing error that is taken up as accurate by the unwary. The classic example is *irregardless,* a jocular dialect play dating back to 1912 on *irrespective* and *regardless;* it's a joke, not a word.

What are we to do with a more insidious joculism, *for free*? A few years ago, when the actor Cliff Robertson was the pitchman for A.T.&T. (which has now dropped its periods in an effort to expunge the word *telegraph*), copywriters frequently had him offering inducements *for free.*

The construction is based on a redundancy, which I remember from the 30's: "I'll give it to you *free for nothing.*" Something is either *free* or *for nothing*—not both. Putting them together was done facetiously, not intended to be taken seriously as Standard English, but it led in the early 40's to *for free.*

Ever since, learned usagists have been pulling chins over the phrase; is it a useful synonymous phrase for the formal *without charge*?

I think not. If you mean *for nothing,* or want to slam home your point with *at no cost to you,* say so. Or, if you like the word *free,* use it freely, but without the unneeded *for* preceding it. *Free of cost* is not exactly redundant, but you can do without the *of cost;* same with *cost-free.* For sheer persuasive power, nothing beats the unadorned *free.*

If you are impelled to pick up *for free,* use it in the knowledge that it is a joculism and may be taken by your listeners to be Standard English, which it is not. The usage is akin to *free gift,* which is rightly a target of the shock troops of the Lexicographic Irregulars who call themselves the Squad Squad.

Its members have already made their choice for Redundancy of the Year. When Representative Mel Reynolds of Illinois was about to be charged with having had a sexual relationship with a minor, he called a news conference to denounce his accuser as an "emotionally disturbed nut case."

Stand and Deliver

The most ill-considered phrase uttered on the floor of the House of Representatives recently came from the Speaker himself.

Urging his fellow Democrats to support President Clinton's economic proposals, Speaker Tom Foley said, "This is the time to stand and deliver."

Presumably, the Speaker meant that the members must courageously stand up and be counted to deliver their votes. However, the phrase *Stand and deliver!* is the command of the highwayman holding up a horse-drawn coach. Its meaning was clear to every driver carrying valuable cargo: *Stand* still and *deliver* up the gold and jewelry.

The phrase today still carries the connotation of mounted theft. It's not a locution a politician wants to apply to a representative's relations with the taxpayers.

While I found your explanation of "stand and deliver" as a highway robbery demand refreshing, I do not believe that the phrase holds the same connotation today. The phrase became updated with the appearance of the 1980's film Stand and Deliver, *in which Edward James Olmos, playing a rogue Los Angeles high school teacher, proposes teaching calculus to what seems to be an incorrigible group of students. During the instruction, he orders his students to "stand and deliver," at which point they work out a homework problem at the blackboard, answer one of his questions, or otherwise prove that they have mastered what they were expected to learn. In that sense, "stand and deliver" carries the sense of "prove what you can do, fulfill by action what you have claimed you are capable of doing." The phrase seems to carry a defensive edge as well, as if one were defending their personal honor by standing up and proving their worth in front of others.*

John McGreevey
Wynnewood, Pennsylvania

State of the Now

The Nitpickers' League has demanded a critique of President Clinton's State of the Union address, which I have resisted because his writers have made a conscious effort to clean up his act.

So just a few precepts: Do not start a sentence with the conjunction *so,* as in "So this year. . . ."

In enumerating, say "third" instead of the Bushian "the third thing."

Do not say "I am persuaded" when you mean "I am convinced"; it seems as if you were sold a bill of goods.

"Democracies don't attack each other" should be "one another," referring to more than two.

When positing anything contrary to fact, get subjunctively moody: "as though the world itself *was*" should be *were.*

Run the whole thing through a cliché-checker. Not all jobs need be *targeted,* all problems *tackled,* all campaigns *launched.*

Alliteration acolytes liked "replaced drift and deadlock with renewal and reform." And this adjuration to my old co-conspirator, Bob Dole, in his rebuttal: How often can you start a sentence with *Now*? Ronald Reagan could not get going without a *Well,* and Dole is trying the same thing with *Now.* As Gertude Stein would say, drop the *now* now.

As a member of the Nitpickers' League I must ask: Is Gertrude Stein hanging out somewhere incognito? Alive and well—well?

Shouldn't the last sentence of your piece have read "As Gertrude Stein might have said" rather than "As Gertrude Stein would say"?

Frank O'Donnell
New York, New York

Status Report

"The issue," President Clinton told a news conference, "is whether men and women who can and have served with real distinction should be excluded from military service solely on the basis of their *status.*"

He went on to announce the staying of discharges "based on *status* alone."

Later, his press aide minimized the numbers of people to which the action would be applied "solely based on *status.*"

Used this way, the word *status,* which means "condition; position relative to others; legal character," is a fuzzifier—not quite a euphemism, but a bureaucratic substitute that takes the sting out of the word or phrase being avoided.

What Mr. Clinton means, and could bring himself to say, is *sexual preference* (the term preferred by those who think homosexuality is usually a proclivity reinforced by conscious choice) or *sexual orientation* (preferred by those who think homosexuality is primarily inborn). These phrases deal with condition, not behavior, and can thus be referred to delicately as *status* in contrast to *activity.*

Let's take a stand: Is the fuzzifier pronounced "STAT-us," as President Clinton prefers, or "STAY-tus," preferred in *Merriam-Webster's Tenth New Collegiate, American Heritage Third* and the *Random House Webster's*?

Clintonites find support in the third edition of *Webster's New World,* which reversed its previous position and chose "STAT-us." Victoria Neufeldt, who edited that dictionary for Simon & Schuster and is now with Merriam-Webster (the status of lexicographers is fluid) says that the more frequent pronunciation in the United States has become "STAT-us." "It parallels the change from "DAY-ta" to "DAT-a" among younger people," says Ms Neufeldt, "especially computer people. I'm from Canada, and still say "STAY-tus" and "DAY-ta," so I guess I'm hopelessly behind the times."

Reserve judgment; in a few years, we'll review the status of the data.

Most scholars who have delved into the subject, including Freud and Kinsey, regard homosexuality mainly as a social status that society has created to control a wide range of sexual behaviors.

According to sociologist Talcot Parsons, a "role" is a combination of "norms," or expected behaviors. A "status" is a collection of roles. The term "homosexual" consists of a number of stigmatic roles, but researchers commonly use the term "role" or "identity" in the singular in the sense of "status."

The terms "homosexuality," "homosexual," "sexual identity," and "sexual preference" have little scientific credibility outside their social use as stigmatic labels. As Kinsey warned us, the term "homosexual" belongs to behaviors, not persons.

William H. DuBay
Costa Mesa, California

I was interested in your notion that Bill Clinton uses status *as a euphemism for sexual orientation, but I think more is at work here.*

Mr. Clinton wants to frame the debate in terms of the general principle that people should not be excluded or persecuted on the basis of who they are (status). "Alone" is included to exclude statuses that affect job performance, such as obesity, low intelligence, etc. That's a smart approach because anyone with any type of minority status—blacks, Jews, Catholics, Greeks, the vast majority of Americans—is interested in defending Mr. Clinton's principle, even if it means tolerating those terrible homosexuals. The Republicans are left standing up for what is fast becoming their sole constituency: straight, white, fundamentalist males with two kids, a six-figure income and a stay-at-home wife.

By the way, you should have been more specific in your definitions of sexual orientation *and* sexual preference. *The only people in a position to merely "think" or hypothesize about homosexuality's origins are heterosexuals. We homosexuals* know *our sexuality is no choice, which is why we say sexual* orientation. *Those heterosexuals who "think" that homosexuality is a* preference *are primarily ideologues uninterested in reality and heterosexual men who think that, by growing out of their adolescent longing for the boy next door, they somehow chose against homosexuality.*

Richard Cendo
Boulder, Colorado

Stiffed Again

Release that puff of smoke from the college of lexicographers; we have a new political verb.

At that rarity of rarities, a presidential news conference, Thomas L. Friedman of *The New York Times* asked whether aid to Russia would be withdrawn if Boris Yeltsin was removed.

"I don't want to get into hypothetical situations," said President Clinton, averting what F.D.R. used to call an "iffy" question, "because I don't want anything I say or do to either undermine or rigidify the situation there."

Quick as a fax, in came this query from Martin Daly of St. Louis: "Did Bill Clinton use the word *rigidify* in his news conference? If so, please respond forthwith."

Firstwith: The adjective *rigid,* rooted in the Latin verb *rigere,* "to be stiff," is a member of the increasingly unpopular *stiff* family, although it may have been influenced by *rectus,* "straight," which led to *rectitude.*

Secondwith: Both as an adjective and in its noun form, *rigidity,* it has these different senses: 1. hard; resistant to change in form when hit or twisted, like "a rigid steel bar"; 2. firm; unyielding, not to be pushed out of place, a sense seized upon by every mattress salesman in business today and the only upbeat, positive sense of the word; 3. difficult to change, inflexible, intransigent, inelastic, unbending, like "a rigid negotiating position"; 4. severe, harsh, like "a rigid disciplinarian," even bitter or cruel, as in the playwright Ben Jonson's "when rigid frosts have bound up brooks and rivers."

Thirdwith: *Rigid* is a word almost always used in criticism these days, though George Eliot, in her novel *Middlemarch* in 1871, used it in praise with "He was one of those rare men who are *rigid* to themselves and indulgent to others." Nowadays, the related *rigorous* is preferred when the desire is to praise, as in *rigorous* exercise with Jane Fonda. If you want to make rigidity look good, you turn to *unwavering* or *principled,* but rarely is *rigid* a compliment.

That's more than you need to know about the adjective *rigid,* this background drawn mostly from the ten-volume *Century Dictionary* of 1897, a wonderful resource now available in some antiquarian bookshops.

Now, forthwith (from the Old English phrase *forth mid,* "along with," later coming to mean "at the same time, immediately, at once") to the verb form, or as some purists resisting change will say, the damnable verbification of an innocent noun.

Suppose you are President, and want to get across the third sense of *rigid,* "inflexible," in an active way. You could always say *to make rigid,* but that's not very creative. You could choose the inclusive *to stiffen,* but that is not sufficiently pejorative, because "to stiffen the sinews" and "to stiffen a backbone" convey a healthy fixity of purpose, and your intention is the opposite, to disparage the inflexibility. How about *to paralyze*? Excessive; that would be overkill.

You, the elected leader of the free world—hell, of the whole world now—have an urgent need for a verb to signify (and cast mild aspersion on) diplomatic sclerosis. The only one that comes to mind is *freeze,* but that sounds too much like price-control lingo and you don't want to kick the stock market out of bed.

What to say? You think to yourself; with 43 percent of the vote, do I have a mandate to create a political verb? Popularity is pushing 60 percent, but the Harris negatives are up over 40 percent—will a blatant act of functional shiftiness turn the English teachers against me?

All this flashes through your mind in an instant, with all the piranhas of the press eager to lunge at whatever you say, and you take the plunge: ". . . to either undermine or *rigidify* the situation there." What the hell, it says what you mean, and nobody will notice that it's not even in some dictionaries.

But we all stiffened with notice. Now the moment of sober second thought: Are we to be rigid prescriptivists or roundheeled descriptivists? Should we embrace *rigidify* or stand our ground against the habit of turning our nouns into verbs?

Here's one vote to legitimate *rigidify.* It is stronger than *freeze,* milder than *paralyze,* more critical than *solidify* and far more conversational than *cause to become rigid.* Besides, the rare verb has been used outside of politics since John Tyler's Administration; the Scottish theologian John Cairns wrote in an 1842 letter, "The muscles of the mind . . . are rigidified by frost and unstrung by heat."

Rack its political use up "Among the New Words," *American Speech* quarterly; in language mavening, we bend lest we break.

C'mon, Safire, you can do better than that. Surely Friedman asked the President whether aid to Russia would be withdrawn if Boris Yeltsin were *removed, not* was *removed.*

Your use of a simple past tense instead of the correct subjunctive confuses and misleads us literati. *A less erudite readership might not have trouble with that construction, but you've got to remember that you're not writing for just anybody and we take our subjunctives seriously.*

Leonardo Neher
Bethesda, Maryland

Stormy Whether—or Not?

This department is blessed not merely by the existence of the Lexicographic Irregulars, with shock troops of the Gotcha! Gangsters, but also by a more irenic quartet of advisers: the "On Language" Board of Octogenarian Mentors, acronym'd Olbom.

What a crew: Jacques Barzun, author of *The House of Intellect* and *The Modern Researcher;* Alistair Cooke, retired as host of *Masterpiece Theater* and long the interpreter of America to the Mother Country; Allen Walker Read, the etymologist of American English who found the origin of *O.K.,* and Frederic G. Cassidy, editor of the *Dictionary of American Regional English,* our answer to Sir James Murray of the *Oxford English Dictionary.* Their collective ages, projected backward in time, would take us to 1649.

Want to see Olbom at work?

"The question is *whether* anti-Castro forces are willing to watch what he says, not what he does" was a citation from *Newsweek* submitted by Bruce Kluger, an editor of *Playboy.* He asks: "Shouldn't *whether* be followed by *or not* at all times? And if *or not* is not needed after *whether,* shouldn't some sort of alternative-choice phrase be added?"

Modern usage books say that the only time *or not* must be used is in an adverbial clause, as in "*Whether or not* you like listening to speeches, you'll tune in to the inaugural address." Otherwise, the *or not* can be clipped, as the writer cited in *Newsweek* did.

Now let's deal that card to a couple of members of Olbom. Allen Walker Read thinks the clipping is O.K.: "The full phrase *whether or not* is appropriate in formal writing, but *whether* by itself is often found in colloquial contexts. Sentences can read smoothly with *whether* by itself."

Jacques Barzun thinks that "rules" about such things as split infinitives and beginning sentences with conjunctions "all are schoolmarm short cuts to bypass the thinking that ought to guide choice in different situations." On the matter of *whether or not,* he applies that thinking to three sentences:

1. "Whether or not he apologizes, he must leave my house."
2. "Whether the event favors us or not, we made a point."
3. "Whether these figures are right, I don't know."

Writes Professor Barzun: "All three are perfectly good sentences. Now, why do I write them as they stand? The first emphatically urges the alternative. The second has the same intention, but the rhythm requires putting *not* at the end of the clause: Try to put it up front and you'll see how weak 'favors us' will sound. The third, unlike the first two, does not affirm or enforce an idea; it raises a doubt, and so the *whether* is left hanging."

Here's Barzun's rule-knocking nuance: "Purpose and rhythm together equal rhetoric, and rhetoric determines the placement of movable parts. Every sentence poses its own problem, which can only be solved by thought." (Lest the Gotcha! Gang wonder why he did not write "solved only by thought," he adds: "Note the idiomatic placement of *only,* which would be overstressed if put in its logical place.")

Now to impossible etymology, the search for roots that lie far from any dictionary. Have you been driven crazy by the prevalence of *you know* in American speech? Where does this useless interjection come from? Why do we use it? To Professor Read:

"It is not commonly known," he replies, "that *you know* was ubiquitous in England in the early nineteenth century, and American travelers often remarked on it. The attached quotation of 1835 is typical."

James Brooks, a Representative from New York, wrote *The New-Yorker* in 1835 (in its pre–Tina Brown incarnation): "Kendal, you know (I don't know whether you know it or not—but *you know* is a phrase an Englishman throws in at the turn of every sentence, when he is hunting for a new idea, or the words to fill the coming one . . .)—but Kendal, you know (I am getting the rascally habit) is great in linsey wolsey."

See? Some linguistic resources even beat the *O.E.D.* on compact disk. Nor does the Olbom limit itself to answers: "What's the origin of *busboy*?" writes Alistair Cooke. "Is it related to *omnibus*?"

John Algeo, far too young for Olbom but a distinguished professor of English at the University of Georgia, thinks Cooke's speculation is correct. The French name for a public conveyance, *voiture omnibus,* "vehicle for everybody," led to the English acceptance of *omnibus* as meaning "for everybody"; it was picked up in political parlance in the 1850's as an *omnibus bill,* sweeping together a little of everything. Professor Algeo speculates that a lowly restaurant employee, called on for everything, may have been called an omnibus; in 1913, the word *busboy* appeared in the United States.

While I had him, I asked Algeo about *you know.* He does not treat the locution with revulsion: "It draws into the discourse the person being addressed. . . .

Another use is to fill up time while the speaker is thinking what to say next. It is, of course, the frequency of use and not the term itself that is irksome."

Finally, I turned to Fred Cassidy, the man from *DARE,* for the pronunciation of the word for a person from Arkansas.

The state is pronounced "AR-kin-saw." The derivation, according to the *Illustrated Dictionary of Place Names,* edited by Kelsie B. Harder, is from the Quapaw tribe of the Sioux, who were called *Ugakhpah,* "downstream people"; French explorers called them *Acansa.* (Do not confuse this with the origin of *Kansas,* from the Siouan *Kansa* or *Kaw,* "people of the south wind.")

"People in Arkansas used to spell it *Arkansaw,*" Professor Cassidy informs me, "and were often called *Arkansawyers* in the days when trees were cut up by hand." A *sawyer* was one who sawed lumber; it was also the name of a log bobbing in the Mississippi River, and may have led to Mark Twain's selection of the name Tom Sawyer. "But the word is no longer acceptable," Cassidy reports. "Now one must say *Arkansans,* alongside *Kansans*."

Bill Clinton, then, from AR-kin-saw, is an ar-KAN-zen.

Dear Bill:

That was a comical-cute piece you had on the Old Codgers. But you'll have to do better than Olbom. *Like the California condor, it will not fly.*

How about OGPU (Octogenarians for Guarding Pure Usage). Better still (for those of us who know what we're talking about)—The Four Horsemen of the Pukka Ellipse! (e.g., She looks as (she would look) if she had *a cold.)*

Once you started on the pronunciation of "Ark'n-saw," I was sure you were going on to the interesting oddity that was always mentioned by the great Miles L. Hanley in his classes on American pronunciation: that the state was called "Arkansaw" because it was settled by Frenchmen; but the river was—still is—pronounced "Ar-kansas" because its headwaters are well to the north, in Colorado—which was settled mainly by Anglos, Germans and,—God knows, Scots (and no doubt—as always in mining country—some Cornish Jacks). They knew as little French as the stout Irish railroadmen who went through Tennessee and re-christened the Frenchmen's L'Eau Froid *(they found a blessed lake there at the end of many hot days of marching),* "Low Freight."

Alistair [Cooke]
New York, New York

Dear Bill:

Is it indecorous or ungrateful of me, in my first act as a member of Olbom, to find fault with the sole begetter of that Crew? Probably both—but duty calls. In the first column of the "Stormy Whether" column, I find "Whether or not *you like listening to speeches, you'll tune in to the inaugural address. Otherwise, the* or not *can be clipped, as the writer cited in* Newsweek *did." Well, perhaps he deserved to be clipped, but hardly in print, or in this of all columns. Gotcha! Gangsters take note.*

As long as I'm being picky . . . In the third column I found, "But Kendel, you know . . . is great in linsey wolsey." Wool, *even in this word, has two* o*'s (see* O.E.D.*).* Wolsey, *even with a small* w, *suggests the archbishop who defied Henry VIII over a little matter of divorce.*

Apologies to the Begetter; a murrain on bad typesetters and proofreaders.

Fred [Frederic G. Cassidy]
Chief Editor
Dictionary of American Regional English
Madison, Wisconsin

You omitted discussion of a formulation which is both Shakespearean and current. That other William wrote (roughly) about whether *'tis nobler in the mind* to *suffer the slings and arrows of outrageous fortune . . .* or to *take arms against them. . . .*

I refer, despite the imperfect citation, to a usage such as "(I can't decide) whether to do A or to do B." Consideration of "or not" doesn't seem to apply to this case.

I had no problem deciding whether to write to you at the Washington or New York offices of The Times.

As ever, I value your thoughts and analyses, whether they are disseminated during the week, on Sundays, in book form, or on radio or television. (There's an unplanned multiplex "whether.")

William J. McKeough
Greenvale, New York

Apropos your article on the popularity of "you know" in 19th-century England, the meaning was quite different, you know.

In England it appears to have been used as a diffident expression of humility, meaning "I realize you have full knowledge of the matter I'm discussing and do not wish to imply that I am teaching you anything." In modern America, it clearly means: "I know what I'm trying to say but can't articulate it because I failed 5th grade English; nevertheless, I hope you know what I'm trying to say, too."

The point is that it's how you speak, not what you know, you know.

Geoffrey Richstone, M.D.
New York, New York

But the river that runs through it is pronounced "the Ar-KAN-zas."

Margaret Haines
Tucson, Arizona

Your brief discussion of the correct identification of people from Arkansas oversimplified a complicated issue.

First, the spelling "Arkansaw" was used in the 1819 legislation creating the territory, although the French and Spanish had consistently spelled the area "Arkansas." William Miller, the first territorial governor, arrived at the Post of Arkansas on a barge flying a flag with "Arkansaw" written on it in several places.

Second, the pronunciation of the word was then much debated. Chester Ashley, who served in the U.S. Senate from 1844 to 1848, pronounced the word with the emphasis on the second syllable. To avoid taking a stand on this issue, he was referred to as the Senator from Arkansas *while Ambrose Sevier was the Senator from* Arkansas. *The state legislature made Sevier's the official pronunciation in 1881 but did not settle the question of how to identify a resident of the state.*

Third, although one sees the vulgar term Arkansawyer *in the nineteenth century and a few proponents have urged its adoption into formal usage, the preferred term through the mid-nineteenth century, nowhere mentioned by your authorities, is* Arkansian. *Elias Cornelius Boudinot, the Cherokee leader, edited a newspaper by that name in Fayetteville in 1859–60, and there are several instances of twentieth century usage. It was used in my* Confederate Arkansas; The People and Policies of a Frontier State in Wartime, *published by the University of Alabama Press in 1976 and still in print. By the way, during the same time period people from Texas were Texians.*

The basic problem is simple. Arkansawyer *has never surmounted its vulgar origins;* Arkansan *sounds too much of Kansas; Arkansian is hallowed in time and closer to the proper pronunciation of "*Arkansas*" but has fallen out of use. Bill Clinton, then, is from "AR-kin-saw," but he could be any one of three things, perhaps appropriately, since Arkansas's history, Hindu-like, often looks at least in three different directions at once (e.g., the 1968 election in which Arkansas voted for George Wallace for President, made Winthrop Rockefeller Governor, and returned William Fulbright to the U.S. Senate).*

Michael B. Dougan
Professor of History
Arkansas State University
State University, Arkansas

Stud Muffin's Buzz-Kill

A *muffin* is an affectionate name for a young woman—"Not now, muffin"—usually taken as a put-down by the daughters of what a previous generation called *cookies.* In a vengeance expressed in campus slang, we now have *stud muffin,* which means "attractive young man." (The *stud* is rooted in the term for a male horse selected for breeding.) A *stud muffin* who works out, I am informed by Charles D. Poe of Houston, can transform himself into a *diesel.*

Welcome to the world of fresh campus slang, drawing on responses to an invitation in this space that went, "If your prof is *crunchy,* don't feel *schwag;* send your local lexicon to Safire's *Buzz-kill.*" Part of the teaser was a definition of *hookup* as "a person with whom one is romantically involved," and *wizard* as "exceptionally sick."

From Cornell University comes this refreshing dash of cold water: "Reading your article felt as if I were listening to a tone-deaf person sing," writes Anna Day of Ithaca, New York. "*Hookup* does not stand for romantic involvement. It is used primarily as a verb, and *to hook up* is to 'get some,' or 'make out.' Previous hookups can be a major source of embarrassment, since the word implies a certain amount of anonymity and a carnality one may not wish to admit to the next morning."

That's how we lexies learn; I had thought it was mere *friendin'.* "Being *crunchy* is the same as being *granola,*" Ms Day, a sophomore, goes on. "It's out-of-control (or *o.o.c.*) P.C., the type that support hunchback [*sic*] whales and don't shave their body hair. It's definitely pejorative and comes from the habit of the granola people of eating trail mix in otherwise civilized surroundings."

We're going too fast. *Granola* is an Americanism from the 1870's for a breakfast-food mixture of rolled oats, sesame seeds, wheat germ, nuts, dried fruit, brown sugar and, in some post-bellum cases, sawdust sweepings and whatever else was lying around the kitchen floor. When chewed, it crunches; when chewed by vegetarians, it does not angry up the blood. *Webster's New World Dictionary,* from Simon & Schuster, helpfully speculates that the word, originally a trademark, was built from the Latin *granum,* "grain," plus the Italian diminutive suffix *-ola.*

Out of control is psychological jargon, the reverse of the 1930's phrase *under control,* and is the title of Zbigniew Brzezinski's latest book on global turmoil (Zbig always uses the latest teen-age slang). The letters *P.C.,* which used to stand for "personal computer" back in the old 286 days, now of course initialize "politically correct," rooted in Maoist thinking. Headline writers cramped for space will welcome *o.o.c.p.c.* to describe such phrases as *temporally impaired* for "late."

Now to *buzz-kill.* Let us not confuse this with *the buzz,* meaning "the talk going around"; that onomatopoeic sense, which imitated the sound of a bee, started out meaning "confused and mingled sound," and gained a gossipy sense in

Shakespeare's *King Lear:* "On everie dream,/Each buz, each fancie"; it was picked up by William Cobbett, the English polemicist and vituperator, who wrote in his 1825 *Rural Rides* that "A sort of buz got about." Now it is the title of a page in *Variety* that sweeps together the latest show-biz chatter, and the first part of *buzzword,* a new term for "jargon" or "vogue word."

The other *buzz* is rooted in the sound some people think they hear in their head when slightly looped or mildly stoned—short of *smashed* by booze or *zonked* on drugs at a *rage,* or party. "A *buzz-kill* is something that kills a buzz," Ms Day notes, "such as having cops break up a party or losing a fake ID. It's generally said to empathize with someone. 'What a *buzz-kill*' would be an appropriate interjection when a friend is telling you about some sobering misfortune." (The term may be related to the earlier *kill-joy.*)

From Berkeley, California, comes this contribution from John J. Reilly, a recent Stanford graduate: "*Nectar,* an intensification of the locution *sweet,* which is most common in surfing culture, describing the esthetic perfection of a subject, usually waves or babes." (A *sweet spot* on a baseball bat is where the batter hopes it will meet the ball.)

From Dartmouth, these words from Richard Dudman: "*scam, n.,* a lover; *blitz, n.,* a message sent via electronic mail; *random, adj.,* strange or weird."

From David Sklar of Wynnewood, Pennsylvania, a high school student: *scudi, n.,* "money," and *blunt, v.i.* (not the noun *blunt,* which means "a cigar laced with marijuana"); the verb denotes "to perform tasks that are drudgery," as in "The reason I put up with *blunting* at McD's is for the *scudi.*"

From Jack Chambers, a professor of linguistics at the University of Toronto, who regularly surveys his students for his "Slang Bag" compilation:

Quad, "a fool," perhaps a clipping of *quadrilateral,* an updating of the 1960's *square.*

To be a friend of Dorothy, "to be homosexual," from the character played by Judy Garland in *The Wizard of Oz,* now a gay cult film. (This term has been used in England for several years.)

Level, "acceptable, approved." A substitute for *cool,* which used to mean "excellent," often expressed as simply *ex.* Gloria Peters, class of '93, finds a newer sense for *cool:* "I hear you and will take appropriate action." Her citation: On the television show *Roseanne,* the leading lady and her husband renew their vows. Instead of answering, "I will," Roseanne responds, "Cool."

Moneypuker, a vivid word picture for "automatic teller machine," unlikely to be taken up in banking advertising.

Professor Chambers adds a nice touch with this quotation from Walt Whitman: "Such is Slang . . . an attempt of common humanity to escape from bald literalism, and express itself illimitably."

But some slanguists are protective about their subject. "I hate to see teen-age argot forcibly injected into mainstream language," observes Ms Day from high above Cayuga's waters. "As soon as it settles into a patois to be translated, you may be sure that the code will change. What is left is wannabe faddish word parroters, mid-life crises people wandering about mumbling, 'Totally rad.' (*Rad* is dated. Very dated.) Get a clue, as we say up here."

Get a clue is an offshoot of *Get a life!,* the conservative imperative exhaustively discussed here previously. Both phrases were preceded by the turn-of-the-century shout *Get a horse!,* which is associated with *stud* and led finally to *stud muffin.*

There may be a female version of stud muffin. *While visiting Los Angeles last summer, some friends from back East took the opportunity to set me straight on the Southern California vernacular—expressions like "stressed," "stoked" and so on. As an example, Jacqueline described a conversation between two Valley Girl types trying on outfits in a changing room. "What do you think," she overheard one ask the other, "I don't look like a little* slut muffin, *do I?"*

Gordon Bock
Gloucester, Massachusetts

Style War: English vs. Murkin

Whose English language is it, anyway? From the tone of the new *BBC News and Current Affairs Stylebook and Editorial Guide,* you'd think the Brits invented it. With unmistakable disdain, the broadcastocrats in London call what we speak "American." As a user of Murkin English, I rise to the defense.

"English is a language that is constantly evolving," writes Tony Hall, the British Broadcasting Corporation's managing director of current affairs, "and we must recognise when change has taken place. That is a task that requires judgement. Hence this style book."

If he wants to spell *recognize* with an *s* or *judgment* with an extra *e,* that's O.K. (an Americanism) with me. But when he writes three times in his foreword about a *style book,* two words, when the book is titled *stylebook,* one word, he betrays a certain inconsistency. Gotta be this or that; can't have it both ways. (The subjects in those clauses are *it* and *you,* both understood; I can constantly evolve, too.) Both the Associated Press and *The New York Times* call their manuals of style *stylebooks,* without wavering; the new *Columbia Guide to Standard American English* calls itself a *usage book.* (Columbia, though more comprehensive, flinches from the controversy about *lifestyle;* A.P. properly treats it as one word, while *The Times* follows *Webster's New World Dictionary, Second Edition,* with *life style,* a locution with neither life nor style.)

"In English," goes the BBC stylebook/style book (putting a comma after the "English"), " 'to look like' means 'to resemble.' . . . In American" (the BBC stylist inexplicably leaves out the comma after the parallel construction) "it means also 'to look likely.' So Americans say: 'It looks like there'll be an election.' " It pains the BBC that "this usage is slowly making its way into English"; the example given is "It looks like raining later." (Americans, and many Brits, would say, "It looks like rain later.") The BBC prefers *looks as though* or *looks as if* to our *looks like.*

That's shooting a grouse in a barrel. The real like/as usage controversy, which the BBC fails to deal with, is the mistaken use of like as a conjunction, "like a cigarette should." The correct way to introduce that clause is with *as.* The way to use *like* in comparisons is as a preposition requiring an object: "Nothing improves the complexion like fog."

After primly resisting the onslaught of American common usage on *looks like,* the BBC goes squishily descriptive on beginning sentences with conjunctions. And what's wrong with starting sentences with *and*? Not a thing, says the BBC: "It may be wrong in grammar books. But it is an everyday occurrence. And it does not obscure meaning." We who labor in Murkin know that beginning a sentence with *and* can be an effective way of highlighting an afterthought, and beginning with *but* offers a stark contrast with the preceding thought. But we are on guard against stylistic choppiness. And two in a row is choppy (British usage may prefer "two in a row *are* choppy").

The BBC cites George Orwell's maxim "If it is possible to cut a word out, always cut it out." A couple of pages later, we have "we allow for stylistic differences to take account of the fact that. . . ." Orwell, revolving in his grave, would have cut *to take account of the fact that* and substituted *because.*

"Some Americanisms add vigour and dynamic expression to the language . . . *teenager, babysitter, know-how, gimmick, stunt, commuter, blurb.*" (Gee, thanks; but why use an ellipsis instead of a colon?) "But the BBC does not adopt Americanisms until they have become commonplace in good spoken English in this country. So we would draw the line [why the conditional *would*? Over goes Orwell again] at *diaper, drug-store, sidewalk,* etc., at Americanisms which [*sic*] simply stretch words needlessly (*transportation*), and at the American habit of turning nouns into verbs (to *hospitalise*)."

It has a good point on the unnecessary *-ation* tacked on *transport.* They join many speakers of Murkin in deploring hyperverbification, a noun coined at this very moment, based on the new verb *hyperverbify.* But what of collective nouns like *government, company, public*? In this paragraph, I have referred to the BBC as both *it* (singular) and *they* (plural); which is correct?

In Murkin, groups take the singular. The BBC *is.* In English, as the BBC restrictively calls its local dialect, you hear "the government *have*" or "the public *are.*" That's their way, as they would put it, or its way, as we would put it; we're both correct in our own bailiwick. And the BBC usefully adjures its announcers to avoid mixing singular and plural pronouns in "false concord." But the broadcaster quotes the usagists Fowler and Gowers as taking no position on whether collectives take singular or plural verbs, and then wimps out. (You can begin successive sentences with conjunctions if they're long sentences; doesn't sound choppy.)

Murkin says: Collectives collect, and the bunched-up bunch is construed as singular. "Nouns that denote a unit take singular verbs and pronouns," decrees the *A.P. Stylebook.* But some plural words—*bushels, data*—become collective nouns when the group is taken as a unit. "The data *is* sound" is right when you are thinking of the data as a unit, but when you conceive of the data as individual items, you can say, "The data *have been* carefully collected."

Murkins use that same sensible practice (we spell *practice* with a *c*) when it comes to *none.* When you mean "not one," it takes the singular: "none *is.*" When you mean "not any," it takes the plural: "none *are.*" Form follows function; construe it the way you intend to, and don't let some cockamamie rule force you into saying what you do not mean. The *New York Times* stylebook has it right: "*None.* Construe as a plural unless it is desired to emphasize the idea of *not one* or *no one*—and then it is often better to use *not one* or *no one* instead of *none.*"

As the BBC does. "None, like no-one," insists this suddenly prescriptive pedant, "always takes a singular verb. 'All of us are human. None of us is perfect.' "

None of these BBC usage rulings are sacrosanct. However, when American English calls for "an audience *with* the Queen," we would do better to say "an audience *of* the Queen." That's the BBC way, and in this instance, Murkins would do well to follow it. (And when we're with her, we should say something like "Looks as if raining.")

I am sorry to hear that the BBC laments the introduction of the supposed Americanism "it looks like rain" into the British language. Perhaps the editors of the BBC stylebook have forgotten that Christopher Robin, while pacing back and forth with his umbrella beneath a blue balloon and a very dirty Winnie-the-Pooh, said, (you can supply the accent), "Tut-tut, it looks like rain." Christopher Robin started his pacing, and Winnie-the-Pooh his quest for honey, in 1926. Isn't it likely that generations of Americans first heard "it looks like rain" while listening to their parents read the words of the British A. A. Milne?

Martha Newman
Austin, Texas

Instead of your newly coined "hyperverbification," might you prefer "superverbification" or a mouth-watering "hyperlogopoiesis"?

Douglas J. Futuyma
Stony Brook, New York

I always carefully point out to people that Murkin, like Strine, should be carefully pronounced with a tip of the hat to the missing syllables. A careful listener can hear every one in the words of a careful speaker.

In our household, where it's a common word, we say Murikin, rather than Murkin.

I'm always amused that French translations of American books, including my own, are usually described as translated from the American.

The discussion of data is the most lucid and sensible that I've ever read.

Peter Norton
Santa Monica, California

Sucking Up

"Transition time is a very sensitive moment for pundits," I wrote recently. "You cannot appear eager to make contact, lest you be accused of *sucking up,* but neither should you. . . ."

A number of readers ("a number of" can mean "two," which is a number) winced at this inelegant locution. "Is this today's street vernacular," asked S. Serebnick of Freehold, New Jersey, "which means 'apple-polishing'?"

This is not the first *yecch!* response to a modern application of the verb; in a piece on high school slang, I reported the frequent use of *to suck face,* meaning "to kiss wetly and noisily." Lotsa shudders from people who forgot what bliss it was when young to oscillate while osculating.

Yes, S. Serebnick, *to suck up* and its predecessor *to suck up to [someone]* does mean "to flatter, curry favor with, obsequiously ingratiate," or as John Hotten defined the term in his 1860 dictionary, "to insinuate oneself into his good graces."

The noun *sucker,* in its slang sense of "thing," is in vogue use. Karen De Witt, a *New York Times* reporter covering the cultural revolution going on in Washington, wrote of a nightspot called Chief Ike's: "Any Saturday night will find 30 to 40 Clinton staff members lined up outside, waiting to hear Stella Neptune, the plastic-clad, gold-brassiered disk jockey, spin disco funk tunes like Parliament-Funkadelic's 'Tear the Roof Off the *Sucker.*' "

Now let's get to what's troubling us: Are *suck up* and the related *sucker* euphemisms for, or based upon, a term heard only in R-rated movies?

Lexicographers believe that the origin of this usage is more innocent than one might think. They point to *suck up*'s possible backformation from *sucker.* A citation from *The Chronicle of the Reign of Henry VI,* written early in the sixteenth century, reads: "Flatterers to the kyng . . . *suckers* of his purse and robbers of his subjectes."

For most of the life of the language, then, *sucker* has meant "toady"; the parasitic sense is most clearly expressed in the current *to suck up.* I would not look shyly away at the use of the term, and readers should note that it hasn't been easy to deal with this sucker.

Surrender, Already

"We have to take our communities back," President Clinton said, and then used a familiar construction: "Community by community. Block by block. . . . Child by child."

And speechwriter by speechwriter. The Clinton usage caused Ed McNally, a member of the Judson Welliver Society of former White House speechwriters, to suggest this President be given "the Joe Biden award" for heavy lifting, in recollection of the 1988 attack on that presidential candidate for rhetorical plagiarism.

Mr. McNally cites this speech by President George Bush on September 5, 1990, in which I suspect he may have had a hand: "Block by block. School by school. Child by child. We will 'Take Back the Streets.' And we will never surrender."

Students of oratory know that was based on Winston Churchill's 1940 Dunkirk speech: "We shall fight on the beaches, we shall fight on the landing grounds, we shall fight in the fields and in the streets, we shall fight in the hills; we shall never surrender."

Before crediting Churchill as the originator of the step-by-step defense, do you suppose that master of the spoken word recalled the phrasing of Georges Clemenceau's defiance in 1918: "I shall fight in front of Paris, within Paris, behind Paris"? Clemenceau himself was paraphrasing the words of Marshal Ferdinand Foch on Amiens.

So much for rhetorical roots to the Bush refusal to give in; what about the derivation of the "child by child" construction?

In 1709, *The Tatler* in England applied the device to the military, advising generals to "Draw out Company by Company, and Troop by Troop," which was more widely understood than the military "in detail."

Chaucer, in 1392, introduced the formula of using the same noun in English to precede and follow the prepositional connector *by* with "to folowe word by word."

We'll get to the ultimate source. Little by little. Quotation by quotation. We will (*shall* is stronger) never surrender.

Chaucer's 1392 "to folowe word by word" may indeed be the earliest such construction in English; but if you are willing to consider other languages, a candidate for the "ultimate source" is the biblical book of Isaiah. Chapter 28, verse 10 includes the phrase "precept by precept, precept by precept, line by line, line by line," in Hebrew, "tzav latzav, tzav latzav, kav lakav, kav lakav." *This recurs in verse 13 of the same chapter.*

Irene Greenwald Plotzker
Wilmington, Delaware

Here goes the source you wonder about in your recent column. It comes from Isaiah 28:10:

For it is precept by precept,
precept by precept,
line by line, line by line,
here a little, there a little. . . .

The alliteration in the Hebrew is thrilling, the message powerful. This is the ultimate source, and I mean ultimate *in every sense of the word. . . .*

Rabbi Israel C. Stein
Congregation Rodeph Sholom
Bridgeport, Connecticut

Swear or Affirm?

Protect and Defend is the title of Jack Valenti's insiderly novel about the turmoil within a future White House, when a Vice President challenges the President for their party's renomination. The phrase comes from the inaugural oath set forth in the Constitution, as the President-elect repeats after the Chief Justice, "I do solemnly swear" to "preserve, protect and defend the Constitution of the United States."

We all heard William Jefferson Clinton follow Chief Justice William H. Rehnquist through the words, but inaugural oath-taking has not always been so simple. William Howard Taft, as Chief Justice in 1929, said "preserve, *maintain* and defend" and Mr. Hoover dutifully went along and repeated it, presuming his investiture would still be legal. This established the precedent: If the swearer-in goofs, follow the goof.

There is some dispute about whether Mr. Hoover actually swore anything. He was a Quaker, and many members of that sect decline to swear oaths, citing the admonition in Matthew 5:34, quoting Jesus: "But I say unto you, swear not at all." The founders provided for that possibility, or for an atheist President, by offering an alternative in the Constitution: "I do solemnly swear *or affirm.*" According to a newspaper story the day before, "Contrary to first reports, Mr. Hoover will swear instead of affirm. . . . He has no aversion to swearing under such circumstances." Archivists at the Hoover Library think he swore.

Not Franklin Pierce in 1853. That one-termer told Chief Justice Roger Taney (pronounced like *tawny*) that he preferred to affirm, presumably citing Matthew. What's the difference? *Affirm* means "avow, promise, attest," but it does not invoke God's name; to *swear* by itself means to swear to God; it is also possible to swear by holding something else sacred for confirmation, as "to swear by my honor, or on my head."

Chief Justices must check out the swear-affirm preference beforehand. They cannot very well intone, "I do solemnly swear or affirm," lest the person being sworn repeat both; it has to be one or the other. And Justices usually ask the President-to-be if he wants to include "so help me God" at the end, a rousing conclusion that is not in the constitutional oath but was ad-libbed by George Washington and has been used by every President since. Even Frank Pierce went for that; it's an appeal for providential aid, and does not count as swearing.

The oath itself played a big part in United States history when Lincoln, in his first inaugural address, told secessionists, "You have no oath registered in heaven to destroy the Government, while I shall have the most solemn one to 'preserve, protect and defend it.' " Lincoln was stretching a point: His "it" referred to the government, while the oath's verbs are plainly directed to the United States Constitution, arguably not the government. Nowhere in that document is there a denial of a state's power to secede, and secessionists claimed the unenumerated right to leave the Union; Lincoln creatively used the oath of office as his device to make it impossible for states to secede without war, and to put the onus for that terrible decision on the Confederacy.

There Are Those Who Say

Some say the most delicious recent metaphor-mangling in Washington came from the lips of Alan Greenspan, chairman of the Federal Reserve, who gained fame as televised balcony-mate of Hillary Rodham Clinton during her husband's economic address to Congress. The Greenspan pledge: "to break the back of the credit crunch."

The *some* that led the preceding paragraph is an example of phantom attribution—a way of making a statement by pretending to report it as the assertion of

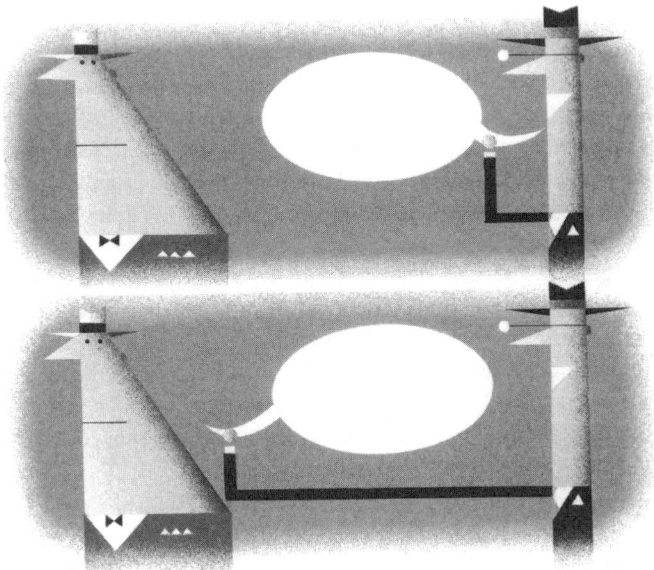

others. Whenever a speechwriter uses the "some say" construction, a speech reader knows that it's safe to agree with, or sternly dissociate himself from, whatever "some" are saying.

Some say is neutral; for really stupid or wrongheaded statements, phantom attribution is made to *there are those who say;* you can bank on *those who* being straw men. *Others say* something far out; *others* live in a whole other world.

In this regard, we present the first effluvia—beyond mere metaphoria—from Foggy Bottom in the Clinton Era. It comes from the "Office of the Assistant Secretary of Defense, Public Affairs," which means that the letter does not come from the Assistant Secretary, but from his office, which is commanded by a desk that writes memos from the desk of.

For as long as I can remember, I have been getting great gobs of unsolicited mail in bulky manila envelopes—occasionally pretty useful—from Les Aspin, who was a hardworking Congressman and is a nice guy. Today, in comes this missive from the Directorate for Public Communication (the K.G.B. loved *directorates;* what else has the Pentagon stolen from Moscow Central?), addressed to "Dear Sir or Madam."

"When Secretary Aspin was Chairman of the House Armed Services Committee, you had expressed an interest in receiving information from him on national security issues." (Maybe I put a check mark on a postcard when I was sleepy or drunk.) "Now that he is the Secretary of Defense," writes Harold Heilsnis, director for public communication—presumably bucking for Chief of the Sixth Directorate of Public Communication and Interactive Relationships—

"*some* [italics mine] have asked to continue receiving material from him on these issues."

Ah, *some* have asked. Who? Close relatives? Old flames? His lips are sealed in his own version of a back-breaking credit crunch. So, is the press agent going to keep sending me the stuff? "We are evaluating the possibility of providing such mailings." (He means "making similar mailings" or "providing such information"; you do not *provide* a mailing as if it were humanitarian relief dropped from the sky.)

"If you wish to receive such materials from Secretary Aspin, please complete the enclosed form," and he attaches one of those government forms that require not only my signature (which I suspect would trigger a full field investigation, tax audit and wiretap warrant) but also demand in capitalized boldface that I return the address label from the envelope I threw away.

In the old days, Les's flack would have dropped me a note asking, "You want to stay on the mailing list?" Gone, gone are the days of plain English, as genuine communication is sucked into the black hole of directorates. I'm afraid those snappy salutes are getting to that old gang of Clinton's.

Tough Sell

When a Democratic Congress received a proposed annual budget from a Republican President, a hospital emergency-room term was invariably used to describe its reception: "Dead on Arrival," D.O.A. for short. With one party in control of both Congress and the White House, the famous phrase was the basis of a pun: "While the Clinton budget will not be Dead on Arrival," said John Kasich, ranking Republican on the House Budget Committee, "there's no question that it's Debt on Arrival." (Punsters instantly recalled the panning of a Clifford Odets drama: "Odets, where is thy sting?")

All agreed, however, that the tax provisions in the President's budget would be a *tough sell.* This phrase, which can denote the *hard sell* delivered with *tough love,* has become the spring entry for cliché of the year.

In Moscow Richard Nixon told Serge Schmemann of *The New York Times* that he had no illusions about persuading an America already turning inward to reverse course and aid reformers in Russia: "It's a very *tough sell.*"

At the end of the Vancouver summit, Strobe Talbott, Ambassador at Large (capitalized but not hyphenated), gave Gordon Peterson of WUSA-TV this assessment of the Clinton plan to invest in Russian democracy: "Of course, he has a *tough sell* . . . but President Clinton knows he has a *tough sell,* and he's starting to make it."

The verb is debatable—do you *make, do, face* or *undertake* a tough sell?—but the noun phrase means "a difficult task of persuasion" and has a generally admirable connotation.

Madison Avenue is its place of origin: Describing a new Sunday newspaper for children in October 1980, one of its executives, Bruno L. Caliandro, noted, "The advertising has been a real *tough sell.*" Two months later, discussing the rise of the TV mini-series, Gary Nardino, president of Paramount Television, was quoted as saying that *The Winds of War* would have been a *"tough sell"* if *Shogun* had flopped. In 1984, John Carman of *The Atlanta Constitution* observed that "A lawyerly series devoted to complex issues is a *tough sell* for TV viewers."

The phrase appeared in the political lexicon in 1987 as Bruce Babbitt, a former Governor of Arizona (now Interior Secretary) carried his campaign for the Democratic nomination for President into New York, where he dared to suggest higher taxes: "I know New York is a *tough sell,*" he said, and did not get its support; Senator Al Gore, who said he favored higher taxes on high-income Social Security recipients, fared better in his own tough sell.

We have witnessed the functional shift of the verb *sell* to the noun *sell,* which began in the nineteenth century and was popularized during the 1950's with *hard sell* and *soft sell.* The *hard* did not mean "difficult," but signified "loud, strident," as in much automobile advertising, extended to "rigorous, uncompromising, harsh," even bordering on "brutal, cruel," as if slamming the potential buyer against the wall. The *soft sell,* on the contrary, was "subtle, gentle," but often carried the connotation of being slightly deceptive; as Fred Mish, editor in chief (lowercased, not hyphenated—where have all the hyphens gone?) of Merriam-Webster, reminds me, the verb *to sell* began with a sense of betrayal of trust.

If you have a *tough sell,* or difficult assignment of persuasion, you will probably want to avoid the *hard sell,* with its authoritarian or panicky tone, which turns off many potential buyers; at the same time, you should avoid the slickness associated with *soft sell.* Easy to do? Nope; that's what makes it a *tough sell.*

Trigger-Happy

Roy Rogers's horse seemed to come thundering down the halls of Congress last month: The word on all lips was *trigger,* not so famously used in politics since Nelson Rockefeller called Barry Goldwater *trigger-happy.*

When you pull a trigger, a gun goes off. From the Middle Dutch *trecken,* "to pull" (same root as *trek,* as in *Star Trek*), the English word began in 1621 as *tricker,* meaning "the lever that springs a trap"; it soon became the name for the small steel catch that releases the hammer or firing pin of a gun when drawn, pressed, pulled or—to use the verb my sergeant preferred—squeezed.

Metaphorically, triggers became heavily involved in Congress with the onset of health care legislation. What to call a device in the law that would measure future fulfillment of a certain level of coverage—and then, if coverage failed to reach that goal, spring a little legislative lever that would bring new pressure to bear? A *time bomb* is pejorative; a *trigger* is not.

But what sort of trigger? From the chairman of the Senate Finance Committee, Daniel Patrick Moynihan of New York, comes this plaintive letter: "Could you access your 'Somewhere a Roscoe . . .' file? The press just now abounds with references to *hard* and *soft triggers* in a health care bill. To what must surely be the distress of handgun aficionados everywhere, we seem to be getting it wrong.

"A *hard trigger* goes off automatically," observes Chairman Pat. "Whereas a *soft trigger* has to be squeezed hard. There is enough confusion about health care. Nor is S. J. Perelman on hand to set us straight."

Dutifully, Senator Moynihan attaches a glossary prepared by the Finance Committee staff. It defines a *hard trigger* as "a mandate (on employers and/or individuals) automatically imposed if a commission determines that the percentage of persons covered by health insurance has not reached a target specified in statute."

A *soft trigger* is a kinder, gentler form of coercion: "Under a soft trigger, Congress reviews recommendations of a commission for increasing coverage rates, if the commission determines that the percentage of persons covered by health insurance has not reached a target specified in statute. There is no requirement for Congress to act." On the CBS program *Face the Nation,* Bob Schieffer defined *soft trigger* more simply as "if you don't have universal health care several years down the road, then Congress will revisit the issue and decide what to do about it."

But wait—there is a refinement known as the *fast-track trigger,* which fits somewhere between hard and soft. *Congressional Quarterly* defines that eventuality this way: "Congress would be presented with legislation designed to achieve universal coverage or control costs. The bills could not be amended or subjected to a filibuster."

Thus, in current political usage, *triggers* are means to commit future Congresses to actions that the present Congress is unwilling to take now. When an idea like this becomes popular, the operative word takes on a glow, and policy wonks come up with a series of modifiers. (A few years ago, the hot legislative word was *cap,* which has since been tossed over the wall.)

"These words *hard trigger* and *soft trigger* are both irregular and misnomer terms not used in the gun business," I am informed by John Armand Caudron, president of Firearms Research and Identification Association in Rowland Heights, California. "What you describe as a *hard trigger* that kicks in automatically may be akin to that of a double-action firearm. It will have a tougher or harder trigger pull because it takes more force to pull than a regular trigger of a cocked firearm. *Soft trigger* could refer to a *hair trigger,* which has a reduced force to drop the hammer or drop the sear, discharging the gun."

Thus, Moynihan is metaphorically right: The political *hard trigger,* which goes off at the slightest touch of failed goals, is really akin to the *hair trigger,* which fires at the gentlest squeeze, whilst the political *soft trigger* takes the kind of hard pulling required in double-action firearms. Congress, as the Chairman of Senate Finances vainly insists, has the whole thing backward.

The recipient of missives from Moynihan must be alert to arcane literary allusions. In this one about triggers, he suggests I access my "Somewhere a

Roscoe . . ." file; he refers to a classic article of that title in the October 15, 1938, *New Yorker* magazine by S. J. Perelman, satirically analyzing the hard-boiled school of private eyes exemplified by Dashiell Hammett's Sam Spade and Raymond Chandler's Philip Marlowe.

Perelman particularly focused on a publication called *Spicy Detective* and its hero, Dan Turner, who took to his apartment "a wow in a gown of silver lamé that stuck to her lush curves like a coating of varnish" named Zarah Trenwick. Just as "she fed me a kiss that throbbed all the way down to my fallen arches," suddenly:

"From the doorway a roscoe said 'Kachow!' and a slug creased the side of my noggin. Neon lights exploded inside my think-tank. . . . She was as dead as a stuffed mongoose. . . . I wasn't badly hurt. But I don't like to be shot at. I don't like dames to be rubbed out when I'm flinging woo at them."

This was the passage from *Spicy Detective,* seized on by the sainted Sidney Joseph Perelman as the essence of the genre, to which the Senate Finance Committee chairman undoubtedly refers. Sure enough, it was in my *roscoe* file, a slang word from circa 1914 meaning "handgun," probably from the male name Roscoe, whose association with the weapon is lost in the evanescent mists of antiquity. (The word *think-tank,* as used in the *Spicy Detective* citation above, in the 30's meant "brain"; losing its hyphen, it later came to be applied to student-free colleges.)

I wish we had Dan Turner with us today to solve a lexicographic mystery. Legislative triggers, whether based on the model of a base-closing commission or on fast-track procedures for approving trade agreements, are said to cause actions to *kick in* at some future date.

Robert Louis Stevenson first used *kick in,* about a door, in the 1881 *Treasure Island;* the first use of the phrase in the sense of "to contribute money" appeared in the United States in 1908, and today political supporters are expected to *kick in* to campaigns. But I suspect a mechanical sense exists, unreported in dictionaries, which causes engines to kick in, or start. For this 30's slang usage, I would ordinarily turn to Zarah Trenwick in her silver lamé gown, but from the doorway a roscoe said "Kachow!" . . .

"Gun" is a term for a cannon.

A pistol, rifle, or shotgun is a "firearm."

Perhaps your sergeant failed to render the traditional military admonition to you:

This is my rifle,
This is my gun,
This is for shooting,
This is for fun.

James D. Storozuk
Fair Lawn, New Jersey

Trophy Wife

"The ultimate ambition of a gold digger is to end up as a *trophy wife,*" Lynn Barber writes in *The Times* of London. Using that phrase in its most pejorative sense, she quotes Sally Burton, who married the actor Richard Burton a year before he died, as one who was not a trophy herself but seemed to know plenty who were: "The golden rule if you are a *trophy wife* is that you do not stray while the old man is still alive."

A somewhat less insulting sense of the phrase appeared in an interview with the actress Bo Derek in the *Chicago Tribune.* Bart Mills, describing her role in a cable-television movie, wrote, "She plays a former megamodel turned *trophy wife* who gets enmeshed in a plot to kill her rich husband." A *megamodel* is a force in the fashion industry, outearning run-of-the-midway supermodels, and is more often gold-dug than gold-digging.

The revised second edition of the *Random House Unabridged Dictionary* provides this cautious definition: "the young, often second, wife of a rich middle-aged man." But that slips past the controversy: Is the *trophy wife* a mere *armpiece,* or even a *bimbo*? Or is she a new and attractive partner in power, successful in her

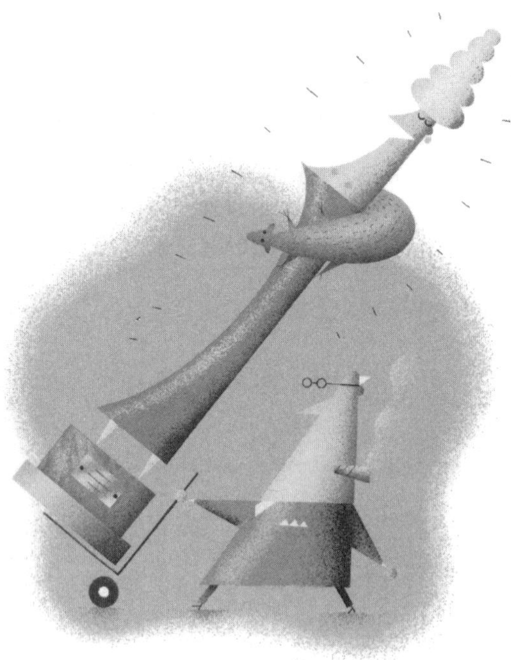

own right? Must she be very thin, or at least physically attractive? Is it a sexist slur?

A *trophy* is an award or honor given for some victory. The meaning of the Greek root is "turning," specifically a turning away from battle, as when an opponent is routed and his battle flags become trophies, symbolic of victory. To have a trophy is fine, but to *be* a trophy is usually considered demeaning.

The term *trophy wife,* now firmly ensconced in the language, was coined by Julie Connelly, a senior editor of *Fortune* magazine. In a cover story in the issue of August 28, 1989, she wrote: "Powerful men are beginning to demand *trophy wives.* . . . The more money men make, the argument goes, the more self-assured they become, and the easier it is for them to think: I *deserve* a queen."

In the initial coinage, the term was in no way synonymous with *bimbo.* "Enter the second wife: a decade or two younger than her husband, sometimes several inches taller, beautiful and very often accomplished," wrote the unmarried Ms Connelly. "The second wife certifies her husband's status and, if possible given the material she has to work with, dispels the notion that men peak sexually at age eighteen. This trophy does not hang on the wall like a moose head—she works. Hard. For starters, she often has her own business."

The woman chosen for *Fortune*'s cover to exemplify this career woman whose husband is part of her career was Carolyne Roehm, a dress designer whose business had revenues of ten million dollars, then married to the leveraged-buyout king, Henry Kravis. They have since divorced; Ms Roehm has retired from the dress business and will be spending the summer in Britain studying Shakespearean tragedy at Oxford University. I was seated next to Ms Roehm at a recent dinner party and seized the opportunity for lexical research.

"Women considered *trophy wives* are accomplished and ambitious," she reported, "in both their careers and their lives. They have some looks, but are neither glamorous nor stupid enough to be called a 'bimbo'; they attract husbands who generally see second wives to be a kind of reward, but who want more than a pretty face."

Thus, the term has two clearly differentiated senses. On what was *trophy wife* bottomed, as they say at the Supreme Court? To *Fortune*'s Ms Connelly: "When I was writing the article, I thought of the real-estate term *trophy building* for a premier place like the Plaza Hotel in New York, and I formed *trophy wife* based on that term."

What about the natural follow-up? "I thought about *trophy husbands,*" Ms Connelly says. "In fact, an issue of *Working Woman* does discuss that, but I decided against it. You might describe Ted Turner as a *trophy husband,* but he's hardly known mainly as someone you wear on your arm."

That suggests that the coiner of *trophy wife,* who originally gave the term a connotation of accomplishment and business acumen, now sees the primary sense as emphasizing a lean pulchritude. "There's a bimbo quality to *trophy,*" she admits, "and that doesn't translate into the male image. A *trophy husband* would be a C.E.O. or a really powerful guy, not some stud muffin." (*Stud,* originally "a protuberance" or "a stand," was applied to male animals used for breeding; *muffin*, in modern slang a cloying endearment for a woman, was combined with *stud* by vengeful females to mean "sexy but airheaded hunk of man.")

Sure enough, the cover of *Working Woman* extends the metaphor in its original, noninsulting sense. TROPHY HUSBANDS is the headline, with a subhead of "Success and Sex: When a high-powered woman meets her match, he's got to be more than attractive, intelligent and charming. He must be rich, powerful and secure." The men chosen to illustrate these admirable characteristics are Ted Turner (husband of actress Jane Fonda), Richard Gere (megamodel Cindy Crawford), Mike Nichols (journalist Diane Sawyer) and Bob Dole (Red Cross chairwoman Liddy Dole).

Although misattributing coinage of *trophy wife* to Tom Wolfe, who described determinedly emaciated spouses as "X-rays" in his novel *The Bonfire of the Vanities*, the magazine vividly defines *trophy husband* with this quotation: "Marry this guy and she becomes one-half of that phenomenon known as the Power Couple."

When attending fashion shows and craft exhibits with my wife, who is a jewelry designer, goldsmith and glass artist, I often put on a badge reading "Artist's Husband." Asked if she thought the attributive noun *trophy* applied, Helene Safire patted my hand and said, "Of course, dear," in a tone that indicates the term never describes veteran husbands.

Working Woman extends the metaphor even further, to *trophy dates:* These unmarried escorts of high-powered or talented women are not *boy toys*, a derogation popularized by Madonna. These desirables include Peter Jennings, David Letterman, Mort Zuckerman, Charlie Rose, Bob Kerrey and the White House aide George Stephanopoulos ("workaholic but great dresser").

As a modern modifier, then, *trophy* most often means "bimbonic" when applied to women, though a second sense remains of "accomplished." Applied to men, however, *trophy* is almost always complimentary. Not fair? "Life is unfair," said President Kennedy, a trophy husband.

Trophy wives are young prizes plucked up by successful aging men who believe that they are entitled to their late-in-life award because of all of their accomplishments. Never mind the faithful wife of 30 or so years who, most likely, stayed at home, raised his *children, cooked his meals, ironed his shirts, cleaned his house, and provided the comfort and stability from which he was able to rise in fame and fortune. After all that, it is no small wonder that she is not the young and vivacious trophy that will flatter his ego. And what is worst of all? The trophy husband actually believes that he deserves the second wife after all that hard work.*

No, I am not a bitter first wife left behind for a young blond. I am a happily married, 37-year-old stay-at-home mother of three, married to a wonderful husband. But I am not unmindful of the weaknesses of the male species and I just couldn't let your piece go unanswered. I think you're terrific.

Sarah Noll
Kansas City, Missouri

I hope that you were baiting a reader response in using the words "firmly ensconced." If so, you succeeded. "Firmly," used as a modifier to "ensconced," is redundant.

Nicholas Woolard
San Ramon, California

Vengeance Is Mine

Here's great news: R. W. Burchfield has reached *revenge.*

Mr. Burchfield is New Zealand's gift to the world of words. As editor of the four-volume supplement to the *Oxford English Dictionary* (now available in a squeezed-down form for use with a magnifying glass, a nice bridge to the day when everyone has a CD-ROM), Burchfield is the source for many of the coinages confidently cited by this department.

He is presently (make that *currently,* because the meaning of *presently* is hopelessly split between "now" and "soon") at work on the rewriting of H. W. Fowler's classic *Modern English Usage.* To some, that is akin to revising the Bible, but Sir Ernest Gowers did that successfully in 1965, and its latest renascence is in good hands with Mr. Burchfield.

"I have reached *revenge* (verb) in my new version," he writes from Oxfordshire, England, after some comments on a political dictionary, "and am not quite sure how even our best writers distinguish it from *avenge* (verb) these days."

Vengeance, as well as *vindication,* is from the Latin *vindicare,* "to set free" or "to claim as one's own." *Avenge* has sometimes had a connotation of gaining just retribution, while *revenge,* in verb form, was more often tainted with a hint of maliciousness. In comic books, "the masked avenger" is a hero. Would "the masked revenger" be a villain, out to get even like the monomaniacal Ahab? Or are the two verbs now interchangeable? That's the usage question.

In my mind, *to avenge* has a neutral connotation; it can mean paying back, or re-tributing, in justice or in pettiness. *To revenge* is in less common use as a transitive verb ("I will revenge this defeat") and more common as a reflexive verb ("I will revenge myself for this embarrassment"). *Avenge* may also be used more often for paying back a wrong done to somebody else ("I will avenge my friend's suffering"), while *revenge* settles a personal score.

I would use *revenge* as a transitive verb only to put a mean edge on my determination to get even.

But that's one man's opinion, arrived at after much chewing over what is just a funny feeling about the verb's *re*-form as being meaner. More important is a current citation, or as Mr. Burchfield puts it, how "our best writers distinguish it" in the ordinary course of work, and not when asked to analyze usage.

Modern Bible translators prefer the phrase *take vengeance* to the verb *revenge.* In Nahum 1:2, where the 1611 King James translators wrote that "the Lord *revengeth,*" the 1970 Oxford translators of the New English Bible rendered the same passage as "the Lord *takes vengeance.*"

One of our best writers today—a modern Charles Dickens—is Herman Wouk. The readership of *The Caine Mutiny* and *War and Remembrance* is vast. (Literary elites and the merchants of murkiness resent this.) Wouk's recent book *The Hope* takes a handful of his flesh-and-blood characters through the latest generation of Israel's wars, and *The Hope* is not only a good read, but it also causes a good think.

"You think I forgive you for stealing Nakhama?" a soldier named Pasternak asks, shaking a thick finger at one of the heroes. "I'll be revenged yet." Wouk writes, "Pasternak half winked one eye and walked off." That wink suggests that the vengeance sought is not serious; thus, one of our best writers prefers *revenge* as a verb to *avenge,* and in this instance *revenge* carries no maliciousness.

I have a hunch that, despite my funny feeling, most good writers would find no difference in meaning between *avenge* and *revenge.*

Vetter Vets *Vet*

"As a practicing veterinarian many years ago," writes Douglas F. McBride of Washingtonville, New York, "I was occasionally called to *vet* a horse. I was accustomed to being called by the noun *vet,* but the use of the word as a verb to describe what I was doing was infrequent."

Hoo-boy, have times changed. Now the verb *to vet* means "to search for weaknesses or flaws"; the noun *vet* continues to mean "animal doctor," but the noun for the person who does the vetting preparatory to clearance of a nominee for public office or candidate for any job is a *vetter.*

Judge Kimba M. Wood, whose sentence to Attorney Generalship was reduced to twenty-four hours, wrote: "Some of my household-help files were received by the White House *'vetters'* at approximately 10 A.M." Use of the word in its gerund form was featured in a *New York Times* editorial that claimed Judge Wood's chances were destroyed by "clumsy *vetting.*"

My questioner wants to know if the new sense is applied only to documents, like household files, or to people as well; he cites my own usage in regard to a judicial panel's choice of a potential Iraqgate special prosecutor: "We can hope it has a choice already *vetted.*" Can you vet a choice who is a person?

Of course you can; if a vet can vet a horse, Dr. McBride, vetters can vet nominees. What we have here is a fine example of what English teachers who coach football teams call "functional shift": A noun becomes a verb and in this case develops a new sense right after the snap. When a doctor *scopes* a patient or a nervous executive *lawyers* a document—even when a vet *curbs* a dog—the subject takes a noun and shifts its function to that of a verb.

To vet the verb *vet:* It began with the Latin *veterinus,* "of cattle and similar domestic animals." (*Vet* as a clipping of *veteran* is based on the Latin *vetus,* "old.") The first sense was the one most familiar to Dr. McBride, "to submit an animal to treatment or examination by a veterinarian." The meaning was extended at the turn of this century to "to examine closely," as in this 1904 use by Rudyard Kipling, who kept a horsy metaphor: "These are our crowd. . . . They've been *vetted,* an' we're putting 'em through their paces."

According to Anne Soukhanov at American Heritage, "The military use of the verb after Kipling was the key to the word's (at least the verb's) gain in international currency outside the British Isles." The dictionary she edits labels it "informal," not "chiefly British"; thanks to the latest burst of usage, lexies will have to start thinking of the word as Standard English.

How is political vetting done? The classic statement of the vetter to the vettee was put by Frank Mankiewicz of the McGovern campaign to a potential running mate, Senator Thomas Eagleton, in 1972: "Tom, is there anything in your background that can give us trouble? Any teenage larks? . . . Anything at all that could raise some questions?"

When the general vetting question was put to Judge Wood by Clinton vetters, it was in the nature of "Do you have a problem with illegal household help?" Because the vettee saw no legal error, the vetters thought that meant no political problem.

The noun is spelled *-er* on the analogy of *go-getter,* not *-or* on the analogy of *bettor,* because the latter is spelled that way to avoid confusion with the comparative *better.* We may expect further extension beyond documents and persons: A quality-control officer for Hanes hosiery may be an *underwear-vetter,* and a German-accented inspector of beds—oh, no.

Views on Sensibilities

Synonymy—the study of shadings of meaning, the fine distinctions between words that carry similar but not the same import—is alive and well at the White House.

John B. Judis of *The New Republic* was interviewing Robert Rubin, the languid dynamo who is President Clinton's economic coordinator. "When I asked Rubin where he got his political views," Mr. Judis wrote, "he winced at the vagueness of the term *views*. Rubin is sensitive to words and phrases the way a sectarian is to creeds. . . . It's a kind of fussiness, but also part of his deadpan earnestness and exactitude."

The reporter tried *opinions, sentiments* and finally—he didn't have a thesaurus in his pocket—*sensibilities*. "*Sensibilities* is a good word," Mr. Rubin allowed, and proceeded to give the sources of his mind-set.

Here is my opinion about a group of words that deal with judgments we make about what we think is true.

By *opinion,* I mean my own conclusion about the rightness of anything, which I am well aware may not be yours. My *view* is even more personal—the way I see a possible truth from inside my own head—and is applied mostly to public issues. My *judgment* is more deliberative, suggesting much chin-pulling in arriving at a position—quite unlike *sentiment* ("Them's my sentiments exactly"), which rests in an emotional response. My *belief*—which can be tentatively held or profoundly a matter of faith—is more certain about truth than an *opinion,* far more sure than my *impression,* though not as certain as my *conviction.*

Where does *sensibility* fit in?

To the roots: *Opinion* comes from the Latin *opinari,* "to think"; *view* from *videre,* "to see"; *sentiment* from *sentire,* "to feel." *Sensibility* deals with that last sense, of the senses; its complex meaning is "awareness of and responsiveness to the emotions of others."

Better known for *Pride and Prejudice,* the novelist Jane Austen also wrote *Sense and Sensibility,* which appeared in 1811. She used *sensibility* as a synonym for *sentimentality,* which she attacked as emotional shallowness; in her alliterative title, she contrasts the weak emotion of sensibility with plain good sense.

In current use, *sensibility* is often defined as "the ability to receive sensations." But it often carries a negative connotation, usually in the plural—"it offended his sensibilities"—of excessive sensitivity.

I ran into Mr. Rubin at lunchtime just outside the White House; he asked me where he could find a decent bagel within walking distance. I steered him to Loeb's New York Deli on Fifteenth Street, but he later told me he couldn't find it; it turned out my directions were wrong. In the case of *sensibilities,* I'd like to make up for my directional gaffe by helping him out.

In my personal view, if Mr. Rubin meant to say "basis of my feelings," *sensibilities* was O.K., but if he meant "the organizing force of my political outlook," it's my belief—more than that, my considered judgment—that he chose the wrong word. But that's a matter of opinion.

Specific reference to Jane Austen's usage of "sensibility" is made in Webster's New International Dictionary of the English Language, Second Edition, Unabridged, *1937 (C. Merriam-Webster).*

I quote, from its definition of the word: "6. Refined sensitiveness in emotion and taste with especial responsiveness to the pathetic,—a trait appealed to in later Georgian literature and art. . . . Sense and Sensibility *. . . Jane Austen."*

You have committed the cardinal sin of trivializing Jane Austen. Her admirers will not forget.

Ben Passen
Boca Raton, Florida

Way Out, Ways In, Right Away

"We've come a ways in journalism, too," I wrote in this space recently. My meaning was that we've come pretty far, but not too far; had I meant to say we had come really far, I would have written *a long way,* with the *way* singular, as in the Virginia Slims slogan "You've come a long *way,* baby."

Why, then, did it seem more natural to write the unmodified *way* as *ways*? Maybe because *we've come a way* would be confused with *we've come away,* with its different meaning of "we've left our moorings." Or maybe I wanted to pull a little mail.

"Why not 'we've come a *way*'?" wrote the easily ensnared Joe Vesely of Deerfield, Massachusetts. "I have a friend who often says *anyways,* and it jolts me slightly as I feel she should be saying *anyway* in context."

On the other hand, the *capo di Gotcha,* Louis Jay Herman of New York, writes, "Your use of *a ways* will, of course, incur the wrath of a bevy of schoolmarms, who will reprehend you for not knowing the difference between singular and plural."

A bevy of cowgirls, according to the country singer Emmylou Harris, agrees with the colloquial usage: "I know the finish line's in sight," go the words to a 1993 Lainie Marsh song on her latest album. "But I still have a *ways* to go." (*Bevy,* the collective noun, is a five-hundred-year-old word of mysterious Middle

English origin; because it is often used to group birds, and is associated with the alliterative *bevy of beauties,* the word has gained a sexist connotation that I herewith reject.)

Most usage books assume that *a way* is the more common usage, but linguistic geographers say it seems that *a ways,* dating back to 1588 in this sense, may be more prevalent, and may teach us about the roots of American English.

"The difference between *way* and *ways* has an interesting areal distribution," says William A. Kretzschmar Jr. of the University of Georgia. He carries on the work of the great word geographer Hans Kurath, and serves as editor in chief of the *Linguistic Atlas of the Middle and South Atlantic States,* known by its acronym, *Lamsas.*

"*Way* occurs in a long band from Richmond through Washington, D.C., to eastern Pennsylvania and Philadelphia, to southeastern New York including New York City," says the man from *Lamsas,* pointing to a map showing additional pockets in Pittsburgh, Albany and Syracuse, as well as on the Eastern Shore and in the northern Shenandoah Valley, with a mere scattering in the South. But the usage of *ways,* as in "a little ways," is heavy all throughout the *Lamsas* area, up and down the Eastern Seaboard and out toward the Midwest. "For the *Lamsas* survey, *ways* is clearly the dominant form, no matter what the handbooks may prefer."

This pattern of difference suggests two things about *way/ways:* "*Way* was a feature in use early in American English, as suggested by its presence in the eastern Pennsylvania, New York Dutch and Eastern Shore rural relic areas," says the linguistic atlas-maker, "and the Southern distribution originating from the old plantation center of Charleston." Today, the form *way* is a feature of the large cities of the Atlantic Corridor, influenced by Philadelphia and New York.

Think about that: The distribution of dialect is not strictly regional, but on occasion is urban vs. rural within a region. (You knew that: City folks speak funny wherever they come from.)

Anyways (a Southern and South Midland dialect form of *anyway,* similar to the jocular *anyhoo* as a variant of *anyhow*), the linguistic atlas-makers have come a ways in studying regional English, though they have a long way to go. (I wonder if the modifier makes all the difference?) Keep at it, *Lamsas;* way to go.

I agree with your characterization of the origin of bevy *as "mysterious."* Webster's New World Dictionary *flatly states that it is from an Old French word for "drinking bout" and is related to* beverage, *but* Webster II *cautiously says "perh. orig. a drinking company" and the other dictionaries in my library (*Webster III, Webster's Collegiate, American Heritage *and* Concise Oxford*) suggest no etymology.*

As you point out, the word right *has the underlying meaning "straight" and is cognate with Latin* rectus. *Nowadays, of course, it normally refers to "straightness" in terms of accuracy and morality. However, the old meaning lingers on in* right angle, upright *(position) and the verb* to right *(e.g., "the boat nearly capsized but then righted itself"). The literal meaning of* rectus *is reflected in the English derivatives* direct *(adj.) and* erect, *while the figurative sense shows through in* correct, rectify *and* rectitude.

Right/rectus *is, incidentally, the past participle of an Indo-European verbal formation represented by Latin* regere *"to guide, direct, rule, govern." The Latin verbal root has produced such English derivatives as* regent, regulate, regular, regimen, regime *and* regiment. *By way of Old French, we get* rule *(originally a straightedge for measuring) and* rail *(a straight wooden or metal bar), both ultimately from Latin* regula.

The same Indo-European root, meaning "to straighten, guide, direct," is the source of Latin rex, *"king," which is cognate with the Sanskrit-derived* rajah.

Louis Jay Herman
New York, New York

I could find no mention in your article that ways *is not the plural that Louis Jay Herman thinks that you will be accused of misusing, but in origin the genitive case used adverbially. Other Standard and non-Standard English examples include* always, besides; *(in disguised form)* once, twice; *(with* -s *ending as a generalized adverbial indicator)* somewheres, whereabouts. *See* O.E.D. *for above.*

Anthony Lloyd
Brooklyn, New York

Welcome to *-icity* City

Nouns, irritated at being turned into verbs at the slightest hat-dropping, have sought vengeance by lashing out at innocent adjectives, forcing them into service as awkward nouns.

At the White House, the *Kopfverdrehers* (a German word for "mind benders," a variant of *spinmeisters*) called in the usual suspects before President Clinton's trip to Europe and Russia. Over lunch in what is now called the old Family Dining Room (where Ulysses S. Grant first heard the news of the Crédit Mobilier scandal), the bigfeet of the Opinion Mafia were permitted to ask very heavy questions about global conceptual frameworks.

Most memorably leaden question was posed by Michael Kramer of *Time* magazine, following in the former columnist Strobe Talbott's ever-ascending footsteps, about the policy-wonk President's proposed "Partnership for Peace." (Late one night, a Clinton speechwriter, gripped by an Agnevian demon, must have slapped his forehead and cried: "I've got it! We can cover up this craven compromise with *alliteration*!")

Mr. Kramer introduced his question with "Mr. President, on the security front. You know the Central European objection—the flaw of the partnership—is the lack of *automaticity* at the end."

Automaticity rippled through the group like butter through a hot knife. The national security adviser—cunning, devious Tony Lake (who has asked that we use those adjectives before his name)—snapped back into focus as we looked at one another with a wild surmise: Was this word the long-awaited replacement for *neo-containment,* or what? What kind of *-icity* is *automaticity*?

I could hardly wait to get back to the *Oxford English Dictionary* in my office. There was one 1870's citation, from a book on brain functions, about man (which was what humankind was once called) "in whom volition is predominant and *automaticity* plays only a subordinate part in motor activities." For recent usage, I ran a Dialog computer search. There, in a 1975 *Knitting Times,* was a story needling an exhibition of machines with "greater pattern potential, higher knitting speeds, more *automaticity* and better production efficiency." In 1993, the medical journal *Chest,* which could present a nice form for *Knitting Times,* argued, "Sarcoid granulomas in the ventricular myocardium can readily become foci for abnormal *automaticity.*" (What do they mean by *readily*?)

With a century-old history, and current usage in disparate publications, *automaticity*'s legitimacy cannot be challenged. Still, it has the ring of rarity; *specificity* was the same way at first, but in the most recent hundred years we came to use that noun, derived from the adjective *specific,* whenever we want to use the nominative to nail something down. The noun form of *authentic* also remains popular; a commercial for Classico pasta sauces says, "Taste the difference *authenticity* makes."

Other examples of adjective-to-noun transitions in vogue: "How come *negativity*?" Ed Turner of CNN writes. "One does not hear *positivity.*"

For "the quality of being negative," I would use something like *nay-saying,* but that's because I'm a nattering nabob of negativism; on a TV commercial for the Psychic Friends Network, a phone-in service to summon spirits from the vasty deep, a network psychic named Chris says she talks to callers to "show them that they can create *positivity* in their life [*sic*]." And the *-ity* form of changing modifiers to things saved Albert Einstein from a theory of relativism.

You are wondering: What happened to *-ness* as the nounifier or nominalizer? *Smooth* and *slick* turned to nouns with *smoothness* and *slickness,* not *smoothicity* or *slickicity.* It's as if some linguistic Al Capone gritted to Frank (The Enforcer) Nitti, "Get *-Ness*!"

What word, then, should pundits use when they favor the entry into NATO of nations that follow agreed-upon procedures of defense alignment and democratic government? The metaphor of machinery—in which *automatic* is synonymous with *involuntary*—jams the gears of diplomacy, and unfamiliar *automaticity* squeaks across the blackboards of our minds. We have other nouns: Assurance. Certainty. Guarantee.

You say: "Smooth *and* slick *turned to nouns with* smoothness *and* slickness, *not* smoothicity *or* slickicity." *Since there are no adjectives* smoothic *or* slickic, *why would the nouns be* smoothicity *or* slickicity? -icity *is a compound suffix in which* -ic *denotes an adjective and* -ity *denotes a noun. If you perversely insisted on endowing those two little Anglo-Saxon words with a Latin noun suffix, you'd get* smoothity *and* slickity *(of course, if you wanted to be fancy, you could make it* smoothitude *and* slickitude*).*

Louis Jay Herman
New York, New York

Regarding automaticity, *the more common word used in the context of the 1870s (I never apostrophize decades; it makes them sound so possessive) reference is* automatism *(strictly speaking, the performance of* nonreflexive *acts without conscious volition). By the way, you neglected to mention* -ism *as a "nounifier." To me, it seems much more popular than* -ness *down there in D.C. (Remember the grandfather in* You Can't Take It with You*? "Where did all these -isms come from anyway?")*

I'm not familiar with Knitting Times, *but the* Chest *review on myocardial sarcoidosis refers to the spontaneous depolarization of cells in the heart. (Tell Ed Turner of CNN that this is called increasing the intracellular "positivity.") Normally, only a few specialized areas of the heart exhibit this property (and they set the pace for the others, although they're called "pacemakers," not "pacesetters"). What the authors mean by* readily *is that injured cells (sarcoid granulomas are little areas of inflammation) can easily (without difficulty or hesitation, but probably not "willingly"—since it's "automatic") begin to act as pacemakers as well.*

This may be the best reason why the use of automaticity *is wrong in the NATO context. For the heart to work well and pump blood out to the rest of the body, each muscle cell must act in a unified and coordinated manner. We can't have too many different pacemakers—one area must set the pace, and the rest must follow!*

James D. Faix, M.D.
Boston, Massachusetts

I was amused to read of the recent exploits of one of my favorite words, automaticity. *In cognitive psychology, the term is a staple of theoretical and research articles. William James in his landmark* Principles of Psychology *(1890) discussed how many forms of mental thought occur automatically, and he cites physiologists dating back thirty years earlier. During the "dark ages" of psychology, 1920–1960, when behaviorism held sway and the study of mental life was frowned upon, no one used the term. But with the cognitive revolution in psychology in the 1960s, research on controlled or conscious versus automatic or nonconscious modes of thought re-emerged and is still flourishing.*

In recent years, one does not have to resort to Knitting Times *or* Chest *to find* automaticity *in widespread use. Gordon Logan, now of the University of Illinois, championed its use in the late 1970s, while Richard Shiffrin of Indiana University preferred* automatism. *I had some battles with journal editors who were in the Shiffrin camp, but consultation of the* O.E.D. *taught me that* -ism *referred to the absolute state, whereas* -ity *referred to the degree or quality. At the time in psychology this was an issue: whether automatic kinds of thought were an all-or-none phenomenon (-ism) or varied in degree of being automatic (-ity). I confess that I didn't like* automatism *because of its too-close similarity to* autism.

John A. Bargh
Professor of Psychology
New York University
New York, New York

What Hath God Unwrought?

When an old word gets summarily executed, this department pays its respects.

"I'm going to miss the word *telegraph,*" says Joe Gemignani, the *New York Times* Sunday Business copy chief. The word was born from the French *télégraphe* in 1794, denoting a semaphore apparatus, a manual signaling device; *tele-* is Greek for "far," and *graphein* Greek for "to write."

The co-inventor of the nautical flag system dubbed it the *tachygraphe,* from the Greek for "rapid," but a French diplomat smoothly renamed it *télégraphe,* presumably because the other word was too tachy.

The first electromagnetic telegraph was designed by Samuel F. B. Morse, whose first public message, from Washington to Baltimore on May 24, 1844, was the biblical passage from Numbers 23:23: "What hath God wrought!"

The exciting technical word was adopted as part of the name of a forward-looking American corporation in 1885. The American Telephone and Telegraph Corporation soon became known as "American Tel and Tel," which was further clipped to its initials "A.T.&T."

The informal shortening of the old nomenclature was not good enough for the

1990's board of directors. Although *telephone* is still a live word, *telegraph* was getting a little hoary.

"While over the years the name achieved a distinctive place in the annals of corporate America," the with-it directors recently wrote to stockholders, "it is also associated with old ways and outdated technologies. Despite some feelings of nostalgia"—with Samuel F. B. Morse vainly tapping out an S O S from his grave—"the board believes it is appropriate at this time to adopt as the company's name the initials AT&T." Stockholders were assured that "the new name—AT&T Corp.—will shed the dated imagery associated with the past."

So the dated old *telegraph* is dead, guillotined by the Robespierres of the information revolution, with none so no-op to do it reverence.

Its obituary was in this style message, vetted by the news desk and flashed by the financial copy desk through this newspaper's up-to-date Atex system: "Please note that the AT&T shareholders today formally approved the company's name change to the AT&T Corporation. This means that we will no longer spell out American Telephone and Telegraph on second references (because that is no longer the name).

"It also means that we will no longer use points in AT&T, because the official name doesn't. And as a result, we will no longer insert a thin space after the ampersand (because there are no points to make the spacing lopsided)."

The fast fist of the telegrapher is forever unclenched; no longer will fighters be able to telegraph their punches. Envision a little headstone in the graveyard of words: "*Telegraph,* 1794–1994. R.I.&P."

The word télégraphe *is one year older than you stated. The suggestion to replace the word* tachygraphe *with* télégraphe *was made by André Francois Miot de Mélito, who was then Chef de Division à l'Interieur in France, in a conversation with Ignace Chappe. Ignace was the elder brother of the telegraph's inventor, Claude Chappe. The discussion between Miot de Mélito and Ignace Chappe took place in early 1793. Matching references to this event appear in both the Memoires of Miot de Mélito and in a book published by Ignace Chappe in 1824.*

The word télégraphe *first entered the public record in a resolution of the French National Convention that records the establishment of a French State Telegraph. That document is dated 26 July 1793. Many documents from this period, however, including the important one from 26 July 1793, spell the word as* Thélégraphe. *It took a few months before the correct spelling had sunk in. France was indeed the first nation to establish a state telegraph.*

Claude Chappe did not share his invention of the semaphore telegraph with anyone, and he was never involved with nautical flag signaling systems. Land-based telegraph systems and nautical signaling systems have always lived separate lives, despite many efforts to unify them. A good number of amateur historians in France have taken up the study of telegraph history. These Chappistes, *as they call themselves, are still sensitive about the distinction between nautical signaling systems, which were later also based on simple types of semaphores, and Chappe-style telegraphs. In conversation, a true* Chappiste *will never tire of correcting the innocent outsider who refers to a Chappe telegraph as a "semaphore." Most semaphores can transmit only a small set of predefined codes. Chappe's device could be used to send arbitrary messages. It was used in this way for over 50 years: by the time the electrical telegraphs took over, the French State Telegraph operated more than 550 Chappe stations.*

Of course, Chappe was not the first to propose the construction of a data network. That history goes back much further. I've recorded a good part of it in a book titled The Early History of Data Networks.

Gerard J. Holzmann
Computing Science Research
AT&T Bell Laboratories
Murray Hill, New Jersey

Whoa, let's not bury the word "telegraph" yet!

Within a few weeks, the word "telegraph" will resound throughout the land at every football practice field, high school and college. Thousands of young men will probably hear the word for the first time and they will not be allowed to forget it.

"Telegraph" is used by coaches to instruct players not to give a play away to the opposing team. Players do this by leaning left or right (some falling backward), by looking in the direction of the called play, by lining up in a different stance, etc.

"Telegraph" has a long life yet.

Bob Mills
Colorado Springs, Colorado

What's So Funny About Bananas?

The word *banana* makes people smile; why?

Maybe it's the spelling. Hubert Horatio Humphrey, who knew he had a tendency to speechify at great length, liked to say, "I'm like the little boy who knew how to spell *banana,* but never knew when to stop."

Perhaps it's the sound that gives the word a comical air. "You say 'ba-NAA-nuh,' I say 'ba-NAH-nuh,' " goes the lyric to the Gershwin song "Let's Call the Whole Thing Off"; it could be the "NAA" pronunciation that triggers the amusement.

Or it could be the fruit itself, a sunny yellow curved in the shape of a smile, as if to say, "Have a nice day." Denuded of its skin, the fruit offers us a *banana peel,* on which one slips to the great hilarity of onlookers.

In old American slang, *banana oil* means "nonsense" (its humorous connotation far different from *snake oil,* meaning "fraudulent"). A *top banana* is a leading comedian. To *go bananas* is to go crazy, and the nonsensical meaning is reflected in the verse of another 1930's song, "But Not for Me," from the Gershwins' *Girl Crazy."*

A *banana republic* was not just a country that produced profits for the United Fruit Company; it was a country with a rinky-dink government, having "backwardness" as its hallmark (until the name was adopted by an American retailer; now it has a yuppie connotation). A *banana boat* is a very slow boat.

Economists know it's funny, too. When Alfred Kahn, Jimmy Carter's anti-inflation czar, was told by his political superiors never to use the word *recession,* he agreed to substitute the word *banana;* he was soon heard muttering about "the worst banana you ever saw."

Perhaps it is the context that gives the word its humor. Let's deal with the word in a serious vein and see if a context of gravity wipes the smile off our face.

A recent front-page article in *The New York Times,* headlined "A Forbidden Fruit in Europe: Latin Bananas Face Hurdles," dealt with the crisis being felt by banana growers in the face of new quotas and tariffs by the European Community protectionists. That's surely serious, affecting profits, jobs, international relations, calling for all due solemnity.

In a letter to *The Times,* Daniel R. Katz, executive director of the Rainforest Alliance, swamped the banana growers with additional charges of using pesticides and fertilizers and converting rain forests into "monocultures" (evidently the bugaboo of multiculturalists). He wrote: "My organization has begun a voluntary program called the Smart Banana Project, to work with banana producers in improving their environmental standards without affecting productivity."

This line caused me to fall out of my chair. Why? Surely Mr. Katz's point—"we support reform of the banana industry, rather than a boycott"—is a serious one, not funny in the least. Then why do we smile at the prospect of the need for *banana reform,* and double up in consideration of the *Smart Banana Project*? If health reform is important, why is not banana reform? If smart bombs are not funny, why are smart bananas? (Just envision those smart bananas, dropped from a banana plane, zeroing in on the banana boycotters in the rain forest; oh, what a lovely war.)

Straighten those faces; let's try again. In the current issue of *The International Economy,* an article by Klaus C. Engelen, an editor of Handelsblatt in Düsseldorf, is headed "Is Helmut Kohl Cracking Up?" The piece discusses the pervasive *Endzeitstimmung,* the mood that the regime is coming to an end, and gives five reasons why Chancellor Kohl, though often highly regarded abroad, is so resented at home.

These reasons for the potential downfall of a Western leader range from "For not shutting the borders sooner on floods of asylum seekers" to "For letting bureaucrats from Brussels cause mass layoffs in Germany's steel plants."

Then comes the crusher: "For standing by as the French protect bananas from their former colonies, forcing the Germans to eat expensive, puny, shabby bananas."

Does Kohl realize he is about to be done in by the fallout from puny bananas? Is there a word in the German language for "shabby bananas," and does Helmut Kohl know it?

I rest my case: There is no way of dealing seriously with the Banana Question. Nobody with a straight face is going to fight for banana reform because bananas, smart or shabby, are inherently funny. ("When you get to my age," says octogenarian Milton Berle, "you don't buy green bananas.") Chomsky, get onto this: It must have something to do with the deep structure of the word itself.

How could you write a piece titled "What's So Funny About Bananas?" and make no mention of the funniest of all banana songs?

It goes back to the 1920's and if memory serves was composed by Billy Rose with the immortal line "Yes we have no bananas, we have no bananas today!"

Murray Illson
Barrington, New Hampshire

The word banana *signaled in semaphore* looks *funny. Normally, a semaphore message is an impressive sight as the sailor rapidly moves his two hand-held flags in various precise positions to indicate letters.*

But sending banana *requires one arm to do the work while the other remains unemployed. Even sillier-looking is the phrase* Panama banana man, *a favorite of the U.S.S.* Glynn *signal gang and a surefire laugh-getter.*

Dereck Williamson
Annandale, New Jersey

I do not know if the Germans have a word for a shabby banana, but they have a wonderful expression which I learned while stationed there in the Army from 1957–59. The saying is "Warum ist die Banana krum?" *I would not bet on the spelling, but the meaning is, "Why is the banana crooked?" It's used as a reply to a stupid question or one that has no real answer.*

Robert R. Singer
Elkins Park, Pennsylvania

In 1980 my wife and I were in Kuilin, China, then virtually unknown to American tourists, and we had some linguistic and travel problems. We were taken by our non-English-speaking Red Brigade–type guide to a center where a charming young Chinese girl, fluent in English, tried to help us. Our on-going tickets provided for us to leave Kuilin directly for Beijing, but regrettably bad weather had blocked all air traffic through the intermediate airport of Changsa and threatened to do so for several days into the future. We wanted to re-route via Canton, an unheard-of request for our guide.

The young girl reiterated the impossibility of doing such a thing, so I played my hole card. I invoked the name of a high official in Beijing. Suddenly the girl said: "Oh, he's top banana" and everything was arranged. I asked her how in the world she, in a provincial city in China, knew that term, and she told me that she had recently guided a U.S. theatrical troupe down the River Li and that they had taught her the term. To put it mildly, it was a surprise to hear it in rural China.

Thomas L. Hughes
Caracas, Venezuela

What's with *With*?

I asked for a seat in *non* so I could enjoy my coffee *with.*

A generation ago, that sentence would have been gibberish. Today it readily communicates meaning: *Non* is instantly recognized as that ever-expanding section of the world given over to the anti-tobacco lobby. The hostess, who never seems to obey her own sign (PLEASE WAIT FOR HOSTESS TO BE SEATED), asks, "Smoking or *non*?" (Because this solicits information about a preference, it is an improvement over the accusatory "One?")

With is "with cream" or half-and-half, or milk, or skim milk, or nondairy creamer, or white paint. *With* is a preposition, its object (cream) understood, and in this function has had a long history; in mid–nineteenth-century England, liquor was sometimes served with sugar, and Charles Dickens had a character in an 1835 story say, "Two glasses of rum-and-water 'warm *with.*' " But what of the new use of *with* as an adverb, now sweeping the country?

"I had begun to think it was my imagination," writes Dottie Hall of Scottsdale, Arizona, "but last week it happened again: 'I thought you'd want to read the material on the plane, so I'll fax it to you now and you can bring it with.' Everywhere I go, sentences seem to be ending in midair: 'I'll fix lasagna and we'll have a salad to go with.' Or 'Do you want me to go with?' Did I miss something? Did a recent blockbuster movie popularize this expression?"

Ms Hall, a marketing consultant, is a perceptive Lexicographic Irregular. (Her report of a new figure of speech about a company on the verge of bankruptcy—"It's circling the drain"—was especially vivid.) The use of *with* as an adverb, or as a preposition without an object, is taking hold.

"If you want a model, I would look to German," observes John Algeo, the neolinguistic observer for *American Speech*. "*Ich halte mit*—'I'm with you,' or *Ich mache mit*—'I'll join in.' But English has a number of prepositions that are also usable as adverbs: 'They drove by the house/They drove by,' or 'We jumped over the fence/We jumped over,' or 'He came to his senses/He came to.' "

The omission of an object after *with*—which effectively turns a preposition into an adverb—is today's hot example of a language's tendency to extend an existing pattern to new elements and words, what the great Danish grammarian Otto Jespersen called "drift."

I confess to having drifted a bridge too far on *with* in a recent political polemic. "A chastened President came before a press corps," I wrote, "to record his acquiescence with political necessity."

"You're not with it when you go prepositioning around with *with* where it doesn't belong," writes Louis Jay Herman, designated hit man of the Gotcha! Gang. "You recently wrote *redolent with*. Now you write *acquiesce with*."

Most usagists accept only *redolent of* and *acquiesce in*. Not *with*.

Redolent means "strongly suggestive of," as in a scent, and was first used figuratively in 1828 with *with*: "Their craft," wrote the theologian Edward Irving, ". . . all redolent with Popish superstition." Rooted in the Latin for "to emit a smell," *redolent* is one step short of the verb *reeks*, which can take a *with*.

Therefore, I would defend the use of *redolent with*, but would acquiesce in Mr. Herman's denunciation of *acquiesce with*; the *with* doesn't belong there. Acquiesce *to*? Maybe; it's being used more and more, but let's stick to *acquiesce in*, a usage judgment you can take with.

As to what's with with, *it may be a hot new usage in Arizona, but it was old news in and around Milwaukee in the 1950s when I was growing up there. Milwaukee and environs have lots of colorful usages, most German-based; that would confirm John Algeo's idea mentioned in your column. At any rate, a perfectly normal teenage conversation at that time might go: "We're going to the beach. Do you want to come with?"*

Barbara B. Simons
Boston, Massachusetts

This regards your discussion of how acquiesce *and* redolent *combine with prepositions.*

The BBI Combinatory Dictionary of English *(John Benjamins, 1986 and 1993) points out the following:*

A. The verb acquiesce *is used with* in *and* to. *A Usage Note adds that some purists feel that* acquiesce to *is old-fashioned. (The* O.E.D. *marks* acquiesce to *as "obsolete.")*

B. The adjective redolent *is labeled as "formal." It is used with* of *and* with. *(The* O.E.D. *cites examples of both constructions.)*

Morton Benson
Havertown, Pennsylvania

The phrase "circling the drain" has been used unofficially in medicine since at least as early as 1987, when I first heard the term. It is sometimes abbreviated C.T.D., which can also stand for "close to death." As you've probably surmised, the term is used to describe patients who rapidly fail but do not die suddenly. I'm not proud of it, but it's true.

Christina Resta, M.D.
New York, New York

Whence *White*?

The word *white,* as a racial description that used to be euphemized as "Caucasian," is being blackened.

In one of his sprightly, insightful (why am I doing a blurb when he hasn't written a book?) essays in *U.S. News & World Report,* John Leo addressed "the demonizing of white men." He opened with a grabber of a lead: "Attention, men of the Caucasoid persuasion."

In a *Washington Post* article about the Financial Accounting Standards Board, Jay Mathews wrote that the F.A.S.B.'s (sometimes pronounced "FAS-bees") "members are drawn from the upper reaches of the accounting profession, and have so far been all male and all European American." My colleague Floyd Norris, in the *Times* financial news section, notes this usage and wonders: "The new euphemism for *white*?"

Caucasia is a region between the Black and Caspian seas that takes in parts of Russia, Georgia, Armenia and Azerbaijan, and is marked by the Caucasus Mountains. The term *Caucasian* was used by the German anthropologist Johann

Friedrich Blumenbach around 1800 to describe whites, who he thought originated there; other nineteenth-century anthropologists expanded the area to Europe and North Africa, with the people of darker as well as lighter skins, but the whole racial category was abandoned by most scientists a century ago.

What, then, to call people who are not what used to be called *black* or *yellow* or *brown* or *red*? I see nothing that has to be euphemized about any of those colors, so long as you don't pretend it represents scientific differentiation. *White* is loosely nearly accurate, though a case can be made for the word chosen by the actor Peter Ustinov when asked his color; he wrote in *"pink."*

An even more finely tuned description of the Northern European dermal hue is E. M. Forster's, in A Passage to India *(p. 62 of the Harcourt, Brace edition of 1924, reprinted): ". . . the so-called white race is really pinko-grey."*

Douglas Leedy
Oceanside, Oregon

Whitewater Words

"All of us got hired here to work for the American people," President Clinton told reporters who were badgering him about charges by Republican leaders in regard to the Whitewater affair, "not to *throw off* on each other."

Lexicographic Javerts have homed in on the South Midland regionalism. The *Oxford English Dictionary* doesn't have *throw off* in the Clintonian sense, but the *English Dialect Dictionary,* by Joseph Wright, published in 1905, has this Dorsetshire usage from before the turn of the century: "Volks be throwen off 'bout it. Vather made vun 'bout it at tea-time." The contextual meaning: "to make fun of."

Mark Twain used it in his 1876 novel, *The Adventures of Tom Sawyer,* when Tom tells Huckleberry Finn in Chapter 25, "But I bet you *I* ain't going to throw off on di'monds."

The phrase is in steady current use; Joan Hall at the *Dictionary of American Regional English* notes that *DARE* defines it as "to say uncomplimentary things about somebody," as in a tape of a Georgian: "Some of 'em thought I was throwin' off on the bus driver, but I didn't mean that."

The Standard English synonyms are "disparage, denigrate, belittle"; a slang variation is "dump on." Mr. Clinton's usage was colorful, appropriate and timely; he can expect political partisans, as well as those goo-goos hung up on ethical standards, to be throwin' off on him for years.

To lovers of political discourse, the Watergate era was the Golden Age of Political Coinage. Never have so many memorable phrases been enshrined in our language in such a short period: The *Big Enchilada* at *CREEP* led the *cover-up,* as the *hardball* and *dirty tricks* played on those on the *enemies list* created a *firestorm* after the *Saturday Night Massacre;* the trail of the *plumbers* led to a *smoking gun* that no *stonewalling* or *limited modified hangout* or claim of *executive privilege* or *deep-sixing* of evidence could contain, and the Administration was left *twisting slowly, slowly in the wind.*

Ah, those were the days of Jill Wine and roses, at least to deep-throated sources and those of us who managed to stay out of jail. Will Whitewatergate be able to rise to such heights of original metaphor? I don't want to throw off on the new crowd, but most of the terminology today is derivative. Some usages bear watching.

Mr. Clinton rejected any Watergate analogy, "except any hysteria that they can *gin up* around it." This is no reference to gin, the alcoholic beverage, but is a shortening of *ginger up,* which Farmer and Henley reported a century ago meant "to make things lively or hum."

Few words have root as a root, but *ginger* is from the Sanskrit word for "antler-shaped root." Some engineers dispute this etymology of *gin up,* claiming its origin was a locution of workers at Eli Whitney's nineteenth-century cotton-picking engine, or cotton gin, but the *ginger* origin is reinforced by the memories of some of my correspondents who recall placing a piece of the root under a horse's tail to make the animal more sprightly at shows.

Cover-up: Mr. Clinton bridles at that word. (I bridle, too, at its hyphenation; can't we gin up some hysteria to drop the hyphen?) To dissociate himself from Watergate memories, Mr. Clinton said, "We're not covering up or anything; we are opening up." Used loosely, the noun *cover-up* means "an action to conceal a mistake"; used with more intensity, the word means "obstruction of justice," a federal crime. The word appeared in a Raymond Chandler story in a 1935 *Black Mask* mystery magazine; it entered the lexicon of political scandal in a 1968 recording made by the financier Louis Wolfson of a conversation with Abe Fortas, in which the Supreme Court Justice said, "Your giving me and my accepting the foundation post was nothing but a *cover-up.*"

When the President heard *cover-up* in a question, he cautioned, "Be careful how you use language." In this matter, close listeners can tell how careful he is being. He uses *credible* as a modifier in protestations of no wrongdoing: "There is no credible evidence and no credible charge that I violated any criminal or civil federal law eight or nine years ago when most of these facts that are being bandied around are discussed." Note, also, the use of *federal* in that sentence.

Firewall: In his *New York Times* column, Frank Rich wryly asked, "*Firestorm* meets *stonewall*?" No. "We have literally erected a *firewall,*" the President said after the firestorm about tip-offs to White House aides from regulatory officials caused initial stonewalling at the White House, "between the White House and other regulatory agencies." The "wall of separation" has long been a trope to describe the American relationship between church and state, and the metaphor gains emphasis by being able to resist fire. (The Clinton use of *literally* in this case was mistaken, unless carpenters and plasterers have been brought in; he meant *figuratively.*)

Modernity in language was displayed by the White House deputy counsel, Joel I. Klein, in his memo to White House staff about gathering subpoenaed documents: "memoranda, records, reports, notes, books, files, summaries or records of conversations, meetings or interviews, summaries or records of telephone conversations, diaries, calendars, date books, telegrams, [now here we boldly go where no White House counsel has gone before] facsimiles, telexes, telefaxes, electronic mail . . . Bernoulli boxes . . . WORM disks . . . floptical disks." Can you imagine the metaphoric uproar if credible evidence of federal (not state) wrongdoing were found on a WORM disk? (It stands for "Write Once, Read Many." You can write on a WORM, unlike a CD-ROM; you cannot erase, the way you can a hard disk.) A floptical disk, I presume, is your ordinary optical disk in the shape of a floppy.

And what of *whitewater* itself? The unsuccessful real-estate company adopted as its name a term first used in 1586 by William Harrison, an English topographer, in describing the swollen torrents of a river denied its direct course: "The water must of necessitie swell with the *white waters* which run downe from the land."

The picture of a couple in a raft or canoe that runs perilously through breakers and rapids, nearing precipitous falls, has been seized on by cartoonists and illustrators of magazine covers. "White Water is also the name of a man's cologne and after-shave from Revlon," James Conroy, a senior vice president at Revlon, points out. "Its name, crafted more than a year ago, had nothing to do with the political situation, but reflects its refreshing, casual, outdoor scent." Perfect Father's Day gift for a sweating White House aide.

Whitewatergate, a natural coinage, is too long to fit in a headline; *the Whitewater scandal* seems excessively critical, at least for now. That leaves us with a neutral borrowing from the French, who last century dealt with *l'affaire Dreyfus,* and most reporters are now calling the Clintons' latest time of troubles *the Whitewater affair.*

WORM disks can indeed be erased, in that the data recorded on the media may be overwritten with ones or random noise. They just may not be written to more than once with new data. Computer system operators have discovered to their chagrin that supposedly uncorruptable WORM media have been, deliberately or otherwise, erased or rendered unreadable.

A floptical drive is a high-density removable media device, using disks that look like normal 3½″ floppies, but have a tracking band (at one point in the prod-

uct's gestation it was optically read, thus the name) imbedded in the surface. I think "floptical" is a trademark. Normally the floptical disks store 20 or 40 megabytes of data.

David Josephson
San Jose, California

Cover-up

In a recent piece about Whitewater words, I wrote, "Used loosely, the noun *cover-up* means 'an action to conceal a mistake'; used with more intensity, the word means 'obstruction of justice.' " Then came the etymology: coinage by Raymond Chandler in a 1935 story in *Black Mask* magazine. I will stand by this coinage despite the *Oxford English Dictionary* supplement's listing of a 1927 book, *Those "Ashes"* by Montague Noble, which uses *cover-up* as a term used in cricket for defending. I also reject a 1920's use of the noun to mean "a garment worn by a woman over her bathing suit"; this also lacks a sinister sense.

Recently, however, I was watching *The Maltese Falcon* on television, in its dismayingly colorized version, and there was Sam Spade's partner, Miles Archer, saying to Miss Wonderly (an alias of Brigid O'Shaughnessy, unforgettably played by Mary Astor) about her fake story of a man running off with her sister, "Could he *cover up* by marrying her?" Sure enough, John Huston's 1941 screenplay picked up the verb use of *cover up* from Dashiell Hammett's novel, written in 1930. Thus, Hammett's verb form was the predecessor of the word Chandler turned into the noun *cover-up* with the sense we know and shiver over today.

And, as the songwriters say, then I wrote, "[*Cover-up*] entered the lexicon of political scandal in a 1968 recording made by the financier Louis Wolfson of a conversation with Abe Fortas, in which the Supreme Court Justice said, 'Your giving me and my accepting the foundation post was nothing but a *cover-up*.' "

From Jacksonville, Florida, by certified mail and with a "showing copy" to my employer that always fails to strike terror in my heart, Mr. Wolfson objects to this citation as being out of context. He submitted an excerpt from a surreptitiously recorded conversation with Justice Fortas, which he says shows there was nothing unethical in the reference.

"Your letter," Fortas said to Wolfson, "and the subsequent acceptance of the foundation post will be put together and will be construed as follows: That your giving me and my accepting the foundation post was nothing but a *cover-up* and that what was really happening was that I was taking a gratuity from you in terms of the statute and supplementing my salary. You see? And that is very bad."

Certainly that puts what seemed, out of context, like a confession into a different light—in context, as how the action would be construed by others. From a lexicographical point of view, however, the Fortas citation remains the earliest known example in print of the use of *cover-up* in the sense of "deliberate obfuscation."

Mr. Wolfson argues that it is erroneous to blame him for the appearance of conflict of interest that some of us opine triggered Justice Fortas's resignation. While I had Wolfson's attention, I wrote back to ask if he believed that the surreptitious recording of a telephone conversation, when the other person on the line has a reasonable expectation of privacy, is ethical.

"Looking back," Mr. Wolfson replied in part, with no return receipt requested, "had I had prior knowledge of this, it never would have taken place. The fact is that this recording was made, without my knowledge, by some members of my family who thought they were being helpful to me. . . . I have never been a party to secretly recording *any conversations* and have always placed among the lowest type of acts anyone doing such a thing."

Secretly made tapes are a frequent source of slang and non-Standard usages. Some single-minded lexicographers hope the nefarious practice continues, thereby providing unself-conscious sources for the language as it is really used. But it would be wrong.

You trace the verb form of cover-up to Dashiell Hammett's 1930 novel, The Maltese Falcon. *You have overlooked an earlier usage recorded by the* Oxford English Dictionary: *Henry Carter Hunting's 1926 book,* The Vicarion, *refers to "something she'd done and thought was covered up, but is found out now!"*

Fred R. Shapiro
Editor
Oxford Dictionary of American Legal Quotations
New Haven, Connecticut

More Whitewater Words

"But did you guys have to put the word *shredding* on the front page," a White House aide complained to a benign pundit, "and even worse, in a headline?"

Shred—one of those Old English words meaning "scrap" or "fragment" that appeared a thousand years ago in *Aelfric's Glossary*—has been getting a bad name lately. It all has to do with a machine.

In the 1927 edition of the Chemical Engineering Catalog, we see advertised a

"Universal Pulping and Shredding Machine . . . intended for tearing apart any fibrous material."

The fibrous material that gave the modern shredding machine a bad name was paper, on which information was printed that could be considered evidence. Right from the start, the benign purpose of the machine was proclaimed in an advertisement in the July 1954 issue of *American Business:* "Shred All, the Waste Paper Shredder: Quickly shreds newspapers, magazines, waste paper . . . into uniform resilient strands ideal for packing purposes." But then came the darker side: "Especially adapted to shredding confidential records."

Lieutenant Colonel Oliver L. North and his assistant Fawn Hall made the machine famous in 1986. When North, later a candidate for the Republican nomination in the United States Senate race in Virginia, was concerned about a forthcoming visit by the F.B.I., he ordered the shredding of his Iran-contra documents. To the chagrin of all those interested in shredding technology, the machine jammed, causing embarrassment.

And now attention is being paid to the destruction of files—perhaps routine, perhaps not—at the Rose Law Firm in Little Rock, Arkansas. The word sends a shudder through the body politic; no wonder its headline use causes consternation in the Whitewater White House.

If *shredding* is inflammatory, another word—*incidental*—is ameliatory, and has become a Clinton favorite.

When asked about meetings with regulatory officials beyond the three that had caused a special counsel to call White House aides before a grand jury, the President acknowledged them but termed them *"incidental,"* not *"substantive."*

These words, found in legal phrases like *incidental damages* and *substantive due process,* are not antonyms.

Incidental means "occurring by chance or without plan"; its antonym is *intentional* or *planned. Substantive* means "firm" or "permanent" or "essential"; depending on the sense intended, its antonym may be *apparent* or *temporary* or *insignificant.*

In law, these adjectives are not mutually exclusive. "An accidental meeting," says Professor Jamin Raskin of the Washington College of Law at American University, "which is *incidental,* could end up in criminal activity, which is *substantive.*" What about the White House's use of *incidental*? "That suggests there was no unlawful intent. To say something is 'not *substantive*' is to indicate that the conduct was not criminal."

How do these words work in terms of, say, obstruction of justice? "If an exchange that was 'not *substantive*' took place, it means that what transpired did not rise to the level of obstructing justice," Professor Raskin explains. "*Incidental* describes the exchange as something that was not deliberate." Thus, President Clinton's choice of *incidental* was a substantive decision.

In a defense of President Clinton on Meet the Press, *Mr. Al Gore actually said: "The President and First Lady have given* every shred *of evidence. . . ."*

Joseph A. Bamberger
Patchogue, New York

I expect that dozens of correspondents (including Anthony Lewis) will have written to you to say that your explanation of "substantive" and its contrasts the other day omitted the most obvious one—which may even be what the President had in mind—namely, the contrast between substantive and procedural questions; that is to say the difference between the content or subject matter of a transaction and the form or procedure by which it is carried through. Some used to say "substantive and adjectival law." So the point about substantive due process is that it came out of procedural due process. Curiously the Concise O.E.D. *does not reveal this usage at all though it appears in the larger work.*

Geoffrey Marshall
The Queen's College
Oxford, England

Whitewaterese

When the recently departed general counsel of the Treasury Department, Jean E. Hanson, characterized a conversation she'd held with Bernard Nussbaum, then the White House counsel, as a "*stay-back* from the Waco *prebrief,*" she inadvertently opened the gates to heavy linguistic investigation.

Lexicographers tune in to Congressional hearings as a great source of Washington jargon and bureaucratic euphemism.

Ms Hanson, a veteran New York lawyer not heretofore known for a poor memory, established a record in the farrago of forgettery. However, lawyers these days are advised by other lawyers never to say, "I don't remember"; it sounds evasive. Five times in one day did she invoke the more artful phrase "I do not have an *independent recollection*" of events recounted in her own memoranda earlier this year. A Harvard law professor, Charles Ogletree, informs me this means "recollection without aid or assistance."

The phrase, not yet in *Black's Law Dictionary,* is usually followed by the testimony that some incontrovertible document "seems to be correct"; if not, the questioner uses the verb *refresh,* as in the 1946 *New Yorker* cartoon supplied to me by

Professor Monroe Freeman of Hofstra University, showing a lawyer sitting on a witness's lap and saying, "Does this, by any chance, refresh your memory, Mr. Fillgate?"

George Stephanopoulos, President Clinton's chief policy aide, tried a variation when a calendar was produced showing him in a meeting with Treasury Secretary Lloyd Bentsen: "I have *no specific memory* of the meeting." The qualifier *specific* protects the witness from the assertion that he doesn't remember it at all. Neil Eggleston, an associate White House counsel, noted the word's legal resonance when he told a Senator, "I don't have any *specific* recollection, and I don't mean that as a word of art."

Senator Alfonse D'Amato, Republican of New York, noted with some asperity that Mr. Bentsen's chief of staff, Joshua Steiner, was backing away from forthright observations written in his diary, as in his report that Mr. Stephanopoulos said of an investigator, "Find a way to get rid of him." Observed the Senator, "Words have meaning, Mr. Steiner." However, he then said he found it "incredulous" that the aide would try to refute his own diary.

Incredulous, from the Latin *credere,* "to believe," means "unwilling to believe"; *incredible* means "hard to believe." There is a difference: I am *incredulous* at your *incredible* statement. The Senator could find backing for his usage in Shakespeare's comedy *Twelfth Night*—"no *incredulous* or unsafe circumstance"—but even the complaisant *Merriam-Webster's Dictionary of English Usage* suggests we restrict *incredulous* to its "disbelieving" sense.

You think it's being a pedant to insist on a difference between *imply,* "to hint," and *infer,* "to draw a conclusion from"? (Correct: I infer that you are implying I am a pedant.)

Representative Pete King, Republican of New York, noted that White House counsel Lloyd Cutler testified that nobody at the White House "ever told him or *implied*" that the White House was negotiating limits on an investigation. But he charged that Deputy Treasury Secretary Roger Altman's diary "had that *inference.*" Wearily, the soon-to-resign Mr. Altman replied: "One could argue that there is a difference between *implied* and *inferred.* I don't know." He does now.

What's a *stay-back*? This is apparently a fresh political term; I have been unable to find it on any of my data bases except as a name. However, we have a clue in the development of the verb "to drop by," or pay a brief visit, to the political noun *drop-by,* as in "I won't attend his embarrassing event, but maybe I'll do a *drop-by* when photographers have gone." A similar construction goes from the verb "to pull aside," to the diplomatic noun, a *pull-aside,* which means "a private meeting at a public event." A *stay-back,* which I hyphenate on the analogy of the above terms, means "a meeting after a meeting, as some of the participants remain behind," according to a Treasury source speaking on stay-background.

But that's not all. "*Stay-back* is an English expression for 'drinks after hours,'" reports Chris Tarrant of Britain's Capital Radio. "By law, the landlord of a pub in

England is supposed to stop serving drink at eleven o'clock at night, but lots of landlords pull the curtains, lock the door to keep the policemen out and let the drinking continue with a handful of regulars until the small hours of the morning. Saturday is obviously the biggest night of the week for staybacks.

"*Saturday Stayback* was a series that used to run on ITV in the U.K. It started at eleven o'clock on Saturday night, featuring comedians and live bands recorded in pubs around Britain."

A *prebrief,* "information disseminated before an event," is the opposite of *debrief,* which is spilled afterward. Both are both nouns and verbs. Both began as Pentagonese, with *prebrief* launched in 1982 ("extensive *prebriefs* and sequential reviews within the Component"). Lawyers picked it up: "A trial brief gives you the ability to *prebrief* the judge," Mark A. Dombroff wrote in a 1983 *Legal Times.* It is now White House jargon for "a briefing held before a presidential trip or meeting to enable the press to understand its significance."

The main controversy in this early stage of Whitewater is the propriety of the Treasury Department's giving the White House advance notice (and where's the Squad Squad on "advance notice"?) of a criminal referral from its ward, the Resolution Trust Corporation, to the Justice Department. To those who think the notification gave the Clintons an advantage that other witnesses or suspects do not enjoy, the warning was a *tip-off* or *alarm bell* or *inside information;* to the President's defenders, the locution for the controversial alert was a *heads up.*

That term was given exhaustive analysis in this space a year ago, when the Deputy Director of Central Intelligence went to his boss, Robert Gates, to—in his words—"give the Director a *heads up*" that the Attorney General would be calling. Although one adjectival sense is "alert, wide-awake," as in a player of "heads-up ball," the usage most common today is the noun for "warning."

The White House choice of *heads up* was adept; it carries the connotation of innocent alert that any political outfielder would give another, lest he get hit in the head by hardball tactics.

You summon the Squad Squad to denounce "advance notice" and yet confer legitimacy on "prebrief." Certainly, as a v.t., "prebrief," particularly as used by Mr. Dombroff, is redundant of "brief" (see Random House Second, *No. 16), but then what does a lawyer know?*

Incidentally, a "trial brief" is always a pretrial document, so Mr. Dombroff is doubly redundant. On the other hand, a "brief" is sometimes filed after argument of a case (as in the United States Tax Court). More often than not, however, it is filed before argument (on appeal), and a British solicitor would not last long if he "briefed" his barrister after the trial.

Daniel S. Knight
Philadelphia, Pennsylvania

Who's Got *Security*?

New Dealers, back in the 30's, had a lock on the word *security.* If any phrase exemplified the yearning of the nation in that Depression era, it was *Social Security.* On the international scene, liberals, who were then interventionist, touted Wilsonian *collective security.* In another sense of the word, the Securities and Exchange Commission was formed to guard against the predators of Wall Street.

At the end of that decade, the conservatives began taking the word back. *Internal security* became the phrase to define the defense against Communist penetration. In the Eisenhower years, *national security* became of great concern, and the President was given a national security adviser who had a whole council to go with him. For a long generation, *security* connoted national defense and was a hot-button word for righties.

The left is now taking the word back. Israel's Labor Prime Minister, Yitzhak Rabin, in the light of widespread worry about the knife attacks of the *intifada,* began balancing *national security* with a need for *personal security.* It was a way to lay the groundwork for an accommodation with local Palestinians and ultimately with the P.L.O.

Personal security was a phrase making it in the United States, too, its use at first dominated by law-and-order advocates who wanted a crackdown on criminals threatening people on the streets. Of late, however—and from the bully pulpit of the White House—the term has been broadened and appropriated by liberals.

The press secretary, Dee Dee Myers (whose first name is Margaret, but the White House is an informal place these days), responded to a question about President Clinton's broadened use of *personal security* in speeches. "I think this is an outgrowth of earlier speeches where the President talked about *personal security,*" she said, "whether it's *health security* or freedom from fear of crime or knowing that you have a good job in an economy that's working."

Thus, Mr. Clinton is using *personal security* as an umbrella term for confidence in police protection, for the end of worry about medical costs to bring what's called *health security* (complete with a *health security card*), and for the economic optimism long known as *financial security.*

"If F.D.R. did his Four Freedoms speech today," wonders Daniel Schorr, senior correspondent of National Public Radio, who called this phenomenon to my attention, "would it be 'Four Securities'?"

This retaking of *security* did not happen by accident; a shrewdly manipulative hand is at work here. It's making right-wingers insecure.

Whole Nine Yards

Frank Gifford, the nation's preeminent (better hyphenate *pre-eminent;* otherwise, it looks as if it sounds like a combination of *preening* and *permanent*) sportscaster, has a book out titled *The Whole Ten Yards,* written with Harry Waters.

Frank's an old buddy and his book is a hoot (the latest sense of *hoot* is defined as "something or someone amusing" in the up-to-the-minute *Merriam-Webster's Tenth Collegiate*), but I hasten to warn readers that the title, while memorable, may contribute to a widespread misapprehension.

The whole nine yards, the expression on which the former football star's catchy book title is based, has nothing to do with football.

One school of etymological thought on this is nautical, where a *yard* is a long spar to support and spread the head of a square sail. (The *yardarm* is the end of that spar, and you are not supposed to booze it up until the sun sinks below it in late afternoon.) Each mast of a three-masted, square-rigged sailing ship carried three yards; when the sails were fully spread, or "under full canvas," the ship had the propulsion of winds caught by *the whole nine yards.*

That's all you know, sneer the drivers of concrete trucks (and you'd better not call them *cement trucks* unless you want truckloads of mail poured, lava-like, over your head). Construction workers insist, and I agree with them, that the phrase comes from the cubic contents of the large, revolving cylinder that mixes cement and sand to make concrete. A job that requires a full truckload calls for *the whole nine yards.* People who know standard measurements say that cubic contents are measured in feet, not yards, but go tell that to the guy in the truck—he'll pour a small load all over your feet.

You will even find seamstresses to say that nine yards used to be the length of a bolt of cloth, and that some fancy dresses took up *the whole nine yards,* but that's as far out as the folk etymology suggesting it means nine-tenths of the way to a first down.

The expression "the whole nine yards" comes from the construction industry where "Ready Mix" and "Cement" trucks had a maximum load of nine cubic yards. Suppliers were loath to send out a truck with less than a full load, so the expression "the whole nine yards" came into use. Now load limits have been changed and eleven-yard loads, and perhaps larger, are allowed. Concrete is always sold and measured by the cubic yard, never by the cubic foot.

I am also sure that the nautical root that you suggest is bogus. Most square-rigged ships carried more than three sails per mast—up to six. For example, a full rigged ship had seventeen squaresails. In fact I can find no standard three-

*masted rig having nine sails and therefore nine yards. (*The Lore of Ships, *LCCC# 63-18428)*

Robert S. Royce
The Hotchkiss School
Lakeville, Connecticut

Woe unto Life

The battle of the predicate nominatives has turned into a slugfest. Some people will never accept *woe is me* as anything but "woe is *unto* me," thereby justifying the *me* as an object of a preposition.

Come at it this way. The Shenandoah University Conservatory presented a new opera, *The Birthday of the Infanta,* at the Kennedy Center in Washington. The librettist, Mary Ewald (arguably, the first woman ever to write a grand-opera libretto), limns the character of the Spanish King with "Life is a cruel country."

Mrs. Ewald is using a metaphor that needs only a *like* to become a simile. Shakespeare's Hamlet soliloquized about "death, the undiscover'd country." Life and death are obviously not countries, but if you suspend logic, and think of life or death as a country, then it could be cruel. Same way as *woe* could be *me.*

(You like *limns*? Good word for "describe," with the same root as "illuminate"; use it in writing, not in speech.)

You refer to Mary Ewald, librettist of the opera The Birthday of the Infanta, *as "arguably, the first woman ever to write a grand-opera libretto." Leaving aside your decision to hyphenate "grand-opera," what about the following:*

Hedwig Lachmann, librettist for Salome *by Richard Strauss*
Adelheid Wette, librettist for Hänsel und Gretel *by Humperdinck*
Colette, librettist for L'Enfant et les Sortilèges *by Ravel*
Myfanwy Piper, librettist for both The Turn of the Screw *and* Death in Venice *by Benjamin Britten*
Mira Mendelson, librettist for War and Peace *by Sergei Prokofiev*

Arguably, there are others.

Douglas M. Haynes, M.D.
Louisville, Kentucky

The Word from the Pope

As language mavens gathered at the New York Public Library recently to hear a panel discuss "Words in the Next Millennium," a crisis was building in the greenroom.

The *greenroom* is the anteroom offstage where performers or lecturers fret, practice their lines or just horse around until the audience starts stamping its feet. (The "attiring room" was noted in Shakespeare's day, and may have been first called *green* at the Drury Lane Theater in London. Some say set designers moved small trees and shrubbery into this room, causing it to be called the *greens room;* others hold that it is rooted in outdoor performances being held on a *greensward;* all is speculation, but it is unlikely that it was so called because the room was painted that color, or was named after a producer named Green.)

Where was I? The linguistic crisis. Two world-class lexicographers were present: Fred Mish, of Merriam-Webster, the corporate descendant of Noah Webster and unabashed bastion of description of the language as it is, and Anne Soukhanov, whose hand guided American Heritage down more prescriptive lines. (A third and fourth, Sol Steinmetz and Jesse Sheidlower of Random House, were in the audience, stamping their feet.)

My plan had been to select words and phrases from that morning's *New York Times* for etymological discussion. I had the newspaper spread out on the table in the greenroom; a chapter of Pope John Paul II's book *Crossing the Threshold of Hope,* was the centerpiece of the Op-Ed page. Circled in red was a word from the following passage: ". . . making use of these very *semina Verbi,* that constitute a kind of common *soteriological* root present in all religions."

Soteriological? Mish and Soukhanov looked at each other blankly. My *Times* colleague, Jeffrey McQuain, who was moderating the panel, offered, "It's the adjectival form of *soteriology,*" which was a big help. After some fast thumbwork in their respective tomes, both lexies came up with the answer: "Theology dealing with salvation" was the Merriam-Webster definition, "especially as effected by Jesus Christ." That's a word the Bishop of Rome would surely be familiar with. But your ordinary newspaper reader, even dictionary writers? Hardly.

With our quick fix from the dictionaries, the panel was able to face the audience of teachers and philologists. The Greek etymon was *soteria,* "deliverance," from *sozein,* "to save," growing out of *sos,* "safe, sound." The *Oxford English Dictionary* has the earliest use recorded in Webster's 1847 dictionary, with a meaning of "a discourse on health," but the theological meaning took over a generation later.

A question of style arises. The Pope, whose publishers have more than a million copies of his book in print in the United States alone, obviously wants to reach a large audience with his book. In the same way, *The New York Times* likes its readers to comprehend the prose it presents. Why, then, use a word that so clearly stumps the experts?

One answer: The excerpt was only an excerpt, and the meaning of the word is explained more fully earlier in the Pope's book. "The rationalism of the Enlightenment," he writes, "strikes at the heart of *Christian soteriology,* that is, theological reflection on salvation (*soteria,* in Greek)." Later, he uses the word as an adjective, defining it in passing: "Christianity is a religion of salvation—a soteriological religion, to use the theological term." Further on, the Pope deepens his church's identification with the Greek word's root: "The very name Jesus, Jeshua ('God who saves'), bespeaks this salvation."

That's how to use an unfamiliar word to make a point; in the Pope's writing, this word is defined at first use, then is made more familiar by its repeated explanation in a book destined for best-sellerdom in Christendom and beyond.

That's just skilled technique. A more principled answer to the question about using a specialist's word in general publication is that it raises the level of discourse. The reader is required to stretch his vocabulary to grasp the writer's point. This goes against the grain of most current writing theory, which puts the burden of communication on the writer to make his meaning plain to a large audience. That's why a *Newsweek* review, troubled by the book's "lofty tone," cautions, "Willing readers may find renewed wonder in *Crossing the Threshold of Hope,* but they'll have to do more than their share of the work."

What's wrong with requiring a reader to work? If you're a world figure, especially the head of a major religion, you can get away with making demands on readers. (The Pope is uniquely entitled to pontificate.) There is a trade-off, however: The working reader has to know that the author is the authentic writer of the prose.

That's what held me throughout the entire book, which I bought after the panel broke up and the edified audience left. This is not a work drafted by a dutiful ghost and edited and approved by the world figure; nor is it a draft from dictation or notes jotted down by a famous person that has been smoothed and revamped by editors to render it more understandable by the intended readership. Though it uses the device of answering questions submitted by the journalist Vittorio Messori, and though it has been translated from Polish to Italian to English, nothing about this style comes across "as told to." Instead, in a throwback to Winston Churchill, it is the work product of the mind of the famous person working alone. The reader is willing to work because the author was willing to work.

Back to my own line of work: The Latin phrase *semina Verbi,* used by the Pope before he let us have it with *soteriological,* means "seeds of the Word." The capitalization of *Verbi,* "the Word," signifies that word means the Word of God; *semina* means "seeds."

The phrase is based on the New Testament parable of the sower, says Jan Ziolkowski, Harvard professor of medieval Latin. In the parable, which is told in three Gospels, a sower spreads some seed on rocks and thorns, and the seed fails; only the seed that falls on good ground flourishes. That parable in the Gospel of Luke uses the expression "The seed is the word of God."

According to Professor Ziolkowski, "In all the interpretations, the sower is a person who spreads the Word—understood sometimes as just Christ himself, other times as others who preach the Word."

Words Out in the Cold

"The third edition of the *American Heritage Dictionary* has no *morals*!" exclaims William J. Slattery of Jamestown, Rhode Island, who is otherwise entranced by the new dictionary.

He is mistaken about the absence of *morals;* that noun does not have its own separate entry, but it is entered under the adjective *moral,* and is crisply defined as "rules or habits of conduct, especially of sexual conduct, with reference to standards of right and wrong." Useful synonymy is added to differentiate among the adjectives *moral, ethical, virtuous* and *righteous.*

The noun *morals* is there in *American Heritage,* in boldface. It is also found as the secondary sense of the noun *moral* in *Merriam-Webster's Tenth New Collegiate* and is alluded to, without boldface, as the plural of *moral* in *Webster's New World.*

However, Ralph G. Beaman of Boothwyn, Pennsylvania, wants to know why I was pleased with *American Heritage,* a dictionary that contains up-to-date items like *spin-doctor* and *cocooning* but lacks such other modern favorites as *glass ceiling, stocking stuffer, party platter, tapa* (in the sense of a snack), *top 40, nose tackle, baked Alaska* and *ta-dah.*

I don't even have to call Anne Soukhanov, its executive editor, to check: These may be nonce words, soon to be gone with the *roller blades.* A word, before being lexed, has to establish itself. (The verb *to lex* has just been used here for the first time, I think, and is unlikely to make it to a second.)

In a few years, will *bra* still retain its new sense of "protection for the front of a utility vehicle"? Will *Mylar* fade with Madonna? Who can say? Meanwhile, dictionaries also serve that only stand and wait; comes the next edition of any major dictionary, and—*ta-dah!*—a *stocking stuffer* for Christmas. (*Xmas* is in.)

Year's Best Lede

You want to learn to write great stuff? Read great writers.

The Op-Ed page is a place for polemics. The purpose of a piece in that medium is not so much to analyze or report as to arouse, inveigh and persuade.

The opening, or lede, must seize the reader's attention and draw him into the argument. One way is with a bald, outrageous or amusing declaration; a better way is with an irresistible anecdote; a third way, the most difficult to bring off, is with subtly poetic writing.

Saul Bellow, the author of *Humboldt's Gift* and *The Dean's December,* who teaches literature at Boston University, tried his hand at an Op-Ed article in *The New York Times* recently. His points, which he made with the sort of grace that carries great force, were (1) that the views of a fictional character should not be taken as the views of the novelist and (2) that what passes these days for "rage" is often manipulative and censorious, shutting down open discussion with charges of defamation or contempt for multiculturalism.

Consider his lede, written in the style of a poetic prayer:

"Snowbound, I watched the blizzard impounding parked cars at midnight. The veering of the snowflakes under the street lights made me think how nice it would be if we were totally covered by white drifts. Give us a week's moratorium, dear Lord, from the idiocies that burn on every side and let the pure snows cool these overheated minds and dilute the toxins which have infected our judgments. Grant us a breather, merciful God."

Impounding is what police do to illegally parked cars, but never before has a *blizzard* done it; that's the sort of original use of language that poets strive for. The subject of the second sentence, another *-ing* term to suggest a continuing action, is *veering.* Do snowflakes ordinarily *veer*? Most of us would use *slant,* but the writer is not most of us and prefers a word that implies a change of direction, which is what makes a blizzard different from a snowfall. He then lays the *pure snows* atop the idiocies that *burn,* thereby metaphorically to cool *overheated* minds; in the process of absorbing that heat, the snow melts and can then *dilute* the infecting toxins.

You don't just toss that off; you think about it, making sure your fresh word picture is internally consistent, as you conclude the lede with a with-it counterpoint to the traditional prayer form by asking God to grant a *breather,* a slang term for "respite" or "easy test between difficult tests."

(Before anyone writes in to note that Bellow's "the toxins which" should be "the toxins *that,*" because *that have infected our judgments* is a restrictive clause, please remember that you get Nobel Prizes for literature, not for grammar.)

Your fear that someone will nitpick Saul Bellow's use of "the toxins which" instead of "the toxins that" is surprising. Even Fowler does not insist on the use of that *over* which *in a restrictive clause.*

Historically, according to Bergen Evans, that *over* which, which *over* that, *went in and out of fashion during the last 400 years. Only grammarians of the prescriptive pedantry vintage insist on the use of* that *in a restrictive clause. You've never been a pedant; why join now?*

Could Bellow have chosen which *for the limp it leaves out of a sentence and omitted the successive* that *for the limp it puts in?* That *or* which *in a restrictive clause is a matter of choice.*

For example, in the King James Bible (1611), Matthew 22:21 reads: "Render therefore unto Caesar the things which are Caesar's; and unto God the things that are God's."

Silas Rhodes
New York, New York

Allow me, as a professor of English, to allay your concerns about Saul Bellow's "grammar." The distinction between that *and* which *in relative clauses is not a grammatical but at best a stylistic one.* Which *has been the ordinary preferred relative pronoun in subordinate clauses since before the time of Shakespeare. In the* Book Review *last Sunday Winston Churchill is quoted as follows: "Let us leave hindsight to history, that history which I am now, myself . . . writing." In the same magazine section as your column is a quotation from E. M. Forster. Referring to personal relations Forster writes: "They are regarded as bourgeois luxuries, as products of a time of fair weather* which *is now past. . . ." Do you really suppose that these two great writers were ignorant of "grammar" and that their ignorance was shared by T. S. Eliot, Ezra Pound, James Joyce, D. H. Lawrence, and Virginia Woolf, all of whom use* which *in exactly the same way? Here is part of a familiar sentence: "When in the Course of human events, it becomes necessary for one people to dissolve the political bands which have connected them with another. . . ." Would the Declaration of Independence have been improved by replacing Jefferson's* which *with the* Times's that*?*

The exclusive use of that *instead of* which *in so-called restrictive clauses has no foundation in either the tradition, the usage, or the idiom of the English language. It is moreover offensive to what is called the concinnity of good prose. And it is interesting to note that the* that . . . that *construction is practiced largely (and not everywhere) in America, while in England, Ireland, Canada, Australia, India, and wherever British English prevails, it is either unknown or ignored.*

Michael Kowal
Associate Professor of English
Queens College
The City University of New York
Flushing, New York

Zero Misteaks

Experts who wallow in the admission of error erode the credibility of their mavenhood. But in a doubt-defying feat of clay, let me rid my conscience of the most egregious of my last year's language gaffes, in both my language columns and my political essays, so as to start the year with a clean slate. (*Thereby to* would be better than *so as to,* but for some reason *thereby* has acquired an overly formal connotation, like *albeit.*)

When President Clinton spoke of "people that are different than we are," I popped him lightly on the use of *different than,* which is not as strong a differentiation as *different from,* but then went on to suggest fixing the end with "people who are different from *ourselves.*"

Lyle W. Sparks of Chicago thought that was an overnice use of the reflexive *ourselves.* "Examples of the proper use of the emphatic or reflexive *ourselves,*" he writes, "are 'We ourselves have committed grammatical error' and 'For the post of language guru, we nominate ourselves.' "

To be correct and direct, the President and I should use "people who are different from *us.*" On some days I'm just not myself. (That's the reflexive form of *me,* used for emphasis; it's different from "not me.")

"Whatever happened to *Burma-Shave*?" I asked in one of my nostalgic moods. "For that matter, whatever happened to *Burma*?" George Meredith of Red Bank, New Jersey, wondered: "Whatever th e difference between *whatever* and *what ever,* what ever happened to people who knew the difference? All gone to Myanmar?"

That's the new name of Burma, adopted in June 1989. I just checked with the spokesman for Myanmar, who says, "Burma was the name given to the country by British colonialists in 1885. The Burmese make up 85 percent of the population, but there are 135 nationalities in our country, and the name Myanmar represents everyone, not just the Burmese."

On *whatever,* both *Merriam-Webster* and *Webster's New World* dictionaries report that one word fits all, but it seems to me that Mr. Meredith has a point: When used in a question, the interrogative pronoun and intensifier should be two words, *what ever.* The meaning is wholly different from the adjective *whatever,* as in "whatever name the dictator of Burma prefers"; whatever the dictionaries say, use the single word in its additional sense of "no matter what."

(What ever happened to the sequential signs along the road that advertised Burma-Shave in doggerel? The shaving cream is gone, the signs are gone, and the roads have been replaced by interstate highways, freeways, whatever.)

Back to more obvious mistakes. "Only by building a floating majority," I wrote with political prescience, could the President "build the momentum . . . to overcome his *bête noir,* gridlock." To which Ihor Sevcenko, Dumbarton Oaks

Professor of Byzantine History and Literature Emeritus at Harvard, responded, "Keep an eye on your proofreader."

This had me scratching my head until an "Oh, no!" came in from Evangeline Bruce of Washington—the beloved Vangy of Georgetown—with "How could you make the *bête* masculine?" The black beast is *la bête noire.* (Proofreaders expecting arcane wordplay in my copy occasionally say to themselves, "This is so obviously wrong that it must be one of his verbal stunts, and I'd better leave it as is so nobody can accuse me of not getting the joke." There was a lot of that kind of papyrus-proofreading in Byzantium.)

I'm good at history, though. In comparing Boris Yeltsin's relentless pressure on a defiant parliament to Oliver Cromwell's blast at legislators unwilling to commit regicide—"It is not fit that you should sit here any longer!"—I noted, "In the ensuing 'Pride's Purge,' a Cromwellian colonel arrested ninety-six reluctant legislators, leaving a 'rump Parliament' to hang the King."

Wrongly executed. "When Charles I walked out one of the oversized windows," corrected Tony Brunton of Bay Shore, Long Island, "onto a hastily erected walkway and platform—which overlooked Whitehall—it was to lose his head rather than hang." Royalty gets decapitated, not hanged.

For a reason having only to do with fumbling fingers, I predicted a great future for "PC-ROM" recently. "For an upgrade of your personal personal computer savvy," instructs Andy Glass, Washington bureau chief and columnist for Cox newspapers, "note that *PC-ROM* is an acronym for 'personal computer read-only memory.' Most often, these chips are cited as the machine's *BIOS,* which stands for 'Basic Input-Output System.' The BIOS is the gizmo that sets things up when you hit the 'On' switch.

"Since *PC-ROM* has been around for more than a decade, eons in computerdom," Mr. Glass continues in his snazzy Ultrashadow font, "I am sure *CD-ROM* is what you really had in mind when you referred to 'the new world of PC-ROM' in noting the growing interest in multimedia systems. *CD-ROM* stands for "compact disk read-only memory."

Yeah, and "read only" means you can't write to the disk, at least not this week. I am correcting this error lest my works be immortalized on CD-ROM and confuse some android reading it in the future.

In a piece on *factoids,* bits of conjecture or misinformation masquerading as facts, I described Mr. Spock of the infinitive-splitting television series *Star Trek* as an *android,* an automaton who was similar to a human but not the same. This was by way of giving the woid on *-oid,* a popular combining form to denote spurious sameness.

"The *Star Trek* character you cited, as Mr. Spock's fans know," wrote Bruce Goldman of Richmond, "is half human and half Vulcan—but all natural—making him a *humanoid,* something like but not quite a human. Commander Data, from *Star Trek: The Next Generation,* is an android. So when you wrote, 'An android is very like a human being but is an automaton,' you published an *analogoid*—something that is like but not quite a real analogy."

Actually, in my filed copy I referred to "Dr. Spock" when I meant "Mr. Spock," which would have drawn angry letters from former children accustomed to feeding on demand. A proofreader was gutsy enough to boldly go where no proofreader had ever gone before, saving me on the honorific before the mistake could hit print; he assumed I knew this—no parent or couch potato could possibly confuse Dr. Spock with Mr. Spock—but was slyly testing him.

ACKNOWLEDGMENTS

The thankees are: Fred Mish of Merriam-Webster, Jesse Sheidlower of *Random House Historical Dictionary of American Slang,* Mike Agnes of Webster's New World and Anne Soukhanov, formerly of American Heritage. OLBOM—the "On Language" Board of Octogenarian Mentors—comprises (not "is comprised of") Jacques Barzun, Fred Cassidy of *The Dictionary of American Regional English,* Alistair Cooke and Allen Walker Read. Sol Steinmetz, who replaced the late Leo Rosten as my guru on Yiddish, isn't eighty yet, but I enlisted him anyway.

Others called upon for lexicographic advice include John Algeo, David K. Barnhart, Cynthia Barnhart, Bryan Garner, Paul Dickson, William A. Kretzschmar Jr. of the *Linguistic Atlas* Project, Joan Hall of *DARE,* James McCawley (the late philological heavy-hitter of the University of Chicago), Allen Metcalf of the American Dialect Society, Wayne Glowka of *American Speech,* Justin Kaplan of *Bartlett's Familiar Quotations,* Ron Gephart of the Library of Congress, Fred Shapiro at Yale Law School, James Simpson of *Simpson's Quotations,* Margot Charlton of the *Oxford English Dictionary,* and Robert Burchfield, former editor of the *O.E.D.* and Constance Hale of *Wired Style.*

My Random Housing includes Kate Medina, Philip Turner, Mary Beth Roche, Amy Edelman, Carie Freimuth, Beth Pearson, Margaret Wimberger, and Patricia Abdale.

These columns first appeared in *The New York Times Magazine,* where my editors have been Jack Rosenthal, Adam Moss, Harvey Shapiro, Michael Molyneaux, Rob Hoerburger, Jeff Roth, Abbott Combs, Jeff Klein, Jaimie Epstein and Bill Ferguson.

In addition to Jeffrey McQuain's and Kathleen Miller's language support, helping me at the *Times* Washington Bureau are my assistant, Ann Elise Rubin, who keeps watch on current words, and Todd Webb, who tries keeping up with the mail. (Although I have an E-mail address, onlanguage@nytimes.com, I still get an ergonomic kick out of feeling handwritten or personally typed letters. My snail-mail address is Safire On Language, *The New York Times* Washington Bureau, 1627 Eye Street NW, Washington, DC 20006.) The Bureau's chief librarian, Barclay Walsh, and the librarians, Marjorie Goldsborough and Monica Borkowski, are as helpful as ever.

The copy editors of my political column, who save me from the Gotcha! Gang and often lead me to language topics, are Steve Pickering, Linda Cohn and Sue Kirby.

My final thankees are the Lexicographic Irregulars, the redundancy reducers of the Squad Squad and the nitpicking troops of the Gotcha! Gang. I appreciate their loyal mock-fury.

INDEX